Autism as an
Executive Disorder

Autism as an Executive Disorder

Edited by

James Russell

Department of Experimental Psychology,
University of Cambridge

OXFORD · NEW YORK · TOKYO
OXFORD UNIVERSITY PRESS
1997

Oxford University Press, Great Clarendon Street, Oxford OX2 6DP

Oxford New York

Athens Auckland Bangkok Bogota Bombay
Buenos Aires Calcutta Cape Town Dar es Salaam
Delhi Florence Hong Kong Istanbul Karachi
Kuala Lumpur Madras Madrid Melbourne
Mexico City Nairobi Paris Singapore
Taipei Tokyo Toronto Warsaw

and associated companies in
Berlin Ibadan

Oxford is a trade mark of Oxford University Press

Published in the United States
by Oxford University Press, Inc., New York

© *Oxford University Press, 1997*

A catalogue record for this book is available from the British Library

Library of Congress Cataloging in Publication Data
(Data applied for)

ISBN 0 19 852349 1 (Hbk)
0 19 852348 3 (Pbk)

Typeset by Hewer Text Composition Services, Edinburgh
Printed and bound in Great Britain by
Biddles Ltd, Guildford and King's Lynn

Preface and acknowledgements

The contributors to this book were certainly not the first to argue that autism—its core features at least—can be viewed as the outcome of profound executive dysfunctioning. (Such ideas probably emerged first in the work of Antonio Damasio and colleagues.) It is, however, fair to say that the work described here is sufficiently without precedent and sufficiently distinctive to constitute a new theory. The main force which shaped it into a theory was, as is often the case, the presence of a different theory—that autism is caused by deficits within (or a lack of) the 'theory of mind' module. However the 'shaping' took different forms in the two groups represented here.

Bruce Pennington and his colleagues in Denver had been researching into executive dysfunctioning within developmental psychopathology a long time before our work began in Cambridge. It was not until 1991, however, that Sally Ozonoff (then at Denver, now at Utah), Bruce Pennington, and Sally Rogers published two landmark papers showing that executive measures were as good, and maybe better, at discriminating autistic subjects from controls than was their performance on theory-of-mind tasks. This did not mean that mentalizing problems are mild in relation to executive problems, but it focused the mind. It inspired studies that asked which of the many aspects of executive functioning are associated with autism and invited us to consider whether executive problems could be major contributor to—or even a cause of—the mentalizing problems. Readers will see that the work has since been flourishing both in Denver and in Utah.

My interest in executive dysfunctions in autism had a different origin. It seemed to me that if there was validity in Piaget's ideas about role of agency in mental development (and in some of the ancient and modern philosophical work on the grounding of first-person thoughts in agency) then it might be possible to explain why executive and mentalizing deficits co-exist in the disorder. When these interests were developing, I was fortunate to have some remarkably talented people as graduate students and research associates. Michelle Turner and Chris Jarrold are represented here, but one who is not is Claire Hughes who became my graduate student before Michelle and Chris began their work in Cambridge. (It is a great pity that prior commitments prevented Claire from writing a piece for this volume.) I should also acknowledge Trevor Robbins' invaluable contribution to Claire's work, as well as his general help and encouragement. (On hearing Trevor end a departmental seminar with the remark—apropos the basal ganglia?— 'As Piaget said, thought is internalised action', I realized that our interests were not as divergent as they seemed.) I am also grateful to the encouragement and discussion I received from Joëlle Proust and for her sharing with me the ideas of her group at 'Centre de Recherche en Épistemologie Appliquée' in Paris. At a meeting of this group I met Joëlle's ex-graduate-student Elisabeth Pacherie who became a contributor to this volume. Her chapter will prove to be an important one, I believe.

I would also like to thank John Campbell for acting as an additional referee for Elisabeth Pacherie's chapter. Finally, I am grateful to the Wellcome Trust who funded Michelle Turner's 'prize studentship' and who have been generously funding my own work since 1993.

Cambridge
January 1997   J. R.

Contents

Contributors

Loisa Bennetto, Department of Psychology, University of Denver, 2155 S. Race St., Denver, CO 80208, USA

Chris Jarrold, Department of Experimental Psychology, Downing St., Cambridge CB2 3EB, UK (Now at the Department of Psychology, Bristol University.)

Elizabeth McMahon Griffith, Department of Psychology, University of Denver, 2155 S. Race St., Denver, CO 80208, USA

Sally Ozonoff, Department of Psychology, University of Utah, Salt Lake City, Utah 84112, USA

Elisabeth Pacherie, CEPERC, CNRS, ,58 rue Championnet, 75018, Paris, France

Bruce Pennington, Department of Psychology, University of Denver, 2155 S. Race St., Denver, CO 80208, USA

D. Taffy Read, Department of Psychology, University of Maine at Farmington, 62 High Street, Farmington, MA 04938-1707, USA

T.W. Robbins, Department of Experimental Psychology, Downing St., Cambridge CB2 3EB, UK

Sally J. Rogers, University of Colorado Health Sciences Center, 4200 E. 9th Avenue, Box B-148, Denver, CO 80262, USA

James Russell, Department of Experimental Psychology, Downing St., Cambridge CB2 3EB, UK

Vivian Shyu, Department of Psychology, University of Denver, 2155 S. Race St., Denver, CO 80208, USA

Michelle Turner, Department of Experimental Psychology, Downing St., Cambridge CB2 3EB, UK (now at the Department of Psychology, Durham University)

1 Introduction

James Russell

My aim in editing this book was to do more than collect between two covers various views and research studies on executive dysfunctions in autism. It was to produce something that was truly a book, something with both unity of purpose and intellectual cohesion. And while nobody could mistake this for the work of one person, I think this aim has been achieved.

What kind of purposes are the contributors 'unified' behind and what do their views 'cohere' around? The immediate answer is that the purpose is to explain why there exists in autism both deficits in the control of action and thought (executive deficits) and difficulties with understanding mental concepts ('theory of mind' deficits); while the coherence is around the view that the executive deficits are, in some sense, primary. In addition, we share the view that research—especially *recent* research—in autism has neglected the existence of behavioural rigidity in its various forms (resistance to change, obsession with regularity, stereotypies, lack of spontaneity).

But inevitably, those who have followed autism research over the past few years will also read this book as a collective reaction to the currently dominant theory of autism. They are right to do so. This theory says that the core psychological cause of autism is lack (or deviance or developmental delay) of the 'theory of mind mechanism' or 'ToMM' (Leslie 1994). People who suffer from autism have, on this theory, an impairment in a particular cognitive module. For some indeed, the disorder of autism is an existence-proof of ToMM. I will call this the 'ToMM-deficit theory'. While it would be wrong to say that all the contributors explicitly reject the ToMM-deficit theory and, in the same terms, each chapter does represent a particular sceptical reaction to it.

I need to be very explicit about what these varieties of scepticism are *not* directed at. Their common denominator is scepticism about a very particular and very ambitious theory, not about the existence of mentalizing deficits in autism. None us is denying that persons with autism have such mentalizing impairments, and none of us would want to say that these difficulties can be, as it were, explained away in terms of executive deficits. That is the first caveat. The second will take much longer to sound. It is that *in rejecting the*

ToMM-deficit theory one does not have to reject the whole idea that our knowledge of mental states has, in the normal case, a theory-like structure. In fact the ToMM-deficit theory expresses a view of mentality that is almost the symmetrical opposite of that favoured by at least one of the original theory theorists, as we shall see.

A 'theory theory' within an executive-deficit approach to autism

This phrase 'theory of mind' was coined by David Premack in a paper on chimpanzee behaviour, but the concept, rather than the phrase, has quite a different ancestry. Adam Morton (1980) applied the term 'the theory theory' to the work of some mid-twentieth century philosophers who wanted to oppose Descartes' picture of mentality without at the same time espousing behaviourism. On the Cartesian view, the subject, in reflecting on his or her mental contents, is supposed to apprehend, directly and incorrigibly, mental kinds such as beliefs or desires. That is to say, introspection was supposed to cut the mental world at its joints. Indeed, reflection upon the contents of consciousness provides us, for the Cartesian, with the kind of bedrock certainty that perception of the external world cannot provide. For the theory theorist, by contrast, mental concepts are theoretical entities, entities yielded by the application of a theory we have constructed to explain ourselves to ourselves. So the introspector, on the theory theory, is not directly perceiving natural kinds but rather exercising a bit of theory-relative know-how when he takes him- or herself to be, say, believing that something is the case.

Who are the theory theorists? Morton writes in a footnote: 'The first stage towards the theory theory is found in some places in Wittgenstein, in Austin, and in Sellars. Putnam's and Fodor's functionalism represents an intermediate stage . . .' (Morton 1980, p. 10). Now some readers may—perhaps in addition to following autism research—also have been following the big debates on the philosophical wing of cognitive science. If so, they will be surprised at this list. For it's not every day one sees philosophers as different as Wittgenstein and Fodor pictured as marching under the same banner. What's happened? Despite the fact that they are indeed both theory theorists, they are leading marches in different directions.

Things will become clearer when we distinguish between a form of theory theory with which any sceptic about the ToMM concept would be happy— this is the Wittgensteinian version—and the form that is foundational to the ToMM-deficit hypothesis—Fodor's. My intention here is not to write a historical footnote about how a term has been used in contradictory ways: it is to show how the claim that our knowledge of mental states requires the

exercise of a theory that is entirely at home with—maybe even *required by*—
an executive-deficit approach to autism.

Here is the sense in which Wittgenstein was a theory theorist. First and
foremost, he was trying to rid us of our misplaced faith not only in the data of
introspection but also in the central role of subjective experience in fixing the
meaning of words. Apprehending and reporting the contents of consciousness will require the subject to use words for mental kinds whose meaning is
not fixed by their reference to mental episodes: their meaning is fixed by
public practice. But this is so not because mental episodes have a kind of
'privacy' which debars the subject from being able to check that what he or
she means by (say) 'pain' or 'think' is the same as what other people mean by
these words. Indeed it is *exactly* this conception of the mental that leads to
the deepest confusions. Take the view that the meaning of the word 'pain' is
fixed by its reference to a particular kind of bodily feeling, a feeling 'private',
that is, to each person, and then consider the following thought-experiment.
There is a man on a desert island who, having never enjoyed human contact,
has no language, but who nevertheless sets about inventing words for his
sensations. One day he has a sensation and calls it 'X'; the next day he has a
similar sensation and decides that this is another example of the X-feeling.
Later still there is a problem case, but he decides that on balance this too is
the X feeling. In naming his sensations the person can never be wrong:
whatever *seems* to be an appropriate use of the term will *be* an appropriate
use of the term. But if he can never be wrong then he can never be right, and if
he can never be right he can never make true statements containing the word
'X'. And so he has no language at all: and so there cannot be a 'private
language'.

The anti-private language argument draws our attention to the fact that
word meanings, in Putnam's phrase, 'ain't in the head'. Obviously enough,
processes go on in the head when we mean things by words, but the meanings
of words are not fixed by the way they map to mental representations.
Accordingly, the language children learn will provide them with theoretical
concepts of many kinds, and the meaning of these will be fixed within the
language and within the variously interweaving rules for its use.

This point applies to the acquisition of a theory of mind in the following
way. On the Wittgensteinian view, a 'theory of mind' would be regarded as a
public theory that the child acquires as he or she learns to speak and to
interact with others both linguistically and non-linguistically. It is an
intersubjective theory that is genuinely *acquired*, rather than an innate
prerequisite for language learning and for social interaction.

How is the theory of mind structured? The meaning of each mental term
exists in relation to the meaning of many (every?) other mental terms within a
system with the coherence and explanatory power of theory. Thus, we would

not say that a child knew what 'pain' or 'enjoy' meant if she often said that people 'enjoy' being in 'pain'. Similarly, the meanings of the so-called 'propositional attitude' terms (believe, know, want, expect . . .) are fixed by their inferential relationships to one another (e.g. if I 'expect' to win then I 'believe' winning is possible for me, but I do not 'know' that I will win). This is not acquired piecemeal, rather, in Wittgenstein's phrase 'light dawns gradually over the whole'.

What does this imply about the innate prerequisites for acquiring mental language? In the first place—this is a major theme of this book—the subject *must be the right kind of mental entity to acquire this theory*, and one might even say that having a mind must precede the theory of it. And this, of course, implies that the nature of mind is not exhausted by our theories of it. Second, with regard to language *per se*, despite what Chomsky has said, Wittgenstein's position has no negative implications for nativist theories of syntax. (One can believe that we have innate, tacit knowledge of the 'move-alpha' rule, the 'subjacency principle', and of all the innate rules Chomsky posits, and still be a Wittgensteinian theory theorist.) This is because Wittgenstein was concerned with verbal concepts and practices not with the formal or 'computational' rules of syntax. What he was rejecting was the view famously proposed by St Augustine that acquiring the semantics of a natural language requires the child to know these semantics already—a kind of private language on to which the public, natural language must be mapped. On the Augustinian view, learning the meaning of 'cat' or 'momentum' or 'think' would demand the presence of innate concepts—a representational format for acquiring these terms, an innate private language.

We now come to a second and quite different sense of 'theory' in 'theory of mind'—the sense used in the ToMM-deficit theory of autism. The work of J. A. Fodor underpins ideas such as 'the module for theory of mind', but a related fact is that he is also well known for rejecting the Wittgensteinian view of language learning (Fodor 1976). He argued that the Augustinian account is indeed correct; that the innate representational format for learning a public (or 'natural' language) is a 'language of thought'; and that the language of thought is a language that does not stand in need of interpretation (a character it shares with the machine code of a digital computer). Knowledge of mental kinds will therefore be innately specified within this format—just like everything else.

Where is the theory theory in all this? As we saw in the Morton quotation, Fodor's view of mental states was functionalist; and for functionalists a mental state is individuated by the way it is caused by perceptual inputs, by the way it causes behaviour, and by its causal liaisons with other mental states. And being individuated by a causal role in this way is not a million miles from being individuated by an *explanatory* role, in the sense that a postulate within a scientific theory (e.g. 'antimatter', 'the articulatory loop') is determined entirely by the role it plays in explaining phenomena in relation to other postulates. The characters of the mental state and of the scientific postulate are, as it were, exhausted by their causal roles within an explanatory enterprise. The upshot is that the subject's knowledge of his or her mental states is a form of theoretical knowledge. But one can be a functionalist without holding Wittgensteinian views about the public, intersubjective nature of this theory.

However, we do not yet have the complete sense of 'theory theory' that is at work within the ToMM-deficit hypothesis. To get this we must add two more ingredients. First, there is the notion of a 'tacit theory' which acquired currency in cognitive science some time during the late 1970s. In this sense, the computations carried out by, say, the visual system or the syntax system can be said to have a theoretical structure. Second, there was further work by Fodor. About 10 years after arguing for the Augustinian view of language acquisition, Fodor (1983) proposed that our tacit-theory-containing perceptual systems have a modular nature; these are the 'input systems', as opposed to the 'central systems'. If—and this is a very big 'if'—we want to think of our theory of mind as a kind of input system, as something that enables us, almost reflexively, to pick out mental kinds in the environment, then it is but a short step to the view that the theory of mind is an innately specified module containing a *sui generis* tacit theory.

This is about as far from Wittgenstein's kind of theory theory as one can get. For Wittgenstein, the theory was a public entity—a set of linguistic, intersubjective practices. On the view just described it is nothing of the kind: it is a tacit, modular 'theory' enabling the subject to parse perceptual inputs into mental kinds; it is ToMM.

With regard to autism, I hope it can now emerge that believing that impoverishments in the autistic theory of mind must be explained in terms of delay or deviance in ToMM, let alone claiming that autism is a kind of existence proof of such a mechanism, means subscribing to a philosophy of mind that is—to put it mildly—*not mandatory*. Moreover, one can believe that our knowledge of mental life is theory-involving while committing ourselves to no particular view about the nature of the innate mental apparatus for acquiring this theory, and consequently about what is innately impaired in autism.

What then if we take a broadly Wittgensteinian approach to this theory? Clearly, we do not have to say, having rejected the Augustianian view, that developing a theory of mind requires us (tacitly) to know it already. But it goes without saying that many things must be true of the subject if he or she is to become a member of this theory-using community. That is to say, the 'pretheoretical' mind must be adequately configured. This is where *agency* comes in; this is where the executive-dysfunction theory of autism comes in.

Agents can control, within limits determined by the environment and by their motor capacities, the nature of their experiences; and the more successful they are at doing so the richer the cognitive substrate will be for having first-person thoughts. They experience being that which determines the moment-to-moment contents of consciousness. (This claim is spelt out in my own chapter.) If this is impaired, the subject will be poorly placed to acquire the public theory of mind. Needless to say there are many pretheoretical cognitive requisites in addition to adequate agency. Some of these *may* turn out to have the character of Fodorian input systems. Although, on the present view, these are certainly not 'precursors' to the theory of mind—the same kind of thing as the main act but only supporting it.

Putting it rather grandly, what lies behind the executive-dysfunction theory of autism is the thought that *Im Angang war die Tat*—the conclusion of Goethe's Faust that 'in the beginning was the deed'. This is a line with such resonance that it can inspire a variety of views, and it would certainly be wrong to say that the claim sketched in the previous paragraph is 'Wittgen-steinian'—despite the fact that Wittgenstein quoted the line (Klagge and Nordmann 1993, p. 394) and that he said it might serve as a motto for his whole later philosophy (Monk 1990, p.306). But there is enough of a parallel, and of an interesting tension, between the view that the acquisition of self-awareness is grounded in agency and Wittgenstein's views about 'the importance ascribed to certain primitive actions and reactions for *concept-formation*' (Winch 1981, p. 176, original italics) to make it worthy of comment.

The Wittgenstein-inspired conception of the theory of mind is as a system of language for talking about mental life and behaviour. This does not mean, as we have seen, that this language must have purchase upon a proto-language which is already in place. But in what sense is this non-linguistic 'something' that psychologically configures us to acquire mental (and non-mental) language involved with agency? In the first sense—the one Goethe had in mind and the one to be found in this book—agents create; and so they will, to some degree, create their experiences and thereby gain a sense of themselves as that which is responsible for them. This creativity can be innately impaired.

Wittgenstein was more interested, however, in social action, a sense of action that encompasses reactions to the doings and emotional displays of other people. There was, for Wittgenstein, a kind of bedrock here, a level at which there can *be* doubt—is this man really in pain or just pretending?—but at which we cannot *begin* with doubt. By contrast, it is language, in so far as language is a system affording falsity as well as truth, which naturally encompasses doubt, uncertainty, and ignorance. Note that some of the child's earliest speech-acts are *questions*.

To illustrate the undoubting, unquestioning role of social reactions Wittgenstein says this. Having described the way a mother will naturally assume her child is in pain when she sees him crying and clutching his cheek and later starts to wonder whether the pain is real, he invites us to consider a mother who *begins* with scepticism. This 'would strike us as queer and crazy—'The game can't begin with doubting' means: we shouldn't call it 'doubting' if the game began with it" (Wittgenstein 1976, p. 414). But some individuals may begin life without this propensity for undoubting reactions; this too may be innately impaired.

Autistic impairments in social action and in natural resonance to the emotional states of others receive little attention in this book. But this certainly does not mean that their explanation should be left to the ToMM-deficit theory. Peter Hobson (1993) has argued that such impairments lie at the heart of autism, and he does so with many references to Wittgenstein and to the work of philosophers influenced by him (e.g. David Hamlyn). The executive-deficit view of autism and Hobson's position are, of course, quite different theories which compete for much of (not all of) the same empirical territory; but I hope to have shown that at a meta-theoretical level they are similar.

But it is now time to stop talking about theory theories, meta-theories, and philosophically inspired theories and start talking about what this book actually contains.

The chapters

As Robbins says at the beginning of his chapter, the ToMM-deficit hypothesis inspires a rather simplistic view of the neural substrate for theory of mind, and thus of the core deficits in autism. In fact, if ToMM is a Fodorian module then it must have, on Fodor's (seventh) criterion, a 'fixed neural architecture'. That is, there must be 'somewhere' in the brain where these *sui generis* computations take place. Modularists have resisted this phrenological fate by proposing a 'cognitive' level between symptoms and neurobiology at which the mentalizing mechanism can be as modular as one might wish. But does this mean that facts about the neurobiology of autism are quite autonomous from these 'cognitive' modules? If so, we have the unwelcome consequence that neurobiology is not going to be allowed to constrain and inspire cognitive theories of autism.

Robbins illustrates how complex the neurobiology of autism has turned out to be, and argues that, because of this, all three neurobiological theories contain elements of truth. Moreover, it is difficult to imagine how such a multifaceted pattern of neural impairments could be modular at any level of description.

The 'executive systems' are, needless to say, the opposite of modular, and, while it is convenient to locate at least some of these in the prefrontal cortex (though given how much of the cortex this covers 'locate' is hardly the word) executive control is achieved by many systems distributed throughout the brain. In other words, the neurobiology of autism has the sort of character one finds in the neurobiology of executive functioning. Indeed, while one must resist pushing the parallel too far, it is interesting to note that each of the three main neurobiological theories of autism locates the core impairment in an area with a significant executive role. These three are: frontostriatal (frontal lesions affect, at least, inhibition, working memory, the generation and monitoring of plans, and they cause stereotypies), mediotemporal (lesions affect aspects of the control of social behaviour, in addition to causing mnemonic and emotional deficits), and cerebellum (efference-copying and attention-shifting affected by lesions). But rather than take this Procrustean course it is perhaps better to read the chapter for what it is. Robbins 'horizontally integrates' the three theories of the neurobiology of autism, points up parallels with schizophrenia, suggests which paths should be followed, and in so doing shows us how neurobiology can inspire and constrain work on the executive dysfunctions in autism

The next two chapters, by Michelle Turner and by Chris Jarrold, are about deficits in the generation of behaviour and ideas—about the 'creativity' to which I referred at the end of the previous section.

One of the four main headings under which autism is diagnosed in DSM-III-R is 'Markedly restricted repertoire of activities and interests', the subheadings of which concern stereotypies, attachments to unusual objects, distress over trivial changes to the environment, unreasonable insistence on routine, and an extremely restricted range of interests. One might sum up these by the phrase 'behavioural rigidity', and the kind of rigidity captured here is just what one would expect from a population severely impaired in generating novel behaviour.

Turner tackles, amongst other things, two major questions inspired by the existence of behavioural rigidity in autism: Are these impairments explicable in terms of mentalizing difficulties? How do these 'everyday' problems relate to performance on formal tests (especially the classic executive tasks)? In the first case, the data she reports speak against the view that behavioural rigidity is caused by impaired theory of mind, and, in the second, she presents some fascinating correlational evidence. For example, the existence of repetitive language and circumscribed interests turns out to be related to difficulties with extradimensional set-shifting. The reader's appetite will be whetted by turning to Table 3.2 on p. 88. This simple table is the precious residue of countless hours testing subjects and interviewing parents—and travelling up and down the UK.

Turner also reminds us of earlier work by Uta Frith and Jill Boucher on the difficulties which persons with autism experience in producing random behaviour. Quite apart from the role these data play in her correctional work they focus our mind upon the cognitive requirements for being random, and suggest new avenues of research into the nature of executive dysfunction not only in autism but in other disorders and in normal development.

Jarrold's approach to generation deficits is different but complementary. Children with autism show little, if any, symbolic play, that is, play in which the child pretends an object or state of the world is other than it is (the Lego-brick, for example, becomes a 'teacup', an empty teacup contains 'tea'). The question is whether this deficit is due to a failure to represent the object at a higher or second-order level such that the representation can be grist to the imagination, or whether the child, though able to do this, lacks the ability to generate ideas for play. That is to say, children with autism may know well enough what it is to pretend but be unable to come up with pretend scenarios. By a similar token, most of us would be hard-pressed to write a plot for a sitcom starring a super-hero for the millennium; but we know what it is to try and what success would look like. Jarrold presents some conceptual arguments against Leslie's (1987) view that pretend play involves the kind of metarepresentation just described and discusses data in favour of the view that the play deficit in autism is one of 'generativity'.

Towards the end of his chapter Jarrold also attempts something of a more speculative nature. Taking his cue from Norman and Shallice's (1986) influential 'supervisory attentional system' model of the prefrontal functions and from some recent neural network simulations of schizophrenic performance on executive tasks, Jarrold distinguishes between three ways in which generation problems could come about. These ideas focus the mind upon what might be impaired in autism at a subpersonal level; and Jarrold's attempts to relate a hypothesis of the core executive deficit in autism to computational modelling is timely and original.

The chapters by Bruce Pennington et al. and by Sally Ozonoff confront the empirical implications of the view that executive dysfunction is 'the primary psychological cause' (Pennington's phrase) of autism. Causal theories of this kind are vulnerable because the less qualified and tentative a theory is, the wider its empirical ramifications.

Pennington and his co-workers review the outcomes of four 'validity tests': (1) if executive dysfunctions are not secondary to other dysfunctions we should expect to find executive impairments in cognitive domains that are not diagnostic of autism; but at the same time (2) executive dysfunction should be seen to underlie impairments which are diagnostic of autism; (3) if executive dysfunctions are causal then they should appear early in life; and (4) if they are causal they should be able to subsume the evidence for other cognitive theories of autism. Pennington reports the results of research by his group in all four areas; although some of the work is still in progress.

While the outcomes are rather mixed, the overall picture is an encouraging one. Under (1) Pennington reports data showing that persons with autism of roughly normal IQ show the kind of memory impairments associated with frontal lesions but not the kind associated with lesions in other brain loci. Under (2), Pennington reports significant associations between executive difficulties, on the one hand, and joint attention, reciprocal social interaction, and imitation and pantomiming, on the other. (Of course this work is correlational, but it is implausible to suggest that, say, joint attention difficulties cause problems with formal executive tests; if there is a causal link it is more likely to be executive→interpersonal.)

Under (3) however, the data are not immediately encouraging. When children around 4 years of age with autism and matched children with developmental delay were compared on a number of executive tasks the result was, broadly speaking, that there were no group differences. (I should caution, though, that the study is not complete.) But, as I argue in my own chapter, there is no reason to find this result discouraging; indeed it may be pointing us to where the locus of executive impairment exists in autism. This is because it seems to be the case that children with autism, unlike other groups of children with frontal impairments such as children with early-treated PKU (Diamond 1996), are only challenged by executive tasks if they contain arbitrary rules. The A-not-B task for example (one of the Pennington battery) contains no arbitrary rules, unlike the Wisconsin Card Sort Test and the Tower of London and other 'classic' frontal tasks. I argue that arbitrary rules pose a far greater challenge to working memory than do tasks without them; and this is neatly in line with Pennington's own proposal (made here and elsewhere) that working memory is the core executive impairment in the disorder. (Although I give a different account of these data in my own chapter.) Under (4) the question was whether executive impairments can be subsumed under what Uta Frith calls impairments of 'central coherence'. Pennington predicted, in line with his working memory theory just mentioned, that as the working-memory load is increased in central coherence tasks the performance of individuals with autism should get worse; while the central coherence deficit theory would make different predictions. The outcome did not clearly favour either the working memory or the central coherence hypotheses, and suggested that the impairments proposed by each 'do not exist at all levels of complexity'. The chapter ends with discussion of a number of meta-theoretical issues and contains a powerful case for a non-modular approach to the neuropsychology of autism.

Ozonoff's chapter confronts the single greatest threat to the hypothesis that executive dysfunction is the main psychological cause of autism, and, more generally, to the claim that mentalizing difficulties in autism are executively rooted. It is this: if other clinical populations of children exist with similar executive difficulties but without autism (or at least without mentalizing problems) then the causal theory collapses. Using this logic, Baron-Cohen (1995, p. 128) cites the fact—if it *is* a fact (see below)—that individuals with Tourette's syndrome have executive problems as evidence against the executive-deficit theory. That is to say: plus executive deficits, minus mentalizing deficits, therefore no causal link. The logic is fine, but, as Ozonoff shows us, the data are not.

What those who wish to dismiss the executive-deficit theory have to show, of course, is that these other populations of children have executive disorders *of the same type and severity as those found in autism and with a similar age of onset*. Well, no such population seems to exist. I have already mentioned PKU children, whose profile of executive difficulties is different from that of children with autism (and also touch on some data from Williams' children in my own chapter). Ozonoff very thoroughly reviews the evidence for executive dysfunctions in ADHD ('hyperactivity'), OCD (obsessive compulsive disorder), and Tourette's. (The case of schizophrenia is less urgent because of its relatively late onset. The evidence for executive impairments in schizophrenia is at least a strong as that in autism, but schizophrenia emerges well after mentalizing abilities have developed. Moreover, schizophrenics do indeed have mentalizing problems: they fail adequately to locate responsibility for their own thoughts, for example. Executive and mentalizing impairment coexist, then, in schizophrenia, as the executive-deficit theory predicts.)

Ozonoff's chapter is admirably concise, and so there is little need to summarize it. It is worth making a couple of points though. With regard to Tourette's syndrome, the evidence for executive impairments is weak and inconsistent. While Baron-Cohen finds evidence for inhibitory deficits—this is of course only one element of executive functioning—two studies do not. Moreover, Tourette's syndrome rarely occurs alone (more often with OCD, ADHD, and autism), and this can render any evidence that might crop up for executive difficulties in Tourette's uninformative. Executive deficits in Tourette's, such as they are, may therefore be the result of co-morbidity. With further regard to inhibition, the evidence from studies with such tasks as Go–NoGo shows that children with autism do not seem to have problems with inhibition *per se*: they are not impulsive, as are ADHD children. Rather, Ozonoff demonstrates, the problem in autism is with mental flexibility— shifting responses from A to B in the third phase of the Go–NoGo task for example.

Finally, it is worth recalling that the objection to the executive-deficit theory implies that other clinical populations with executive dysfunctions *do not also have mentalizing problems*. This assumption is not only a dangerous one to make, it is probably wrong. Recently, for example, Happé and Frith (1996) have shown that while children with conduct disorder are not impaired on standard false-belief tasks they do show autism-like impairments on tests of everyday social understanding. Indeed 'there was evidence of impairment in social insight, not dissimilar to that found in able individuals with autism' (p. 385). This is what the executive-deficit theory would predict. Moreover, the false-belief task is a crude instrument that makes executive as well as mentalizing demands, and so it is naïve to say that if a child passes it then she 'has' a theory of mind and if she fails then she does not. In consequence, one cannot say that if a population of children passes the task at the mental age of 4 years then that population has no mentalizing problems. (Happé (1994) is one of the few people to have devised and used more sensitive measures suitable for populations with higher mental ages.)

The final two chapters—by the French philosopher Elisabeth Pacherie and by me—have the same problem at heart. If there is a conceptual link between agency and self-consciousness what is its nature and what implications does it have for autism? While Pacherie's starting-point is Jeannerod's work on motor control and while the ideas she develops depend, to some degree, on positions defended by other philosophers (notably John Searle and Christopher Peacocke) her thesis is striking and original.

Pacherie's aim is to describe a form of conscious awareness of agency that, while being non-conceptual, is structured in such a way as to make the acquisition of a concept-exercising agency possible. The Jeannerod-inspired claims are: that there is a functional equivalence between motor preparation and motor imagery, that the motor image is the conscious counterpart of motor representation, and that the content of this normally unconscious motor representation becomes conscious when actions are delayed or blocked. The development of the thesis also depends upon a distinction which Searle draws between 'prior intentions' (I intend to do something, then I do it) and 'intentions in action' (in acting I am in control of my body in such a way that my intentions and my bodily movements have a kind of unity). Finally, the notion of contents of experience being non-conceptual but structured comes from a parallel that Pacherie makes with Peacocke's ideas about the so-called 'protopropositional' contents of perception. This is the form of non-conceptual experience that must be enjoyed if perceptual concepts are to have any purchase. By virtue these, the visual experience of, say, a square and a diamond, are different (Peacocke notes the different kinds of symmetry we see in them). That is to say, the contents of experience can contain properties and relations that are salient to us without our exercising concepts of these perceived contents (e.g. we may lack the concepts of square and diamond). For Pacherie, the level of the motor image in agency is the non-conceptual but structured counterpart to the level of protopropositional content of perception.

One of the main points Pacherie makes when she shows us the kind of cash-value these ideas have for the psychology of autism is that—broadly paraphrasing—unless there is the right kind of bridge between prior intentions and intentions in action the normal consciousness of agency will be lacking, and thus the normal consciousness of oneself as an acting self will be lacking. It is, on her thesis, the motor image which provides such a bridge, and, needless to say, the lack of it will explain failure on executive tasks in so far as these require the on-line translations of intentions into actions.

She also raises the exciting possibility that Jeannerod's ideas may help us understand why persons with autism find it difficult to perceive the intentionality of other agents. Under normal conditions, on Jeannerod's view, seeing another agent perform an action excites in us a motor representation of a similar kind to that which would have existed had we acted ourself. However, because we do not, in fact, act—the action is 'blocked' in that sense—the motor representation comes into consciousness. This is an alternative to the view that one of the building blocks of theory of mind development is an innate module exclusive to parsing the actions of others. On Jeannerod's view, by contrast, there is a motor representational system that covers both the first and third person; and so agency perception is not independent of the exercise of one's own agency.

It is coincidental that my proposals and Pacherie's are somewhat similar; though perhaps coincidence is not the word, given that we are talking about the same bit of Nature! The starting-points and ways of arguing are very different, but the conclusions are similar and the goal is the same. In my chapter I too try to describe a form of non-conceptual but structured experience of agency whose impairment will prevent the normal acquisition of agency concepts. I do not use Pacherie's terminology, however, and refer instead to the development of 'pretheoretical self-awareness' as grounding first-person thoughts and thus the acquisition of a theory of mind. The first part of the chapter builds upon ideas I set out in a recent book (Russell 1996).

I begin with the process of efference-copying and broaden this into a discussion of action-monitoring—a concept wide enough to include everything from visuomotor processes in the fruit fly to self-monitoring in source memory. I argue that action-monitoring mechanisms not only make basic motor control possible (e.g. postural stability) but additionally support the development of self-world dualism and the correlative ability to locate responsibility for self-caused changes in perceptual inputs within one's own body. (My debt to Chris Frith's work, in the latter case, is obvious.) My discussion of pretheoretical self-awareness focuses upon bodily aware-

ness, non-representational knowledge of volition, and the necessary identity
of the willing and the knowing self.

A second, though far from exact, parallel with Pacherie's thesis is to be
found in the discussion of Richard Held's claim that efference-copying
requires the production of 'visual schemata' of motor commands which
are matched against the visible results of bodily movements. (I also discuss
the evidence for children with autism being impaired in the construction of
these schemata.) These visual schemata are not the same as Jeannerod's
motor images, although the two postulates would seem to be mutually
dependent. In any event, the Held-derived and the Jeannerod-derived ideas
converge upon the claim that children with autism will have an impaired
body schema; and the existence of imitation deficits in autism supports this.

After a review of the evidence for action-monitoring impairments in
autism I argue, on the basis of the work of Bruce Pennington and colleagues, of Sally Ozonoff, of Claire Hughes, and of work I have carried out with
Chris Jarrold, that the executive tasks which challenge children with autism
are the ones requiring the subject to act on the basis of an *arbitrary* rule while
inhibiting a prepotent response. I then argue that, because arbitrary rules are
ideally encoded in natural language and because failing to encode them in
this way will leave the subject prey to prepotency effects, autism may be
associated with a paucity or absence of self-regulatory language. I admit
along the way that the claim is speculative and that the conceptual and
developmental link between pretheoretical awareness and regulatory language has yet to be spelt out. That said, it is worth remembering that
language impairments are a criterial feature of autism. It is also worth
remembering that one of the more influential approaches to autism before
the ToMM-deficit theory came on the scene was Michael Rutter's (1979)
view that autism is, in large part, a consequence of linguistic impairment (for
a recent re-assessment of it see Bailey *et al.* 1996). Finally, I hope that the
links between this claim and the ideas developed at the beginning of this
Introduction about the theory of mind development being indissociable from
the acquisition of language do not need to be spelt out.

Practical implications?

It is clear that most of the research reported in this book is theory-driven to
the core. And perhaps for some of those responsible for the day-to-day care
of autistic children and adults our concerns may seem too theory-driven by
half. There is, after all, the ever-present danger of using research literature on
a mental disorder as the exercising ground for academic hobby-horses; and
maybe it is not enough simply to avoid this danger. Perhaps there is an onus
on those who press for a particular view of the disorder to say what their

views imply about the possibility of remediation and about the best methods of care. One of two things can tentatively be said.

First, with regard to remediation, it might be said that the executive-deficit theory inspires somewhat more optimism than the ToMM-deficit theory. If the primary psychological cause of autism is that the individual 'lacks' the module for theory of mind, one is faced with the task of devising neurochemical treatments that could bring such a module into being. Remember that modules are *sui generis* so they cannot be, as it were, woven from other kinds of neurocomputational cloth. Alternatively, we are forced to imagine that a dormant module could be revived having never been used, and that too is biologically implausible.

On the executive-deficit theory, by contrast, one can say the following: (1) the pretheoretical mind is inadequately configured due to impairments in executive systems distributed through much of the brain; (2) we should consider the neurobiological parallels between autism and schizophrenia (discussed by Robbins) as well as the parallels in executive dysfunctioning; and note that (3) schizophrenia is caused, in part, by neurochemical imbalances originating in development which could, in theory at least, be corrected. In the light of this, one can at least imagine that it would be possible to reconfigure the executive systems by correcting the balance of chemical neurotransmitters. This is, of course, a very tall order indeed; and, as Robbins mentions, the autistic-like negative symptoms in schizophrenia are, at present, largely resistant to drug treatment. But if some of the claims made in this book are correct, drug-based treatments of executive dysfunctioning would enable the individual to achieve a mental life which would make late access to this theory possible.

Meanwhile, what do the two theories imply about care—about techniques for making the life of the person with autism go as well as possible? For those who hold a more modest form of the ToMM-deficit hypothesis, it is 'delay' and 'deviance' rather than 'lack' of ToMM that will be emphasized. If something is delayed it can be brought on, and if it is deviant it may be set straight; and so there have been attempts to 'teach' theory of mind to subjects with autism (e.g. Swettenham 1996). This training has had some success, but it is only effective with the false-belief, task-based scenarios on which the child is trained: it does not generalize. This suggests that the child is picking up a set of procedures with limited understanding of their wider significance. However, it would be quite wrong to dismiss these attempts, not least because such teaching may sometimes help the individual, in a subtle way, to experience the social world as a more predictable place.

The executive-deficit theory does not inspire training programmes as naturally as the ToMM-deficit theory. One could imagine how, say, augmented feedback might facilitate some forms of executive control; but, if the impairments are as profound as we are claiming, it is difficult to be optimistic about their success. So what is the upshot? Instead of trying to make individuals with autism become more like individuals without it, the theory encourages us to make the environment of autistic persons, as far possible, the 'objective correlative' of their inner mental rigidity. In other words, we provide them with a social life with order, predictability, and that affords the opportunity for mechanical and idiosyncratic interests. Of course there are practical constraints on how far one can go here. It is presumptuous, for example, to recommend that carers should never, say, encourage an autistic child who only eats a certain brand of white, sliced bread to try something else, or more seriously, should always comply with his demands no matter how much it upsets other people. But children with autism, if the theory is correct, are not wilful in the sense we apply to normally developing children; or rather their form of 'wilfulness' reveals their core psychological deficit. Until drug treatments emerge, accommodating their environment to their uniquely inflexible mental life is probably one of the main things we can do to help them lead a happy life.

Acknowledgements

I am grateful to Sally Barrett-Williams for extensive discussion on the first part of this introduction and to Trevor Robbins for his comments on the whole thing. I thank Jane Heal for advice about the Wittgenstein literature.

REFERENCES

Bailey, A., Phillips, W., and Rutter, M. (1996). Autism: Towards an integration of clinical, genetic, neuropsychological, and neurobiological perspectives. *Journal of Child Psychology and Psychiatry*, 37, 89–126.

Baron-Cohen, S. (1995). *Mindblindness: An essay on autism and theory of mind*. MIT Press, Cambridge, MA.Diamond, A. (1996). Evidence for the importance of dopamine for prefrontal cortex functions early in life. *Philosophical Transactions of the Royal Society: Biological Sciences*, 351, 1483–94.

Fodor, J. A. (1976). *The language of thought*. Harvester Press, Hassocks, UK.

Fodor, J. A. (1983). *The modularity of mind: An essay on faculty psychology*. MIT Press, Cambridge, MA.

Happé, F. G. E. (1994). An advanced test of theory of mind: understanding of story characters thoughts and feelings by able autistic, mentally handicapped and normal children and adults. *Journal of Autism and Developmental Disorders*, 24, 129–54.

Happé, F. G. E. and Frith, U. (1996). Theory of mind and social impairment in children with conduct disorder. *British Journal of Developmental Psychology*, 14, 385–98.

Hobson, P. (1993). *Autism and the development of mind*. Lawrence Erlbaum, Hove.

Klagge, J. and Nordmann, A. (ed.) (1993). *Philosophical occasions*. Basil Blackwell, Oxford.

Leslie, A. M. (1987). Pretence and representation: The origins of 'theory of mind'. *Psychological Review*, 94, 412–26.

Leslie, A. M. (1994). Pretending and believing: issues in the theory of ToMM. *Cognition*, 50, 211–38.

Monk, R. (1990). *Ludwig Wittgenstein: The duty of genius*. Cape, London.

Morton, A. (1980). *Frames of mind: Constraints on the commonsense conception of the mental*. Clarendon Press, Oxford.

Norman, D. A. and Shallice, T. (1986). Attention to action: Willed and automatic control of behaviour. In R. J. Davidson, G. E. Schwartz, and D. Shapiro (ed.) *Consciousness and self-regulation: Advances in research*, Vol. 4., pp. 24–49. Plenum Press, New York.

Russell, J. (1996). *Agency: Its role in mental development*. Erlbaum (UK) Taylor and Francis, Hove.

Rutter, M. (1979). Language, cognition, and autism. In R. Katzman (ed.) *Congenital and acquired cognitive disorders*. Raven Press, NY.

Swettenham, J. (1996). Can children with autism be taught to understand false belief using computers? *Journal of Child Psychology and Psychiatry*, 37, 157–65.

Winch, P. (1981). Im Anfang war die Tat. In I. Block (ed.) *Perspectives on the philosophy of Wittgenstein*. Basil Blackwell, Oxford.

Wittgenstein, L. (1976). Cause and effect: Intuitive awareness. *Philosophia*, 6, 415–31. (Trans. Peter Winch.)

PART I

The neurobiology of autism

2 Integrating the neurobiological and neuropsychological dimensions of autism

T. W. Robbins

Introduction

The challenge to research into childhood autism lies in relating what appears to be a set of apparently somewhat independent symptoms, such as impaired communication and language deficits, problems with mentalizing about people's minds ('Theory of Mind', ToM), mental retardation, neurological signs and stereotyped behaviour, to corresponding deficits in brain systems. This research approach can be viewed as one of 'vertical integration' (Churchland 1986) in which theories in one domain are strengthened by structural congruences in another. A similar theme has been voiced by Morton and Frith (1995) and in a recent theoretical review (Happé and Frith 1996). One example of this 'vertical' approach would be the attempt to link findings employing purely cognitive or neuropsychological paradigms to results obtained using the neurobiological techniques from such fields as neuroimaging, neurochemistry and neuropathology. Unfortunately, this approach often reduces to a search for possible modular 'brain centres' associated with what are assumed to be the dominant, core or 'primary' defining symptoms of the disorder. This can lead to controversial stand-points in the case of autism, such that there is a specific brain module for the ToM which is absent or poorly developed. A related and equally simplified 'vertical' notion would be that the deficiencies in 'executive' functioning observed from the application of tests generally used to assess brain-damaged subjects for autism must be related to a malfunction of a brain region typically associated with such problems in the control and regulation of behaviour, the prefrontal cortex. It does not seem very likely that executive functioning is modular, probably representing instead a set of control processes that are widely distributed across neural systems, including the heterogeneous anatomical components of the prefrontal cortex and their connections with other brain structures (Pandya and Yeterian 1995).

However, autism generally presents as a set of symptoms, the precise significance of which, relative to another, remains to be established—as in the case of the ToM impairments and the more general problems in 'executive function' also present in the disorder. Analogously, the main neurobiological findings in autism seem to implicate many possible foci which are probably affected to varying extents in different individuals. These are problems of 'horizontal' integration, and it seems evident that a complete understanding of the disorder has to achieve an orderly account in both the 'vertical' and 'horizontal' dimensions. This understanding would ultimately range in the vertical dimension from the genetic and cellular to the social and clinical levels. In the horizontal dimension, it would be important to understand the full range of symptoms from 'mentalizing' to dyskinesias.

A review of the relevant, often conflicting, neuropathological, neurochemical and neuroimaging evidence relating to child autism makes it clear that we are currently distant from an understanding of this syndrome in neural terms, certainly when compared with what is understood at the clinical and neuropsychological levels (Bailey *et al.* 1996). This excellent review, and the relatively recent, comprehensive survey of major neurobiological findings in autism (Bauman and Kemper 1994a) remove the need for this chapter to be a critical compilation of evidence. Instead, I will selectively survey some of the main data and current theories of the neural basis of autism, in the context of the integrative strategy outlined above which is already being pursued in the analysis of other disorders, such as adult schizophrenia.

While autism and schizophrenia, despite certain overlapping features, are considered as distinct clinical entities, they also have many parallel features. Like autism, schizophrenia is a syndrome with multiple, seemingly unrelated and sometimes bizarre, symptoms, including those of language and social communication. Both are associated with cognitive deficits (or mental retardation in the case of autism), but both can occur in a context of high levels of intellectual functioning. Both have associated neurological symptoms such as dyskinesias. The precise aetiology of both is still a matter of intense investigation, but they are powerfully affected by genetic factors probably affecting brain development. Both are treated, with varying degrees of success, with drugs that antagonize dopamine receptors, the rationale being that psychotic and stereotyped behaviours are attenuated by such treatment. The dopamine receptor-blocking agent haloperidol is of only limited efficacy in autism, whereas the negative symptoms of schizophrenia are resistant to therapy with such conventional neuroleptic drugs. Other neurotransmitter changes have been suggested to occur in both, for example of serotonin (or 5-hydroxytryptamine, 5-HT), and of opioids in the case of autism (see Anderson 1994). Above all, what strikes the naïve observer about child autism and schizophrenia is their considerable degree of heterogeneity, which produces major problems, for example, in comparing different studies and even in finding appropriate control groups. However, accounting for this heterogeneity surely must figure strongly in any theory, whether it is one postulating unitary, or multiple, neural substrates.

Quite powerful ideas about the neural basis of schizophrenia have emerged from a convergence of different types of neurobiological information. For example, there is now considerable evidence of impairments in both frontal and temporal lobe (including limbic) dysfunction in schizophrenia, particularly in the interactions of these structures with one another and with subcortical structures such as the striatum, and the mesencephalic dopamine system, especially under stressful circumstances (Jaskiw and Weinberger 1992). Most importantly, this information is now being integrated with cognitive and neuropsychological data on schizophrenia to help provide a viable neural account of the disorder, particularly from new initiatives such as functional neuroimaging.

A survey of the major neural theories of autism

Fuelled mainly by informed speculations about the known functions of different brain regions, and on the basis of neuropathological and neuroimaging data, autism has been associated with dysfunction in three major neural axes: the temporal lobe and limbic system (e.g. Dachevalior 1994; Bauman and Kemper 1985); the frontal cortex and striatum ('frontostriatal' systems) (e.g. Damasio and Maurer 1978); and the cerebellum and brainstem (e.g. Bauman and Kemper 1985; Courchesne et al. 1988). The numbers of subjects involved generally has been (necessarily) quite small, first because children with autism do not generally come quickly to autopsy, and second because of the ethical and logistic limitations imposed by using techniques of magnetic resonance imaging (MRI) and positron-emission tomography (PET) in children (Filipek et al. 1992). Thus, many of the relevant data actually derive from adult subjects with autism, and therefore have to be extrapolated to the development of child autism with some caution. As will be seen, the three main types of theories lean on somewhat different types of evidence; post-mortem neuropathology and animal neuropsychology in the case of the medial temporal hypothesis; structural imaging and neuropathology in the case of the cerebellar hypothesis; and neuropsychological theory, supported by neuroimaging and neurological data, in the case of the frontostriatal hypothesis.

The medial temporal lobe hypothesis

Bauman and Kemper's (1985) painstaking neuropathological analysis of serial sections in eight autistic subjects coming to autopsy has shown the existence of greater numbers of small, closely packed cells in the medial temporal lobe (see Fig. 2.1) in such limbic structures as the entorhinal cortex, hippocampus (all four fields of Ammon, CA1–4), medial septum and amygdala, although much of the temporal neocortex itself appears normal. The inference generally drawn from these data is that there there has been a neurodevelopmental retardation leading to a malfunctioning of these circuits during development, with consequent symptoms that may resemble, but not be identical to, the types of deficits produced by actual brain lesions. Isolated cases supporting this hypothesis have been reported in the literature of autism with neuropatho-logical features in medial temporal lobe structures such as the amygdala (Bachevalier 1994). Frequently, autism is associated with medial temporal lobe epilepsy or tuberous sclerosis (see Bachevalier 1994). However, so far, there has been relatively little in the way of quantitative data provided on these temporal lobe abnormalities (Bailey *et al.* 1996).

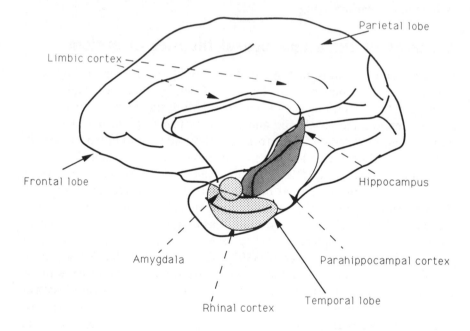

Fig. 2.1 Schematic diagram of the medial aspect of the temporal lobe in a rhesus monkey brain to show the underlying amygdala and hippocampus. Note the overlying rhinal and parahippocampal cortex in this medial view.

There has also been a relative paucity of neuroimaging studies showing abnormalities in medial temporal lobe structures, despite reports from post-mortem studies of reductions in hippocampal volume in autism. Early studies utilizing pneumoencephalographic techniques to measure the size of the brain ventricles have reported dilatation of the left temporal horn, perhaps consistent with the post-mortem observations (Hauser *et al.* 1975). Again, isolated cases with many autistic features resulting from temporal lobe tumours have been reported (e.g. Hoon and Reiss 1992). But the suggestion that structural changes in the medial temporal lobe are common in autism has not been well supported by observations made with CT or MRI scanning techniques (Bailey *et al.* 1996; Courchesne *et al.* 1993; Saitoh *et al.* 1995). It is possible that more dynamic forms of neuroimaging will prove to be more sensitive to possible changes. For example, a recent study using single-photon emission tomography (SPET) of 31 children and adolescents with autism and autism-like syndromes found consistent reductions in regional cerebral blood flow in the temporal lobes, regardless of whether or not the subjects had epilepsy (Gillberg *et al.* 1993). There were also more general, smaller reductions in cerebral blood flow in the parietal and temporal regions, in accordance with earlier data of Lelord *et al.* (1991).

The other main form of support for the temporal lobe hypothesis comes by analogy with behavioural or cognitive syndromes produced by temporal lobe damage in human subjects and monkeys. Bachevalier (1994) has argued persuasively from this perspective, particularly from observations made on monkeys receiving neonatal lesions of the temporal lobe. Newborn rhesus monkeys had the amygdalohippocampal complex removed by aspiration in two stages, a procedure which also damages large portions of the entorhinal and perirhinal cortices (see Fig. 2.1; but see Murray 1996 and Suzuki 1996 for more detailed anatomical diagrams). Positive control monkeys received bilateral removals of area TE (inferotemporal cortex). Subsequently, the behaviour of these animals was carefully observed during the course of subsequent development in social contexts, as well as in formal tests of recognition memory using the delayed matching-to-sample procedure.

The medial temporal lobe lesioned monkeys failed to develop normal social behaviour at the expense of 'locomotor stereotypies and self-directed activities'. These effects contrasted with the loss of apparent fear and disinhibited behaviour associated with the Kluver–Bucy syndrome in adult animals with similar lesions. They could also be distinguished from the effects of TE lesions which led mainly to hyperactivity and did not persist into adulthood. In cognitive terms, the medial temporal lobe lesions produced effects which are found in adult monkeys: impairments in delayed non-matching to sample (DNMTS), but sparing of performance on a test of visual 'habit' learning, as measured by the acquisition of concurrent visual discriminations with 24 hour delays between trials with the same stimuli. The gross behavioural effects of temporal lobe lesions are certainly reminiscent of some of the features of autistic behaviour in humans. Impairments in 'declarative ' memory, as measured by the DNMTS test, have certainly been reported in autistic subjects (Ameli *et al.* 1988; Dawson 1996), but are perhaps not the most obvious cognitive symptom in this condition. Indeed, Bennetto *et al.* (1996) have not found this test to be very sensitive to autistic deficits. The sparing of skill-based, 'procedural' knowledge in autism implied by the hypothesis has been little studied.

Overall, the temporal lobe theory receives some support and has a degree of neuropsychological credibility, but it is not compelling in identifying the unique neural substrates of autism, for reasons that will become further apparent below.

The cerebellar hypothesis

This hypothesis also arose from neuropathological and neuroradiological observations. Williams *et al.* (1980) initially discovered a selective loss of cerebellar Purkinje cells in a single autistic patient. These findings, together with associated reductions in cerebellar granule cells, have since been confirmed throughout the cerebellar hemispheres and vermis (Bauman and Kemper 1985, 1994b). The majority of neuroimaging findings have also confirmed that there is cerebellar hypoplasia (Courchesne *et al.* 1988; see reviews in Courchesne 1995; Hashimoto *et al.* 1995). Particularly impressive has been the enormous MRI study by Hashimoto *et al.* (1995) of 102 autistic patients and 122 controls aged from about 3 months to 20 years. The autistic patients included both mentally retarded and high-functioning individuals, with a preponderance of the former. However, they found evidence not only of reduced cerebellar volume, but also of other brainstem posterior fossa structures, the medulla oblongata, pons and the midbrain (see Fig. 2.2). The differences in size between autistic and control groups for the pons and cerebellar vermian lobules I–VII eventually disappeared with age, suggesting that development was simply retarded. In contrast, initial differences in size were sustained in the midbrain, medulla oblongata and vermis VIII–X. These results indicate a neurodevelopmental deficit, possibly resulting from pre-natal trauma, rather than postnatal neurodegeneration. Hashimoto *et al.* (1995) were also able to identify 10 infants (less than 3 years of age) with developmental delay and poor eye contact and give them prospective MRI scans, prior to the later confirmed diagnosis of autism. These additional observations show that these neural changes are present at the earliest signs of infantile autism. What, however, is currently lacking is any direct evidence of cerebellar or brainstem deficits using functional imaging techniques, including PET. An early study of metabolism using [^{18}F]fluorodeoxy-D-glucose (FDG), found no obvious abnormalities (Heh *et al.* 1989).

It is thus especially important to attempt to relate the structural changes to other features of autism in order to gauge their causal significance. The brainstem abnormalities are consistent with evidence of altered auditory

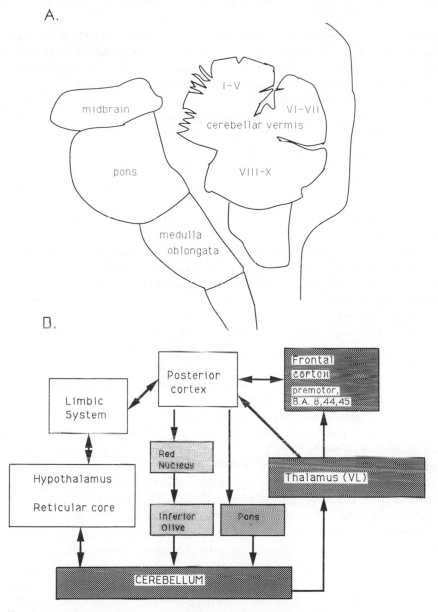

Fig. 2.2 (A) Schematic sagittal section through a human brain to show interrelationships among the posterior fossa structures (similar to what would be seen following inspection of an MRI scan with defining anatomical boundaries added for the purposes of quantification (see, for example, Hashimoto *et al.* 1995)). (B) Diagram to show major input–output neural connections for the cerebellum. B.A., Brodmann's area; VL, ventrolateral.

brainstem evoked potentials and short-latency somatosensory potentials (e.g. Ornitz 1987). The brainstem and midbrain abnormalities may explain the possible changes in chemical neurotransmitter systems of the reticular formation in autism and the associated impairments in attention and arousal to which Kanner himself alluded (Kanner 1943). The possible involvement of these systems is significant in the light of (it has to be pointed out, largely unsuccessful) attempts to treat autism with drugs which affect 5-HT, noradrenaline and dopamine systems (Anderson 1994). However, the possible dysregulation of these systems would also have implications for the functioning of diverse forebrain regions, especially the prefrontal cortex (see Robbins and Everitt 1987,1995) and therefore represents a possible factor which may interact with the medial temporal and frontostriatal hypotheses.

An obvious weakness of the cerebellar hypothesis is that it lacks vertical integration with respect to the core symptoms of autism, as at first sight autistic children do not show traditional cerebellar signs. One way of addressing this deficiency is to link the anatomical deficits to changes occurring elsewhere in more plausible brain regions such as the limbic system, parietal cortex (e.g. Courchesne *et al.* 1993; Ornitz, 1983) and even the prefrontal cortex, via the ventrolateral thalamus (Leiner *et al.* 1991). Another way is to postulate a core functional deficit in autism which is related to cerebellar function, and which contributes to clinical symptoms such as impaired social communication. Courchesne and colleagues have mounted an impressive case that the cerebellar deficits themselves might correspond to certain attentional deficits in autistic children. For example, Courchesne *et al.* (1994a) provide data to support the hypotheses that: (1) the cerebellum might normally help to coordinate attentional processes analogous to the role it has in motor control; and (2) that abnormalities of this structure in autism lead to attentional deficits that contribute to the familiar impairments in cognitive and social functioning. They compared groups of autistic children ($n = 8$, mean age 13.9 years, verbal IQ $= 59$) with normal adolescents and mental-age-matched children, and a comparison group of patients with cerebellar lesions in a rather unusual cross-modal (visual/ auditory) attentional shifting paradigm. A possible shortcoming of their study is that it does depend crucially on a comparison with the cerebellar lesion group; thus far, there have been relatively little data to support strongly a specific role for the cerebellum in attentional shifting, as distinct from motor control, or even other possible cognitive functions of the cerebellum including timing, conditioning and associative learning (Canavan *et al.* 1994; Fiez *et al.* 1992; Leiner *et al.* 1991). It remains possible that the substrate for the attentional deficit is, in fact, some other neural correlate of cerebellar changes, possibly in brainstem reticular structures (see above). Courchesne *et al.* (1994) also consider the possibility of parietal involvement, based on their observations of associated parietal lobe deficits in autism (Courchesne *et al.* 1993). However, a subgroup comparison of autistic patients with and without such posterior cortical damage did not reveal any significant differences on the attentional shifting task. Moreover, the voluntary, cross-modal and conditional nature of the task contingencies leaves open the possibility that frontal lobe, including premotor, regions contribute to this attentional shifting deficit. It is of interest that the cerebellum gains quite direct anatomical access to those regions of the prefrontal cortex (e.g. Brodmann area 8) that have been implicated in conditional discrimination learning, via the thalamus (Leiner *et al.* 1991, see Fig. 2.2 and p.40).

A more general possibility is that the cerebellar and brainstem abnorm-alities in autism are related mainly to the common mental retardation observed in the disorder. Hashimoto *et al.* (1995) perhaps had the potential to address this hypothesis directly and powerfully, but they came to no clear-cut conclusions. From their literature review and analysis, however, it would appear that abnormalities in cerebellar/brainstem or midbrain development are often linked, though not invariably so, to mental retardation in autism.

Analysis of the cerebellar hypothesis has been further complicated by the report of hyperplasia (i.e. surplus development of neurones), as well as hypoplasia, in the cerebellar vermis of autistic patients, indicating a con-siderable degree of heterogeneity in the neuropathology of posterior fossa structures in autism (Courchesne *et al.* 1994b). So far, however, this heterogeneity has not been convincingly related to any aspect of the symptomatology of the disorder. It is possible, for example, that the opposite neural changes might result in common or contrasting forms of dysfunction at the symptomatic level.

The frontostriatal hypothesis

Unlike the other two major theories, the possible role of the frontal cortex and the basal ganglia in autism was first conjectured mainly on the basis of neurological evidence such as the common occurrence of dystonias, dyski-nesias, gait disturbance, facial asymmetries and other psychomotor signs (Damasio and Maurer 1978). More recently, the deficits in autism in certain aspects of executive functioning (Ozonoff *et al.* 1991) as well as in solving tests of the 'theory of mind' (ToM) (Baron-Cohen *et al.* 1985) have re-focused interest on these important functional systems. Damasio and Maurer (1978) speculated that the 'mesolimbic' cortex, i.e. the mesial frontal cortex and structures of the medial temporal lobe, were vulnerable in autism, as well as the striatum (caudate and putamen). The major strength of their theory is not only that it can explain the common neurological sequelae, but also the more ritualized stereotyped movements and higher level repetitive behaviour, which are frequently associated with malfunctioning of the striatum, generally from an overactivation of its dopaminergic projection.

There is also evidence from the psychopharmacological literature in animals that stereotyped responses can result from a dimunition of inhibitory control from the prefrontal cortical afferents to the striatum (see Robbins *et al.* 1990 for a review). In fact, it seems possible that different forms of stereotypy would result from damage to temporal lobe structures such as the hippocampus and damage to the frontal cortex, probably because of the precise topography of their projections on to the striatum. For example, the oral responses in rats that predominate in the stereotyped behaviour induced by high doses of amphetamine depend on the release of dopamine from the dorsal striatum (caudate–putamen) which has rich connections with the frontal cortex, whereas perseveration of limb movements may depend to a greater extent on the release of dopamine from the ventral striatum (nucleus accumbens) which receives mainly limbic input (see Robbins *et al.* 1990 for a review). The gross convergence of information processed by the temporal lobe and frontal cortex via circuitry to the structures of the basal ganglia (Alexander *et al.* 1986; Suzuki 1996) illustrates another way of considering the 'horizontal' integration of the neural evidence relating to autism, as anticipated by the theorizing of Damasio and Maurer (1978) on the basis of much more limited neuroanatomical information.

This information about the neural substrates of drug-induced stereotypy in laboratory animals is useful heuristically in considering the significance of this common symptom in autism. First, it is apparent that the drug-induced stereotypies also have much in common with the dyskinetic responses that may feature in autism. Second, in the animal literature on the effects of amphetamine in rats and monkeys, it is of interest that impairments in social behaviour are often associated with the drug-induced stereotypy. Indeed, this drug-induced stereotyped behaviour has been described as having an 'autistic' quality (Schirring 1979). The question is whether this apparent link has any more general significance for the clinical disorder. It is evident that the occurrence of stereotypy generally precludes the performance of other complex sequences of behaviour (Lyon and Robbins 1975). However, rarely, the drug-induced stereotypies can be incorporated into bizarre, repetitive forms of social behaviour in both rats and monkeys. Thus, we presume that stereotypy itself does not necessarily *produce* autistic behaviour, but is nevertheless often correlated with it. Evidence is provided for this by the careful observations of Scraggs and Ridley (1978) which showed that the social isolation occurs at lower doses than required to produce overt stereotyped behaviour. Moreover, blockade of stereotypy with neuroleptic drugs (dopamine receptor anatagonists) does not necessarily reinstate normal social behaviour (Ridley *et al.* 1979; Scraggs and Ridley 1979). This is consistent with evidence that drugs such as haloperidol are of limited efficacy in the treatment of autism.

Another possible causal relationship between social behaviour and stereotypy is indicated by the finding that rearing rats in social isolation increases the propensity to stereotyped behaviour (Sahakian *et al.* 1975) and that this can be linked to enhanced functioning of subcortical dopamine systems, often in the context of reciprocal dimunitions in prefrontal cortical dopaminergic activity (Robbins *et al.* 1996). Thus, it seems appropriate to suggest that stereotypy in autism might also reflect the dysregulation of frontostriatal functioning, possibly as a consequence of previous and current exposure to environmental and social stressors.

In theoretical terms, the explanation of stereotypy, as pointed out by Robbins and Sahakian (1983), is of interest in terms of the Norman and Shallice (1980) formulation of 'attention-to-action'. This theoretical system involves the interaction between a 'supervisory attentional system' (SAS) and a 'contention scheduling system' to determine response output. The interaction between these two abstract systems can be related to one between the cerebral cortex (especially prefrontal cortex) and the striatum (Robbins and Sahakian 1983). Stereotyped behaviour can be viewed in at least two ways: (1) it could result from a 'release' of 'supervisory attention' over primitive schema controlling behaviour under conditions where there is a lack of sensory eliciting stimuli or 'triggers' to interrupt responding, caused, for example, by impoverished stimulation from the environment; or (2) it could arise because of the excessive release of a modulatory neurotransmitter (such as dopamine, in the case of amphetamine-induced stereotypy) which occludes executive control by a massive dysregulation of the contention scheduling that normally allows behaviour to be sequenced in a relatively automatic manner. Obviously, stereotypy could also result from a combination of these factors. Also, it is apparent that it is not necessary to invoke such a specific form of executive functioning as ToM to account for this behaviour. As such, the occurrence of stereotypy in autism perhaps provides a powerful argument for the importance of more general executive functions such as response inhibition and the regulation of levels of subcortical activation.

As in the case of amphetamine-induced behaviour in humans and other animals, and in forms of human psychopathologies ranging from schizophrenia, and obsessive–compulsive disorder (OCD) to Gilles de la Tourette's syndrome, it is also apparent that stereotyped behaviour in autism can occur across a broad range of levels of integration, from simple responses to complex rituals and thought sequences (Robbins *et al.* 1990; see Turner, this volume). Although the nature of such behaviour is often reported to be qualitatively distinct from that observed in autism (McDougle *et al.* 1995), it is significant that these apparently different forms of psychopathology have been similarly linked to dysfunctions of corticostriatal functions, often with accompanying abnormalities in brain neuromodulatory systems (in the case of OCD, 5-HT) (Insel 1992). Recent empirical work by Turner (Chapter 3) provides a new approach to the analysis of stereotypy in autism that emphasizes possible relationships with deficits in executive control arising from a novel neuropsychological approach, stemming partly from the aim of bridging work between experimental animals and humans (see also p. 36).

Evidence from neuroimaging

Assessing the frontostriatal hypothesis 16 years on, there is little available post-mortem evidence, but some relevant information from the neuroimaging domain. The common finding in structural imaging studies is that there is no obvious abnormality in the size of the lateral, mesial, or orbitofrontal regions of the prefrontal cortex, but the quite frequent (43% of cases) presence of abnormalities of various kinds in the parietal cortex (Courchesne et al. 1993). There has been little convincing evidence from metabolic scanning of the resting state, where results generally indicate very variable and often minor changes scattered over the entire cerebral cortex. A good example is that of Schifter et al. (1994), who concentrated on scanning a heterogeneous sample of 13 autistic children with both structural (CT or MRI) and functional (PET, using FDG) methods. Only 5 of the 13 subjects had qualitatively abnormal PET scans; of these 5, 4 also had abnormalities detected with structural imaging, but none of the patients had any frontal deficits whatsoever. In a comparable sample of 18 children and adolescents, De Volder et al. (1987) had earlier found evidence of heterogeneity in both the prefrontal and parieto–occipital–temporal association areas: six children showed relative 'hypofrontality', whereas two exhibited 'hyperfrontality'. Although the basal ganglia have perhaps been less commonly investigated, some early findings of structural abnormalities (Gaffney et al. 1989; Jacobson et al. 1988) perhaps now need to be examined more directly. However, in scrutinizing the detailed data for striatal resting metabolism provided by De Volder et al. (1987) there is little current support available.

To counterbalance this generally unpromising picture for the frontostriatal hypothesis in the structural neuroimaging domain, recently there has been some evidence of alterations in autism using more modern technology. Utilizing SPET with ^{99m}Tc-HMPAO as a (hexamethylpropylene amine oxime or 'Ceretec') ligand, George et al. (1992) found that four adult autistic patients had globally decreased perfusion, but disproportionate reductions in the right temporal and midfrontal cortex. Although the study was conducted in the resting state, the subjects unusually were allowed to keep their eyes open. A recent study has scanned five autistic children with the xenon-133 method for SPET at two different developmental stages: 3–4 years of age (just after metabolic maturation of the frontal cortex in normal children) and three years later (Zilbovicius *et al.* 1995). These children exhibited an apparent delayed maturation of activity in the prefrontal cortex; mean frontal rCBF was reduced on the first scan but was normal by the time of the second. It should be realized that the prefrontal cortex probably 'matures' in several distinct stages; certainly in terms of executive functioning, optimal levels of performance for each task are attained at very different ages throughout development (Diamond 1990), and this is also probably consistent with how the structure develops neurobiologically. There has also been some preliminary evidence of frontal abnormalities in terms of phospholipid metabolism measured using magnetic resonance spectroscopy (Minshew *et al.* 1993).

A more direct functional imaging paradigm was utilized by Buchsbaum and colleagues (1992) in which seven reasonably high-functioning adults with child-onset autism were investigated with PET while performing a visual vigilance (continuous performance) task. While the mean 'hypofrontality' index was not significantly different between the two groups, inspection of individual data showed clear abnormalities. In all seven subjects, one or more brain regions, including the right frontal lobe in three individuals, the right striatum (putamen) in two individuals and right frontal white matter in a further two, were shown to have regional glucose metabolic rates less than or greater than 3 standard deviations from the mean of the control group. This is a particularly significant study for three main reasons. First, because the same subjects had earlier been shown to have no metabolic abnormalities in the resting state (Heh *et al.* 1989), clearly indicating the powerful perspective afforded by the task-related functional imaging perspective. A second striking feature is that the level of task performance was similar in the controls and patients. Thus, the normal objections deriving from analogous research in schizophrenia (e.g. McGuire and Frith 1996) that blood flow changes merely passively reflect task performance rather than underlying neural abnormality would not appear to hold. A final reason for taking note is that although this study did find such clear-cut significant results, it has not apparently been followed up by many others. Either the results have proven difficult to replicate, or the investigators in this field, unlike those faced with similar challenges to marry psychopathology with brain abnormality (e.g. especially in the case of schizophrenia (Weinberger *et al.* 1986)), have not taken appropriate heed of the potential of this paradigm.

Evidence from neuropsychology

The findings described above for functional neuroimaging make it clear that understanding the neuropsychology of autism, a topic which preoccupies much of this volume, is crucial to the 'frontostriatal' hypothesis. Even in the context of the complications of mental retardation in autism, as well as the social and language impairments, a number of facts about the cognitive deficits are becoming clear. There is considerable evidence for 'executive' deficits in autism, defined as impairments in the control processes by which cognitive performance is normally optimized (Baddeley 1986; Robbins 1996). The difficulties of quantifying and defining executive failure and especially of equating it specifically to frontal lobe dysfunction are well known. In general, a reasonable defence can be made of the specificity of the executive deficits in autism, especially because performance is often intact or even superior in certain forms of visuospatial functioning (e.g. the 'Block Design' test from the WAIS—see Happé and Frith 1996). This sparing of visuospatial forms of cognition is important in defining the specificity of possible 'executive' deficits, as it is a common claim that such functioning reflects 'fluid' intelligence (Duncan 1995), and visuospatial cognitive ability is commonly used to quantify this general intelligence factor.

I would argue instead that the category of executive function probably includes a variety of distinct, though interactive, capacities such as working memory, planning, fluency, response inhibition, shifting attentional set and vigilance, probably with overlapping and distinct neural substrates (see Robbins 1996). Many of these capacities can be indexed by performance on, by now, quite familiar tests: delayed-response type (Diamond 1990) or self-ordered memory tasks, the Tower of Hanoi, and its variants most suited to assessing planning function, the Tower of London and the Stockings of Cambridge tasks, verbal fluency, the Wisconsin Card Sort Test (WCST) of attentional set-shifting, as well as the continuous performance test of sustained attention (see Pennington and Ozonoff 1996 for an overview). Recently, we have begun to apply our own variants of tests of these capacities (see Fig. 2.3), including the computerized Stockings of Cambridge task, a

---

Fig. 2.3 Diagrammatic representation of some of the computerized tests used for the neuropsychological assessment of autistic children from the CANTAB battery. (a) A test of self-ordered, spatial working memory (results not presented here; used by Turner, M., unpublished findings). (b) 'Stockings of Cambridge' task—an analogue of the Tower of London test (Shallice and Burgess 1996). One of the 'easy' (3 move problems) is shown. (c) Attentional set-shifting task. There are two perceptual dimensions, shape and superimposed white lines, elements of which can occur in any configuration. The subject is trained with reinforcing feedback to learn basic and then compound discriminations of shape (or line), and then exposed to two transfer tests with novel exemplars: an intradimensional shift, which examines transfer of the discrimination to the same dimension, and an extradimensional shift, which examines transfer to the alternative, previously irrelevant, dimension. See Hughes *et al.* (1994) for further explanation. (Reproduced by permission from Lange, K.W. *et al.* (1992). *Psychopharmacology*, **107**, 394–404.)

a)

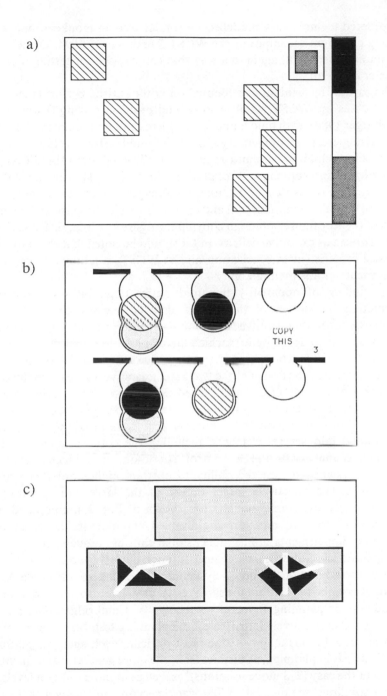

b)

c)

self-ordered memory task modelled on similar tests in monkeys, and a set-shifting paradigm decomposing the WCST (Hughes *et al.* 1994; Turner 1996; and unpublished data) again in a way that can be used for testing monkeys (Dias *et al.* 1996).

The earliest relevant studies focused on adult autistic performance using such tests as the WCST, Trail making, and problem solving (Rumsey and Hamburger 1988), with mild language problems and no significant deficits in many visuoperceptual or memory skills. Prior and Hoffmann (1990) were the first to assess children with autism (aged 10–17 years) using the WCST, the Milner Maze and copying and recall of the Rey figure. The autistic children were impaired on aspects of all tests, notably perseveration on the WCST, impaired use of strategy and trial and error learning in the maze and deficient recall of the Rey figure (although copying the figure was intact). These can all be interpreted as executive deficits, but it should be noted that there was also evidence of deficient categorization on the WCST, resulting from possible impairments in abstracting ability.

The finding of apparently impaired abstracting ability is crucial to interpreting the nature of the WCST deficits, because the viability of hypotheses based on executive functioning depends critically on the absence of background cognitive deficits which directly lead to impairments on tests such as the WCST, which have many cognitive elements. These considerations underpinned the design of the two main executive tests used in the study by Hughes *et al.* (1994) that had received extensive prior validation in adult patients with frontal and temporal lobe excisions, basal ganglia disorders and dementia. For one of these tests, the basic requirements of the WCST were decomposed into several elements, including the core requirement of an extradimensional shift and a control condition, intradimensional shift expressly designed to test the ability to abstract higher order perceptual dimensions. The selectively larger deficit of the large autistic group of children at the extradimensional stage shown in Fig. 2.4, compared with both normal controls and learning-disabled children, in the absence of differential impairments in intradimensional shifting, argues quite strongly for a specific set-shifting deficit. Thus, although there was no separate test of non-executive function (as noted by Pennington and Ozonoff (1996)), this control was embedded within the same test, a principle also employed for the second test of planning function (Stockings of Cambridge). The autistic group was also selectively impaired on the planning test, but in terms of the economy of solutions mainly at the most difficult level, again suggesting a specific deficit in planning, as distinct from the more general requirements of the test at the easy (2–3 move solutions), as well as at more difficult levels (4–5 move solutions, see Fig. 2.4). What was especially interesting was the lack of significant correlation within the autistic group of the set-shifting and planning deficits. This lack of correlation between executive tests is quite well known from the mainstream neuropsychological literature on the effects of frontal lobe damage, and suggests the strong possibility of dissociations between different aspects of executive functioning, which would not be at all inconsistent with the neural organization of the prefrontal cortex and its neural connections (Shallice and Burgess 1996; and see Robbins 1996, Fig. 2.5).

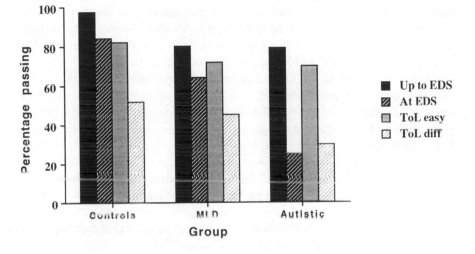

Fig. 2.4 Summary of data on the tests of intra/extradimensional set shifting and performance on the Stockings of Cambridge test of planning for groups of normal children ($n = 47$), matched for verbal and non-verbal age with groups of non-autistic, minimal learning disabled (MLD) ($n = 38$) and autistic ($n = 35$) children and adolescents. Data are expressed as the percentage passing all stages of discrimination learning immediately prior to the extradimensional shift stage (EDS), and at the EDS itself (a model of the core requirement of the Wisconsin Card Sorting Test). Also shown are the percentages of subjects achieving perfect soultions for the 'easy' (2–3 move) and 'difficult' (4–5 move) solutions on the test of planning. Not all subjects attempted all tests; in particular, failure prior to the EDS stage precluded testing at that stage. (Data taken from Hughes *et al.* 1994, with permission from the author and publisher.)

This form of correlational analysis has been extended by Ozonoff *et al.* (1994; see also Ozonoff, Chapter 6) who showed that autistic children were much more impaired in the WCST type of test than in another test of executive dysfunction, based on the inhibition of responding (a Go–NoGo task). This dissociation is especially significant in view of the fact that other notable developmental psychopathologies, such as attention deficit disorder, exhibit greater evidence of impairment in behavioural inhibition (see Pennington and Ozonoff 1996 for a review). It suggests not only that executive mechanisms can be dissociated at an information processing level of analysis, but also, potentially, of regional differences in dysfunction even within the frontal cortex itself. This hypothesis may help to drive further analysis of the neural, as well as the cognitive, bases of autism.

The approach may also help to resolve the difficult issue of one of the core forms of cognitive deficit in autism, on tests of ToM (Baron-Cohen et al. 1985). On the one hand, many aspects of tests of this capacity appear to depend on basic cognitive and executive processes; thus impairments in performing such tests could be reduced to possibly simpler deficits (see Russell, this volume). Thus the apparent deficits in the development of a 'theory of mind' could result simply from a failure to develop executive capacities in childhood. On the other hand, the special nature of the social cognitive deficits in autism would seem unlikely to be explained simply in terms of standard impairments following specific forms of cortical (including prefrontal) and subcortical damage, even in the developing child. The debate has recently been reviewed by Bailey et al. (1996). A key study has been that of Ozonoff et al. (1991) of high-functioning autistic individuals (8–20 years of age) performing tests both of theory of mind capacities of increasing sophistication ('first' and 'second-order' tests) and standard executive functions such as the WCST. Two of the most salient findings were first, the greater incidence of executive than ToM deficits in the autistic group; and second, the significant intercorrelation of these deficits in autism, but not in the control group, when IQ was controlled.

In neural terms, such findings are relevant to theories that there may be some modular capacities of the prefrontal cortex that selectively control aspects of social cognition, perhaps by integrating information from a variety of sensory and visceral modalities, and controlling the selection of appropriate behavioural sequences in the light of previous experience. One theory might argue that this module is invariably damaged in autism, and that the other executive deficits arise from more variable, incidental damage to nearby regions (e.g. Baron-Cohen 1995). However, the results of Ozonoff et al.'s study suggest that the neural structures subserving the more basic executive functions are most likely to be disturbed in autism, with the structures controlling the social aspects of cognition being affected to a more variable extent. It is, of course, more than likely that this modular approach to the ToM and executive deficits is misplaced, and that other, more subtle modes of organization are appropriate, such as the hierarchically, or hetararchically interactive neural networks suggested by anatomical and neurobiological analyses (Pandya and Yeterian 1995; Petrides 1996; Roberts et al. 1995).

The design of the Ozonoff et al. (1991) study has an even greater significance for understanding the neurobiological correlates of autism, as it included measures of a wide range of other capacities in autism, including verbal memory, perception of emotion and spatial cognition. The autistic group was impaired in all but the final domain. Of particular interest was that the deficit in emotion perception was only statistically related to 'first-order' ToM deficits, suggesting a further fractionation of the cognitive capacities, even in the realm of social cognition. The importance of such findings is that they suggest possibilities of new functional imaging situations for probing regional changes in cerebral blood flow with much greater sensitivity than before, especially given the advent of new imaging technologies, including a PET using oxygen-labelled water (^{15}O) for measuring rCBF and functional MRI (fMRI), with greater temporal resolution than hitherto. These technical advances allow several scans to be made during the same session. Thus, control tasks can be carried out in conjunction with the main experimental task in order to allow the isolation of the cognitive capacities of interest, for example, by subtractive comparisons of different patterns of rCBF under control and experimental conditions. Alternatively, assuming adequate statistical power, it may be possible to test a subject in several different functional domains within the same session. Methods of fMRI will allow greater spatiotemporal resolution and the possibility of repeated scans, provided that the ethical problems posed by the physical constraints of the MRI environment can be surmounted for non-anaesthetized children.

A look into the future

The main themes in this following section are suggested by possible parallels in schizophrenia research, specifically from the use of functional imaging with cognitive paradigms to provide more sensitive means of assessing the functional status of different brain regions, novel means of analysing PET or fMRI data in terms of functional connectivity and neuropsychological and clinical data in terms of clusters that can be related, in turn, to brain systems.

Neuroimaging in a cognitive context

Already, advances are being made in the application of cognitive paradigms to functional imaging. For example, one study has used a paradigm based on the silent reading of stories with and without ToM connotations to reveal changes in rCBF in the frontal lobe, probably in Brodmann area 8 of the left mesial prefrontal cortex (Fletcher *et al.* 1995). Moreover, a recent study, undertaken by the same group, of five cases of young adult men with Asperger syndrome, showed that no task-related activity was evident in this region, although adjacent areas were activated normally (Happé *et al.* 1996).

Fletcher *et al.* (1995) point out that the region of activation corresponds to a similar area defined in a study by Mazoyer *et al.* (1993) in which many of the stories read aloud by the subjects had themes relevant to ToM including competition, deception and intrigue. However, it is also reasonable to point out that the exact anatomical identity of this region is still unclear, and other functional imaging studies have found that apparently very different symptoms, such as hallucinations, may be related to the left medial prefrontal cortex (Frith 1996). In addition, it is possible that the activation may be due to cognitive abilities not equated across the ToM and control tasks, such as the ability to make conditional ('if–then') inferences or other forms of rule-based reasoning (Frye *et al.* 1995). There is, in fact, evidence that similar regions help to mediate conditional discrimination learning in a non-social context in both monkeys and humans, based on evidence from the effects of brain lesions (Petrides and Milner 1982). Thus, there are grounds for believing that this brain region mediates more general aspects of conditional reasoning or logical inference that would also be required to solve ToM tasks. This does not, of course, imply that this is the only brain region that might contribute to conditional associative learning; it is of particular interest in view of the cerebellar hypothesis discussed above that cerebellar disease also apparently impairs such learning (Canavan *et al.* 1994). It is, however, reassuring that the correlational evidence of functional imaging can be complemented by evidence of the likely causal role of the region in a given function, as inferred from the deleterious effects of its damage or removal.

A similar ToM theme has been evident in the functional imaging work undertaken by Baron-Cohen *et al.* (1994). They have employed SPET with a 'regions-of-interest' paradigm to show that the orbitofrontal cortex appeared to show greater activation during the reading of words denoting mental states. However, it seems just possible from Damasio's (1994) somatic marker hypothesis that this activation results, in part, from the detection of a somatic or visceral arousal signal by neurones in this region that would be mediated by activity in ascending chemical systems of the reticular core. It has indeed been shown that somatic marker deficits can contribute to impairments in more general decision making in non-social, as well as social, contexts (Damasio 1994).

Notwithstanding the difficulties of analysis, ToM tasks will surely continue to be a prime area of research in the imaging context. Analogous functional activation procedures will be developed to probe the basic executive, and non-executive, deficits in high-functioning autistic individuals, but there is also a need to identify the optimal paradigm for cases with mental retardation. Previous experience with standard cognitive situations will be invaluable in this regard. For example, there have been studies of the Tower of London planning tasks in adults that might prove suitable even for autistic children

(Baker *et al.* 1996). A variant of the WCST is surely already being tried with autistic individuals, as this has been one of the key tasks underlying the development of the 'hypofrontality' hypothesis in schizophrenia (Berman *et al.* 1995; Weinberger *et al.* 1986). Similarly, there has been considerable interest in working memory paradigms sensitive to prefrontal cortical dysfunction, and these again would be suitable in view of the evidence of deficits in aspects of both verbal and spatial working memory in autistic children (Bennetto *et al.* 1996; Pennington and Ozonoff 1996; but see also Russell *et al.* 1996). A critical issue concerns the specificity of such deficits with respect, for example, to minimal learning-disabled (MLD) comparison groups. In the recent studies by Russell *et al.* (1996) and Turner (1996) high-functioning autistic children were impaired relative to normal controls, but not when compared with MLD controls. However, it may be worth pursuing a detailed analysis of some of these paradigms in autistic children, as they are being used increasingly in functional imaging studies. Thus, for example, in the study by Turner (1996) the test of self-ordered working memory employed has been studied intensively with PET in normal adult volunteers (Owen *et al.* 1996). In view of the cerebellar deficits in autism that have been associated with impairments in a modality switching task, this may be a suitable probe for possible cerebellar deficits; indeed such an experiment would provide a test of cerebellar involvement in this form of attention regulation. The temporal lobe hypothesis could also be tested by employing suitable test paradigms. Delayed matching-to-sample is an obvious alternative in view of the literature on this for both human subjects and monkeys (Murray 1996; Owen *et al.* 1995). However, it is possible that tests of the perception of emotion will also be valuable, for example in assessing the possible involvement of limbic structures of the medial temporal lobe.

This exciting prospect of a combination of advances in imaging technology and the cognitive neuropsychology of autism can be expected rapidly to overtake the projections made here. However, the comparison with schizophrenia research offers not only further models for possible progress with these powerful tools, but also a few sobering thoughts and cautions. For example, one controversy in schizophrenia research has centred on the interpretation of functional imaging data, where changes in rCBF mirror actual performance deficits on tasks such as the WCST and verbal fluency (cf. Frith 1996; Weinberger and Berman 1996). The question is then whether the changes in rCBF are mere artefacts of impaired performance. When performance has been equated in various ways, the differences between schizophrenics and control subjects often disappear. This has been one of the reasons for the suggested demise of the 'hypofrontality' hypothesis of schizophrenia (cf. Gur and Gur 1995). However, while it can be conceded that subjects who cannot effectively attempt a test such as the WCST will probably not show the usual prefrontal cortical activation, it may also be true that poor performance on such a test may not *necessarily* lead to frontal hypoactivation (Weinberger and Berman 1996). Thus, while the possible dangers in interpretation are highlighted, it is also possible that removing performance deficits in patient groups in a functional activation context is akin to 'throwing the baby out with the bath-water'. These same problems of interpretation in functional imaging paradigms must now be tackled in the context of autism. It is noteworthy in the pioneering study described on p. 33, by Buchsbaum *et al.* (1992) using a variant of the continuous performance test, that differences in test performance were *not* apparently a complicating factor in the different patterns of cortical metabolism seen in autistic and control individuals. This does raise the tricky issue then of deciding whether a change in cortical metabolism or rCBF in a given brain region actually has any functional significance, but this would be answered, in part, by evidence from converging sources, such as the deleterious effects of a lesion of the same region.

Functional connectivity from neuroimaging

Advances in the statistical analysis of imaging data have also opened up new theoretical possibilities for investigating the relationship between psycho-pathology and neural systems. An obvious, but important point is that processing in structures such as the medial temporal lobes, cerebellum and the prefrontal cortex occurs within these structures in the context of their neuroanatomical connections with other brain regions. In the case of the frontal cortex, several important relationships can be discerned which are probably important determinants of its capacity to act in an executive capacity at a systems level. For example, this region has important reciprocal connections with structures in the posterior cortex such as the parietal and temporal cortex, the limbic system, the striatum, and chemically defined systems of the reticular core (Fig. 2.5). This connectivity can potentially fulfil such functions as holding information 'on-line' while coordinating different capacities in posterior cortical structures, the selection of action, the shifting of set and the regulation of attention and arousal. The dorsolateral prefrontal cortex forms distributed neural networks with structures such as the parietal cortex, hippocampus and caudate nucleus, whereas the orbitofrontal cortex may participate in a network including the cingulate cortex, amygdala and ventral striatum (Goldman-Rakic 1987). In the context of autism, it would therefore not be surprising to find evidence of common dysfunction in such intercon-nected structures, including the medial temporal lobe, parietal cortex, striatum and prefrontal cortex. However, the fact that the cerebellum mainly projects to premotor regions of the cortex, means that common cerebellar and frontal deficits in autism would be difficult to construe in this way.

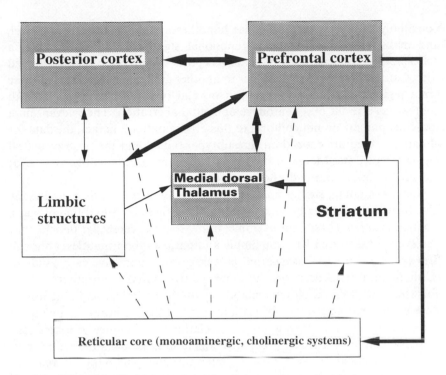

Fig. 2.5 Schematic diagram to show the major patterns of neural interconnectivity of the prefrontal cortex.

The relevance of this approach to schizophrenia has recently been outlined by McGuire and Frith (1996). They point out that the normal reciprocal relationship between the prefrontal cortex and temporal cortex functional imaging paradigms is diminished in schizophenia, perhaps consistent with the lack of functional neural connectivity between these structures (Friston and Frith 1995), as a result of aberrant neural development. This lack of functional connectivity at the neural level is what is expressed functionally as a dysexecutive syndrome, or as psychotic symptoms, as a result of impaired information processing in the cortex of the schizophrenic patient. It is even possible, through suitable functional imaging paradigms, that functional connectivity between distinct prefrontal regions could be assessed, or novel sites of activation identified which are correlated with poor test performance (e.g. Frith 1996; Weinberger and Berman 1996).

This approach can also potentially make use of relevant neurochemical data such as the status of glutamate receptors in the temporal lobe and frontal cortex (Deakin *et al.* 1989; McGuire and Frith 1996), as connectivity between different regions of the cerebral cortex is probably almost wholly dependent on this excitatory neurotransmitter. Thus, such data could potentially be used to test particular hypotheses at the neural systems level, and make inferences about its functional significance. For example, a deficiency of postsynaptic glutamate receptors in one brain region coupled with a surfeit of immature neurones in another area might suggest that these brain regions had failed to establish normal functional connections with another, as a result of a neurodevelopmental aberration. The relevant data for schizophrenia do not conform to this precise pattern; in fact, the data for glutamate receptors depend on the subtype studied and the precise cortical region sampled (see McGuire and Frith 1996 for refs), but analogous data for the autistic brain simply do not seem to exist.

Notwithstanding, similar analyses could be applied to autism, and many investigators have already been thinking along these lines in different ways. Courchesne et al. (1993), for example, imply that the cerebellar deficits they observe are associated with the limbic and parietal abnormalities, although firm evidence for such associations is lacking. An impressive early study of rCBF in autism focused on this issue of functional connectivity. Thus, Horwitz et al. (1988) explored metabolic patterns of activation in the resting state by correlating glucose utilization across different brain regions in 14 autistic patients and controls using correlational techniques to assess connectivity. Careful statistical procedures, including 'jack-knifing' and 'bootstrapping' techniques were used to minimize the possibility of spurious associations. The main results were that: (1) more correlations were reduced rather than increased in the autistic group compared with controls; and (2) the location of these changes in correlation involved parietal–frontal regions, as well as correlations of these areas with subcortical regions. This prescient study seems especially timely for studies of autism in the functional context.

Cluster analysis of autistic symptoms

One of the most consistent findings in schizophrenia research has been the discovery of a number of distinct symptom clusters using principal component analysis (Liddle 1987a). Moreover, the symptom clusters thus defined have been quite consistent in showing factors that can readily be labelled 'reality distortion/thought disorder','disorganization' and 'psychomotor poverty' (e.g. Johnstone and Frith 1996). The theoretical importance of this form of analysis can be seen in several ways. First, it provides a way of beginning to understand the huge interindividual variability in schizophrenia; a patient's symptoms may be described, in part, by different loadings for these three main factors. Second, it provides a way of generating hypotheses about the neural substrates of schizophrenia. An early paper proposed that the three clusters could be ascribed to deficits, respectively, in the temporal cortex, orbitofrontal cortex and dorsolateral prefrontal cortex (Liddle 1987b). Whilst the initial tests of this hypothesis using neuropsychological testing did not provide strong support for the particular neural scheme envisaged, later studies with more appropriate cognitive tests with PET did support the main concept of different major neural foci for the main clusters. The sites of differential activation in the three main functional imaging contexts were a little different, but not far removed from the original speculations (Liddle 1990).

The exact relevance of these neural sites to autism is of course tangential; the main possible point of overlap may be with the 'disorganization' and 'psychomotor retardation' domains, the former because of its association with executive deficits (Johnstone and Frith 1996) and the latter because the construct of psychomotor retardation captures most of the negative symptoms of adult schizophrenia which, of course, include autistic features. The more obvious relevance lies in the possibility of performing similar analyses with detailed data from a large autistic sample, including degree of mental retardation, presence of epilepsy, performance on tests of emotional perception, social cognition, memory and executive functioning. Ideally, as may yet be the case for schizophrenia, these psychological and clinical variables would be supplemented by additional data of likely relevance from the same individuals, including modern means of assessing the status of metabolic activity in different brain regions via functional imaging, neurotransmitter receptors, expression of relevant proteins and mRNA species, obtained either post mortem, or perhaps through *in vivo* imaging techniques. The heterogeneity of symptoms in autism might then begin to be understood in neural terms and, in turn, be related to possible aetiological factors.

Conclusions

From what I have discussed above, it is clear that the three apparently very different hypotheses concerning the neural basis of autism may each have more than a germ of truth in them. The impetus to 'horizontal integration' across these hypotheses may then prove just as viable a prospect as the much vaunted 'vertical integration' referred to in the Introduction that would link the clinical and psychological features of autism to abnormalities in brain systems and neurochemistry.

I have not been able to say very much about the possible implications of this approach for understanding the aetiology of autism, but it is apparent that characterizing the phenotype of such a complex disorder will undoubtedly aid its genetic analysis (Bailey *et al.* 1996) and further focus the search for possible aetiological factors (Coleman 1987). One model for the aetiology of such diversity of symptoms may be general impairments in neuronal metabolism produced by the overproduction of aberrant proteins or deficiency in one or more of them. This could even be expressed as an impairment in a single neurotransmitter system, although, at present, this seems unlikely in autism. Such general effects, however, would have ramifying effects on a number of distinct forms of processing carried out by brainstem and forebrain structures, given the commonalities and differences of organization that exist in different brain regions. Another model for aetiology might be a variable spectrum of coexisting abnormalities in different brain systems that are caused by multiple factors. It is easy to build yet more complex aetiological models by combining the main features of these extreme cases.

This chapter has attempted to summarize what is known about the neural basis of autism and to project future advances from what have proven to be productive lines of investigation in adult schizophrenia. How useful this example will prove, and how applicable it will prove to be to the different types of problem presented by the study of autism, remains to be seen.

Acknowledgements

I should like to thank Chris Jarrold for getting me started on this project, Jim Russell for excellent suggestions regarding the ms. and Michelle Turner and Barbara Sahakian for discussion. Our empirical work was supported by the Wellcome Trust.

REFERENCES

Alexander, G. E., DeLong, M., and Strick, P. S. (1986). Parallel organization of functionally segregated circuits linking basal ganglia and cortex. *Annual Review of Neuroscience*, **9**, 357–81.

Ameli, R., Courchesne, E. C., Lincoln, A., Kaufman, A. S., and Grillon, C. (1988). Visual memory processes in high-functioning individuals with autism. *Journal of Autism and Developmental Disorders*, **18**, 601–15.

Anderson, G. M. (1994). Studies on the neurochemistry of autism. In *The neurobiology of autism* (ed. M. L. Bauman and T. L. Kemper), pp. 227–42. Johns Hopkins University Press, Baltimore.

Bachevalier, J. (1994). Medial temporal lobe structures and autism: a review of clinical and experimental findings. *Neuropsychologia*, **32**, 627–48.

Baddeley, A. D. (1986). *Working memory*. Clarendon Press, Oxford.

Bailey, A., Phillips, W., and Rutter, M. (1996). Autism: Towards an integration of clinical, genetic, neuropsychological and neurobiological perspectives. *Journal of Child Psychology and Psychiatry*, **37**, 89–126.

Baker, S. C., Rogers, R. D., Owen, A. M., Frith, C. D., Dolan, R. J., Frackowiak, R. S. J., et al. (1996). Neural systems engaged by planning: A PET study of the Tower of London task. *Neuropsychologia*, **34**, 515–26.

Baron-Cohen, S. (1995). *Mindblindness: an essay on autism and theory of mind*. MIT Press, Cambridge, MA.

Baron-Cohen, S., Leslie, A. M., and Frith, U. (1985). Does the autistic child have a 'theory of mind'? *Cognition*, **21**, 37–46.

Baron-Cohen, S., Ring, H., Moriarty, J., Schmitz, B., Costa, D., and Ell, P. (1994). The brain basis of the theory of mind: the role of the orbitofrontal region. *British Journal of Psychiatry*, **165**, 640–9.

Bauman, M. L. and Kemper, T. (1985). Histoanatomic observations of the brain in early infantile autism. *Neurology*, **35**, 866–74.

Bauman, M. L. and Kemper, T. (ed.) (1994a). *Neurobiology of autism*. Johns Hopkins University Press, Baltimore.

Bauman, M. L. and Kemper, T. (1994b). Neuroanatomic observations of the brain in autism. In *Neurobiology of autism* (ed. M. L. Bauman and T. Kemper), pp. 119–45. Johns Hopkins University Press, Baltimore.

Bennetto, L., Pennington, B. F., and Rogers, S. J. (1996). Intact and impaired memory functions in autism. *Child Development*, **67**, 1816–35.

Berman, K. F., Ostrem, J. L., Randolph, C., Gold, J., Goldberg, T. E., Coppola, R., et al. (1995). Physiological activation of a cortical network during performance of the Wisconsin Card Sorting Test: a positron emission tomography study. *Neuropsychologia*, **33**, 1027–46.

Buchsbaum, M. S., Siegel, B. V. Jr., Wu, J. C., Hazlett, N., Sicotte, N., Haier, R., et al. (1992). Brief report: Attention performance in autism and regional metabolic rate assessed by positron emission tomography. *Journal of Autism and Developmental Disorders*, **22**, 115–25.

Canavan, A. G. M., Sprengelmeyer, R., Dienes, H.-C. and Homberg, V. (1994). Conditional associative learning is impaired by cerebellar disease in humans. *Behavioral Neuroscience*, **108**, 475–85.

Churchland, P. S. (1986). *Neurophilosophy: toward a unified study of the mind-brain*. MIT/Bradford Press, Cambridge, MA.

Coleman, M. (1987). The search for neurological subgroups in autism. In *Neurobiological issues in autism* (ed. E. Schopler and G. B. Mesibaw), pp. 163–78. Plenum Press, NY.

Courchesne, E. (1995). New evidence of cerebellar and brainstem hypoplasia in autistic infants, children and adolescents: the MR imaging study by Hashimoto and colleagues. *Journal of Autism and Developmental Disorders*, **25**, 19–22.

Courchesne, E., Yeung-Courchesne, R., Press, G. A., Hesselink, J. R., and Jernigan, T. (1988). Hypoplasia of cerebellar lobules VI and VII in infantile autism. *New England Journal of Medicine*, **318**, 1349–54.

Courchesne, E., Press, G. A., and Yeung-Courchesne, R. (1993a). Parietal abnormalities detected with MR in patients with infantile autism. *American Journal of Roentgenology*, **160**, 387–93.

Courchesne, E., Townsend, J., Akshoomoff, N. A., Saitoh, O., Yeung-Courchesne, R., Lincoln, A.J., et al. (1994a). Impairment in shifting attention in autistic and cerebellar patients. *Behavioral Neuroscience*, **108**, 848–65.

Courchesne, E., Saitoh, O., Yeung-Courchesne, R., Press, G. A., Lincoln, A. J., Haas, R. H., et al. (1994b). Abnormality of cerebellar vermian lobules VI and VII in patients with infantile autism; identification of hypoplastic and hyperplastic subgroups with MR imaging. *American Journal of Roentgenology*, **162**, 123–30.

Damasio, A. (1994). *Descartes' error*. Putnam Press, NY.

Damasio, A. and Maurer, R. G. (1978). A neurological model for childhood autism. *Archives of Neurology*, **35**, 777–86.

Dawson, G. (1996). Brief report: neuropsychology of autism: A report on the state of the science. *Journal of Autism and Developmental Disorders*, **26**, 179–84.

Deakin, J. F. W., Slater, P., Simpson, M. D. C., Gilchrist, A. C., Skan, W. J., Royston, M. C., et al. (1989). Frontal cortical and left temporal glutaminergic dysfunction in schizophrenia. *Journal of Neurochemistry*, **52**, 1781–6.

De Volder, A., Bol. A., Michel, C., Congneau, M., and Goffinet, A. M. (1987). Brain glucose metabolism in children with the autistic syndrome: Positron tomography analysis. *Brain Development*, **9**, 581–7.

Diamond, A. (1990). The development and neural bases of memory functions as indexed by the AB and delayed response tasks in human infants and infant monkeys. *Annals of the New York Academy of Sciences*, **608**, 266–317.

Dias, R., Robbins, T. W., and Roberts, A. C. (1996). Dissociation in prefrontal cortex of attentional and affective shifts. *Nature*, **380**, 69–72.

Duncan, J. (1995). Attention, intelligence and the frontal lobes. In *The cognitive neurosciences* (ed. M. Gazzaniga), pp. 721–33. MIT Press, Cambridge, MA.

Fiez, J. A., Petersen, S. E., Cheney, M. K., and Raichle, M. (1992). Impaired non-motor learning and error detection associated with cerebellar damage. *Brain*, **115**, 155–78.

Filipek, P. A., Kennedy, D. N., and Caviness, V. S. Jr. (1992). Neuroimaging in child neuropsychology. In *Handbook of neuropsychology*, Vol. 6 (ed. I. Rapin and S. J. Segalowitz), pp. 301–29. Elsevier Science Publishers, Amsterdam.

Fletcher, P. A., Happé, F., Frith, U., Baker, S., Dolan, R., Frakowiak, R.S.J., et al. (1995). Other minds in the brain: a functional imaging study of the 'theory of mind'. *Cognition*, 57, 109–28.

Friston, K. J. and Frith, C. D. (1995). Schizophrenia: a disconnection syndrome? *Clinical Neuroscience*, 3, 89–97.

Frith, C. D. (1996). The role of the prefrontal cortex in self-consciousness: the case of auditory hallucinations. *Proceedings of the Royal Society of London*, 'B', 351, 1505–12.

Frye, D., Zelazo, P. D., and Palfai, T. (1995). Theory of mind and rule-based reasoning. *Cognitive Development*, 10, 483–527.

Gaffney, G. R., Kuperman, S., Tsai, L. Y., and Minchin, S. (1989). Forebrain structure in infantile autism. *Journal of the American Academy of Child and Adolescent Psychiatry*, 28, 534–7.

George, M. S., Costa, D. C., Kouris, K., Ring, H., and Ell, P. (1992). Cerebral blood flow abnormalities in adults with infantile autism. *The Journal of Nervous and Mental Disorders*, 180, 413–17.

Gillberg, I. C., Bjure, J., Uvebrant, P., Vestergren, E., and Gillberg, C. (1993). SPECT (Single photon emission computed tomography) in 31 children and adolescents with autism and autistic-like syndromes. *European Child and Adolescent Psychiatry*, 2, 50 9.

Goldman-Rakic, P. S. (1987). Circuitry of primate prefrontal cortex and regulation of behavior by representational memory. In *Handbook of physiology. The nervous system* (ed. F. Plum), pp. 373–417. American Physiological Soc., Bethesda, MD.

Gur, R. C. and Gur, R. E. (1995). Hypofrontality in schizophrenia. RIP. *Lancet*, 345, 450–2.

Happé, F. and Frith, U. (1996). The neuropsychology of autism. *Brain*, 119, 1377–400.

Happé, F., Ehlers, S., Fletcher, P., Frith, U., Johannson, M., Gillberg, C., Dolan, R., Frackowiak, R., and Frith, C. (1996) 'Theory of mind' in the brain. Evidence from a PET scan study of Asperger syndrome. *Neuroreport*, 8, 197–201.

Hashimoto, T., Tayama, M., Murakawa, K., Yoshimoto, T., Miyazaki, M., Harada, M., et al. (1995). Development of the brainstem and cerebellum in autistic patients. *Journal of Autism and Developmental Disorders*, 25, 1–18.

Hauser, S. L., DeLong, G. R., and Rosman, N. P. (1975). Pneumographic findings in the infantile autism syndrome: a correlation with temporal lobe disease. *Brain*, 98, 667–88.

Heh, C. W. C., Smith, R., Wu, J., Hazlett, E., Russel, A., Asarnow, R., et al. (1989). Positron emission tomography of the cerebellum in autism. *American Journal of Psychiatry*, 146, 242–5.

Hoon, A. H. and Reiss, A. L. (1992). The mesial-temporal lobe and autism: Case report and review. *Developmental Medicine and Child Neurology*, 34, 252–65.

Horwitz, B., Rumsey, J. M., Grady, C. L., and Rapoport, S. I. (1988). The cerebral metabolic landscape in autism: intercorrelations of regional glucose utilization. *Archives of Neurology*, 45, 749–55.

Hughes, C., Russell, J., and Robbins, T. W. (1994). Evidence for executive dysfunction in autism. *Neuropsychologia*, 32, 477–92.

Insel, T. R. (1992). Toward a neuroanatomy of obsessive–compulsive disorder. *Archives of General Psychiatry*, 49, 739–44.

Jacobson, R., Le Couteur, A., Howlin, P., and Rutter, M. (1988). Selective sub-cortical abnormalities in autism. *Psychological Medicine*, **18**, 39–48.

Jaskiw, G. E. and Weinberger, D. R. (1992). Dopamine and schizophrenia—a cortically corrective perspective. *Seminars in the Neurosciences*, **4**, 179–88.

Johnstone, E. C. and Frith, C. D. (1996). Validation of three dimensions of schizophrenic symptoms in a large unselected sample of patients. *Psychological Medicine*, **26**, 669–80.

Kanner, L. (1943). Autistic disturbances of affective content. *Nervous Child*, **2**, 217–50.

Leiner, H. C., Leiner, A. L., and Dow, R. S. (1991). The human cerebro–cerebellar system; its computing, cognitive and language skills. *Behavioural Brain Research*, **44**, 113–28.

Lelord, G., Garreau, B., Syrota, A., Bruneau, N., Pourcelot, L., and Zilbovicius, M. (1991). SPECT rCHF, Doppler transcranial ultrasonography and evoked potential studies in pervasive developmental disorders. *Biological Psychiatry*, **29**, 292s.

Liddle, P. (1987a). The symptoms of chronic schizophrenia: a re-examination of the positive–negative dichotomy. *British Journal of Psychiatry*, **151**, 145–51.

Liddle, P. F. (1987b). Schizophrenic syndromes, cognitive performance and neuro-logical dysfunction. *Psychological Medicine*, **17**, 49–57.

Liddle, P. F. (1990). Regional cerebral metabolic activity in chronic schizophrenia. *Schizophrenia Research*, **3**, 23–4.

Lyon, M. and Robbins, T. W. (1975). The action of central nervous system stimulant drugs: a general theory concerning amphetamine effects. In *Current developments in psychopharmacology*, Vol. 2 (ed. W. Essman and L. Valzelli), pp. 79–163. Spectrum, NY.

McDougle, C. J., Kresch, L. E., Goodman, W. K., Naylor, S. T., Volkmar, F. H., Cohen, D. J., et al. (1995). A case-controlled study of repetitious thought and behaviour in adults with autistic disturbance and obsessive–compulsive disorder. *American Journal of Psychiatry*, **152**, 772–7.

McGuire, P. K. and Frith, C. D. (1996). Disordered functional connectivity in schizophrenia. *Psychological Medicine*, **26**, 663–8.

Mazoyer, B. M., Tzourio, N., Frak, V., Syrota, A., Murayama, N., Levrier, O., et al. (1993). The cortical representation of speech. *Journal of Cognitive Neuroscience*, **5**, 467–79.

Minshew, N. J., Golstein, G., Dombrowski, S. M., Panchalingam, K., and Pettegrew, J. M. (1993). A preliminary 31p-MRS study of autism: evidence for undersynthesis and increased degradation of brain membranes. *Biological Psychiatry*, **33**, 762–73.

Morton, J. and Frith, U. (1995). Causal modelling: a structural approach to developmental psychopathology. In *Manual of developmental psychopathology*, Vol. 1 (ed. D. Cicchetti and D. Cohen), pp. 357–90. John Wiley, NY.

Murray, E. (1996). What have ablation studies told us about the neural substrates of stimulus memory? *Seminars in the Neurosciences*, **8**, 13–22.

Norman, D. and Shallice, T. (1980). Attention to action: willed and automatic control of behavior. Center for Human Information Processing, Technical Report No. 99. University of California, San Diego.

Ornitz, E. M. (1983). The functional neuroanatomy of infantile autism. *International Journal of Neuroscience*, **19**, 85–124.

Ornitz, E. M. (1987). Neurophysiologic studies of infantile autism. In *Handbook of autism and pervasive developmental disorders* (ed. D. J. Cohen, A. M. Donnellan, and R. Paul), pp. 148–65. Wiley, NY.

Owen, A. M., Sahakian, B. J., Semple, J., Polkey, C. E., and Robbins, T. W. (1995). Visuospatial short term recognition memory and learning after temporal lobe excisions, frontal lobe excisions or amygdala hippocampectomy in man. *Neuropsychologia*, **33**, 1–24.

Owen, A. M., Evans, A. C. , and Petrides, M. P. (1996). Evidence for a two-stage model of spatial working memory processing within the lateral frontal cortex: a positron emission tomography study. *Cerebral Cortex*, **6**, 31–8.

Ozonoff, S., Pennington, B. F., and Rogers, S. J. (1991). Executive function deficits in high-functioning autistic children: relationship to theory of mind. *Journal of Child Psychology and Psychiatry*, **32**, 1081–105.

Ozonoff, S., Strayer, D.L., McMahon, W. M., and Filloux, F. (1994). Executive function abilities in autism and Tourette syndrome: an information processing approach. *Journal of Child Psychology and Psychiatry*, **35**, 1015–32.

Pandya, D. P. and Yeterian, E. H. (1995). Morphological correlations of human and monkey frontal lobe. In *Neurobiology of human decision-making* (ed. A. E. Damasio, H. Damasio, and Y. Christen), pp. 13–46. Springer, NY.

Pennington, B. F. and Ozonoff, S. (1996). Executive functioning and developmental psychopathology. *Journal of Child Psychology and Psychiatry*, **37**, 51–87.

Petrides, M. P. (1996). Lateral frontal cortical contribution to memory. *Seminars in the Neurosciences*, **8**, 57–63.

Petrides, M. P. and Milner, B. (1982). Deficits on subject-ordered tasks after frontal- and temporal lobe lesions in man. *Neuropsychologia*, **20**, 249–62.

Prior, M. and Hoffmann, W. (1990). Brief report: neuropsychological testing of autistic children through an exploration with frontal tests. *Journal of Autism and Developmental Disorders*, **20**, 581–90.

Ridley, R. M., Baker, H. F., and Scraggs, P. R. (1979). The time course of the behavioural effects of amphetamine and their reversal by haloperidol in a primate species. *Biological Psychiatry*, **14**, 753–65.

Robbins, T. W. (1996). Dissociating executive functions of the prefrontal cortex. *Proceedings of the Royal Society of London*, 'B', **351**, 1463–71.

Robbins, T. W. and Everitt, B. J. (1987). Psychopharmacological studies of arousal and attention. In *Cognitive neurochemistry* (ed. S. Stahl, S. D. Iversen and E. Goodman), pp. 135–70. Oxford University Press, Oxford.

Robbins, T. W. and Everitt, B. J. (1995). Arousal systems and attention. In *The cognitive neurosciences* (ed. M. Gazzaniga), pp. 703–25. MIT Press, Cambridge, MA.

Robbins, T. W. and Sahakian, B. J. (1983). Behavioural effects of psychomotor stimulant drugs: clinical and neuropsychological implications. In *Stimulants: clinical, behavioural and neurochemical perspectives* (ed. I. Creese), pp. 301–38. Raven Press, NY.

Robbins, T. W., Mittleman, G., O'Brien, J., and Winn, P. (1990). Neuropsychological significance of stereotypy induced by stimulant drugs. In *Neurobiology of beha-*

vioural stereotypy (ed. S. J. Cooper and C. Dourish), pp. 25–63. Oxford University Press, Oxford.

Robbins, T. W., Jones, G. H., and Wilkinson, L. S. (1996). Behavioural and neurochemical effects of early social deprivation in the rat. *Journal of Psychopharmacology*, **10**, 39–47.

Roberts, A. C., Collins, P., and Robbins, T. W. (1996). The functions of the prefrontal cortex in humans and other animals. In *Modeling the early human mind* (ed. P. Mellars and K. Gibson), pp. 67–80. McDonald Inst. Monographs, Cambridge.

Rumsey, J. M. and Hamburger, S. D. (1988). Neuropsychological findings in high functioning men with infantile autism, residual state. *Journal of Clinical and Experimental Neuropsychology*, **10**, 201–21.

Russell, J., Jarrold, C., and Henry, L. (1996). Working memory in children with autism and with moderate learning disabilities. *Journal of Child Psychology and Psychiatry*, **37**, 673–86.

Sahakian, B. J., Robbins, T. W., Morgan, M. J., and Iversen, S. D. (1975). The effects of psychomotor stimulants on stereotypy and locomotor activity in socially deprived and control rats. *Brain Research*, **84**, 195–205.

Saitoh, O., Courchesne, E., Egaas, B., Lincoln, A. J., and Schreibman, L. (1995). Cross-sectional area of the posterior hippocampus in autistic patients with cerebellar and corpus callosum abnormalities. *Neurology*, **45**, 317–24.

Schifter, T., Hoffman, J. M., Hatten, H. P., Hanson, M. W., Coleman, R. E., and DeLong, G. R. (1994). Neuroimaging in infantile autism. *Journal of Child Neurology*, **9**, 155–61.

Schirring, E. (1979). Social isolation and other behavioural changes in a group of adult vervet monkeys (Cercopithecus aethiops) produced by low, non-chronic doses of d-amphetamine. *Psychopharmacology*, **64**, 219–24.

Scraggs, P. R. and Ridley, R. M. (1978). Behavioural effects of amphetamine in a small primate: relative potencies of the d- and l- isomers. *Psychopharmacology*, **59**, 243–5.

Scraggs, P. R. and Ridley, R. M. (1979). The effect of dopamine and noradrenaline blockade on amphetamine-induced behaviour in the marmoset. *Psychopharmacology*, **62**, 41–5.

Shallice, T. and Burgess, P. (1996). The domain of supervisory processes and the temporal organization of behaviour. *Proceedings of the Royal Society of London 'B'*, **351**, 1405–12.

Suzuki, W. A. (1996). Neuroanatomy of the monkey entorhinal, perirhinal and parahippocampal cortices: Organization of cortical inputs and interconnections with amygdala and striatum. *Seminars in the Neurosciences*, **8**, 3–12.

Turner, M. (1996). Repetitive behaviour and cognitive functioning in autism. PhD thesis, University of Cambridge.

Weinberger, D. R. and Berman, K. F. (1996). Prefrontal function in schizophrenia: confounds and controversies. *Proceedings of the Royal Society of London, 'B'*. **351**, 1495–503.

Weinberger, D. R., Berman, K. F., and Zec, R. F. (1986). Physiological dysfunction of dorsolateral prefrontal cortex in schizophrenia. I Regional blood flow evidence. *Archives of General Psychiatry*, **43**, 114–24.

Williams, R. S., Hauser, S. L., Purpura, D. P., DeLong, R., and Swisher, C. N. (1980). Autism and mental retardation: neuropathological studies performed in four retarded persons with autistic behavior. *Archives of Neurology*, **37**, 749–53.

Zilbovicius, M., Garreau, B., Samson, Y., Remy, P., Barthélémy, C., Syrota, A., et al. (1995). Delayed maturation of the frontal cortex in childhood autism. *American Journal of Psychiatry*, **152**, 248–52.

PART II

Impairments in generating behaviour

3 Towards an executive dysfunction account of repetitive behaviour in autism

Michelle Turner

The growing evidence for executive deficits in autism has led to the suggestion that executive dysfunction may be of primary importance to the autistic syndrome. The evidence for such deficits in both normally intelligent, or high-functioning, and learning-disabled individuals with autism is compelling across tasks of planning, establishment and maintenance of attentional set, and inhibition of prepotent responses. One of the major attractions of this theory has been its suggested potential to explain some of the characteristics of autism that have eluded direct explanation from other theories. In particular, it has been proposed that primary impairments in the control and regulation of behaviour may be able to explain the characteristic presence of repetitive behaviour in autism.

Whilst there have been no attempts to articulate any such account in detail, the joint pursuit of executive functioning and repetitive behaviour in autism has the potential to enrich both lines of study. First, exploring how the executive account may explain repetitive behaviour in autism is likely to valuably inform and encourage the study of repetitive behaviour. The neglect of repetitive behaviour has been noted by many writers (e.g. Bailey *et al.* 1996; Baron-Cohen 1989; U. Frith 1989; Russell 1996), yet there has been little impetus to encourage the study of these behaviours. Directing the focus of the executive account to explore how deficits in the regulation of behaviour may be linked to repetitive behaviour may also valuably identify and highlight those specific areas of executive functioning likely to be impaired in autism. One of the greatest problems for the executive hypothesis of autism has been the fact that this is a broad concept in an area in which deficits can be identified in many different clinical groups.

A further advantage likely to be conferred by a research approach which aims to link the study of executive functioning and repetitive behaviour is the chance to examine how symptomatology and cognitive impairment are linked. If a cognitive deficit is causally important in the development of the autistic syndrome then a number of strong predictions are entailed. First, it must be predicted that any such deficit is universal to autism. Second, it must be predicted that any such deficit is autism-specific. These predictions have been the focus of many current research strategies which have attempted to determine the relative prevalence of cognitive deficits in areas such as executive functioning and 'theory of mind' in individuals with autism and non-autistic control subjects. However, a third, and equally important prediction of any causal account, is that any variance in the degree and nature of the deficit will be associated with variability and severity of the symptomatology that is suggested to stem from this deficit. Recently, there has been some attempt to validate and test this prediction for the theory of mind account (U. Frith *et al.* 1994). If this prediction is supported, there is strong evidence that the cognitive deficit and the symptom are fundamentally related, whether or not the deficit is autism-specific.

Tests of this latter prediction will be a recurrent theme throughout this chapter as I review different explanations of repetitive behaviour in autism. This review considers both recent attempts to explain repetitive behaviour as the consequence of a cognitive deficit, and also suggests two ways in which repetitive behaviour may follow from impaired functioning of executive processes. However, the chapter begins with a look at the definition and phenomenology of repetitive behaviour in autism.

What is repetitive behaviour?

The term repetitive behaviour is an umbrella term which encompasses a wide range of behaviours including stereotyped movements, marked distress in response to changes in small details of the environment, an insistence in following routines in precise detail, and preoccupation with narrow, circum-scribed interests. However, at least three characteristics unite these appar-ently disparate classes of behaviour and define them as repetitive behaviour. These are: (1) the high *frequency of repetition* in the display of the behaviour; (2) the *invariant* way in which the behaviour or the activity is pursued; and (3) that the behaviour is *inappropriate* or *odd* in its manifestation and display. Thus, any account of repetitive behaviour must be able to explain why the behaviour is repeated frequently, why the form of the behaviour should remain unchanged, and why the behaviour is inappropriate or unusual and does not develop in the usual manner. Any such account must also be able to explain the diversity of repetitive phenomena seen in autism, and also the marked resistance to intervention and subsequent response substitution (Epstein *et al.* 1985; Harris and Wolchik 1979) commonly reported in the treatment literature.

However, despite the fact that it is possible to identify many common threads in the display of repetitive behaviour, detailed study of these behaviours can only be achieved if the full spectrum of behaviour, which may be captured under this broad definition, can be subdivided into discrete classes of behaviour which are clearly defined. Whilst many terms have been used to refer to different forms of repetitive behaviour, they have often been poorly defined and inconsistently used in the literature. The term 'obsession' has been used to refer to behaviours as disparate as high rates of finger twiddling, continually lining up objects, insisting that certain objects must be kept in certain places, and very narrow fields of interest. Other terms such as 'self-stimulation' perilously presuppose the origin and function of the behaviour. Although two classification systems have been proposed in the recent literature (C. Frith and Done 1990; Ridley 1994), both these group together behaviours which are relatively heterogeneous in form (see Turner 1995). The use of such broad criteria fails to allow for the fact that different classes of repetitive behaviour may be more or less typical of different clinical groups, or even different subgroups, of individuals within the autistic spectrum. Moreover, studying broad categories of behaviour may obscure the way in which repetitive behaviours differ in individuals of different ages or ability levels, the way in which these behaviours change with different situational factors, or most importantly from the present point of view, the way different factors may be important in the development and maintenance of different classes of behaviour.

The lack of a sound empirical base makes it difficult to know just what criteria may allow for meaningful distinctions between different classes of behaviour. Different writers have emphasized various features of repetitive behaviour: the frequency or degree of repetition; the inappropriateness of the act or movement; and the complexity of the behaviour. Instead, the classificatory system I have outlined in earlier work (Turner 1995) groups behaviours which are consistently similar in their form, content, or common presentation as members of a single class. This taxonomy is derived both from the autism literature and the literature for spontaneously occurring repetitive behaviour in normal and clinical populations. These subdivisions reflect terms that are commonly employed in the literature, and in this sense are not new. However, I have attempted to provide clear and explicit definitions for 11 narrow classes of repetitive behaviour in an attempt to reduce the ambiguity inherent in this literature. This taxonomy is outlined in Table 3.1.

The neglect of repetitive behaviour

The importance of repetitive behaviour to the autistic syndrome has been emphasized since Kanner first described the syndrome in 1943. Kanner

Table 3.1 A taxonomy of reptitive behaviour

Label	Definition	Typical example
Tardive dyskinesia	Rhythmic abnormal involuntary movements, most typically of the jaw, mouth, lips, and tongue, but also of the limbs and trunk	Lip smacking; sucking movements; pill rolling movements of the fingers
Tics	Abrupt, brief, recurrent, and involuntary movements and/or vocalizations which can be suppressed by the individual for a short time. In contrast to stereotyped movements, tics vary in their intensity and are non-rhythmic in nature	Jerky movements of discrete facial muscles; eye blinking; shoulder shrugging
Stereotyped movements	Apparently voluntary rhythmic movements of the body which are repeated in an invariant manner, and are inappropriate to the current context	Hand flapping; body rocking; finger flicking
Self-injury	Any apparently voluntary, repetitive, topographically invariant act that causes probable pain, or actual harm, to the self	Head banging; biting the self
Stereotyped manipulation of objects	Topographically invariant manipulation of objects repeated in a manner that is inappropriate given the nature, and usual function, of the object	Spinning objects; repetitively examining a toy; lining objects up in rows
Abnormal objects attachments and preoccupations	Any persistent attachment to, or preoccupation with, an object, or part of an object, which is not used to provide comfort or security to the individual in the normal sense. May include unusual objects	Persistent preoccupation with carrying a stick, a rubber glove, etc
Insistence on sameness of environment	An insistence on one or more minor features of the environment remaining unchanged despite no obvious, or logical, basis. Attempts at change are met with marked resistance	Insisting that the curtains remain open or closed, or that ornaments remain in certain positions; insistence on always playing the same record; insistence on wearing the same T-shirt

Rigid adherence to routines and rituals	Any routine or ritual which is characterized by total invariance and inflexibility, and which is adhered to in every relevant situation	Insisting on dressing in the same highly stereotyped fashion; insisting on buying a newspaper on every trip to the shop, regardless of whether or not one has previously been purchased (even though the child may have no interest in reading the newspaper him- or herself)
Repetitive use of language	Any phrase or linguistic device which is either (1) copied from other sources, or (2) is presumed to be self-generated but is used repeatedly across different times and situations in an inappropriate manner	Immediate or delayed echolalia; repetitive use of the same phrases or questions (palilalia); verbal rituals
Circumscribed interests	The repetitive and all-absorbing pursuit, or discussion, of one narrowly circumscribed topic or activity	Reading maps and talking about different countries and their flags on a daily or hourly basis (although the child may show no interest in seeing films of these countries on television)
Obsessions and compulsions	Obsessions are defined as recurrent thoughts or images that are perceived as intrusive, senseless, and distressing. Compulsions are defined as stereotyped acts performed in response to an obsession to avert or prevent a perceived impending threat or disaster	Preoccupation with dirt and contamination and consequent repetitive washing and disinfecting to counteract the perceived threat of disease

identified the obsessive insistence on sameness of behaviour, activity, and routine seen in autism as one of two cardinal symptoms which he suggested to be core features of the disorder. Since that time, the central role of repetitive behaviour in autism has been confirmed by epidemiological study. Wing and Gould (1979), in their study of all the children living in the London borough of Camberwell, confirmed that stereotyped movements and repetitive patterns of activity co-occurred with social abnormalities of the autistic type, reporting that 'all the children with social impairments had repetitive stereotyped behaviour' (p. 25 therein). This result, along with the fact that repetitive behaviour is a necessary prerequisite for a diagnosis of autism, suggests that repetitive behaviour is as fundamentally important to the autistic syndrome as the social and communication impairments that have long been the focus of interest and research.

However, the fact remains that repetitive behaviour in autism has been relatively little studied. This situation seems to have arisen for two reasons. First, repetitive behaviour is described not just for individuals with autism, but individuals from other clinical and non-clinical groups. Second, it has been long assumed that these behaviours are a secondary symptom of the disorder, invoked by the individual as a coping mechanism in response to altered levels of arousal. Each of these possibilities will be considered in turn.

A marker of non-specific impairment

Even a cursory examination of the literature for repetitive behaviour reveals that many instances of this behaviour are reported for non-autistic individuals. Repetition of behaviour and activity is a feature of normal behaviour, most especially during childhood, but also at times of boredom and anxiety (de Lissovoy 1962; Kravitz and Boehm 1971; Lindsay et al. 1982; Mitchell and Etches 1977; Rago and Case 1978; Sallustro and Atwell 1978; Soussignon et al. 1988; Thelen 1979, 1981; Werry et al. 1983). Moreover, certain classes of repetitive behaviour have been described as a characteristic feature of many clinical conditions including mental retardation, schizophrenia, blindness and deafness, obsessive–compulsive disorder, dementia, Parkinson's disease, and Tourette's syndrome (see Frith and Done 1990; Ridley 1994; Turner 1995, for reviews). However, abnormalities of language and social functioning are also characteristic of many of these conditions. Thus, the fact that repetitive behaviour is not confined to autism does not in itself prove that these behaviours are an uninformative feature of the autistic syndrome. Rather, this simply suggests that the presence of repetitive behaviour is no more a litmus test for autism than any general disruption to language or social skill.

However, it is the fact that repetitive behaviour is a characteristic feature of learning disabilities, even where there is no associated autistic impairment, that has most served to minimize the significance of repetitive behaviour to autism. Whilst it is true that the majority of individuals with autism are learning-disabled, the conclusion that these behaviours may be little more than indicators of intellectual impairment, or a non-specific sign of organic dysfunction, has been premature. First, this position is inconsistent with the fact that repetitive behaviours persist in those individuals with autism who have intelligence in the normal, and even the superior, range (Bartak and Rutter 1976; Szatmari et al. 1989; Tantam 1991). Second, this position is at odds with apparent qualitative differences, in that certain classes of repetitive behaviour commonly reported in autism (such as insistence on sameness of environment or routine) are not commonly described for non-autistic, learning-disabled individuals (Turner 1997a). Finally, despite the fact that few studies have been undertaken to explore the phenomenology of repetitive behaviour in autism as distinct from learning disability, a small number of studies provide evidence to suggest that repetitive behaviour is significantly more common in autistic than non-autistic individuals matched for age and ability level. Hermelin and O'Connor (1963) reported that even amongst individuals with marked learning disabilities, individuals with autism are found to engage in significantly more, and longer, bouts of stereotyped movements than learning-disabled individuals of equivalent intellectual impairment. In a recent study of high-functioning autistic individuals, Szatmari et al. (1989) reported that repetitive movements, insistence on sameness behaviour, repetitive use of language, and circumscribed interests were significantly more common than for non-autistic control subjects referred to an outpatient psychiatry clinic.

Following on from these studies, my recent PhD work has sought to compare the relative prevalence, frequency, and duration of repetitive behaviours in autistic and non-autistic comparison individuals. This research was conducted using the Repetitive Behaviours Interview, an interview designed to assess repetitive behaviour in each of the 11 classes of behaviour listed in Table 3.1. Two groups of autistic individuals were studied: 22 high-functioning children and adults with autism who had a verbal IQ of above 75 (the HFA group), and a further 22 learning-disabled individuals with autism who achieved a VIQ of below 75 (the LDA group). Two groups of age-, sex-, and ability-matched comparison subjects were also included. The high-functioning comparison (HFC) subjects were recruited from an outpatient psychiatric population, whilst the learning-disabled comparison (LDC) subjects were recruited from special schools[1]. For both high-functioning and learning-disabled subjects, repetitive behaviour of most classes was reported to be significantly more common in the autistic, relative to the comparison, subjects. It is particularly telling that 98% of the autistic subjects were reported to display repetitive behaviour in three or more of 11 classes of behaviour probed by the interview, in comparison with only 17% of the comparison subjects. In support of the claim that these behaviours are a pervasive and enduring feature of the autistic syndrome, the results of the interview revealed few effects of age and ability on the display of repetitive behaviour. This finding is clearly at odds with any suggestion that these behaviours are no more than a simple index of intellectual ability, and instead supports Kanner's (1943) original assertion that repetitive behaviour is a core feature of the autistic spectrum.

A secondary coping mechanism

The second reason that repetitive behaviour has been ignored in autism stems from the long-held assumption that these behaviours function as a coping mechanism and, as such, are no more than a secondary feature of the disorder. Whilst it has been alternatively suggested that this coping mechanism may serve to reduce chronically high arousal levels (Hutt and Hutt 1965, 1970; Hutt et al. 1964; Zentall and Zentall 1983) or, conversely, to relieve underarousal brought about by a presumed lack of stimulation from the world (e.g. Goodall and Corbett 1982; Schopler 1965), the overarousal account has enjoyed the most popularity. On this view, repetitive behaviours are adaptive behaviours employed by the autistic individual as a homeostatic mechanism that regulates arousal levels. Specifically, Hutt and Hutt suggest that repetitive behaviour serves as a displacement activity to block sensory input and thus reduce arousal.

This hypothesis has been widely influential in shaping the views of clinicians, teachers, and parents of autistic children, yet its foundations remain shaky. The first problem for this account is born of circularity. The assertion that autism is characterized by high arousal levels stems from the observation that autistic individuals engage in high rates of repetitive behaviour. However, the presence of this behaviour is then explained as an adaptive response to chronic overarousal. Clearly, this circularity can only be resolved by independently measuring arousal levels in autism. However, there is no firm evidence that individuals with autism are any more (or less) aroused than other clinical groups. The second problem has been the failure to test the predictions of this account in any rigorous fashion. The overarousal account predicts that situations which increase arousal levels will also lead to increased displays of repetitive behaviour. However, the three studies which have tested, and purport to support this prediction in autism (Charlop 1986; Colman et al. 1976; Hutt and Hutt 1965), are all beset by methodological problems (see Turner 1997a). Further predictions, for example concerning the temporal relationship between increases in arousal levels and the display of repetitive behaviour, remain to be tested.

A third problem is that much of the existing literature does not fit with this hypothesis. A coping account would seem inconsistent with the pervasive display of these behaviours across different environmental conditions. This account would also appear unable to explain the high rates of repetitive behaviour observed in individuals with autism when they are alone in an unstimulating environment such as a time-out room (Charlop *et al.* 1983; Runco *et al.* 1986). Whilst we cannot rule out the possibility that extreme arousal levels serve to increase rates of repetitive behaviour in individuals with autism, just as they do in normal subjects (C. Frith and Done 1990; Rago and Case 1978; Soussignon *et al.* 1988) and in animals of other species (Mason 1991; Mason and Turner 1993), there is no evidence to support the assertion that the primary function of repetitive behaviour in autism is to modulate arousal levels.

However, perhaps the chief problem with this account (and all other accounts borrowed from the learning-disabilities literature applied to explain the phenomena of repetitive behaviour in autism) lies in its very origins of work with non-autistic populations. Although repetitive behaviour may index the presence of certain factors, or the operation of certain mechanisms, in non-autistic populations, we cannot assume that the display of repetitive behaviour in autism indicates that similar processes are at work in the autistic disorder. Any account so derived is ill-equipped to explain the qualitative and quantitative differences that appear to exist in the display of these behaviours in autism and learning disability. Moreover, any such account is unable to explain why these behaviours are so ubiquitous, pervasive, and enduring in autism, when the same does not appear to hold for non-autistic individuals with learning disabilities. However, this is not to dismiss these accounts out of hand. On the contrary, each of these accounts may contain more than a grain of truth and each appears well placed to explain certain instances of repetitive behaviour (see Turner 1997a, for review). However, if we want to provide a full explanation of the pervasive tendency to repetition that characterizes autism and sets it apart from other clinical disorders, then we must look towards those hypotheses which account for repetitive behaviour in autism through a mechanism that is suggested to be specific to autism.

Non-executive accounts of repetitive behaviour in autism

As recent theories have sought to explain the autistic syndrome at the psychological level as the consequence of impaired or altered cognitive functioning, there have been some attempts to articulate how these cognitive deficits may lead to the behavioural manifestation of autism. In particular, two hypotheses have been proposed to explain the development and display of repetitive behaviour in autism as the result of cognitive processing which, it is suggested, is fundamentally different to that in many other (if not all other) non-autistic individuals. These accounts are the influential 'theory of mind' hypothesis (e.g. Baron-Cohen 1995; Baron-Cohen *et al.* 1985; U. Frith 1989) and the 'central coherence' theory (U. Frith 1989; U. Frith and Happé 1994).

Repetitive behaviour as the result of impaired mentalizing ability

In a paper published in 1989, Baron-Cohen suggested that the theory of mind account was consistent with the display of repetitive behaviour in autism. Specifically, Baron-Cohen suggested that a theory of mind deficit leading to an impaired ability to understand others' mental states, and thus predict their behaviour, renders the social environment unpredictable and frightening for individuals with autism. Baron-Cohen proposed that repetitive behaviour may develop in autism as a coping strategy to reduce the level of anxiety that results from an impaired ability to comprehend the social world. More recently, a similar account has been proposed by Carruthers (1996). Like Baron-Cohen, he suggests that many of these behaviours serve to withdraw the individual from the social world which they are unable to understand. Carruthers goes on to suggest that different classes of repetitive behaviour may have subtly different origins. He suggests that insistence on sameness may be explained as the autistic child attempts to gain control over his or her world by producing rigid, if arbitrary rules, whilst circumscribed interests may arise 'partly from loneliness (and) partly as a further reaction to the opaque nature of the social world' (p. 268 therein). He explains the odd topics of many autistic interests as the result of the fact that many normal interests (e.g. films) depend on well-developed social understanding. Carruthers suggests that an impoverished appreciation of the social environment leaves the individual with autism with little choice but to develop interests around non-social and routine topics.

This hypothesis valuably generates a number of testable predictions, of which I will consider just two. First, this account predicts that, on a moment-to-moment basis, the level of repetitive behaviour displayed will be related to the unpredictability of the current situation and the degree of interpersonal contact involved. Specifically, this account predicts that levels of repetitive behaviour will be highest when the individual is in a novel or unpredictable social situation, or when faced with new people, and lowest when the individual is in a highly familiar environment that does not involve others. Whilst no studies have been undertaken to test this prediction in any direct fashion, several studies have compared the rates of stereotyped behaviour during periods of social interaction and periods in which limited or no interpersonal demands are made. In direct contradiction of this prediction, each of these studies has reported that rates of stereotyped behaviour are lowest during periods of social interaction and highest during periods of no such interaction (Clark and Rutter 1981; Dadds *et al.* 1988; Donnellan *et al.* 1984; Volkmar *et al.* 1985). Moreover, Clark and Rutter (1981) reported that the highest rates of adaptive *non*-stereotyped activity were observed in situations in which high levels of interpersonal demands were imposed.

A second prediction can be derived from the general premise that if a cognitive deficit lies at the root of repetitive behaviour, variance in the hypothesized deficit should be associated with variability in the display of repetitive behaviour. Thus, if a lack of mentalizing skill is causally responsible for the high rates of repetitive behaviour observed in autism, it must be predicted that those individuals who evidence some mental-state understanding should engage in relatively less repetitive behaviour than those who have little or no ability to understand and infer the mental states of others. Carruthers notes that it is unlikely that all individuals with autism suffer from a total theory of mind failure. Instead, he suggests that many individuals will be contending with partial failure (and hence part-functioning) of their mind-reading system. This is consistent with the fact that many autistic individuals can pass first- and even second-order theory of mind tests (Bowler 1992, Happé 1991; Ozonoff *et al.* 1991; Prior *et al.* 1990; Sparrevohn and Howie 1995; Tager-Flusberg and Sullivan 1994;) and also that some individuals show evidence of real-life mentalizing ability (Dawson and Fernald 1987; U. Frith *et al.* 1994).

I have recently tested the prediction that those autistic individuals who display some evidence of mental-state understanding in passing standard first-order theory of mind tests, should show relatively less repetitive behaviour than those autistic individuals who fail such tests. Each of the autistic subjects was administered a battery of four tasks (a variant on the standard Sally-Anne task (Baron-Cohen *et al.* 1985), an additional version of this task using three locations (one of which was never visited), the Limited Knowledge task (Leslie and U. Frith 1988), and the Smarties task (Perner *et al.* 1989)); the Repetitive Behaviours Interview described above was administered to each of their carers. This interview yielded four summary scores[2] giving an index of the display of repetitive behaviour in each of four categories: (1) repetitive movements (this included stereotyped movements and stereotyped manipulation of objects); (2) insistence on sameness behaviour (this included insistence on the sameness of environment and insistence upon specific routines and rituals); (3) repetitive use of language; and (4) circumscribed interests. Statistical analyses were undertaken to compare the repetitive behaviour summary scores of those autistic individuals that passed three or more of the four tasks (the 'passers') and those that passed fewer than three tasks (the 'failers'). These analyses revealed that, for each of the four domains of repetitive behaviour considered, repetitive behaviours were no more common in theory of mind 'failers' than 'passers'.

The failure to find support for either of the predictions considered must cast serious doubt over whether there is any direct association between mentalizing skill and the display of repetitive behaviour in autism. However, even aside from these failures the theory of mind account appears to be an inadequate explanation of repetitive behaviour in autism. Despite the fact that this account is firmly rooted in recent psychological theory of cognitive functioning in autism, it still does not provide a *direct* explanation of the origin and display of repetitive behaviour. Thus, it is difficult to see how the theory of mind account can explain many of the essential characteristics of repetitive behaviour such as the pervasive and enduring nature of the behaviour, its striking invariance, or why the autistic individual is never found to engage in a balanced range of activities (even if social interaction and social play are excluded).

Repetitive behaviour as the result of the lack of a drive for 'central coherence'

On U. Frith's (1989) central coherence account, the superior performance of autistic subjects on tasks such as the Block Design task is explained in terms of their inability to integrate perceptual information. Individuals with autism are described as experiencing a 'fragmented' perceptual input which is characterized by local, rather than global, coherence. This can lead to a focus on seemingly insignificant details of the environment, and a failure to take the wider context or meaning of a situation into account. It is easy to see how this account could be extended to explain the narrowness of repetitive behaviour in autism, as well as the obtuse topics that may become features of circumscribed interests, and the rote fashion with which these interests are pursued. Similarly, this account is consistent with the common insistence that even minor features of the physical environment remain unchanged, and the savant skills that have been described in a small proportion of autistic individuals. Both of these classes of behaviour could be described as examples of restricted or local coherence in the absence of a normally functioning ability to search for significant and meaningful aspects of a given situation. Thus, in contrast to the accounts that have been considered up until this point, this hypothesis can explain some of the essential features of repetitive behaviours in autism, most especially the highly specific and circumscribed nature of these behaviours and the manner in which they appear to be devoid of any meaning or wider relevance.

If this hypothesis is to explain the display of repetitive behaviour in autism, we must predict an association between central coherence and the display of repetitive behaviour—such that this behaviour is most marked in those individuals whose thinking is especially characterized by a lack of the normal drive for central coherence. In particular, it might be predicted that these individuals, for whom 'local' rather than 'global' coherence is particularly salient, should display marked insistence on sameness and highly restricted circumscribed interests. To test this prediction, I have recently explored the relationship between central coherence and the display of repetitive behaviour in the earlier described samples of high-functioning and learning-disabled individuals with autism. I compared the summary scores derived from the Repetitive Behaviours Interview of those autistic individuals scoring above and below the median on one of the tests suggested to be sensitive to the strength of 'drive for central coherence', the Children's Embedded Figures task. Statistical analyses revealed that for each of the four domains of repetitive behaviour reflected in the repetitive behaviour summary scores, there was no difference in the reported display of repetitive behaviour between those autistic individuals who achieved high scores on the embedded figures task and those who received low scores. Thus, on the basis of this result, there seems to be little support for the suggestion that repetitive behaviour is mediated by the weak drive for central coherence that is purported to characterize autistic thinking.

There are also other impediments to accepting this hypothesis as a full theory of the display of repetitive behaviour. It is not easy to see how this account can be extended to explain low-level repetitive behaviour such as stereotyped movements, stereotyped manipulation of objects and echolalia. U. Frith makes an attempt to account for these behaviours by suggesting that autistic individuals also 'plan and execute actions in fragmentary forms' (U. Frith 1989, p. 116), yet this would seem to be quite distinct from a lack of drive for central coherence which relates primarily to the understanding and integration of incoming information. Moreover, this account cannot readily explain the high degree of repetition or the remarkable invariance that is characteristic of this behaviour without recourse to alternative concepts and theories. Finally, the predictive value of this account appears to be limited. It is not clear whether this account can make any predictions about the situations in which these behaviours are most likely to occur, or the factors that should increase or reduce the display of these behaviours.

Repetitive behaviour as a symptom of executive dysfunction

Whilst it has been suggested that an executive dysfunction account may explain repetitive behaviour, there has been relatively little speculation about just how this may be achieved. Suggesting that these behaviours may result from executive dysfunction in general terms really tells us nothing, since the term is both too broad and too vague to suggest any mechanism by which this might be achieved, or to generate specific and testable predictions. However, if we begin by assuming that one of the main roles of any executive system is to regulate and control volitional acts, then at least two basic processes are required. Any such system must be able to both *generate* appropriate behaviour and to *inhibit* ongoing action which is undesired. In short, the subject must at least be able to trigger the 'start' and 'stop' of behaviour at will. There is a clear parallel here with the way in which the 'supervisory attentional system' (SAS) is suggested to achieve conscious control of action in the model of Norman and Shallice (1980). These authors suggest that conscious control can only be achieved through the modulation of the lower-level unconscious and automatic control process of 'contention scheduling'. Thus, on this account, the SAS can only exert its influence on behaviour through the channels of inhibiting or increasing the activation level of an action schema in the contention scheduling process.

In this section I want to advance the hypothesis that disruption to either (or both) of these processes could lead to the development and display of repetitive behaviour in autism. I will begin by considering the possibility that repetitive behaviour may stem from impaired inhibitory control of action. The subsequent section considers the hypothesis that this class of behaviour may be mediated by an impaired capacity to produce novel self-generated behaviour.

Repetitive behaviour as a failure of behavioural inhibition

Inhibition is central to the control and regulation of behaviour. In the SAS model, the ability to inhibit ongoing and prepotent acts is seen as crucial to the normal, flexible, and adaptive regulation of behaviour. If the SAS lost the ability to inhibit action plans, self-generated or volitional behaviour would become seriously disrupted and characteristically perseverative. From this account it is easy to see how a failure of inhibition may be the psychological substrate of repetitive behaviour. An inability to inhibit actions, thoughts, and behaviour would ensure that once an individual was engaged in some activity, or following one line of thought, this behaviour would be pursued to an abnormally persistent and rigid degree. Thus, unlike the accounts of repetitive behaviour described above which see repetitive behaviour as some type of self-imposed coping mechanism, this account sees repetitive behaviour as the direct, naturalistic counterpart of the tendency to perseveration.

Although there are many parallels between repetitive and perseverative behaviour, there are also key differences which make this an important distinction. Whilst the term 'repetitive behaviour' refers to the repetition of a *spontaneous* action or behaviour, the term 'perseveration' refers to *elicited* or *response* behaviour. In this way, perseveration may be defined as the inappropriate repetition of an act or verbalization which has been elicited by some prior command or environmental event. Perseveration is a common phenomenon in the neuropsychological literature where it is described for a range of tasks and in a range of clinical populations. Moreover, it is well documented that perseverative responding can be of a number of different types and occur at distinct and dissociable levels of behavioural control (Goldberg 1986; Kapur 1985; Luria 1965; Sandson and Albert 1984). For example, Kapur reported a double dissociation between two forms of perseveration in two patients with anterior tumours. One patient perseveratively repeated items from previous trials on a verbal memory task, but was unimpaired on the classic task of attentional set shifting, the Wisconsin Card Sorting test (WCST). The second patient made no intrusion errors on the memory task, but was unable to switch attentional set and sort the stimuli cards from the WCST according to a new sorting principle. This patient perseveratively sorted every card by the original sorting principle despite explicit negative feedback from the experimenter. The first patient can be described as showing simple response perseveration or 'recurrent perseveration', whilst the second patient demonstrated perseveration of attentional set, or 'stuck-in-set perseveration' (Sandson and Albert 1984).

The behavioural inhibition hypothesis not only predicts that experimentally induced perseveration should be highly correlated with naturalistic data for the display of repetitive behaviour, but also that different classes of repetitive behaviour will be associated with different categories of perseverative deficit. Specifically, it might be predicted that simple response perseveration would index the presence of relatively low-level repetitive behaviour such as stereotyped movements and stereotyped manipulation of objects. In contrast, stuck-in-set perseveration may be associated with higher-level repetitive behaviour such as circumscribed interests, rigid adherence to routines and rituals, and repetitive language. In this way repetition, like perseveration, could occur either at the level of repeating the same low-level sequence of behaviour over and over again, or at the level of being stuck in an area or topic so that variable action sequences are deployed, but the topic never changes.

This account also generates a number of other predictions. First, this hypothesis predicts little modulation of repetitive behaviour due to changes in the level of arousal or anxiety experienced by the individual. In contrast, it predicts that specific environmental manipulations would lead to an alteration in the level of repetitive activity produced. In task situations providing strong cues to guide the direction of attention, or in circumstances which elicit well-learnt behaviours, this account would predict lower levels of repetitive behaviour relative to situations in which no such guidelines or structure are provided. Few studies have explored this possibility, but there is some evidence consistent with this proposal. In a study of the effects of treatment structure on children with autism, Schopler *et al.* (1971) reported that repetitive behaviour occurred with reduced frequency when an adult structured a learning session relative to when the child chose what to do. Similarly, Bartak and Rutter (1973) observed that of three institutions caring for individuals with autism, the one that provided the most structured environment was the most successful in managing the residents and their behavioural difficulties. Finally, Olley (1987) reported that the use of strong cues to guide students through an activity, and all its component steps, are very effective in increasing the task behaviour of autistic children.

The following sections explore this hypothesis in greater detail. The first section asks whether there is unambiguous evidence of inhibitory failure leading to perseveration in autism. This section is subdivided to consider perseveration at the level of response behaviour and perseveration of attentional set, separately. The second section directly tackles the prediction that perseverative responding should be associated with a display of repetitive behaviour by describing the results of a recent study designed to explore this issue.

Evidence for a failure of inhibition in autism

Recurrent perseveration

Although perseveration of response behaviour is commonly described in the neuropsychological literature, this class of responding has not been clearly reported in individuals with autism. However, perseverative responding of this nature indicates a very severe degree of impairment and is rare even amongst patients with frontal lobe lesions. Inhibitory impairments often exist in these patients, but are not apparent on tasks where the experimenter provides clear structure and elicits individual responses with cues such as questions. In contrast, when these patients are given less structured tasks in which they are asked to produce multiple responses, perseverative responding is frequently observed (Eslinger and Grattan 1993).

Whilst such tasks have only been rarely used in autism, there is evidence that is, at least, reminiscent of recurrent perseveration in the early studies of pattern production in autism. In these studies the subject was required to produce a series of responses from a small range of response choices. In one task, subjects were simply asked to guess the colour of each new card in a regular pack of playing cards as each card was dealt in turn (U. Frith 1970). In a second task, subjects were presented with a two- or four-bar xylophone and the instructions to 'Play a nice tune, anything you like' (U. Frith 1972). The response sequences produced by the autistic group were characterized by repetition, and were both more rule-bound and showed greater restriction of elements than the sequences produced by learning-disabled or young normal subjects. Moreover, Frith reported that some of the autistic subjects produced the one response choice over and over in a rigid fashion. This pattern of exclusive repetition was not seen in any of the control subjects. This pattern of excessively restricted and repetitive responding in autistic subjects, relative to age- and ability-matched control subjects, has been confirmed by further studies (Baron-Cohen 1992; Boucher 1977; Turner 1995).

The paradigm used in my own work was a modified version of a computerized Two-choice response task used by C. Frith and Done (1983) in a study of individuals with schizophrenia. In this modified task, subjects were presented with two response locations and simply asked to guess whether the next target would appear in the left or right box. Target locations were determined randomly by the computer, but subjects were not told this and were instead encouraged to try and find as many target bricks as they could. The response sequences of about 10% of the HFA subjects and 30% of the LDA subjects were characterized by repetition of one of the response choices to an excessive degree. This same pattern of responding was not reported for any of the comparison subjects.

However, whilst the responding of the autistic subjects is reminiscent of response perseveration, it is not truly perseverative as it does not meet the defining criteria of *inappropriate* responding. In tasks of pattern production there is no right or wrong sequence, and producing the same response choice over and over is a simple and efficient response to the demands of the task. Similarly, in the Two-choice task, repeating the same response at every trial is a simple way of maximizing the chances of success. Thus, although exclusive repetition of a single response choice is rarely, if ever, observed in normal subjects and appears to be a telling sign for impaired cognitive function, on the basis of this task alone it is difficult to determine whether a moderate tendency to repetition is attributable to executive dysfunction or the use of an efficient strategy.

In response to the problems of interpretation posed by the Two-choice task I have also used a further task, the Sequence task, to explore the capacity for inhibitory regulation of simple response behaviour in autistic and non-autistic subjects in greater detail (Turner 1995). The Sequence task differs from the Two-choice paradigm in two key ways. First, in the Sequence task subjects are required to produce response *sequences* rather than a series of single response choices. Four boxes are presented on a computer screen and subjects are asked to make as many different sequences as they can by touching each box once and once only. Second, subjects are explicitly asked to avoid repetitions and produce as many *different* sequences as possible.

Therefore, to perform successfully on this task subjects must inhibit previously rewarded, and thus salient, response sequences and continue to produce novel response sequences.

This study revealed few statistically significant differences between the performance of the HFA and the HFC subjects, but clear evidence for an autistic deficit amongst the learning-disabled subjects. The LDA subjects produced significantly fewer novel responses than LDC subjects, and significantly more perseverative responses, including higher numbers of repetitions of the immediately preceding response sequence.

Although it is impossible to assert with certainty that the impaired performance of the LDA subjects is due to a failure of inhibition, the pattern of findings is inconsistent with some other possibilities. In particular, the high number of immediate repetitions produced by the LDA individuals is inconsistent with an explanation in terms of poor working-memory capacity. Some of the LDA subjects repeated the same sequence, consecutively, as many as 12 times despite persistent reminders to try something different. Moreover, the responding of some of these subjects gave the impression that without prompting they would have continued to repeat the same sequence on all 24 attempts. No comparison subjects repeated a sequence more than twice in succession. After three consecutive repetitions subjects were reminded to try 'a different sequence'. This prompt did induce some of the autistic subjects to produce a novel response after a string of consecutive repetitions, but then they often proceeded to repeat this sequence perseveratively, or simply reverted to the pattern of repeating the previous sequence trial after trial. Finally, some of the comments made by LDA subjects during testing are consistent with a failure to inhibit the salience of the previous response. Many expressed frustration at always repeating the same sequence, or announced half-way through a sequence, 'Uh-oh, I've done this one', yet would continue with a previously produced sequence. The comment of one LDA boy was particularly telling and appeared to describe the frustration of many of these subjects: 'Its hard to stop doing pink, blue, green, yellow—it's stuck in my head'. This evidence is consistent with other reports of an inconsistency between both language and action in autism (Ozonoff, personal communication), and after frontal lobe injury (e.g. Milner 1963).

Stuck-in-set perseveration

Several studies into autism have reported perseveration of the stuck-in-set variety when using tests of attentional set-shifting. The most commonly used task has been the WCST, but this has yielded an ambiguous and contradictory pattern of results. Two studies have reported that high-functioning children and adolescents with autism make more perseverative errors, but no

more non-perseverative errors, than age- and ability-matched control subjects (Ozonoff *et al.* 1991; Prior and Hoffman 1990). Three further studies
have reported that high-functioning autistic subjects achieve significantly
fewer correct category shifts, than control subjects, whilst making significantly more perseverative and non-perseverative errors (Rumsey 1985;
Rumsey and Hamburger 1988; Szatmari *et al.* 1990). However, the fact
that the autistic adults in these latter studies are of significantly lower IQ than
the control subjects calls the validity of these findings into question. When
Szatmari *et al.* re-analysed their data to include only those subjects with a
full-scale IQ of 85 or greater (to equate the groups for ability level), no
differences were found in the performance of the autistic and control
subjects. Two further studies have failed to find any deficit in the performance of high-functioning children and adults with autism relative to
comparison subjects (Minshew *et al.* 1992; Schneider and Asarnow 1987).

Recently, Hughes *et al.* (1994) have explored the capacity to shift attentional set in learning-disabled autistic individuals relative to age- and ability-
matched control individuals using a different task. The Intradimensional,
Extradimensional (IDED) set-shifting task differs from the WCST in that it
is presented to subjects in a simplified stage-wise format. The task begins
with subjects required to learn a simple discrimination between two pink
geometrical shapes which differ only in form. After six successive correct
responses are reached (at this and all subsequent stages) the subject is
required to reverse the learnt rule and respond to the previously incorrect
stimulus in the target stimulus dimension. The next stage introduces an
additional stimulus dimension, white lines, which are paired with the shapes.
At this stage the contingency remains the same (i.e. the same shape remains
correct). The next stage is the first of the two crucial transfer stages. In the
intradimensional shift stage (IDS) the subject is presented with new exemplars for both of the stimulus dimensions. Although the subject must learn a
new contingency, it is with respect to the same stimulus dimension (shape). In
contrast, at the second of the transfer stages, the extradimensional shift stage
(EDS), new exemplars of each dimension are again introduced, but this time
the contingency is derived from the line, and not the shape, dimension. Thus,
at this stage subjects must ignore the shape stimuli and instead determine
which of the white lines is the new target stimulus. It is only at this stage that
the subject is required to make a true shift of attentional set from one
stimulus dimension (i.e. shapes) to the other (i.e. lines).

The chief advantage of this procedure is that it enables the experimenter to
break down the many complex demands of the WCST and isolate the precise
difficulty of the subject. Using this new paradigm, Hughes *et al.* (1994)
confirmed that the primary difficulty of learning-disabled autistic individuals
is in making an extradimensional shift of attention from one stimulus

dimension to the other. Hughes *et al.* reported that the autistic subjects were significantly less likely than the chronological and mental age matched control subjects to successfully complete the task, and this was due to differences at the EDS stage, but not at any of the earlier stages of the task. Moreover, the autistic subjects produced more errors than the non-autistic, learning-disabled group at the EDS transfer stage, but not at the preceding IDS transfer stage. The same pattern of results has been reported using the same task in patients with frontal lobe lesions (Owen *et al.* 1991) and patients with Parkinson's disease (Downes *et al.* 1989).

However, despite the usefulness of this paradigm in demonstrating a clear deficit in extradimensional set-shifting in autism over and above the deficits in more fundamental attentional and learning processes, one can still question whether this deficit is only explicable as stuck-in-set perseveration to the previously relevant dimension. Whilst one explanation of this deficit is that subjects have difficulty at the EDS stage of the task because of an inhibitory failure in shifting attention away from the previously reinforced dimension, as Hughes *et al.* note, a further possibility is that this deficit may stem from a deficit in engaging attention to the previously irrelevant dimension. This confound is a consequence of the fact that the same two stimuli dimensions are used throughout all stages of the task.

To address this confound, a modified version of the IDED task has been developed in which subjects perform two separate conditions of the task (Owen *et al.* 1993). In the first, the previously irrelevant stimulus dimension is replaced with a new one at the EDS stage of the task. This condition is labelled the 'perseveration' condition as subjects have no exposure to the new and correct dimension. Thus, failure to make the extradimensional shift successfully cannot be attributed to prior learning about this dimension; rather failure at this stage must reflect difficulty in moving attention away from the old previously relevant dimension. In the second 'learned irrelevance' condition, the previously reinforced dimension is replaced with a novel dimension at the EDS stage. Success on this condition involves shifting attentional set to the previously irrelevant dimension (cf. Mackintosh 1983). Failure to successfully make the attentional shift in this condition cannot reflect perseveration to the incorrect dimension as subjects have no prior experience of this dimension, rather failure must reflect an inability to switch attention to a dimension which was previously incorrect. Using this task, Owen *et al.* (1993) reported that the extradimensional shifting difficulty of patients with frontal lobe lesions is overwhelmingly one of perseveration to the previously relevant dimension. In contrast, the difficulties experienced by Parkinson's disease patients receiving the anti-Parkinsonian drug L-dopa was almost exclusively attributable to a susceptibility to learned irrelevance. I have recently administered this modified version of the IDED task to the autistic and non-autistic comparison subjects described in my earlier studies in an attempt to identify whether the set-shifting difficulty of autistic subjects is of a perseverative or non-perseverative nature (Turner 1995). A different pattern of results was revealed for the high-functioning and the learning-disabled subjects. The learning-disabled autistic subjects were found to make significantly more errors than the learning-disabled comparison subjects at the EDS stage of the task in the perseveration condition, but not in the learned irrelevance condition. That is, the LDA subjects only showed a set-shifting deficit when the previously reinforced dimension was present. When this dimension was removed from the task at the EDS stage and replaced with a novel dimension, the LDA subjects were unimpaired at shifting their attention to make a discrimination on the basis of the previously irrelevant dimension. Thus, on the basis of these results, the attentional set-shifting deficit of the LDA subjects appears to be truly one of perseverative responding to the previously relevant dimension.

In contrast, there was no difference between the performance of the high-functioning autistic and the high-functioning comparison groups at the EDS stage in either condition. However, there were signs that some of the HFA subjects were experiencing set-shifting difficulties at the EDS stage that were restricted to the perseveration condition. Two of the 22 HFA subjects failed to reach the criterion at the EDS stage in the perseveration condition, yet all reached criterion at this stage in the learned irrelevance condition. Moreover, some of the HFA subjects appeared to be correctly passing the EDS stage without making any shift of attentional state. Three subjects spontaneously remarked that they were passing the task via a process of conditional association, making comments like: 'When the square is big it's that one and when the square is little it is that one'. This non-shifting route to success is made possible in the Modified IDED task, as the change of stimulus dimension that occurs at the EDS stage of this task provides a very clear visual signal to suggest that 'something' about the task has changed.

In summary, there seems to be good evidence that the attentional set-shifting impairment of the learning-disabled autistic subjects at the EDS stage of the IDED task is attributable to perseverative responding to the previously reinforced dimension. The situation is less straightforward for the high-functioning autistic subjects, given the mixed pattern of results on the WCST and the uncertain results from the Modified IDED task. However, the pattern of results obtained is at least consistent with a failure of inhibition for some autistic subjects when task requirements demand that the subject switches the focus of their attention from one dimension of a complex stimulus to another.

Thus, taking the results from the Modified IDED task and the Sequence task together, it appears there is evidence for a failure of inhibition leading to perseveration in autism. This perseverative responding has been elicited in learning-disabled individuals with autism and is both of the stuck-in-set and recurrent types. It is notable that those individuals who had difficulty with the perseveration condition of the Modified IDED task were, by and large, neither the same individuals who showed markedly perseverative responding on the Sequence task nor the individuals who displayed excessive repetition of response on the Two-choice task (who were, with few exceptions, the same individuals). Whilst this partial dissociation simply parallels results of neuropsychological findings described earlier, it is of considerable interest that this dissociation has been reported within the one population of developmentally disordered individuals.

Perseverative responding and repetitive behaviour

As described earlier, the behavioural inhibition hypothesis of repetitive behaviour in autism predicts that there will be an association between the degree and class of inhibitory deficit and the display of repetitive behaviour. Moreover, this hypothesis predicts that different classes of perseverative deficit will be associated with different classes of repetitive behaviour. Specifically, it predicts that recurrent perseveration, or perseveration of a previous response, will be associated with the presence of low-level stereotyped movements, whilst perseveration of the stuck-in-set variety will be associated with higher level classes of repetitive behaviour—such as repetitive discussion of the same topic or repetitive pursuit of the same activity.

Correlational analyses and median split comparisons were undertaken and provided striking support for these predictions. Considering the Two-choice task first, for the autistic, but not for the comparison, subjects there was a clear pattern of association between excessive repetition of one response choice on this task and parental report of stereotyped movements, but no other class of repetitive behaviour, as reflected in the repetitive behaviour summary scores derived from the Repetitive Behaviours Interview. This finding is consistent with C. Frith and Done's (1983) report of an association between rule-bound responding and total movement disorder in their schizophrenic subjects.

Although the only evidence of an inhibitory deficit on the Sequence task was found in the performance of the LDA subjects, significant correlations between the display of repetitive behaviour and the number of immediate repetitions produced on this task were obtained for both the LDA and the HFA subjects. Specifically, the number of immediate repetitions produced was positively correlated with the display of repetitive movements for both autistic groups, and circumscribed interests for the HFA subjects only. Median split comparisons confirmed this pattern of results, revealing that those subjects producing the lowest numbers of novel responses, and also the highest number of immediate repetitions, showed the highest rates of repetitive movements and the most restricted and extreme circumscribed interests. No such links were observed between task performance and the display of other classes of repetitive behaviour for the autistic subjects, nor for task performance and any class of behaviour for the non-autistic comparison subjects.

It is relatively easy to see how an impaired ability to inhibit previously emitted responses may be related to the display of repetitive movements, as repetitive movements are likely to be the naturalistic equivalent of simple tendencies to repeat movements and responses in task situations. Thus, just as autistic subjects seem unable to modify and adapt their response behaviour in line with task demands, they may be unable to inhibit and modify environmentally triggered or spontaneously produced actions to produce varied patterns of responding. Similarly, at least some manifestations of circumscribed interests could be seen to arise as a naturalistic counterpart of recurrent perseveration, since an important part of the definition of a circumscribed interests is that the subject carries out the same activity over and over in an invariant fashion. Thus, a tendency to repeat the same sequence several times in succession in the Sequence task may have parallels with the autistic individual who is fascinated by 'Thomas the Tank Engine' and repeats lines from the books over and over. However, other manifestations of circumscribed interests seem to be closer to the phenomena of stuck-in-set perseveration. Thus, the autistic subject who is fascinated with road signs and draws them repetitively, typically draws a variety of such signs. What is striking about this behaviour is not the repetition of one behavioural sequence, but the failure to break from this topic to produce a drawing of anything else. Thus, as suggested earlier, it may be predicted that those subjects who produce high rates of EDS errors in the perseveration condition of the Modified IDED task will be more likely to show such a pattern of association than the subjects producing low rates of such errors.

In support of this prediction, those autistic individuals who produced high rates of EDS errors in the perseveration condition of the Modified IDED task were significantly more likely than those who made low numbers of such errors to display repetitive use of language and circumscribed interests as assessed by the repetitive behaviour summary scores. In contrast, there was no such relationship between task performance and the display of stereo-typed movements and sameness behaviour for the perseveration condition, nor for performance at any stage of the learned irrelevance condition and any of the four summary scores. Moreover, there was no association between performance on either condition of this task and the display of any class of repetitive behaviour for the comparison subjects. This pattern of results is consistent with the suggestion that a difficulty in shifting the focus of attention may specifically underlie the display of 'higher-level' repetitive behaviour in autism, such as repeated talk on one topic and restricted and rigid pursuit of circumscribed interests. This contrasts sharply with the pattern of association between responding on the tasks employed to tap inhibition of simple response behaviour (the Two-choice and Sequence tasks) and parental report of repetitive behaviour where significant correlations were (largely) restricted to the 'lower-level' phenomena of stereotyped movements.

Repetitive behaviour as the result of an impaired generative ability

The ability to respond to the environment in a flexible and adaptive way depends not just on the ability to control and regulate behaviour through the inhibition of inappropriate activity, but also on the ability to generate appropriate goals and courses of action. If the ability to generate novel behaviour and ideas was permanently disabled we might predict that we would not only use a small set of action plans, but also repeat them time and time again. Thus, in autism, executive dysfunction may render individuals unable to generate novel action plans and so they are forced to repeat the same acts over and over. In this way, maybe it is because it is difficult for autistic people to be spontaneous and creative in their use of objects, toys, and their leisure time, that they are commonly found carrying out the same activity over and over again.

A generativity deficit has many advantages in explaining important characteristics of repetitive behaviour in individuals with autism. It can readily explain the development and maintenance of these behaviours along with the limited usefulness of many of the behavioural intervention strategies that are frequently reported in the literature. Moreover, this account would seem well placed to explain the diversity of repetitive phenomena in autism, since an impaired generative ability would be predicted to affect functioning at all levels of behaviour. In this way, impaired generative ability could variously lead to the repetition of a simple fragmentary movement or the repetition of a full and complete sequence of behaviour. Furthermore, this account would also explain why a tendency to repetition is so pervasive across all areas of functioning in autism. For example, it would explain how the play of autistic children is typically repetitive in nature, and also why individuals with autism commonly carry out the same activities in the same order even when this behaviour is not unusually rigid. Finally, this is at least consistent with the degree of repetition and invariance characteristic of repetitive behaviour. If a generative mechanism is seen to lie at the root of flexible and adaptive functioning in the normal individual, then the loss or malfunction of these mechanisms would be expected to result in minimal modification to established behaviour patterns. Further, it would be predicted that, in the absence of alternative activities to fill a behavioural vacuum, these activities would be repeated over and over again. This account, like the regulation of activity one, does not see repetitive behaviour as a secondary coping mechanism.

This account generates several testable predictions. First, we might expect autistic individuals to engage in a restricted range of activities generally, quite apart from the display of repetitive activities. Second, we might expect to see higher levels of repetitive activities when autistic individuals are alone and unoccupied without external prompts to guide their choice of activity. Finally, it would be expected that when alternative, clearly specified options are presented to an autistic individual, the level of repetitive activities exhibited should decrease, and the level of adaptive behaviour displayed should increase.

In line with the first prediction, individuals with autism typically have very small behavioural repertoires (Lovaas et al. 1974). Moreover, at least in individuals with Down's syndrome, the size of the individual's behavioural repertoire has been found to be correlated with the level of stereotyped movements exhibited by these individuals (Francis 1966), such that those individuals who displayed the highest rates of stereotyped movements were observed to engage in the most restricted range of behaviour. Consistent with the second prediction, there is good evidence that individuals with autism display high rates of repetitive behaviour when high demands are placed on their generative ability, either because they are alone and unoccupied, or because there are few cues to guide their behaviour (Charlop et al. 1983; Runco et al. 1986). Studies which have attempted to identify cyclic variation and ultradian rhythms in the stereotyped movements of non-autistic, learning-disabled individuals have also pointed to the peaks in these behaviours that correspond to periods of transition and little organized activity in the routine of these individuals (Kaufman and Levitt 1965; Lewis et al. 1981; Tierney et al. 1978). The only study to look for a similar pattern in individuals with autism is that of Sorosky et al. (1968). Although the authors failed to find any evidence of ultradian rhythms in the stereotyped movements of these individuals, they were specifically focusing on cycles of less than 2-hours' duration and so may have failed to identify variations that accompany significant changes in routine (e.g. low activity periods at mealtimes and at staff-handover periods).

Finally, some evidence supports the prediction that when autistic children are provided with alternative activities, the level of repetitive behaviour displayed drops dramatically. Two independent studies have found that a programme designed to teach appropriate play activities to children with autism led to a marked reduction of stereotyped behaviour which generalized across settings and was maintained at follow-up (Azrin *et al.* 1973; Eason *et al.* 1982). However, in direct contrast, Wells *et al.* (1977) found that behavioural techniques which reduce levels of stereotyped behaviour do not always lead to an increase in the levels of appropriate toy play. The problem with such intervention techniques is that their reductionist nature serves to limit an already highly restricted behavioural repertoire. As Lovaas (1970, cited in Zentall and Zentall 1983) has suggested, behaviour modification techniques have been more effective in reducing stereotyped behaviour than in establishing appropriate behaviours.

Evidence for a generativity impairment in autism

If the hypothesis that individuals with autism are poor at generating novel ideas and responses is correct, then they should be poor at generating ideas and novel responses spontaneously, without prompting, in experimental tasks. Thus, these individuals may perform relatively well on structured tasks in which there are questions, cues, etc. to guide their response, but they would be predicted to produce low rates of responses when few or no cues and only very general instructions are provided. Moreover, as the cues provided are less useful in prompting or eliciting behaviour so the task should become increasingly likely to elicit deficits in individuals with autism.

However, it may be argued that this prediction simply echoes the earlier prediction derived from the behavioural inhibition hypothesis. Both hypotheses predict poor performance on unstructured tasks in which subjects are asked to produce multiple responses to a single cue. Yet, the fact that both of these accounts should predict deficits on such tasks is not surprising. These two abilities, whilst distinct, are in some senses two sides of the same coin. Each is crucial at times when the individual is required to produce volitional behaviour in an environment which provides few cues or clues to guide and prompt this behaviour. Moreover, in such situations both the generation and inhibition of volitional behaviour are necessarily highly interrelated, as the inhibition of one act must precede the generation and activation of any alternative course of action. Therefore, it follows that, in those empirical tasks which may best elucidate each class of deficit, either impairment may be expected to lead to poor performance. However, this is not to say that these hypotheses are empirically indistinguishable—indeed, I would argue that these hypotheses are (largely) dissociable. Whilst both might predict deficits on tasks in which subjects are asked to produce multiple responses to a single cue, the nature of these deficits would be expected to be rather different in each case. A failure of inhibition would be predicted to lead to response-production characterized by the repetition of earlier responses or the production of responses that are highly thematically related. In contrast, a pattern in which subjects displayed clearly reduced (as opposed to inappropriate) fluency is consistent with a primary impairment in the capacity to self-generate novel responses or new modes of responding.

Few studies have directly explored the possibility of an impaired generative capacity in autism. However, there is some evidence that successive drawings produced by children with autism show a greater degree of thematic relatedness than equivalent drawings by non-autistic control children (Lewis and Boucher 1991). Other studies have utilized the Word Fluency task in which subjects are asked to produce as many words as they can in response to a cue (usually a letter or a semantic category) in one minute. Some studies have reported that individuals with autism are impaired relative to non-autistic, age- and ability-matched control subjects (Minshew et al. 1992; Rumsey and Hamburger 1988), whilst others have failed to find any such differences (Boucher 1988; Minshew et al. 1995; Scott et al. 1995).

However, the Word Fluency paradigm does not provide a good test of the capacity to generate multiple *novel* responses. Whilst this task is one of generativity, in the sense that it requires subjects to produce many different responses to a single cue, it does not require the subject to generate responses *de novo*. The task does not require the subjects to go beyond their knowledge and generate new and imaginative responses, or interpret the cue provided in a new or unusual manner. Rather, it simply requires the subjects to trawl their lexicon and retrieve suitable exemplars of the given category. This distinction is perhaps best illustrated by the study of Boucher (1988). Whilst Boucher reported no difference between the performance of learning-disabled autistic and age- and ability-matched control children on a standard task of category fluency, in a further task in which subjects were asked to think of as many miscellaneous words as they could in 60 seconds (subjects were instructed to name 'as many words as you can think of, any words at all') she reported a marked performance deficit in the autistic subjects. The difference between this and the former task is that the miscellaneous task provides the subject with no cues which can be used as 'bait' in any mental trawl of the lexicon. At this point, it may be argued that the subjects may succeed on this task without 'thinking up' any responses in this way at all. That is to say, the subjects may achieve a good performance by merely looking around the room and naming the items present, or reciting well-learnt information. However, even here subjects must generate such a strategy or tactic to improve their performance. Thus, without a cue to aid performance the subjects in Boucher's miscellaneous condition are reliant upon their generative ability to achieve a satisfactory score.

It is surprising that few have followed up this line of enquiry by developing and employing further tests of generative ability in the study of the executive abilities of individuals with autism. Tests of *ideational fluency* have been commonly used in the neuropsychological literature to tap not only the ability to access stored knowledge, but also the ability to generate new responses. These tasks require the subject to produce as many different interpretations of a situation as possible. I have recently used two such paradigms to study generative ability in autistic and non-autistic comparison subjects (Turner 1997b). The first paradigm was the typical Uses of Objects task, in which the subject is asked to name as many as possible uses of a given object (e.g. a newspaper) within a certain time. It is possible either to produce common uses of the object (e.g. read it, use it to start a fire) or to produce highly imaginative ones (e.g. as wallpaper, to keep warm). Whilst both types of response are correct, it is only the latter class of response that requires the subject to be truly generative, in the sense of looking at the situation from new perspectives and seeing new possibilities, thus generating new responses as opposed to recalling stored knowledge. If subjects have poor generative ability they would be expected to produce few responses and, in particular, to be impaired at producing the latter class of highly imaginative response.

The second paradigm was the related Pattern Meanings task described by Wallach and Kogan (1965). In this task the subject is presented with five meaningless line drawings and asked to suggest all the things that each pattern could be. The generativity deficit hypothesis would predict that individuals with autism will be impaired at generating multiple interpretations, and particularly at providing imaginative or interpretative responses. In each task the subject was given 2.5 minutes in which to produce responses for each cue item.

Both paradigms yielded essentially similar findings. At both ability levels, the autistic subjects produced significantly fewer responses than the comparison subjects. Moreover, the HFA subjects were found to display such a marked deficit on these tasks that they produced significantly fewer responses than the LDC subjects, despite a mean IQ some 40 points higher than that of the learning-disabled controls. The same pattern of results was obtained when the analyses were restricted to the number of new themes produced, or the number of responses that could be identified as being highly imaginative.

It is significant that many of the most able, and some of the eldest, HFA subjects were among the most impaired on this task. The only adult in this study to have held gainful employment was one of the three most impaired subjects on this task. After completing the Use of Objects task he commented that thinking of things 'has always been my biggest problem'. Similarly, two subjects attending mainstream school were also among the most impaired on these tasks. These three subjects produced as few as one or two responses on some trials.

A third task of generativity employed in the present study was the Design Fluency task of Jones-Gotman and Milner (1977). In this task there are two conditions. In the first 'free' condition subjects are given a blank sheet of paper and asked to produce as many designs as they can in a 5-minute period. In the second 'fixed' condition, subjects are asked to repeat the task, but this time to produce only responses made up of four lines. In both conditions, subjects are explicitly forbidden from producing common or well-known designs that depict a recognizable object or symbol.

There was no difference in the total number of designs produced by the autistic and the comparison subjects in either condition. However, when performance was assessed by the number of *novel* designs produced, the comparison subjects were found to achieve significantly higher scores than the autistic subjects in both test conditions. This discrepancy was largely attributable to high rates of incorrect designs, repetitions of previous designs, and production of highly redundant designs in the autistic, relative to the comparison, subjects. These results are in direct contrast to the results of the earlier ideational fluency tasks. In the Use of Objects and Pattern Meanings tasks the autistic subjects produced significantly fewer responses than the comparison subjects, but there was no significant tendency for the former to produce any more repetitions or redundant responses than the latter.

The high rates of repetitions and redundant responses produced by the autistic subjects on this task serve as a reminder that poor performance on fluency tasks is not an unequivocal sign of generativity impairment. As suggested earlier, this pattern of responding is more consistent with an explanation in terms of a failure to inhibit previous responses than a failure to generate any responses. In particular, high rates of repetitions of previous responses are consistent with an inability to inhibit previous, and thus prepotent, responses; whilst high rates of redundant responses may indicate a failure of the normal ability to shift attentional set, leaving the individual 'stuck' in one line of thought or approach to the problem. In contrast, the combination of a low number of responses and low rates of repetitions and redundant responses obtained with the ideational fluency tasks may be more safely attributed to a generativity deficit. Thus, despite many commonalties between the ideational and design fluency tasks, each leads to different, and apparently contradictory, conclusions. However, two explanations may reconcile the discrepancy between the results of these tasks.

The first is that the reduced fluency in the ideational fluency tasks is attributable to the linguistic nature of these tasks; and that reduced fluency in people with autism is due not to an impaired capacity to generate novel responses, but to their relatively poorer language skills. However, two lines of evidence run counter to this possibility. First, several of the autistic subjects who were the most impaired on the ideational fluency task were those subjects with the highest verbal IQ and clearly the best verbal skills. Second, this account leaves the discrepancy between the high rate of errors in responses on this task and the low rate of such responses on the other tasks unexplained.

Clearly, on tasks such as the Use of Objects task the subject must first begin by generating some idea in a full and complete way. However, subjects may complete the Design Fluency task by beginning each design before they have fully formulated an idea, thus, to some extent, generating their response 'on the hoof'. It is possible that this approach is more likely to result in high rates of perseverative responding as the subject is more susceptible to 'capture' by the salience of the previous response (or the motor programme that produced that response). In support of this possibility, two of the autistic subjects expressed frustration when completing the Design Fluency task. Both subjects produced very high rates of repetitions and as they finished each design commented that it was a repetition of the immediately prior design, but seemed unable to do anything to prevent this. This finding is very reminiscent of a similar phenomenon reported for a small number of autistic subjects undertaking the Sequence task. As in the present paradigm, a number of autistic subjects exhibited exasperation at their inability to produce responses which were different from their preceding responses. Both are non-verbal tasks of the ability to generate multiple responses and both allow subjects to begin their response before the idea is fully formulated. Use of a further paradigm may enable these alternative explanations for the discrepancy to be distinguished. The Gesture Fluency task (Jason 1985) is a non-verbal task in which the subject is required to produce multiple and varied hand gestures. If the nature of the response deficit on tasks of fluency is determined by whether or not the task demands that the subject fully formulates or conceptualizes the response prior to responding, one would expect to find a pattern of impairment on the Gesture Fluency task akin to that reported for the ideational fluency measures. In contrast, if response modality is the critical component in these tasks, one would expect to find little evidence of reduced fluency on the Gesture Fluency task.

Reduced fluency and repetitive behaviour

Finally, considering the pattern of association between performance on the three experimental tasks of generativity described above and the naturalistic display of repetitive behaviour, as assessed by the Repetitive Behaviours Interview, allows us to directly examine the hypothesis that repetitive behaviour in autism is mediated by a failure of the normal ability to generate novel and spontaneous behaviour. For both groups of autistic subjects, but not the comparison subjects, correlational analyses revealed that the number of novel responses produced in the ideational fluency tasks was significantly negatively associated with the repetitive behaviour summary scores for the display of sameness behaviour and circumscribed interests, but not for stereotyped movements or the repetitive use of language. This conclusion was reinforced by the results of median split comparisons. These comparisons confirmed that those autistic individuals who produced few novel responses on the Use of Objects task displayed significantly more extreme sameness behaviour and circumscribed interests relative to those subjects who produced high rates of such responses. This result was also confirmed for circumscribed interests using the number of novel designs produced in the Design Fluency task to achieve the median split. Thus, this pattern of findings is consistent with the hypothesis that a generative failure may be particularly related to a lack of variety and novelty in behaviour. Consistent with the results of analyses which sought to link the display of repetitive behaviour and performance on tasks of behavioural inhibition, the specificity of the associations between generativity failure on certain tasks and the display of certain classes of repetitive behaviour is very striking.

The account of repetitive behaviour provided by the parents of many of the subjects also provides support for the generativity hypothesis. Many carers described that repetitive behaviour was exacerbated in situations where the individual was alone or unoccupied. Although this pattern of results is also consistent with other alternative hypotheses (not least the failure of inhibition account), the pattern of report suggested that, in autistic individuals, the lack of alternative stimulation was associated with increased rates of repetitive behaviour more than any other single factor.

Repetitive behaviour and executive functions in autism: a reappraisal

When suggesting that repetitive behaviour in autism may be the direct and naturalistic manifestation of impaired executive control, I hypothesized that this could occur in at least two ways. First, I suggested that an impaired capacity for the normal inhibitory control of behaviour could lead to repetition in action and thought as the individual, unable to regulate action and attention in the normal manner, becomes 'locked into' one line of behaviour. Second, I suggested that an inability to produce novel behaviour in a self-generated fashion would be predicted to lead to a lack of variety in responding which may be manifested as repeated display of behaviours from a small and well-rehearsed behavioural repertoire. The evidence reviewed in this chapter is broadly consistent with each of these possibilities.

Thus, both hypotheses find support in the results of studies which have compared the naturalistic display of repetitive behaviour in individuals with autism in contrasting environmental situations. Moreover, the results of my own studies described in this chapter offer some support for each account. One of the most striking features of these latter results is the highly specific pattern of association between task performance and the display of different classes of repetitive behaviour. This is summarized in Table 3.2. This table shows that, as predicted, repetitive movements were significantly associated with recurrent perseveration on both the Two-choice and Sequence tasks, whilst repetition of language (most commonly accounted for by repeated talk on the same topic) was associated with perseveration of the stuck-in-set type at the EDS stage of the Modified IDED task. In contrast, insistence upon sameness behaviour was found to be associated with deficits on the ideational fluency tasks. Finally, the presence of circumscribed interests was found to be associated with both impaired extradimensional set-shifting in the perseveration condition of the Modified IDED task and reduced fluency on the generativity measures.

Table 3.2 Summary of statistically significant associations between task performance and parental report of repetitive behaviour in individuals with autism ('$\sqrt{}$' indicates statistically significant ($p < 0.05$) association between behaviour and task performance as revealed by correlational analyses and median split comparisons; '–' indicates no such statistically significant association)

Class of behaviour	Recurrent perseveration (Sequence task)	Stuck-in-set perseveration (Modified IDED task)	Generativity (Ideational and Design fluency)
Repetitive movements	$\sqrt{}$	–	–
Sameness behaviour	–	–	$\sqrt{}$
Repetitive use of language	–	$\sqrt{}$	–
Circumscribed interests	$\sqrt{}$	$\sqrt{}$	$\sqrt{}$

Given the failure of this review to find support for either the failure of inhibition or the generativity account at the expense of the other, it follows: (1) that different accounts apply to different subgroups of individuals; (2) that different accounts explain different classes of repetitive behaviour; or (3) that repetitive behaviour is multiply determined. It seems likely that there is some truth to each of these possibilities. First, some of the autistic individuals studied clearly had relatively more trouble with one class of tests than the other. Moreover, on the basis of the present results it appears that some classes of behaviour (repetitive movements, sameness behaviour and, repetitive use of language) are preferentially associated with impairments on one class of task, whilst the display of circumscribed interests was associated with poor performance on all tests used. As the class of circumscribed interests is probably the most heterogeneous class of repetitive behaviour in the present taxonomy, it seems plausible that this category may include behaviours of diverse origins. Accordingly, it may be possible to further subdivide the class of circumscribed interests to reflect the nature and relative complexity of the interest pursued. Alternatively, it may be that as this class of behaviour includes some of the most complex of repetitive behaviours there are multiple determinants for these behaviours.

As an explanation of many features of the autistic syndrome, the conclusion suggested from this pattern of results is that both hypotheses are inextricably connected and complimentary. At a basic level, it appears that both accounts are needed to explain the full spectrum of repetitive behaviour observed in autism. Moreover, each account seems relatively better suited to explaining different features of spontaneous behaviour in autism. The behavioural inhibition account is consistent with the high degree of repetition and the invariance of many repetitive behaviours, whilst the generativity account describes why, at all times, the behaviour of individuals with autism is predictable and lacks initiative and creativity. Finally, the closeness of the predictions of each account reinforces the fact that these abilities are two sides of the same coin. Thus, the present results can be best summarized as showing that the naturalistic display of repetitive behaviour is associated with general disruption to a system such as the SAS of Norman and Shallice (1980) which is responsible for controlling volitional activity. One of the strengths of the SAS account lies in the way it is able to account for features of autism that have been little explored but which, none the less, are characteristic of the disorder. This account is well able to explain the lack of initiative and poverty of speech (Dykens *et al.* 1991; Rumsey *et al.* 1985) frequently reported in autism, along with the finding that the spontaneous play of children with autism is highly repetitive and thematically restricted relative to that of non-autistic individuals (Black *et al.* 1975; Fein *et al.* 1991; Jarrold *et al.* 1993). Just as the theory of mind approach has drawn attention to many of the characteristic features of autism and valuably inspired much research, so this account emphasizes, in an equally striking way, many other, but potentially equally important, features of the disorder.

The suggestion that repetitive behaviour may be best explained as the consequence of a general disruption to executive processing systems used in the generation and regulation of novel and spontaneous behaviour also offers the potential to explain some of the heterogeneity that exits in the display of repetitive behaviour. If individuals with autism vary in the extent to which the capacity for behavioural inhibition and the ability to generate new modes of behaving are affected, then this account may be able to explain different behavioural profiles in individuals of similar ages and ability levels. It is unlikely that any executive system is a unitary system, or that it has a single and discrete neurobiological locus (see Robbins, Chapter 2). Instead it is likely that executive functions are mediated by distinct and diverse anatomical regions which may be prone to differential insult depending on the nature of the aetiology or the age at which it is sustained. However, impaired executive control is unable to explain all features of repetitive behaviour in autism in an effortless fashion. In particular, it is difficult for this account to explain the characteristic presentation of some forms of repetitive behaviour. For example, an executive dysfunction account would appear unable to explain the way that the interests of autistic individuals typically focus on apparently trivial details of the subject matter and are pursued in such a highly circumscribed fashion. Moreover, it is not clear that this account is well suited to explaining insistence on sameness of environment. In contrast, these features of repetitive behaviour appear consistent with many of the predictions of the central coherence account. Whilst I failed to provide support for any direct association between a reduced drive for central coherence and the display of repetitive behaviour, it may be that this hypothesis is relevant, along with many others, in determining at least some of the characteristics or features of repetitive behaviour in autism. None of the hypotheses reviewed are mutually exclusive, and it is possible that a behaviour which may develop as a result of executive dysfunction is also shaped or maintained by other processes and factors.

Finally, there are other features of repetitive behaviour that none of the accounts reviewed here are well able to explain. For example, these accounts are ill-equipped to explain why some forms of repetitive behaviour are so consistent across different individuals and even different cultures. Moreover, anecdotal reports of markedly repetitive behaviour from the earliest months of life are difficult to square with the cognitive accounts of repetitive behaviour offered here. At such a young age the cognitive systems suggested to underlie these behaviours would not be expected to be fully functional in normal infants.

Could the display of repetitive behaviour explain the presence of executive deficits?

It must be stressed that although the results from my study are consistent with an executive account of repetitive behaviour outlined above, the correlational nature of these findings limits the support they can give to this account. Whilst this research has demonstrated a link between the display of repetitive behaviour and deficits on tasks of generativity and behavioural inhibition in individuals with autism, it can say nothing about the nature of this relationship. These results are equally consistent with two further possibilities, each of which must be adequately addressed.

First, it is possible that causality may run in the opposite direction such that executive function deficits are the consequence of the display of repetitive behaviour. Specifically, it may be that repetitive behaviours develop in autism as the direct result of some, as yet, unspecified pathology. The effect of these behaviours may be to reduce the normal range of varied experience to such an extent that the individual is unable to develop normal volitional skill in the usual manner. Whilst this account is equally consistent with the correlational evidence described in this chapter, it does generate predictions which may enable it to be distinguished empirically from the opposite executive hypothesis. If executive difficulties arise as the direct consequence of the individual engaging in high rates of repetitive activities, it would be predicted that environmental manipulations intended to ameliorate the effects of executive difficulties would have no impact on the display of repetitive behaviour. Thus, further experiments designed to compare the rates of repetitive behaviour in environmental situations, with and without cues to structure the environment and direct the individual's behaviour, offer the potential to discriminate between these hypotheses. If cueing was found to elicit lower rates of repetitive behaviour this would lend support to the original hypothesis that repetitive behaviour results from fundamental executive impairments. Failure to find any difference between the presence and absence of cues would be consistent with the hypothesis that repetitive behaviour is the direct result of pathology which induces repetition in behaviour. Whilst this type of rigorous testing has not been undertaken, the results of studies described earlier provide some evidence to suggest that the display of repetitive behaviour is lessened in environments where clues and cues are provided which serve to minimize the planning and attentional demands of many tasks (Bartak and Rutter 1973; Olley 1987; Schopler et al. 1971), and that this behaviour is observed at unusually high levels when the individual is alone with few cues to guide them (Charlop et al. 1983; Runco et al. 1986).

A second possibility is that the apparent link between repetitive behaviour and performance on tasks of behavioural inhibition and generativity is mediated by some third factor. This may be found either at the level of psychological functioning, or at the level of brain function or neurochemistry. In the case of a neurobiological third factor it is possible that the same neural systems and/or neurochemical pathways may mediate both executive task performance and the display of repetitive behaviour in the absence of any functional links between these behavioural domains. Other alternatives are also plausible, including the possibility that anatomically adjacent brain areas may be involved in both domains, or that separate systems mediating both domains are equally sensitive to the timing or nature of some neurobiological insult which is the primary aetiology in autism. The results of studies which compare the level of repetitive behaviour displayed by individuals with autism with and without intervention designed to minimize the executive demands of the environment, may also allow this hypothesis to be empirically disentangled from the original position. If task performance and the display of repetitive behaviour are functionally unrelated we predict there would be no effect of such environmental manipulation on the display of repetitive behaviour. However, the hypothesis that these behaviours are the direct result of executive deficits would predict a highly specific pattern of association.

Whilst each of these accounts may be consistent with a general pattern of association between repetitive behaviour and task performance, the highly specific pattern of association between task performance and the display of repetitive behaviour, and the results of those studies which have compared the display of behaviour in different environmental situations, suggest that the original hypothesis is the strongest contender at the present time. However, more research is needed to explore this issue further and to cement the specific pattern of association between these domains of functioning from different research avenues.

Explaining repetitive behaviour in autism and other clinical conditions

Further research must also address the similarities and differences between the display of repetitive behaviour in autism and other clinical groups. It is noteworthy that the deficits described in this chapter for people with autism have also been reported in many of the other clinical populations also associated with the display of repetitive behaviour. Thus, one or more of the executive deficits reported in this chapter for individuals with autism have been described for others with acquired lesions to the frontal lobes, Parkinson's disease, schizophrenia, dementia of the frontal type, Tourette's syndrome, and obsessive–compulsive disorder (see Turner 1995 for a review). Since repetitive behaviour has received little systematic study in these populations it is difficult to accurately describe just how repetitive behaviour in autism compares with that in these other conditions, but I think few would disagree that there are both quantitative and qualitative differences between repetitive behaviour in autism and other clinical conditions. In autism relative to other clinical conditions, repetition and sameness of behaviour appears more frequent, more intense, and more pervasive in its influence on all areas of functioning. Thus, a major challenge to further work in this field must be to explore why, if the same executive dysfunction is found in non-autistic individuals, these individuals do not display the broad spectrum of extreme and pervasive repetitive behaviour that is observed in autism.

At this stage there seem to be two possible explanations. The first is that autistic and non-autistic individuals may show different executive deficits, or may fail tasks for different reasons. Pennington and Ozonoff (1996) provide evidence to suggest that the pattern of deficits may be different in autism and other developmental psychopathologies, yet a similar analysis has not been conducted to compare executive deficits in autism with some of the other (admittedly adult) clinical populations these individuals most closely resemble. The fact that different populations may fail the same task for different reasons has been emphasized by the earlier cited study of Owen et al. (1993). A similar approach to breaking down tasks and exploring different clinical groups may be useful for other tasks such as generativity tasks, where, as it has been argued earlier, poor performance may be the consequence of distinct deficits.

The second possibility may lie in the fact that autism, unlike the other clinical conditions mentioned above, is a developmental disorder and it is this fact which leads to the characteristically extreme and pervasive display of repetitive behaviour observed in autism. If individuals with autism never develop executive function abilities it is perhaps not surprising that the repetitive behaviour shown by this group is so marked and pervasive. A similar analysis has been provided by Frith and Frith (1991) for an explanation of differences in social cognition ability in autism and schizophrenia, but such a proposal suffers from being difficult to evaluate experimentally. However, the fact that executive deficits and repetitive behaviour are present in a range of clinical conditions suggests that future research may usefully focus on trying to explain repetitive behaviour in non-autistic as well as autistic individuals. Thus, it may be fruitful to group and study individuals who display similar repetition of behaviour both where these individuals carry a diagnostic label of autism and also where a different diagnosis has been made. This 'symptom' as opposed to 'syndrome' approach has recently been advocated within the schizophrenia literature (e.g. Buchanan and Carpenter 1994; Costello 1992). By extending this approach to compare the psychological basis of repetitive behaviour in clinically diverse conditions we have the potential to undertake the most rigorous test of the executive dysfunction hypothesis of repetitive behaviour. This approach would provide a valuable opportunity to study the links between symptom and psychological substrate at all levels and shades of repetition in thought and action.

Notes

1. These same subjects were used in each of the studies conducted by myself to be described in this chapter.
2. These scores were weighted to reflect the prevalence of the behaviour and the frequency, or in the case of insistence on sameness behaviour, the severity, of this behaviour.

Acknowledgements

I would like to thank Jim Russell and Trevor Robbins for discussion and comments on this work and Chas Fernyhough, Rebecca Saltmarsh, and Liz Sykes for their comments on the draft of this manuscript. The empirical work described in this chapter was undertaken whilst the author was in receipt of a Wellcome Trust Prize Studentship and a Cambridge Overseas Research Student Award.

REFERENCES

Azrin, N. H., Kaplan, S. J., and Foxx, R. M. (1973). Autism reversal: eliminating stereotyped self-stimulation of retarded individuals. *American Journal of Mental Deficiency*, **78**, 241–8.

Bailey, A., Phillips, W., and Rutter, M. (1996). Autism: towards an integration of clinical, genetic, neuropsychological, and neurobiological perspectives. *Journal of Child Psychology and Psychiatry*, **37**, 89–126.

Baron-Cohen, S. (1989). Do autistic children have obsessions and compulsions? *British Journal of Clinical Psychology*, **28**, 193–200.

Baron-Cohen, S. (1992). Out of sight or out of mind? Another look at deception in autism. *Journal of Child Psychology and Psychiatry*, **7**, 1141–55.

Baron-Cohen, S. (1995). *Mindblindness: an essay on autism and theory of mind*. MIT Press, Cambridge, MA.

Baron-Cohen, S., Leslie, A. M., and Frith, U. (1985). Does the autistic child have a 'theory of mind'? *Cognition*, **21**, 37–46.

Bartak, L. and Rutter, M. (1973). Special educational treatment of autistic children: a comparative study. I: Design of study and characteristics of units. *Journal of Child Psychology and Psychiatry*, **14**, 161–79.

Bartak, L. and Rutter, M. (1976). Differences between mentally retarded and normally intelligent autistic children. *Journal of Autism and Childhood Schizophrenia*, **6**, 109–20.

Black, M., Freeman, B. J., and Montgomery, J. (1975). Systematic observation of play behavior in autistic children. *Journal of Autism and Childhood Schizophrenia*, **5**, 363–71.

Boucher, J. (1977). Alteration and sequencing behaviour, and response to novelty in autistic children. *Journal of Child Psychology and Psychiatry*, **18**, 67–72.

Boucher, J. (1988). Word fluency in high-functioning autistic children. *Journal of Autism and Developmental Disorders*, **18**, 637–45.

Bowler, D. M. (1992). 'Theory of mind' in Asperger's syndrome. *Journal of Child Psychology and Psychiatry*, **33**, 877–93.

Buchanan, R. W. and Carpenter, W. T. (1994). Domains of psychopathology: an approach to the reduction of heterogeneity in schizophrenia. *Journal of Nervous and Mental Disease*, **182**, 193–204.

Carruthers, P. (1996). Autism as mind-blindness: an elaboration and partial defence. In *Theories of theories of mind* (ed. P. Carruthers and P. K. Smith), pp. 257–73. Cambridge University Press.

Charlop, M. H. (1986). Setting effects on the occurrence of autistic children's immediate echolalia. *Journal of Autism and Developmental Disorders*, **16**, 473–83.

Charlop, M. H., Schreibman, L., Mason, J., and Vesey, W. (1983). Behavior-setting interactions of autistic children: a behavioral mapping approach to assessing classroom behaviours. *Analysis and Intervention in Developmental Disabilities*, **3**, 359–71.

Clark, P. and Rutter, M. (1981). Autistic children's response to structure and to interpersonal demands. *Journal of Autism and Developmental Disorders*, 11, 201–17.

Colman, R. S., Frankel, F., Ritvo, E., and Freeman, B. J. (1976). The effects of fluorescent and incandescent illumination upon repetitive behaviors in autistic children. *Journal of Autism and Childhood Schizophrenia*, 6, 157–62.

Costello, C. G. (1992). Research on symptoms versus research on syndromes: arguments in favour of allocating more research time to the study of symptoms. *British Journal of Psychiatry*, 160, 304–8.

Dadds, M., Schwartz, S., Adams, T., and Rose, S. (1988). The effects of social context and verbal skill on the stereotypic and task-involved behaviour of autistic children. *Journal of Child Psychology and Psychiatry*, 29, 669–76.

Dawson, G. and Fernald, M. (1987). Perspective taking ability and its relationship to the social behavior of autistic children. *Journal of Autism and Developmental Disorders*, 17, 487–98.

de Lissovoy, V. (1962). Head banging in early childhood. *Child Development*, 33, 43–56.

Donnellan, A. M., Anderson, J. L., and Mesaros, R. A. (1984). An observation of stereotypic behavior and proximity related to the occurrence of autistic child–family member interactions. *Journal of Autism and Developmental Disorders*, 14, 205–10.

Downes, J. J., Roberts, A. C., Sahakian, B. J., Evenden, J. L., Morris, R. G., and Robbins, T. W. (1989). Impaired extra-dimensional shift performance in medicated and unmedicated Parkinson's disease: evidence for a specific attentional dysfunction. *Neuropsychologia*, 27, 1329–43.

Dykens, E., Volkmar, F., and Glick, M. (1991). Thought disorder in high-functioning autistic adults. *Journal of Autism and Developmental Disorders*, 21, 291–301.

Eason, L. J., White, M. J., and Newsom, C. (1982). Generalized reduction of self-stimulatory behavior: an effect of teaching appropriate toy play to autistic children. *Analysis and Intervention in Developmental Disabilities*, 2, 157–69.

Epstein, L. J., Taubman, M. T., and Lovaas, O. I. (1985). Changes in self-stimulatory behaviors with treatment. *Journal of Abnormal Child Psychology*, 13, 281–94.

Eslinger, P. J. and Grattan, L. M. (1993). Frontal lobe and fronto-striatal substrates for different forms of human cognitive flexibility. *Neuropsychologia*, 31, 17–28.

Fein, D. A., Wainwright, L., Morris, R., Waterhouse, L., Allen, D. A., Aram, D. M., et al. (1991). Symbolic play development in autistic and language-disordered children (abstract). *Journal of Clinical and Experimental Neuropsychology*, 13, 53.

Francis, S. (1966). An ethological study of mentally retarded individuals and normal infants. Unpublished PhD thesis, University of Cambridge.

Frith, C. D. and Done, D. J. (1983). Stereotyped responding by schizophrenic patients on a two-choice guessing task. *Psychological Medicine*, 13, 779–86.

Frith, C. D. and Done, D. J. (1990). Stereotyped behaviour in madness and in health. In *Neurobiology of stereotyped behaviour* (ed. S. J. Cooper and C. T. Dourish), pp. 232–59. Clarendon Press, Oxford.

Frith, C. D. and Frith, U. (1991) Elective affinities in schizophrenia and childhood autism. In *Social psychiatry: theory, methodology and practice* (ed. P. Bebbington). Transaction Press, New Brunswick, NJ.

Frith, U. (1970). Studies in pattern detection in normal and autistic children: II. Reproduction and production of color sequences. *Journal of Experimental Child Psychology*, **10**, 120–35.

Frith, U. (1972). Cognitive mechanisms in autism: experiments with color and tone sequence production. *Journal of Autism and Childhood Schizophrenia*, **2**, 160–73.

Frith, U. (1989). *Autism: explaining the enigma*. Blackwell, Oxford.

Frith, U. and Happé, F. (1994). Autism: beyond 'theory of mind'. *Cognition*, **50**, 115–32.

Frith, U. Happé, F., and Siddons, F. (1994). Autism and theory of mind in everyday life. *Social Development*, **3**, 108–24.

Goldberg, E. (1986). Varieties of perseveration: a comparison of two taxonomies. *Journal of Clinical and Experimental Neuropsychology*, **8**, 710–26.

Goodall, E. and Corbett, J. (1982). Relationship between sensory stimulation and stereotyped behavior in severely mentally retarded and autistic children. *Journal of Mental Deficiency Research*, **26**, 163–75.

Happé, F. G. E. (1991). Theory of mind and communication in autism. Unpublished PhD thesis, University of London.

Harris, S. L. and Wolchik, S. A. (1979). Suppression of self-stimulation: three alternative strategies. *Journal of Applied Behavior Analysis*, **12**, 185–98.

Hermelin, B. and O'Connor, N. (1963). The response and self-generated behaviour of severely disturbed children and severely subnormal controls. *British Journal of Social and Clinical Psychology*, **2**, 37–43.

Hughes, C., Russell, J., and Robbins, T. W. (1994). Evidence for executive dysfunction in autism. *Neuropsychologia*, **32**, 477–92.

Hutt, C. and Hutt, S. J. (1965). Effects of environmental complexity on stereotyped behaviours of children. *Animal Behaviour*, **13**, 1–4.

Hutt, C. and Hutt, S. J. (1970). Stereotypies and their relation to arousal: a study of autistic children. In *Behaviour studies in psychiatry* (ed. C. Hutt and S. J. Hutt), pp. 175–204. Pergamon Press, Oxford.

Hutt, C., Hutt, S. J., Lee, D., and Ounsted, C. (1964). Arousal and childhood autism. *Nature*, **204**, 908–9.

Jarrold, C., Boucher, J., and Smith, P. (1993). Symbolic play in autism: a review. *Journal of Autism and Developmental Disorders*, **23**, 281–307.

Jones, G.W. (1985). Gesture fluency after focal cortical lesions. *Neurophsychologia*, **23**, 463–8.

Jones-Gotman, M. and Milner, B. (1977). Design fluency: the invention of nonsense drawings after focal cortical lesions. *Neuropsychologia*, **15**, 653–74.

Kanner, L. (1943). Autistic disturbances of affective contact. *Nervous Child*, **2**, 217–50.

Kapur, N. (1985). Double dissociation between perseveration in memory and problem solving tasks. *Cortex*, **21**, 461–5.

Kaufman, M. E. and Levitt, H. (1965). A study of three stereotyped behaviors in institutionalized mental defectives. *American Journal of Mental Deficiency*, **69**, 467–73.

Kravitz, H. and Boehm, J. J. (1971). Rhythmic habit patterns in infancy: their sequence, age of onset and frequency. *Child Development*, **42**, 399–413.

Leslie, A. M. and Frith, U. (1988). Autistic children's understanding of seeing, knowing and believing. *British Journal of Developmental Psychology*, **6**, 315–24.

Lewis, M. H., Maclean, W. E., Johnson, W. L., and Baumeister, A. A. (1981). Ultradian rhythms in stereotyped and self-injurious behavior. *American Journal of Mental Deficiency*, **85**, 601–10.

Lewis, V. and Boucher, J. (1991). Skill, content and generative strategies in autistic children's drawings. *British Journal of Developmental Psychology*, **9**, 393–416.

Lindsay, S. J. E., Salkovskis, P. M., and Stoll, K. (1982). Rhythmical body movement in sleep: a brief review and treatment study. *Behavior, Research and Therapy*, **20**, 523–6.

Lovaas, O. I., Schreibman, L., and Koegel, R. L. (1974). A behavior modification approach to the treatment of autistic children. *Journal of Autism and Childhood Schizophrenia*, **4**, 111–29.

Luria, A. R. (1965). Two kinds of motor perseveration in massive injury of the frontal lobes. *Brain*, **88**, 1–10.

Mackintosh, N. J. (1983). *Conditioning and associative learning*. Clarendon Press, Oxford.

Mason, G. J. (1991). Stereotypies: a critical review. *Animal Behaviour*, **41**, 1015–37.

Mason, G. J. and Turner, M. A. (1993). Mechanisms involved in the development and control of stereotypies. In *Perspectives in ethology*, Vol. 10 (ed. P. P. G. Bateson, P. H. Klopfer, and N. S. Thompson), pp. 53–85. Plenum Press, NY.

Milner, B. (1963). Effects of different brain lesions on card sorting. *Archives of Neurology*, **9**, 90–100.

Minshew, N. J., Goldstein, G., Muenz, L. R., and Payton, J. B. (1992). Neuropsychological functioning in non-mentally retarded autistic individuals. *Journal of Clinical and Experimental Neuropsychology*, **14**, 749–61.

Minshew, N. J., Goldstein, G., and Siegel, D. J. (1995). Speech and language in high-functioning autistic individuals. *Neuropsychology*, **9**, 255–61.

Mitchell, R. and Etches, P. (1977). Rhythmic habit patterns (stereotypies). *Developmental Medicine and Child Neurology*, **19**, 545–50.

Norman, D. A. and Shallice, T. (1980). Attention to action: willed and automatic control of behaviour. Center for Human Information Processing, Technical Report No. 99. University of California, San Diego.

Olley, J. G. (1987). Classroom structure and autism. In *Handbook of autism and developmental disabilities* (ed. D. J. Cohen and A. M. Donnellan), pp. 411–17. Wiley, NY.

Owen, A. M., Roberts, A. C., Polkey, C. E., Sahakian, B. J., and Robbins, T. W. (1991). Extra-dimensional versus intra-dimensional set shifting performance following frontal lobe excisions, temporal lobe excisions or amygdalo-hippocampectomy in man. *Neuropsychologia*, **29**, 993–1006.

Owen, A. M., Roberts, A. C., Hodges, J. R., Summers, B. A., Polkey, C. E., and Robbins, T. W. (1993). Contrasting mechanisms of impaired attentional set-shifting in patients with frontal lobe damage or Parkinson's disease. *Brain*, **116**, 1159–75.

Ozonoff, S., Pennington, B. F., and Rogers, S. J. (1991). Executive function deficits in high-functioning autistic individuals: relationship to theory of mind. *Journal of Child Psychology and Psychiatry*, **32**, 1081–1105.

Pennington, B. F. and Ozonoff, S. (1996). Executive functioning and developmental psychopathology. *Journal of Child Psychology and Psychiatry*, **37**, 51–87.

Perner, J., Frith, U., Leslie, A. M., and Leekam, S. R. (1989). Exploration of the autistic child's theory of mind: knowledge, belief, and communication. *Child Development*, **60**, 689–700.

Prior, M. and Hoffman, W. (1990). Neuropsychological testing of autistic children through an exploration with frontal lobe tests. *Journal of Autism and Developmental Disorders*, **20**, 581–90.

Prior, M., Dahlstrom, D., and Squires, T. L. (1990). Autistic children's knowledge of thinking and feeling states in other people. *Journal of Child Psychology and Psychiatry*, **31**, 587–601.

Rago, W. V. and Case, J. C. (1978). Stereotyped behavior in special education teachers. *Exceptional Children*, **44**, 342–4.

Ridley, R. M. (1994). The psychology of perseverative and stereotyped behaviour. *Progress in Neurobiology*, **44**, 221–31.

Rumsey, J. M. (1985). Conceptual problem-solving in highly verbal non-retarded autistic men. *Journal of Autism and Developmental Disorders*, **15**, 23–36.

Rumsey, J. M. and Hamburger, S. D. (1988). Neuropsychological findings in high-functioning men with infantile autism, residual state. *Journal of Clinical and Experimental Neuropsychology*, **10**, 201–21.

Rumsey, J. M., Rapoport, J. L., and Sceery, W. R. (1985). Autistic children as adults: psychiatric, social, and behavioural outcomes. *Journal of the American Academy of Child Psychiatry*, **24**, 465–73.

Runco, M. A., Charlop, A. H., and Schreibman, L. (1986). The occurrence of autistic children's self-stimulation as a function of familiar versus unfamiliar stimulus conditions. *Journal of Autism and Developmental Disorders*, **16**, 31–44.

Russell, J. (1996). *Agency: its role in mental development*. Erlbaum (UK), Taylor and Francis, Hove.

Sallustro, F. and Atwell, C. W. (1978). Body rocking, head banging, and head rolling in normal children. *Journal of Pediatrics*, **93**, 704–8.

Sandson, J. and Albert, M. L. (1984). Varieties of perseveration. *Neuropsychologia*, **22**, 715–32.

Schneider, S. G. and Asarnow, R. F. (1987). A comparison of cognitive/neuropsychological impairments of nonretarded autistic and schizophrenic children. *Journal of Abnormal Child Psychology*, **15**, 29–46.

Schopler, E. (1965). Early infantile autism and receptor processes. *Archives of General Psychiatry*, **13**, 327–35.

Schopler, E., Brehm, S., Kinsbourne, M., and Reichler, R. J. (1971). Effect of treatment structure on development in autism. *Archives of General Psychiatry*, **24**, 415–21.

Scott, F., Baron-Cohen, S., and Leslie, A. (1995). If pigs could fly! An investigation of counterfactual reasoning and imagination in autism. Paper presented at the *1995 Society for Research in Child Development conference*, Indianapolis.

Sorosky, A., Ornitz, E., Brown, M., and Ritvo, E. (1968). Systematic observations of autistic behavior. *Archives of General Psychiatry*, **18**, 439–49.

Soussignon, R., Koch, P., and Montagner, H. (1988). Behavioural and cardiovascular changes in children moving from kindergarten to primary school. *Journal of Child Psychology and Psychiatry*, **29**, 321–33.

Sparrevohn, R. and Howie, P. M. (1995). Theory of mind in children with autistic disorder: evidence of developmental progression and the role of verbal ability. *Journal of Child Psychology and Psychiatry*, **36**, 249–63.

Szatmari, P., Bartolucci, G., and Bremner, R. (1989). Asperger's syndrome and autism: comparison of early history and outcome. *Developmental Medicine and Child Neurology*, **31**, 709–20.

Szatmari, P., Tuff, L., Finlayson, M. A. J., and Bartolucci, G. (1990). Asperger's syndrome and autism: neurocognitive aspects. *Journal of the American Academy of Child and Adolescent Psychiatry*, **29**, 130–6.

Tager-Flusberg, H. and Sullivan, K. (1994). Predicting and explaining behaviour: a comparison of autistic, mentally retarded and normal children. *Journal of Child Psychology and Psychiatry*, **35**, 1059–75.

Tantam, D. (1991). Asperger syndrome in adulthood. In *Autism and Asperger syndrome* (ed. U. Frith), pp. 147–83. Cambridge University Press.

Thelen, E. (1979). Rhythmical stereotypies in normal human infants. *Animal Behaviour*, **27**, 699–715.

Thelen, E. (1981). Kicking, rocking and waving: contextual analysis of rhythmical stereotypies in normal human infants. *Animal Behaviour*, **29**, 3–11.

Tierney, I. R., McGuire, R. J., and Walton, H. J. (1978). Distributions of body rocking manifested by severely mentally deficient adults in ward environments. *Journal of Mental Deficiency Research*, **22**, 243–54.

Turner, M. A. (1995). Repetitive behaviour and cognitive functioning in autism. Unpublished PhD thesis, University of Cambridge.

Turner, M. A. (1997a). Repetitive behaviour in autism. (Submitted)

Turner, M. A. (1997b). Fluency performance in high-functioning and learning disabled individuals with autism. (Submitted)

Volkmar, F. R., Hoder, E. L., and Cohen, D. J. (1985). Compliance, 'negativism', and the effect of treatment structure in autism: a naturalistic behavioral study. *Journal of Child Psychology and Psychiatry*, **26**, 865–77.

Wallach, M. A. and Kogan, N. (1965). *Modes of thinking in young children*. Holt, Rinehart and Wilson, NY.

Wells, K. C., Forehand, R., and Hickey, K. (1977). Effects of a verbal warning and overcorrection on stereotyped and appropriate behaviors. *Journal of Abnormal Child Psychology*, **5**, 387–403.

Werry, J. S., Carlielle, J., and Fitzpatrick, J. (1983). Rhythmic motor activities (stereotypies) in children under five: etiology and prevalence. *Journal of the American Academy of Child Psychiatry*, **22**, 329–36.

Wing, L. and Gould, J. (1979). Severe impairments of social interaction and associated abnormalities in children: epidemiology and classification. *Journal of Autism and Developmental Disorders*, **9**, 11–29.

Zentall, S. S. and Zentall, T. R. (1983). Optimal stimulation: a model of disordered activity and performance in normal and deviant children. *Psychological Bulletin*, **94**, 446–71.

4 Pretend play in autism: executive explanations

Christopher Jarrold

Introduction—the relevance of pretend play to psychological theories of autism

There is little doubt that children with autism have substantial problems in producing pretend play. The United Kingdom's National Autistic Society cites a 'lack of creative pretend play' as one of the manifestations of the disorder; diagnostic criteria in DSM-III-R (APA 1987) include 'absence of imaginative activity'; and recent epidemiological research indicates that an absence of pretend play at 18 months of age is predictive of a subsequent diagnosis of autism (Baron-Cohen et al. 1992).

This pattern is confirmed by empirical studies of levels of pretence exhibited by children with autism (see Jarrold et al. 1993 for a review). The majority of children with autism appear not to produce flexible and creative pretence (Atlas 1990; Doherty and Rosenfeld 1984; Hadwin et al. 1996; Wing 1978; Wing et al. 1977). Comparative studies which have contrasted the play of children with autism against that of mentally handicapped and normal controls, matched for mental age, have revealed a deficit in terms of the number of pretend acts produced (Jarrold et al. 1996; Libby et al. 1995; Sigman and Ungerer 1984), the quality of pretend play produced (Riguet et al. 1981), and the proportion of children producing pretence (Baron-Cohen 1987). Although Lewis and Boucher (1988) found no difference in the amount of time spent in pretend play between a group of children with autism and verbal-mental-age matched handicapped and normal controls, this may have been the result of near-floor levels of pretence among these controls. Indeed, a recent replication has confirmed that children with autism do spend less of their time in pretend play than children with moderate learning difficulties matched for verbal mental age (Jarrold et al. 1996).

There can be little doubt then, that children with autism are impaired in their production of pretend play. However, the cause of this impairment is not clear. Until recently it was generally accepted that a failure to produce pretence was due to an impaired ability to engage in 'metarepresentational' thought. Metarepresentation is defined as representing how oneself or another represents the world as being (Pylyshyn 1978). Theory of mind tasks, in which a child typically has to make inferences about another's beliefs, are seen by most to require metarepresentation (Leslie 1987, 1988; Leslie and Roth 1993; Perner 1991), and the fact that individuals with autism perform extremely poorly on such tasks (e.g. Baron-Cohen 1991; Baron-Cohen *et al.* 1985; Leslie and Frith 1988; Perner *et al.* 1989) has led to the suggestion that a failure to metarepresent is central to autism (Baron-Cohen 1995; Leslie and Frith 1990; Leslie and Roth 1993). In fact, both Baron-Cohen and Leslie argue that an intact theory of mind rests on the operation of a modular system dedicated to the construction and manipulation of metarepresentations (a 'Theory of Mind Module'; ToMM[1]), which is impaired in autism. An important point which should be made here is that although Baron-Cohen and Leslie would not want to argue that the ToMM is 'monolithic' (Leslie and Roth 1993), and would instead claim that it might break down into subsystems, or develop from more primitive modules (Baron-Cohen 1995; Baron-Cohen and Ring 1994), the fact that the system *is* 'modular' does imply an 'all or none' quality. By this account someone can either metarepresent or they cannot, and the argument is that children with autism cannot.

The relevance of these issues to our understanding of pretend play in autism was highlighted in Leslie's (1987) seminal paper in which he claimed that pretend play is metarepresentational in nature. According to Leslie, when a child makes sense of another's (or indeed their own) pretend actions, they do this by representing the other 'as pretending'. More specifically, they represent how the pretender represents the relation between the play prop (e.g. a banana) and the imagined object (e.g. a telephone) (Leslie and Roth 1993; see Jarrold *et al.* 1994b). This is metarepresentation because it involves 'representing how oneself or another represents the world as being' (see above). Under this account a failure to pretend in autism is easily explained—children with autism are impaired in constructing and/or manipulating metarepresentations—pretend play requires exactly this ability—hence children with autism have severe problems with pretence.

If this were the whole story, then there might be little to be learned from an in–depth study of pretend play skills in autism. However, there are a number of reasons for questioning this metarepresentational account and these will be outlined in the next section. The following section will then discuss whether an alternative explanation of pretend play deficits in terms of 'executive dysfunction' in autism is instead more plausible. I will then describe recent work which has attempted to test directly an executive account of pretend play deficits, and will provide evidence of a failure to generate pretend acts in autism. Later, the argument is posed that a problem of 'generativity' can potentially explain the range of problems seen in the pretend play of children with autism, and is consistent with deficits of spontaneity and flexibility in other domains as well. This first half of the chapter will perhaps be most relevant to those with an interest in pretence in autism. The final section of this chapter is, however, more general in so far as it outlines ways in which a generativity deficit might be located within the theoretical framework of 'executive deficits'.

Problems with the metarepresentational-deficit account

There appear to be three main problems concerning a metarepresentational-deficit explanation of children with autism's problems of pretence. The first raises a theoretical concern which centres on the very claim that pretend play is metarepresentational in nature. A number of authors have argued that Leslie overestimates the cognitive demands of pretend play (Harris 1991, 1993, 1994; Jarrold et al. 1994b; Lillard 1993; Perner 1991). In essence the counterclaim is that young children do not need to represent their own or another's pretend attitude to the world (metarepresentation), at least not for forms of pretend play observed before four years of age (Lillard 1993). Instead it has been suggested that younger children can carry out pretence by treating the pretend episode 'as-if' it were true, rather than by representing the relation between the true and imaginary state of affairs (Perner 1991). Similarly, understanding pretend play in others may involve no more than making a counterfactual reading of a situation which makes no sense if interpreted literally (Harris 1994). Space prevents a detailed discussion of these theoretical issues (see Jarrold et al. 1994b), and indeed, while this line of argument conflicts with Leslie's, it does not, on its own, amount to strong evidence against his views. In fact, there would be a degree of circularity in invoking these theoretical points as a reason for rejecting the metarepresentational account—one is forced to argue that pretend play is not metarepresentational if one accepts the empirical evidence against Leslie's position (outlined below), and yet still wishes to claim that children with autism are metarepresentationally impaired, given their problems with theory of mind tasks. Theoretical concerns about the status of pretence, although important, will therefore be set aside, and empirical data that appear to contradict the predictions of the metarepresentational-deficit account will be considered instead.

Children with autism can pretend

The essence of the metarepresentational hypothesis is that children with autism simply cannot engage in pretence. Any evidence of pretence in autism is therefore at odds with the theory. Somewhat surprisingly then, some pretend play is seen in some children with autism in most of the studies described above; while the others do not give sufficient detail to determine maximum levels of performance. Of 10 children with autism, two exhibited pretence in Baron-Cohen's (1987) study (compared to 17 of 20 mental-age matched controls). While none of the 10 children with autism assessed by Hadwin *et al.* (1996) showed spontaneous pretence during an initial assessment, all showed some evidence of pretence during a teaching session in which pretend play was encouraged and prompted, with five producing pretence spontaneously under these conditions. Similarly, if one excludes from Wing's (1978) sample any children who would not normally be expected to show pretend play given their developmental level (see Jarrold *et al.* 1993), there remain only 3 of 31 'psychotic' children with autistic symptoms who show no symbolic play at all. Sigman and Ungerer (1984) divided their play session into 10-second intervals, and found that, on average, their group of children with autism showed pretence in 1.3 of these intervals (compared to 4.8 for controls), and Jarrold *et al.* (1996) found that their sample of children with autism spent on average around 7% of their free play time engaged in pretence[2] (compared to 19% for controls).

In itself, this clearly falls short of being evidence for intact, pretend play skills in autism, because the levels of pretend play seen are certainly very low. However, this is unsurprising as the studies mentioned generally assessed children with relatively low mental ages, under conditions that did not prompt a great deal of pretence in controls. The important point is that a metarepresentational account would appear to predict a *total absence* of pretence in autism.

Having said this, there are two criticisms which could certainly be advanced by a proponent of the metarepresentational view. First, it might be argued that the pretend play seen in these cases does not amount to genuinely metarepresentational pretence, but is rather a learnt behaviour which only *appears* metarepresentational. The behaviour of children with autism is characteristically stereotyped and repetitive, and an experimenter might easily mistake an action for creative and novel pretence which is instead a direct copy of something the child has seen before, or has done many times themselves. Support for this suggestion comes from Wing's (1978) study. Of the 31 children described above as capable of pretending, 27 were classed as showing 'stereotyped' pretence only. A second possible criticism is that it may be oversimplistic to view a metarepresentational account as predicting an inability to pretend in all children with autism. Instead it would only predict an absence of pretence in those children with a metarepresentational deficit. While most children with autism have severe problems on theory of mind tasks, there is always a small percentage of any sample who pass these tasks (around 20%; U. Frith *et al.* 1991). Autism may therefore reflect severely delayed acquisition of metarepresentational ability, rather than a total failure to acquire metarepresentational understanding (Baron-Cohen 1991; Holroyd and Baron-Cohen 1993; see Happé 1995), and it may be that the children who show some evidence of pretence are those who have acquired metarepresentational competence, albeit at a severely delayed stage.[3]

The fact that some children with autism show some ability to pretend may therefore not be so damaging for the metarepresentational account. Much more problematic is growing evidence that children with autism show *unimpaired* pretend play skills in certain circumstances. Riguet *et al.* (1981) and Ungerer and Sigman (1981) both suggested that assessing spontaneous play behaviour might underestimate children with autism's competence for pretence. They found that structuring play sessions, by introducing cueing and modelling of pretend acts did increase levels of pretend play in their samples of children with autism (see also Hadwin *et al.* 1996). However, these groups remained impaired relative to controls (see Sigman and Ungerer 1984). In contrast, Lewis and Boucher (1988) found unimpaired 'elicited' and 'instructed' pretend play in children with autism, in terms of both the quantity and quality of the pretend acts produced in response to these manipulations. Aspects of Lewis and Boucher's methodology have been criticized (Baron-Cohen 1990; although see Boucher and Lewis 1990; Jarrold *et al.* 1993), but a recent replication and extension of this work has confirmed that children with autism spend significantly less of their spontaneous play time in pretend play than do controls, and produce significantly fewer spontaneous pretend acts, but are unimpaired in their ability to carry out pretend instructions (Jarrold *et al.* 1996).

Further evidence of unimpaired pretend play skills in autism under maximally structured testing conditions comes from findings of unimpaired ability to carry out prompted or instructed object substitution (Charman and Baron-Cohen 1997; Jarrold *et al.* 1994a; Lewis and Boucher 1995), and of intact ability to comprehend pretend acts carried out by an experimenter. Jarrold *et al.* (1994c) showed children with autism a number of pretend episodes in which a glove puppet poured a pretend substance on to another toy animal. These children were unimpaired, relative to language-matched normal and learning disabled controls, in their ability to name these imaginary substances, and in describing the pretend consequences of the episodes. One problem with this experiment though was that the control groups performed surprisingly poorly, and so it may be that their performance was artificially lowered by methodological aspects of the procedure. That said, identical results were found by Kavanaugh and Harris (1994) in a study which did not suffer from these shortcomings.

That children with autism are able to produce normal levels of pretend play, and are able to make sense of pretend acts carried out by another person, clearly presents a challenge to the metarepresentational account in so far as it predicts a global inability to produce and comprehend pretence in children with autism. The only way in which the metarepresentational deficit theory could explain these results would be by suggesting that these experiments do not test 'pretend play proper'—that the experimenter is providing *sufficient* cues for the children to carry out the tasks by means of less sophisticated, non-metarepresentational processes. At present, however, the strength of this argument is difficult to judge (see Jarrold *et al.* 1994c, 1996).

The deficit extends to functional play

Functional play is defined as '. . . the appropriate use of an object or the conventional association of two or more objects such as using a spoon to feed a doll or placing a teacup on a saucer.' (Ungerer and Sigman 1981, p.320). A number of authors have argued that play of this form should not be classed as 'symbolic' or pretend play proper as one cannot be sure whether the child is really using one object to 'symbolize' another, or has instead learnt the appropriate use of a miniature toy (Elkonin 1966; Huttenlocher and Higgins 1978). Leslie (1987) also argues that a distinction should be drawn between functional play and true pretence, but goes further than previous authors in claiming that there is a fundamental and qualitative difference between the two behaviours. He notes that: 'In both functional play and error acting as if, the as-if component really only exists from the observer's point of view. From the actor's point of view, the actions are serious. But in pretence the actor is acting as if from the actor's point of view as well.' (p.414). In terms of his theory, functional play, unlike pretence, can be carried out without recourse to metarepresentations. Baron-Cohen (1987) makes this claim more explicitly: 'Pretend play is also assumed to require second-order representations . . . In contrast, a first-order representational capacity is sufficient for reality or functional play.' (p.146). Clearly, by this analysis, children with autism's problems in pretence should not extend to functional play.

However, there is increasing evidence to the contrary: Sigman and Ungerer (1984) found a deficit in both the 'symbolic' and functional play of their sample of children with autism. They produced fewer functional acts and spent less of their time in functional play than did controls. Similarly, Lewis and Boucher (1988) found that children with autism spent less time in spontaneous functional play than controls. Baron-Cohen (1987) did not, by contrast, find a functional play deficit, but this may be explained in terms of the criteria he adopted for rating play as being functional. These included the simple naming of toys, and it is, at the very least, arguable whether this corresponds to 'appropriate use of an object'; one would certainly expect children with autism to be able to name toys even if they had severe problems in playing with them creatively. For this reason, the fact that 80% of Baron-Cohen's sample of children with autism showed 'functional play', so defined, is not surprising, and does not imply that functional play is intact in autism. Finally, in our recent research we have also found that children with autism spend significantly less of their free play time engaged in functional play than do controls (Jarrold *et al.* 1996). Fig. 4.1 shows the proportion of time spent in pretend, functional, manipulative and 'no play', with two different sets of materials, by children with autism and language-ability-matched controls. Across both toy sets children with autism spent significantly less time in both pretend and functional play.

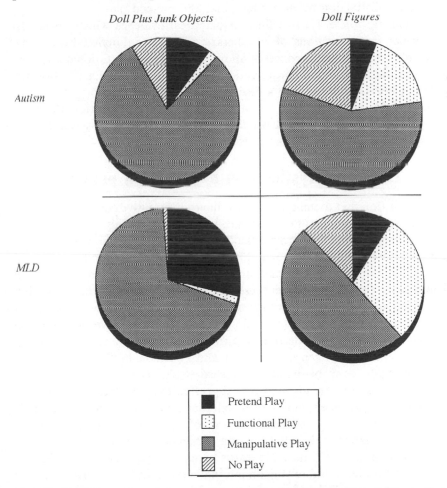

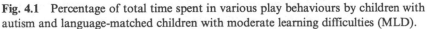

Fig. 4.1 Percentage of total time spent in various play behaviours by children with autism and language-matched children with moderate learning difficulties (MLD).

As indicated, the suggestion that children with autism's deficits in play spread beyond pure pretence is at odds with the metarepresentational account. It might be argued that the purpose of distinguishing pretend and functional play was not to separate behaviour that certainly involved pretending from that which certainly did not. Instead Huttenlocher and Higgins' (1978) suggestions were aimed at separating pretend play from behaviours which *may not* involve true pretending. It is therefore possible that functional play could include a degree of pretend activity, and it might be this aspect of functional play behaviour which is seen less amongst children with autism. While plausible, this line of argument is not consistent with the metarepresentational hypothesis, which, as noted above, proposes a qualitative distinction between functional and pretend play.

To sum up, there are two lines of empirical evidence which appear to contradict the predictions of the metarepresentational-deficit hypothesis. Regardless of theoretical concerns about the metarepresentational status of pretence, these empirical considerations provide sufficient justification for asking whether children with autism's problems in pretend play are better explained by an alternative hypothesis. The following section discusses whether an executive account provides a more satisfactory explanation of the deficits in pretence seen in autism.

Is an executive dysfunction explanation plausible?

The suggestion that pretend play might have an executive component can be traced back to Vygotsky (1966). Prior to Leslie's (1987) analysis, pretend play had typically been viewed as a gradually developing behaviour; Piaget (1962), for example argued for a gradual differentiation between 'signifier' (the real object or action used by the child) and 'signified' (the absent object or action being 'represented'). Subsequent research has shown that this differentiation can take two main forms: 'decentration'—moving from the self as the agent in pretence to using another (e.g. a doll) as an agent (e.g. Lowe 1975; Watson and Fisher 1977) and 'decontextualization'—moving away from using realistic objects in pretence (e.g. Elder and Pederson 1978; Jackowitz and Watson 1980). Even before this empirical work, Vygotsky had indirectly identified these two trends, and had suggested that they reflect the child's growing ability to free meaning from external, situational constraints. In his terms, decentration is the emancipation of meaning from action, while decontextualization is the emancipation of meaning from objects. Vygotsky wrote that '[in play] . . . the child learns to act in a cognitive, rather than an externally visible, realm, relying on internal tendencies and motives, and not on incentives supplied by external things.' He went on to argue that this contrasts with the behaviour of 'Certain brain-damaged patients' whose actions are determined by the external environment. These themes have recently been taken up by Harris (1991, 1993, 1994). He argues that the developmental trends in pretence away from action determined by the external context reflect the child's growing ability to impose internal executive control on their behaviour. Further, he argues that executive deficits prevent children with autism from imposing this control, and hence from producing spontaneous pretend play.

Harris' account is preferable to the metarepresentational hypothesis in a number of ways. First, it takes more account of the normal pattern of pretend play development. As it accepts that pretend play develops gradually, with its roots in play which is tied to the external situation, it does not make an *a priori* and qualitative distinction between functional play and pretend play. It is therefore, in principle at least, more consistent with evidence of a functional play deficit in autism. Second, it is able to explain the contrast seen between the impoverished production of pretence seen in children with autism, and their unimpaired comprehension of pretence and their ability to produce pretence in structured situations. Harris (1993) notes that his account predicts impaired spontaneous pretence but also that, with external prompting, children with autism should be able to pretend. In these cases he claims that instructions to pretend 'shift the locus of control to the external contextual frame provided by the adult'.

Harris's account is, however, incomplete in some respects. While he provides a clear explanation of why pretence might be executive, or have executive components, he is not specific about what these components are. A number of quotes from his 1993 paper highlight the problem (my italics): 'The basic claim to be developed is that autistic children are deficient in *planning* their actions and responses' (p. 233); 'Autistic children, it will be claimed, have special difficulties in *over-riding* external or habitual control in this autonomous, planful fashion' (p 233); 'An explanation of the autistic child's impoverished pretend-play, therefore, is that the ability to achieve this *shift in the locus of executive control* is distorted or grossly delayed' (p. 234); '. . . the hypothesis implies that autistic children will have difficulty in spontaneously *generating* and *imposing* their own make-believe conceptions on a given context' (p 238). In a way, Harris invokes too many executive deficits for us to be clear about exactly where children with autism's problems in pretence really lie.

One way in which an executive dysfunction hypothesis might be clarified is by focusing on each of these aspects of pretence separately. An assumption inherent in this approach is that executive control can be fractionated into a number of individual functions; the final section of this chapter outlines the theoretical basis for this assumption. Meanwhile, the next section outlines research which my colleagues and I have carried out to see whether children with autism have particular problems in either of two, potentially-distinct aspects of pretending: (1) problems in inhibiting a prepotent, functionally appropriate response to an object rather than using it 'as-if' it were something else, and (2) problems in generating pretend acts.

Evidence for the role of executive deficits

A failure to inhibit

As noted above, Harris' views contain a potential explanation of why a failure to inhibit inappropriate action might hamper the production of pretend play in children with autism. Harris suggests that in normal pretend play, children have to override or inhibit the actions elicited by an object, and instead impose their own make-believe actions upon that object. One prediction that follows from this suggestion is that the process of overriding will become more difficult the more strongly an object elicits a particular action or 'schema'. In other words, children will find it harder to pretend that a pencil is a telescope than to pretend, say, that a similarly shaped piece of wood is a telescope: the pencil has a well-defined function which elicits particular behaviours while the piece of wood elicits no particular action.

The effects of an object's natural uses are, in fact, observed in normal pretend play development; and they reflect the process of decontextualization mentioned previously. Copple *et al.* (1984) showed that 4- and 5-year-olds are sensitive to the function of toy props in object substitution. They engaged children in one of two pretend scripts. In each case the experimenter provided the target for substitution asking the child, for example, to find a 'spoon' from amongst a set of possible props. The functional role that the spoon played differed between scripts; in script 1 the spoon was required for scooping out some ice-cream, in script 2 it was needed for stirring. The authors found that in the majority of cases children selected a prop which was able to fill this functional role. For example, an egg shell was used for a 'scooping spoon' and a stick for a 'stirring spoon'.

A gradual development in the ability to override salient function, or 'functional decontextualization', has been shown in a number of studies. Ungerer *et al.* (1981) found that 18-month-old children preferred to use objects with no clearly defined function, rather than functional objects, in substitutions; a preference which was less marked at 34 months of age. Elder and Pederson (1978) found that 30-month-olds (but not 36-month-olds) were impaired in their ability to use objects appropriately in pretend substitutions when the objects differed from the specified target in both function and perceptual appearance. They note that in these cases the children often used these objects appropriately rather than in pretence, and suggest that the fact that these props each had their own distinct function played a part in making these substitutions more difficult for the youngest children. Finally, Jacowitz and Watson (1980) found that groups of children of mean ages 16 and 23 months progressed sequentially through the following levels of 'substitutability': (1) similar form plus similar function; (2) similar form plus dissimilar function or similar function plus dissimilar form; (3) dissimilar form plus ambiguous (non-functional) function; (4) both dissimilar form and function. Although these studies confound problems of both perceptual and functional differences between target and substitute, the evidence nevertheless suggests that children do have some problems in overriding an object's function in pretence.

It therefore seems plausible that children with autism produce little pretence because, as a result of executive deficits, they are unable to override the action schemas elicited by the function of objects around them. It is the 'banana-ness' of the banana, for example, which prevents them from pretending that it is a telephone. To test this proposal we carried out the following experiment (see Jarrold *et al.* 1994a for full details). A total of 24 children with autism, aged between 4 and 13 years, were matched to control groups of children with moderate learning difficulties and normally developing children on the basis of individual, verbal mental-age scores. Verbal mental ages ranged from around 30 to 94 months, with a mean of around 54 months for each group.

The experiment borrowed its methodology from a study by Golomb (1979). She was able to determine which objects children perceived as being most suitable for a pretend substitution by giving children a range of props, asking them to select the most appropriate one for a substitution, and then after removing that choice, asking the child to choose again. By repeating this procedure all the props could be ranked in order of perceived 'substitutability'. In our study, children were shown five acts: a cardboard figure was shown brushing its teeth with a toothbrush; eating a toy pizza; eating a sweet; putting on a scarf; and carrying a book to school. Each of these acts was modelled using a 'real' prop, although in most cases these were miniature objects, and then the children were asked to choose their own prop in order to carry out each pretend act.

In each case, children were initially presented with five props from which to choose: one of which matched the 'real' target in terms of physical size and colour, but that had its own clear function, for example a pencil for the toothbrush scenario. This prop was termed the counterfunctional (CF) prop. The four other props all had no clear function, and were termed nonfunctional (NF). They matched the 'real' target and the CF prop in their colour, but varied in their size. The first NF prop (NF1) was the same size as the 'real' object and the CF prop, but the other three NF props (NF2, NF3, NF4) became sequentially less similar, with their size varying systematically on one dimension. For example, in the toothbrush scenario, the NF props were all pieces of dowelling with the same diameter as the pencil (the CF), but they varied systematically in length, with NF1 being as long as the pencil and the toothbrush (see Fig. 4.2).

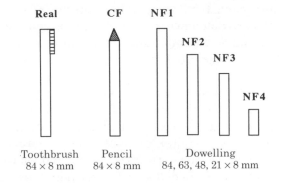

Fig. 4.2 Example object set for 'inhibition experiment'.

After a child had chosen a particular prop, their choice was noted and that prop was then removed from that set. The other scenarios were then presented. The remaining items in the first set of objects were then re-introduced, and children were again asked to pick an appropriate prop and to act out the pretend act. This procedure was repeated, with the child's choices being removed from the remaining props at each turn, until all the props were ranked in order of their suitability for substitution as perceived by the child. We hypothesized that control children would select the CF relatively early on, given its perceptual similarity to the target object, although they might prefer the NF1 prop in the light of the evidence of functional decontextualization described above. We also expected them to pick the NF props in strict order of perceptual similarity to the target—an effect of perceptual decontextualization. On the other hand, we predicted that if children with autism had trouble in overriding an object's salient function in pretence then they would be reluctant to choose the CF prop, and would instead select more NF props in preference.

In fact, the position at which the CF prop was chosen did not differ across the groups. This was true when performance was averaged across all five scenarios ($p = 0.50$), or when considered for each scenario separately ($p = 0.75$). In other words, children with autism, on average, selected the counter-functional prop as early as did the controls; and, in fact, showed no particular reluctance to select the CF prop in any of the five scenarios. The similarity in performance across groups was confirmed when scores for all five types of prop were examined.[4] This analysis allowed us to investigate patterns of 'perceptual' and 'functional' decontextualization in each group. Each prop was given a score from 1 to 5 corresponding to when it was selected, i.e. the prop chosen first received a score of 1, and the prop selected last received a score of 5. All groups showed significantly higher scores for NF2, NF3 and NF4 than for CF and NF1 props, a pattern which indicates perceptual decontextualization, but provides little evidence of functional decontextualization. Decontextualization effects were extremely similar for all the groups. This can be seen in Fig. 4.3 which plots average scores for each prop type for the children with autism and one control group of children with moderate learning difficulties.[5]

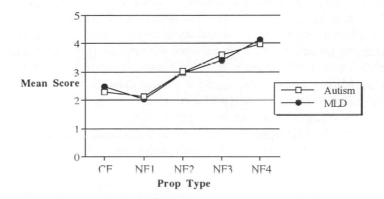

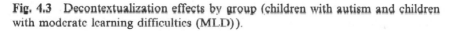

Fig. 4.3 Decontextualization effects by group (children with autism and children with moderate learning difficulties (MLD)).

These results clearly indicate that children with autism are unimpaired, relative to a variety of control groups, on all aspects of this particular task. They show no special reluctance to select the counterfunctional object for pretence, and their pattern of choices across the range of available props is entirely similar to controls. These findings go against the suggestion, implicit in Harris' views, that pretend play might be problematic for children with autism because of a problem in overriding the action elicited by an object's function in favour of a non-literal, pretend action.

A failure to generate

If we accept that for children with autism the problems in pretence do not lie in inhibiting the prepotent action prompted by an object's function, then we are left with the problem of pinpointing the aspect of pretending which might be 'executively' difficult for them. Harris' suggestions again provide a potentially useful starting point. As already noted, he writes: '. . . the hypothesis implies that autistic children will have difficulty in spontaneously generating and imposing their own make-believe conceptions on a given context' (Harris 1993 p. 238). If imposing a make-believe scheme is not particularly difficult, because children are able to inhibit the functional response elicited by an object, then perhaps it is the process of *generating* that scheme which is the locus of the problem.

There is, in fact, some support for the proposal that children with autism have problems in generating pretend acts. Sigman and Ungerer (1984) found that in a spontaneous play setting children with autism did not spend significantly less time in pretence than mentally handicapped and normal controls (although there was a clear trend towards impairment), but they did produce fewer 'symbolic' acts than mentally handicapped controls (there was again a clear trend towards impairment relative to normal controls). In a structured play setting children with autism produced significantly fewer 'symbolic' acts than both control groups. Further, the children with autism produced fewer functional play acts than controls in both experimental conditions. A subsequent study by Mundy *et al.* (1986) found a similar deficit in the production of symbolic play acts among children with autism, although these children did not produce significantly fewer functional acts in this case.

Similar findings emerged from our own observational study (Jarrold *et al.* 1996; experiment 1), where children with autism produced pretend acts at a slower rate than controls. This difference only approached significance when considered across both of the toy sets employed—arguably because of the low levels of pretend play observed in all groups with the doll figures toy set (see Fig. 4.1). When the doll plus junk objects set was considered separately, children with autism were found to produce pretend acts at a significantly slower rate than controls. There was also a trend for functional acts to be produced at a slower rate among children with autism across both toy sets.

These results suggest that children with autism might have substantial problems with generating pretend acts (and functional play acts also). In fact, it could be argued that deficits observed and measured in terms of time spent in a particular play activity might be secondary to this problem in producing play acts. In other words, children with autism might spend less time pretending spontaneously than do controls because they generate fewer pretend acts to begin with. Alternatively, if children with autism continue one play activity for a protracted period of time they might spend as long in this activity as do controls while producing far fewer acts. It would seem likely that studies reporting no deficit in functional play in autism might be picking up this phenomenon, and be missing the fact that children with autism produce fewer diverse functional play acts than controls. It is important therefore that observational studies assess both the duration of play and the number of discrete acts produced in order to present the complete picture of play deficits in autism.

More direct evidence for a problem in generating a number of novel pretend acts in any play situation comes from two more recent studies. Charman and Baron-Cohen (1997) first engaged children with autism in two functional play scripts, either feeding a doll with a toy spoon or with a toy cup, after which they tested their ability to use substitute props in a similar situation. Although children with autism were unimpaired relative to matched controls in their ability to carry out the previously specified play act with a substitute object, they produced significantly fewer novel uses of the prop (only 9% of substitutions were novel ones compared to 45% for controls). In the same vein, Lewis and Boucher (1995) recently reported new data collected at the time of their 1988 study showing that children with autism were unimpaired, relative to matched controls, in their ability to produce 'symbolic' responses to a series of instructed substitutions or play acts. However, Lewis and Boucher did find that children with autism tended to produce fewer 'original' play acts in a separate condition designed to elicit a series of different play acts with particular props.[6]

Stronger evidence for generativity problems comes from our own test of this ability in pretend play in autism (see Jarrold *et al.* 1996; experiment 3 for full details). In this study we compared 15 children with autism, aged between 5 and 13 years, with children with moderate learning difficulties and normally developing children, matched individually for verbal mental age. Verbal mental ages ranged from 31 to 94 months, with an average for each group of 57 months. Each child's ability to generate pretend acts was assessed in two testing sessions. In one condition—'without props'—children had to generate pretend acts without any external aids, while in the second condition—'with props'—eight objects were available to them to provide potential cues for pretence. These were: a large, metal cake tin; a plastic card-index box; a football scarf; a plastic colander; a clear plastic ruler; a candle; a small, cylindrical metal tub; and a plastic serving spoon. Testing took place in a small room in the child's school from which all objects had either been removed or covered by large white sheets in order to minimize external cues which might prompt pretence.

Each session began with the experimenter modelling three pretend acts for the child, after which the child was asked to show the experimenter 'what they could pretend to do'. Children were then encouraged to continue pretending. If the child did nothing for 15 seconds, or said that they could think of no more acts, then the experimenter modelled a further act as a prompt. This was done twice if necessary, and if a third extended pause or refusal occurred the session was terminated at that point. Otherwise sessions were ended after 6 minutes had elapsed. A record was kept of the number of novel pretend acts produced over time by each child in each condition.

A small number of children from each group did 'drop-out' of each condition before the full 6 minutes had elapsed. Therefore, six separate analyses were performed, one for each minute of time elapsed. These compared the cumulative number of pretend acts produced up to that time point by all remaining children, across groups and conditions. There was no significant effect of condition (with or without props) at any time point, and no significant group by condition interactions. However, there was a significant effect of group at 4, 5 and 6 minutes, due in each case to lower scores among the children with autism than the other two groups. These group differences remained significant when verbal mental age was entered into the analyses as a covariate. This was done to control for possible discrepancies in mental age as children dropped-out of the experiment over time. In fact, under these covariance analyses, the group differences in performance after 1, 2 and 3 minutes were close to, or just significant. Children with autism's generally poorer level of performance is emphasized by Fig. 4.4, which graphs cumulative totals of pretend acts produced, averaged across both conditions. Error bars (95% confidence limits for means) are given for the children with autism for totals after 4, 5 and 6 minutes.

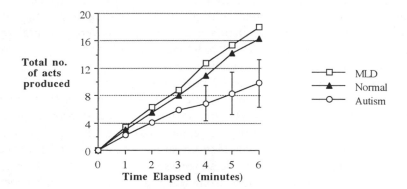

Fig. 4.4 Mean number of acts produced over time.

Clearly the children with autism experienced significant problems in both conditions of this experiment. Importantly, they did produce some pretend play (see Fig. 4.4), but, as was observed in the observational study described above, produced pretend acts at a slower rate than controls. The results of this direct test of generativity in play are therefore consistent with those observed by Lewis and Boucher (1995) and by Charman and Baron-Cohen (1997), and with the evidence of a reduced rate of act generation in observational studies (Jarrold *et al.* 1996; Mundy *et al.* 1986; Sigman and Ungerer 1984).

A generativity deficit?

The experiments described in the previous section suggest that children with autism have problems in generating the pretend schemes necessary for flexible and creative pretend play, but show no particular problem in inhibiting responses which might be elicited by an object's functions. The question of whether this distinction between 'generating' pretend acts and 'inhibiting' elicited functional acts maps on to any sensible fractionation of executive processes will be considered in the following section of this chapter. However, this present section will expand on the implications of a generativity deficit by reviewing how a generativity problem can explain the broad range of experimental findings regarding pretend play in autism, and by briefly considering whether a generativity deficit might extend beyond the domain of pretend play and be more generally pervasive in autism.

A plausible hypothesis is that children with autism have severe difficulty in generating the ideas necessary for flexible and creative pretence. A problem, however, is that this hypothesis is underspecified, because it says nothing about the actual processes involved in coming up with an idea for pretence. For example, a generativity problem might itself arise from a lack of experience of potential play acts, from an absence of spontaneous and creative 'thought', or from a failure of translating thought into action. Also, we cannot, at this stage, distinguish clearly between the generation of *ideas* for play or of the *actions* which go to make up the play act itself. Some of these points will be considered in the following section of this chapter when the executive underpinnings of generativity are considered, but it is important to note that the hypothesis remains useful, even if under-specified, because it makes empirical predictions which stand in stark contrast to those that follow from the metarepresentational-deficit account (see Lewis and Boucher 1995).

A failure to generate pretend acts is clearly consistent with the impaired levels of spontaneous pretence seen in autism. In particular, it specifically predicts a main impairment in the number of pretend acts carried out. This, in turn, will often lead to children with autism spending less time in pretence than other groups, but this is not a necessary consequence of the hypothesis. It is possible, although perhaps unlikely, that children with autism might produce fewer pretend acts than other children, but persist with each act for a longer period of time. Unlike the metarepresentational-deficit account, the generativity hypothesis does not predict a *global inability* to produce pretence. Instead it argues that pretend play will be *problematic*, but not impossible, for children with autism. The metarepresentational account therefore struggles to account for the fact that a certain amount of pretence is seen in our own generativity test (see Fig. 4.4). The generativity hypothesis is consistent with the production of some pretence by children with autism, it only predicts that production of pretend acts will take place at a delayed rate.

Unlike the metarepresentational account, the generativity hypothesis is not obliged to draw a qualitative distinction between functional and pretend play, a distinction which is at odds with the normal pattern of the gradual development of pretence. It can therefore explain why the problems which children with autism have in creative play appear to extend beyond 'symbolic' pretence to functional play as well. Further, the generativity hypothesis argues for a *production* problem in autism, and therefore predicts that individuals will have no difficulty in comprehending or making sense of pretend acts that are carried out by another person, again in line with the empirical evidence. In contrast, the metarepresentational explanation must predict impaired *comprehension* of pretence, in addition to impaired production.

One final difference between the two accounts is that the generativity hypothesis predicts unimpaired production of pretend play in autism under certain circumstances, namely when the idea for pretence is specified for the child. It is important to note that this is not the same as claiming that any increase in 'structure' within the testing situation will lead to improved performance. Elicitation or encouragement to pretend should not make things any easier if ideas for pretence are not provided by the experimenter, although these manipulations might raise levels of pretend play slightly without removing the deficit seen in autism (see Jarrold *et al.* 1996). However, if the experimenter specifies or instructs a pretend act then children with autism should have no difficulty in carrying this out (Charman and Baron-Cohen (1997); Jarrold *et al.* 1994a, 1996; Lewis and Boucher 1988, 1995). A generativity deficit might also be masked if the props given to a child admit or prompt a large number of acts themselves. This is what was seen in Lewis and Boucher's (1995) study where there was only a trend towards impaired generation of acts. One of the props in this case was a toy doll, which (as the authors note) allowed for a large number of simple functional play acts (produced by simply moving the doll's body and limbs). It is interesting to note that while many props might prompt a number of functional acts, which might arise from simple manipulation, one can argue that no prop can ever provide a very good prompt for pretend acts. Although an object's perceptual form might mean that it is more suitable in one pretend script than another, the fact that pretence is by its very nature non-literal means that the child must still work to come up with some other 'identity' for the prop—a pretend act can never arise from the simple conventional manipulation of an object. Also a pencil could be a gun, a toothbrush, a telescope, a magic wand, etc. *ad infinitum*, and so cannot be a strong prompt for any one particular pretend act. One might therefore predict that a generativity deficit might be more clearly seen in pretend than in functional play, which is broadly what is reported in the literature.

As a final point, the generativity deficits observed in studies of pretend play are in line with evidence of a general problem in generating novel activity in autism. Lewis and Boucher (1995) provide a review of some of this work. They highlight the distinction between impaired free recall and unimpaired cued recall of material seen in children with autism (Boucher 1981; Boucher and Lewis 1989; Boucher and Warrington 1976) as evidence of a failure to spontaneously generate appropriate retrieval strategies. Similarly, individuals with autism show impaired word fluency for miscellaneous words, though not for generating words within a category (Boucher 1988). There is also evidence of impaired generation of ideas for drawings in autism (Lewis and Boucher 1991). A study by Turner (1995a) has also shown clear evidence of deficits on three fluency tasks designed to test generative ability. These involved generating as many different uses for functional and non-functional objects, coming up with as many interpretations of ambiguous stylized drawings, and drawing as many non-representational designs as possible in limited periods of time. In contrast, Scott and Baron-Cohen (1996) found no evidence of a generativity deficit in autism on two tasks; generating uses of an object and verbal fluency. However, the absence of an impairment in this case may be due to floor effects among controls, who produced, on average, fewer than two uses of the object per minute, and fewer than one and a half words every minute. Two control groups were employed in this study: normally-developing children aged between 4 and 5 years and children with learning difficulties of an equivalent verbal mental age; arguably, both tasks are too difficult for children at this developmental level. Certainly the word fluency task, in which words beginning with a certain letter (F, A or S) had to be generated, would seem to be particularly inappropriate for children with a language age of only 4 years. A final point is that Scott and Baron-Cohen only examined performance on each task for a total of 2 minutes, which may not be long enough to allow a generativity deficit to be clearly seen (see Fig. 4.4).

These studies therefore provide some evidence to suggest that a generativity deficit may be relatively pervasive in autism, and, at the least, may extend beyond the domain of pretend play. However, it would be premature to elevate problems of generativity to the level of a fundamental psychological explanation of autism. Instead, the approach adopted in the next section will be to consider whether generativity problems can be accommodated within an executive dysfunction framework.

How a generativity deficit fits with notions of executive dysfunction

Previous sections of this chapter have suggested that children with autism have problems in generating play acts in pretence, but not in inhibiting prepotent actions elicited by objects' functions. This section will attempt to describe ways in which a problem in generativity might result from executive dysfunction in autism. It will also consider whether the proposed dysfunction is consistent with the general pattern of symptoms, and of executive deficits in particular, which are observed in autism. To this end, a model of executive control will be developed, which has three separate levels of control. Ways in which dysfunction within each of these three levels might lead to apparent problems in generativity will then be outlined. The model itself is borrowed from Shallice and colleague's work in this area (Norman and Shallice 1986; Shallice 1988, 1994; Shallice and Burgess 1991), while my thoughts about ways in which the model might break down to produce problems in generativity are heavily in debt to Gordon Brown (personal communications; Brown et al. 1994).

A basic model of executive control

'Executive control' essentially refers to the process of conscious and deliberate top-down control of action. This is seen most explicitly in Shallice and colleague's model, in which the supervisory attentional system (SAS) provides top-down control over the process of action selection (contention scheduling). Central to Shallice and colleague's arguments is the assumption that behaviour can be divided into two 'streams'—one exercised under conscious control, and one that occurs 'automatically' in the absence of conscious control. The actions selected in each case are the same; what differs is whether top-down executive control is exercised in the process of action selection. To give an example, I might 'automatically' turn the wheel of a car as I approach a bend on a stretch of road which I know well, or I might 'deliberately' make the same turning action to pull off a road to get a cup of coffee at a service station. Given that I can select appropriate actions even when my mind is elsewhere, the process of action selection must be able to function 'normally' even in the absence of top-down control. In this sense, contention scheduling, although part of the executive control process as a whole, stands apart from the higher level SAS.

The role of the SAS within Shallice's model is to select and represent goals (e.g. Cohen and Servan-Schreiber 1992; Diamond 1990; Goldman-Rakic 1994; Pennington 1994). It is clear that the SAS must necessarily be involved with both of these processes. The whole purpose of an executive system is to guide behaviour with reference to internally specified goals; the SAS must therefore represent or hold on-line goal states if this is ever to occur. Similarly, to the extent that executive control involves altering behaviour so that the external world comes to match the internally specified goal state (cf. MacKay 1978), monitoring of the external world and planning of action must also be carried out by the SAS. A number of authors have characterized the process of goal-representation in terms of information being held on-line in working memory (Diamond 1990; Pennington 1994). Consistent with this suggestion, empirical studies have shown that representational working memory of this form is mediated by the prefrontal cortex (Diamond 1990, 1991; Goldman Rakic 1987, 1994). However, there is a sense in which using the term 'working memory' in this context does not advance our understanding very far. On the one hand it is simply another way of saying that the SAS represents goals in order to guide behaviour. The term might additionally be used to denote the fact that the SAS has a limited capacity (cf. Baddeley and Hitch's working memory model; Baddeley 1986; Baddeley and Hitch 1974), but this is not an important issue for the current model. Consequently, I will generally use the term 'goal-representation' rather than refer to 'working memory', while accepting that many would see the two as analogous.

What is more important is the need to be specific about the type of information represented by the SAS. Broadly, and perhaps rather loosely, speaking these are 'goals', but it should be noted that goals may be 'endogenous', and arise internally and spontaneously, or be more reactive. In the context of formal neuropsychological tasks, such as the Wisconsin Card Sort Test, goals are often defined by the interaction of the experimenter's instructions and the subject's inferences about the particular requirements of the task. In these instances the importance of appropriate goal-selection (through monitoring feedback information) is clearly seen, and the goals that come to be represented are really 'task demands' or rules. A number of authors, and particularly those who develop computer-based simulations of performance on this type of executive task (Cohen and Servan-Schreiber 1992; Dehaene and Changeux 1989, 1991), use terms like 'context representation' to refer to the process of holding this type of task-defined, goal state on-line.

Simulation studies, in fact, provide further support for the view that the SAS is involved in this form of goal (or 'rule', or 'context') selection and representation. Evidence for the importance of appropriate goal-selection (monitoring) comes from two studies in which performance on the Wisconsin Card Sort Test (WCST) has been modelled using connectionist networks. Dehaene and Changeux (1991) developed a network which was able to carry out the WCST successfully until the unit-clusters which provided negative feedback were lesioned, when frontal patterns of perseveration emerged. Levine *et al.* (1992) also simulated frontal performance by reducing the effectiveness of feedback in their network. In this case they reduced the 'gain of signals' from nodes corresponding to the experimenter's reinforcement ('right', 'wrong'). This parameter, gain, determines the extent to which signals are amplified (see Cohen and Servan-Schriber 1992)—with high gain, inhibitory signals become more inhibitory, and excitatory signals become more excitatory. Consequently, reducing gain reduces the discriminability of a signal.

Other simulations have focused on the process of goal-representation, with similar results. Dehaene and Changeux (1989) modelled young infant's performance on delayed response tasks (cf. Diamond 1990) with a connectionist network containing two levels, one concerned with sensorimotor inputs and outputs, and the other with memory and rule coding. Only lesions to the latter layer of units produced impaired performance akin to that shown by infants, and attributed to delayed maturation of prefrontal areas. Kimberg and Farah (1993) used a production rule system to model performance on the WCST, as well as on motor sequencing, Stroop and source-memory tests. Their simulation produced 'frontal' performance following the weakening of '. . . associations between working memory representations that include representations of goals, stimuli in the environment, and stored declarative knowledge' (p. 414). While it is not entirely clear that a weakening of associations between these elements actually corresponds to a deficit in 'working memory', as has been claimed (Pennington and Ozonoff 1996), Kimberg and Farah do note that entirely similar deficits would occur upon reduction of '. . . the activation available within working memory or the transmission of data activation from working memory' (p 423). Finally, Cohen and Servan-Schreiber (1992) developed connectionist networks to simulate the frontal performance seen in patients with schizophrenia on the Stroop task, a Continuous Performance Test and a test of lexical disambiguation. In each case frontal performance resulted from a reduction in the gain parameter of 'context' units, which either maintained a representation of the task demands and instructions (Stroop test) or of previous contexts (CPT, lexical disambiguation). In line with the points about 'gain reduction' made above, Cohen and Servan-Schreiber interpret their manipulation in terms of a '. . . degradation of the internal representation of context' (p.62).

These simulations confirm that 'frontal' patterns of task performance are seen in systems with deficient goal-selection and/or goal-representation. It is worth noting that very similar results emerge from either deficit, whether in selection/monitoring or in representation/working memory. Another point to make is that both types of problem have been modelled in two different ways, on the one hand in terms of an obliteration of that process (lesion to specific units in the model) and, on the other, in terms of a reduction in efficiency of the process (modelled by a reduction in the gain parameter of specific units). These two distinctions, between selection and representation, and between obliteration and degradation, will be developed further when the implications for problems of generativity of dysfunction within the SAS are considered.

To return to Shallice's model, a final property of the system follows from the fact that there must be some form of interface between the representation of goals and the selection of goal-appropriate action. The SAS must exercise top-down control on action selection by interacting with the process of contention scheduling: control must obviously be exercised, not just represented. It is at this intermediate level, as it were 'between' the SAS and contention scheduling, that the processes of inhibition and activation come into play. Both allow control to be exercised on the process of contention scheduling. In Shallice's model, contention scheduling works on the basis of one particular action schema being activated over and above all others (Norman and Shallice 1986). External stimuli elicit particular actions by activating them directly, and if these actions are inappropriate then the activation level of that particular schema must be lowered by top-down inhibition. (It is worth noting that an action can only ever be inappropriate with reference to previously specified goals, hence the claim that inhibition *follows* from goal-representation.) Similarly, if one action has been selected then, in the absence of any other external cues, it will remain active leading to perseveration of action, unless inhibited internally. However, inhibition can only ever be a means by which one can prevent oneself from doing something inappropriate (e.g. eating yet another chocolate from an open box in front of you). A separate process must be necessary to produce behaviour which does not arise as a direct response to the external environment (e.g. getting up to leave the room). In this case, when an action schema is to be selected in the absence of external cues, internal top-down activation must be imposed on contention scheduling (Shallice 1994). This distinction, between inhibition as a reactive process and activation for the execution of internally generated goals, has, in fact, been drawn by many authors (Frith 1987; Goldberg 1985; MacKay 1978; Passingham 1993).

To sum up, three potentially separable levels within Shallice's approach have been identified. There is the SAS which selects and represents goals; there are the processes of activation and inhibition by which top-down control is exercised; and there is the process of contention scheduling, which is the domain upon which executive control is exercised. Fig. 4.5 presents a simple summary of this model. The following three subsections will outline ways in which problems in generativity might arise from dysfunction at each of these three levels within the model. In each case the broader implications of the proposed dysfunction will also be discussed. The levels of the model will be considered in 'bottom-up' order, beginning with problems at the level of action selection.

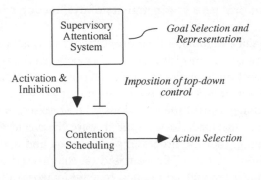

Fig. 4.5 A simplified version of Shallice and colleagues' model.

A problem in action selection

Contention scheduling is a dynamic process, with action schemas competing for activation with each other. As already described, particular action schemas will be activated to a greater or lesser extent from three potential sources—the external environment, the person's current activity and their goals. Inhibition from top-down goals may also occur, and Norman and Shallice (1986) argue that within the level of contention scheduling lateral inhibition must operate between schemas, so that as one action is selected the activity of other schemas is dampened down, allowing the appropriate action to 'win out'. Contention scheduling can therefore be viewed as an integrative process, in which both inhibitory and excitatory factors are added together. A dynamic system of this form will have certain parameters set to determine the relative contributions of these inputs, and the threshold levels required for an action to be selected. If the system is biased heavily towards excitatory inputs (i.e. the relative effects of lateral inhibition and top-down inhibition are weak), then contention scheduling will be unselective—actions will arise easily in response to external stimuli for example, and impulsivity will result. Alternatively, if the system is biased towards inhibitory inputs (and the relative contribution of excitatory inputs from the external environment of from the SAS is weak) then contention scheduling will be overconservative. In this case, action schemas will struggle to reach threshold activation levels, and inertia will follow.

Clearly, the latter situation would result in a problem of generativity. If contention scheduling has a relatively inhibitory bias, then it will be more difficult for top-down activation to raise action schemas to threshold levels of activation. An inhibitory bias in action selection in autism might therefore explain the problems seen in pretend play. However, there are two other implications that follow from this suggestion which also need to be considered in the light of what we know about autism, and the general pattern of executive deficits seen in the disorder. Firstly contention scheduling is normally able to operate either in the presence or absence of top-down control. A problem in action selection would therefore be observed in all situations, and not just when executive control is required. This would imply that in autism we should expect a general problem of inertia, and a failure to make impulsive 'errors' or slips of action. Even when executive control is applied, an inhibitory bias in action selection should mean that control exercised via inhibitory processes should be particularly effective, or at the least, successful. This account therefore predicts problems of generativity, but no problems of impulsivity, in line with the results of our studies of executive factors in pretend play in autism described above.

However, this appears to be inconsistent with what is generally seen in autism. Many studies have clearly shown that children with autism do make inappropriate responses prompted by the external environment (Hughes 1996; Hughes and Russell 1993; Russell et al. 1991). Problems of set-shifting seen on the WCST (Ozonoff et al. 1991; Prior and Hoffman 1990; Rumsey 1985; Rumsey and Hamburger 1988, 1990; Szatmari et al. 1990; see also Hughes et al. 1994) would also seem to indicate a failure to inhibit a previously reinforced but currently inappropriate response. However, these failures of inhibition could be viewed as secondary to a more fundamental problem in generating an appropriate response (see Russell, Chapter 8). Perseveration and flexibility are, in a sense, two sides of the same coin— perseveration might occur because of a failure to inhibit a response, or because of an inability to produce an alternative behaviour. Ozonoff et al. (1994) argue for something along these lines in autism (see also Ozonoff, Chapter 6), after showing that children with autism have more problems in switching behaviour than in simply inhibiting an action in a 'Go–NoGo task'. They write: 'Our results help rule out basic defects in the ability to inhibit responses . . . The present results do suggest that clear deficits in cognitive flexibility exist in autistic individuals' (Ozonoff et al. 1994, p.1029). Similarly, Pennington and Ozonoff (1996), following an extensive review of the range of executive deficits seen in a variety of developmental disorders, argue that '. . . deficits in inhibition are prominent in ADHD but not in autism, in which there are marked deficits in cognitive flexibility' (p. 79).

This second implication of a generativity deficit at this level of control is that there is no reason to suppose that problems exist higher in the system. In other words, this account suggests that individuals with autism should be able to represent goals, but be unable to execute them. This parallels Frith's (1987) account of Parkinson's disease, in which poverty of action (but not of 'volition') is seen. As Frith writes: '. . . the Parkinson's disease patient wishes to act, but cannot generate the movements' (p.641). In line with the suggestions made here, Frith interprets this as a problem at the level of action selection, which he argues, implicates damage to the striatum (Frith 1992; Frith and Done 1988). Brown *et al.* (1994) also claim that the motor problems seen in Parkinson's disease reflect disruption within the striatum.

A problem in imposition of control

A second way in which a problem of generativity might arise within the executive system is at the interface between goals represented in the SAS and the translation of these goals into action via contention scheduling. As discussed, executive control is exercised by processes of activation and inhibition, and the hypothesis to be developed in this subsection shares similarities with the previous one, in that it concerns the balance between inhibitory and excitatory processes. However, a more radical suggestion can be made at this slightly higher level of control, which is that there may be a selective impairment to the systems which impose control via activation, with a sparing of the systems which impose inhibitory control.

For this to be possible these systems must be separable. Goldberg (1985) has argued for something akin to this, by suggesting that internally driven action relies on a 'medial' premotor system involving the supplementary motor area (SMA) and basal ganglia, while reactive, externally driven action rests on a 'lateral' system which includes the ventrolateral arcuate premotor cortex. There is also empirical evidence for the neurological distinctiveness of these two systems. First, Passingham and his colleagues have examined the voluntary motor behaviour of monkeys following lesions to the premotor cortex (Chen *et al.* 1995; Passingham *et al.* 1989; Thaler *et al.* 1995). In line with Goldberg's suggestions they have shown that lesions to the medial premotor cortex and anterior cingulate produce a marked reduction in the number of learned, but internally generated, actions; lesions to the lateral premotor area produced much less of an impairment (Thaler *et al.* 1995). Second, a number of studies have used positron emission tomography to examine patterns of regional cerebral blood flow (rCBF) in humans during tasks which elicit internally or externally cued actions. C. D. Frith *et al.* (1991) asked normal adults to say particular words, or to make certain actions, in one of two conditions—either the response was specified by the experimenter (repeating a word, flexing a touched finger) or the subject had to generate a response (giving a word beginning with a certain letter, moving any finger). In both verbal and manual versions of the task, having to generate a response led to significant increases in rCBF in the dorsolateral prefrontal cortex and anterior cingulate cortex. In a similar manner Peterson *et al.* (1988) compared levels of rCBF when subjects either had to repeat a noun they had seen or heard, or give an appropriate use for the specified object. They found that having to generate an appropriate response led to increased blood flow levels in the left inferior frontal area and the anterior cingulate gyrus.

Finally, Deiber *et al.* (1991) measured levels of rCBF while subjects moved a joystick in response to a tone under five different experimental conditions. In a baseline condition subjects simply moved the joystick forward when they heard a tone. In two 'externally cued' conditions the type of tone specified the direction of movement, while in two 'internally cued' conditions the subject either followed through a prelearnt sequence of moves or had to generate a random movement. A comparison of the internally cued versus externally cued conditions showed that blood flow increased in the anterior SMA, left prefrontal lobe and right parietal lobe for internally generated actions. In particular, the random condition was associated with significant increases in rCBF in the prefrontal cortex (bilaterally), the SMA and the anterior cingulate sulcus. Many other studies have shown an increase in activation in the SMA (among other areas) during tasks which can be thought to involve a degree of voluntary self-generation (Colebatch *et al.* 1991; Fox *et al.* 1985; Jenkins *et al.* 1994; Orgogozo and Larsen 1979; Roland *et al.* 1980, 1982).

These studies support the suggestion that internally driven actions are mediated by a different neural mechanism than externally specified ones, and give some indication of what that mechanism might be. The generation of actions appears to lead to increased regional cerebral blood flow in three particular areas—the prefrontal cortex, the supplementary motor area and the anterior cingulate. The lesion studies described above also highlighted two of these areas as being involved in the initiation of voluntary action—the medial premotor cortex (supplementary motor area) and the anterior cingulate. This converging functional and anatomical evidence fits neatly within Goldberg's (1985) conceptual framework. He suggests that the medial premotor route (internally driven action) links with the dorsomedial prefrontal cortex, while the lateral premotor system connects with the orbital frontal cortex. This, in turn, is consistent with suggestions that the orbital frontal cortex is responsible for inhibition of externally driven responses (Diamond 1990; Fuster 1989). Further, the anterior cingulate and the SMA are also linked within Goldberg's medial system. It is therefore possible that problems of generativity in pretend play in autism arise from a selective impairment in the imposition of excitatory control on action selection in response to self-generated goals. A selective impairment of this kind would imply some form of damage to the medial rather than lateral premotor system within Goldberg's (1985) framework, in particular within the dorsomedial prefrontal cortex, the supplementary motor area (medial premotor cortex) and/or the anterior cingulate.

In common with the previous hypothesis, this account would imply that individuals with autism should have no problems in exercising inhibitory control. While in line with the results of our own studies (described in pp. 000–00), it again struggles to explain why individuals with autism do seem to be impulsive in certain situations (unless one accepts that these problems in inhibition are secondary to generativity deficits). The major difference between the two accounts advanced so far is that a problem at this higher level does not imply general inertia, as, in this case, the process of contention scheduling should function normally in the absence of any top-down control. This implies that individuals should react to external stimuli, and in particular, that they should be able to initiate action if prompted to do so by an external source, such as an experimenter giving them instructions. Once again this account would predict that individuals with autism should be able to represent goals 'higher-up' in the executive system, but would have trouble translating goals into action.

A problem in goal-selection and -representation

At the highest level of the model outlined in Fig. 4.5 is goal-selection and -representation. The consequences of dysfunction at this level of control were discussed earlier with reference to computer models which have simulated 'frontal' performance on a range of tasks by either lesioning the units responsible for goal-selection and -representation, or by degrading the signal passed on by such units. Although these studies concentrate largely on the failure to inhibit the previously reinforced responses which follow from these manipulations, problems of activation would also occur in these situations. An inability to select or represent goals within the SAS would mean that top-down executive control would never be exercised on the process of contention scheduling. Actions then would only ever be selected if they were elicited by the external environment, or if currently active. Inertia, as well as impulsivity and perseveration, would consequently result. To give an example, if the chief executive in a company never issued any instructions to any other members of the organization then (in the absence of another person willing to take control) no new activities would ever be started, and no current behaviour or strategy would be halted.

A less drastic possibility is that goals might be 'poorly represented' within the SAS. In this case the SAS might still impose control signals on to contention scheduling, but these signals would be degraded or poorly specified. Again this would lead to problems of both generativity and impulsivity—because, as already discussed, the purpose of the SAS is to initiate appropriate action and inhibit inappropriate behaviour. If our chief executive did issue instructions, but did this rather half-heartedly or un-clearly, then change to the status quo would be possible, but there would still be a reduced chance of a new procedure being initiated, or a current activity being halted. This type of deficit corresponds to those models which weaken control signals by reducing their gain parameter. As discussed, reduced gain not only makes inhibitory signals less inhibitory, but it also makes excitatory signals less excitatory. Consequently, some form of impairment at this level of control, be it total or partial, would lead to problems in generating new behaviour as well as in inhibiting inappropriate action.

An advantage of the notion of a degradation of control is that it could explain why individuals with autism are able to inhibit inappropriate responses and are able to generate appropriate responses in some in-stances. Poorly specified control only makes activation or inhibition of activity 'more difficult', not impossible. Therefore inhibition will be possi-ble, providing the external context provides some support for this (e.g. if particular task demands are made more explicit), and initiation of action will similarly be possible if the external situation prompts or elicits particular behaviours in some way. The ability to inhibit counterfunctional behaviour seen in the study of inhibition in pretence which I described earlier can therefore be explained, as here the children are told what the identity of the prop should be. Further, the ability to generate some pretence, but at a slower rate than controls, as seen in the second study reported earlier, is consistent with the notion that initiation of activity in the absence of strong external cues should be executively difficult, but not impossible. Other implications of dysfunction at this level of control are that it points to neurological problems within the prefrontal cortex specifically. It also implies that goals or context are poorly represented in prefrontal working memory in autism, rather than being well specified but not initiated. There is, in fact, some evidence that impaired generativity in autism arises from an absence or paucity of ideas, rather than an inability to translate ideas into action (Turner 1995b; see Russell 1996, p.245).

A final question which must be considered at this point is whether dysfunction should be viewed in terms of a problem in goal-selection or -representation. Clearly either type of problem would lead to the same form of psychological deficits (see the discussion of modelling studies earlier) and this in itself suggests that the two processes are closely linked. Problems in goal-selection will lead to inappropriate goals being represented; if negative feedback from a task such as the WCST is not properly monitored then the rules held in mind will not be updated successfully. Also, poorly specified goals might follow from a failure to monitor a situation adequately. In this way, problems in representation may well be a necessary consequence of poor goal-selection or monitoring. However, this relationship would seem to be unsymmetrical, as goals might well be adequately selected but then poorly represented or held in mind.

At present, we do not know enough about autism to decide whether problems of goal-representation might be primary, or rather follow from more fundamental problems in appropriate goal-selection. Pennington and colleagues (Bennetto *et al.* 1996; Pennington 1994; Pennington and Ozonoff 1996) argue heavily in favour of a prefrontal working memory deficit in autism, but the actual evidence for working memory deficits in autism is mixed (Bennetto *et al.* 1996; Russell *et al.* 1996). Russell (1996) argues instead in favour of a fundamental monitoring problem in autism. However, his account, in common with Frith's theoretical approach to schizophrenia (Frith 1987, 1992; Frith and Done 1988), concentrates on the link between the monitoring of internally generated action and an awareness of agency. This is monitoring at a slightly different level of the control process—in Frith's terms the monitoring of launched intentions operates between the level of goal-representation and action selection. Frith also argues for a relatively specific monitoring problem in schizophrenia, and sees no problems in monitoring actions themselves (as opposed to the intention to act), or the state of the external environment. The link from monitoring to formation of goals or plans is also intact in his model. However, as far as autism is concerned, Russell's views are obviously consistent with the suggestion that general monitoring deficits might lead to poorly specified top-down executive control.

Summary

There appear then to be at least three ways in which problems of generativity might arise in autism as a consequence of executive dysfunction. These correspond to the three 'potentially separable' levels of Shallice's model identified above (Fig. 4.5). The first is a problem at the level of contention scheduling, and, specifically, of an inhibitory bias in the process of action selection. This would produce a generativity deficit because abnormally high levels of top-down activation would be necessary in order to override these inhibitory effects, and to prompt behaviour. As contention scheduling is the process by which all actions are selected, regardless of whether top-down control is being exercised or not, then this account must predict general inertia in autism. It also predicts that goals should be able to be represented, and consequently accessible, but not readily enacted. This type of generativity deficit would be similar to that seen in Parkinson's disease, where there is poverty of action but intact will to act, and would appear to implicate damage to the striatum.

The second suggestion is similar, as it concerns the relative trade-off between inhibitory and excitatory control processes, but focuses at the level of imposition of control. The claim is that excitatory top-down control is imposed on the process of contention scheduling via a specific neural pathway. It is therefore possible that this system might be selectively damaged, with a sparing of the ability to impose inhibitory control. This would lead to generativity problems, though again it would imply that the goals that might drive behaviour should themselves be adequately represented. The hypothesized locus of impairment in this case would be within Goldberg's (1985) medial system which links the dorsomedial prefrontal cortex with the supplementary motor area.

Both of these first two hypothesis predict impaired generativity, but spared inhibitory control Although not necessarily a problem as far as an explanation of pretend play deficits is concerned (see above), this is inconsistent with the evidence of both generativity and impulsivity deficits in autism in certain situations. This clearly is a problem unless one is prepared to accept that an apparent failure to inhibit is secondary to a more fundamental deficit in 'flexibility' (so an individual perseverates because he or she cannot generate alternative behaviour; see previous discussion). The third hypothesis, namely of dysfunction in the level of goal-selection and -representation, does not suffer from this problem, because a failure to generate behaviour and impulsivity would co-occur if goals were poorly represented. While autism might be associated with a total failure to represent goals within the SAS, a more plausible way of phrasing the hypothesis is in terms of degraded goal-representation. The connectionist networks, which simulate 'frontal' behaviour by reducing the gain of units involved in selecting or representing goals, provide a useful model for this. What remains unclear is whether goals might be poorly represented because of problems in holding them on-line over time (working memory) or because of a failure to adequately monitor the external environment in the first place. However, in either case the locus of dysfunction within the brain would be the prefrontal cortex.

Of these three accounts, it is the third which perhaps fits best with our current understanding of autism. While flexibility is being seen as an increasingly important aspect of the disorder, it seems unlikely that all the evidence of impulsivity in autism can be reduced to a consequence of inflexibility as the first two accounts would require. Also, what evidence there is suggests that a failure to generate in autism may not reflect an inability to translate intact goals into action, but rather a paucity of goals in the first place. The third account is also entirely consistent with the pretend play data outlined in previous sections of this chapter, where it appears that providing the *idea* for pretence is the key to circumventing difficulties in children with autism. One drawback is that the third account might well be viewed as little more than a re-statement of what we already know, namely that autism is associated with degraded top-down executive control. My hope, however, is that the final section of this chapter, in common with other recent approaches (e.g. Pennington 1994; Pennington and Ozonoff 1996; Russell 1996), has highlighted ways in which this debate might be taken further, in order to allow us to be more specific about the nature of the executive deficits associated with autism.

Notes

1. Leslie (Leslie and Thaiss 1992) argues that the ToMM is 'domain specific' in that it only deals with 'mental' metarepresentations. Although others (e.g. Perner 1991) would argue that theory of mind rests on more general metarepresentational abilities, the term 'metarepresentation' will only be used here to refer to the mental domain.
2. It should be noted that Jarrold *et al.* use a somewhat liberal measure of pretend play activity, which includes behaviours which appear to be 'pretend', but which could not be confirmed as such because of a lack of verbal elaboration of the activity. However, even under a more conservative criterion children with autism spend *some* time in pretend play (3% vs. 6% for controls; Jarrold 1993).
3. Three additional points should be made here. First, some would claim that even those individuals who successfully pass theory of mind tasks do not possess true metarepresentational competence, but instead 'hack-out' a solution by alternative means (Bowler 1992; U. Frith *et al.*, 1991; Ozonoff *et al.* 1991). Second, Boucher (1996) has also argued against delayed development of metarepresentational competence in autism, claiming that if a metarepresentational deficit is central to autism then autistic symptoms should lessen in severity as this ability comes 'on-line'. Finally, an important point is that even if delayed development of metarepresentational ability in autism is accepted, this does not imply that the acquisition of metarepresentational skill is a gradual, quantitative process. Instead, it implies a delay in the point at which a qualitative change occurs.
4. This analysis is presented in detail in Jarrold (1993).
5. The performance of all groups was so similar that only two can be shown on the figure without obscuring the performance of the children with autism.
6. Lewis and Boucher suggest that their results provide only 'qualified support for an impaired generativity explanation' because a significant impairment in terms of the number of original acts produced was only observed with one of the two props available, and even then, only relative to one of the two control groups.

Acknowledgements

The studies reported in the first five sections of this chapter were carried out in collaboration with Jill Boucher and Peter Smith, and I am grateful to them for their guidance in developing the ideas discussed in these sections. Paul Harris provided useful advice on aspects of this work, as did Jim Russell. I am also grateful to Jim for his careful editing of the whole chapter, and for encouraging me to develop the theoretical ideas outlined in the final section. As already noted, many of the arguments in this last section arose directly from discussions with Gordon Brown, and I would also like to thank him, Jill Boucher and Teresa McCormack for their helpful comments on a previous draft of the chapter.

REFERENCES

American Psychiatric Association (1987). *Diagnostic and statistical manual of mental disorders—3rd revised edition (DSM-III-R)*. American Psychiatric Association, Washington, DC.

Atlas, J. A. (1990). Play in assessment and intervention in the childhood psychoses. *Child Psychiatry and Human Development*, 21, 119–33.

Baddeley, A. D. (1986). *Working memory*. Clarendon Press, Oxford.

Baddeley, A. D. and Hitch, G. J. (1974). Working memory. In *The psychology of learning and motivation* (ed. G. Bower), 47–90. Academic Press, NY.

Baron-Cohen, S. (1987). Autism and symbolic play. *British Journal of Developmental Psychology*, 5, 139–48.

Baron-Cohen, S. (1990). Instructed and elicited play in autism: A reply to Lewis and Boucher. *British Journal of Developmental Psychology*, 8, 207.

Baron-Cohen, S. (1991). The development of a theory of mind in autism: Deviance and delay? *The Psychiatric Clinics of North America*, 14, 33–51.

Baron-Cohen, S. (1995). *Mindblindness: an essay on autism and theory of mind*. MIT Press, Cambridge, MA.

Baron-Cohen, S. and Ring, H (1994). A model of the mindreading system: neuropsychological and neurobiological perspectives. In *Children's early understanding of mind: origins and development* (ed. C. Lewis and P. Mitchell), 183–207. Lawrence Erlbaum Associates, Hove.

Baron-Cohen, S., Leslie, A. M., and Frith, U. (1985). Does the autistic child have a 'theory of mind'? *Cognition*, 21, 37–46.

Baron-Cohen, S., Allen, J., and Gillberg, C. (1992). Can autism be detected at 18 months? The needle, the haystack, and the CHAT. *British Journal of Psychiatry*, 161, 839–43.

Bennetto, L., Pennington, B. F., and Rogers, S. J. (1996). Intact and impaired memory functions in autism. *Child Development*, 67, 1816–35.

Boucher, J. (1981). Immediate free recall in early childhood autism: Another point of behavioural similarity with the amnesic syndrome. *British Journal of Psychology*, 72, 211–15.

Boucher, J. (1988). Word fluency in high functioning autistic children. *Journal of Autism and Developmental Disorders*, 18, 637–46.

Boucher, J. (1996). What could possibly explain autism.? In *Theories of theories of mind* (ed. P. Carruthers and P. K. Smith), pp. 223–41. Cambridge University Press.

Boucher, J. and Lewis, V. (1989). Memory impairments and communication in relatively able autistic children. *Journal of Child Psychology and Psychiatry*, 30, 99–122.

Boucher, J. and Lewis, V. (1990). Guessing or creating? A reply to Baron-Cohen. *British Journal of Developmental Psychology*, 8, 205–6.

Boucher, J. and Warrington, E. K. (1976). Memory deficits in early infantile autism: Some similarities to the amnesic syndrome. *British Journal of Psychology*, 67, 73–87.

Bowler, D. M. (1992). 'Theory of mind' in Asperger's syndrome. *Journal of Child Psychology and Psychiatry*, **33**, 877–93.

Brown, G. D. A., Britain, A. A., Elvevåg, B., and Mitchell, I. J. (1994). A computational approach to fronto-striatal dysfunction in schizophrenia and Parkinson's disease. In *Neurodynamics and psychology* (ed. M. Oaksford and G. D. A. Brown), 35–82. Academic Press, San Diego.

Charman, T. and Baron-Cohen, S. Brief report: Prompted pretend play in autism. *Journal of Autism and Developmental Disorders*, **27**, 325–32.

Chen, Y.-C., Thaler, D., Nixon, P. D., Stern, C. E., and Passingham, R. E. (1995). The functions of the medial premotor cortex: II. The timing and selection of learned movements. *Experimental Brain Research*, **102**, 461–73.

Cohen, J. D. and Servan-Schreiber, D. (1992). Context, cortex, and dopamine: A connectionist approach to behavior and biology in schizophrenia. *Psychological Review*, **99**, 45–77.

Colebatch, J. G., Deiber, M.-P., Passingham, R. E., Friston, K. J., and Frackowiak, R. S. J. (1991). Regional cerebral blood flow during voluntary arm and hand movements in human subjects. *Journal of Neurophysiology*, **65**, 1392–401.

Copple, C. E., Cocking, R. R., and Matthews, W. S. (1984). Objects, symbols and substitutes: The nature of the cognitive activity during symbolic play. In *Child's play: Developmental and applied* (ed. T. D. Yawkey and A. D. Pellegrini), 105–23. Lawrence Erlbaum Associates, Hillsdale, NJ.

Dehaene, S. and Changeux, J. P. (1989). A simple model of prefrontal cortex function in delayed-response tasks. *Journal of Cognitive Neuroscience*, **1**, 244–61.

Dehaene, S. and Changeux, J. P. (1991). The Wisconsin Card Sort Test: Theoretical analysis and modelling in a neuronal network. *Cerebral Cortex*, **1**, 62–79.

Deiber, M.-P., Passingham, R. E., Colebatch, J. G., Friston, K. J., Nixon, P. D., and Frackowiak, R. S. J. (1991). Cortical areas and the selection of movement: A study using positron emission tomography. *Experimental Brain Research*, **84**, 393–402.

Diamond, A. (1990). The development and neural bases of memory functions as indexed by the AB and delayed response tasks in human infants and infant monkeys. In *Annals of the New York Academy of Sciences*, Vol. 608. *The development and neural bases of higher cognitive functions* (ed. A. Diamond), 267–317. New York Academy of Sciences, NY.

Diamond, A. (1991). Guidelines for the study of brain–behavior relationship during development. In *Frontal lobe function and dysfunction* (ed. H. S. Levin, H. M. Eisenberg, and A. L. Benton), 339–78. Oxford University Press.

Doherty, M. B. and Rosenfeld, A. A. (1984). Play assessment in the differential diagnosis of autism and other causes of severe language disorder. *Journal of Developmental and Behavioral Pediatrics*, **5**, 26–9.

Elder, J. L. and Pederson, D. R. (1978). Preschool children's use of objects in symbolic play. *Child Development*, **49**, 500–4.

Elkonin, D. (1966). Symbolics and its function in the play of children. *Soviet Education*, **8**, 35–41.

Fox, P. T., Fox, J. M., Raichle, M. E., and Burder, R. M. (1985). The role of cerebral cortex in the generation of voluntary saccades: A positron emission tomographic study. *Journal of Neurophysiology*, **54**, 348–69.

Frith, C. D. (1987). The positive and negative symptoms of schizophrenia reflect impairments in the perception and initiation of action. *Psychological Medicine*, **17**, 631–48.

Frith, C. D. (1992). *The cognitive neuropsychology of schizophrenia*. Lawrence Erlbaum Associates, Hove.

Frith, C. D. and Done, D. J. (1988). Towards a neuropsychology of schizophrenia. *British Journal of Psychiatry*, **153**, 437–43.

Frith, C. D., Friston, K., Liddle, P. F., and Frackowiak, R. S. J. (1991). Willed action and the prefrontal cortex in man: A study with PET. *Proceedings of the Royal Society of London B*, **244**, 241–6.

Frith, U., Morton, J. A., and Leslie, A. M. (1991). The cognitive basis of a biological disorder: Autism. *Trends in Neurosciences*, **14**, 433–8.

Fuster, J. M. (1989). *The prefrontal cortex: anatomy, physiology, and neuropsychology of the frontal lobe*. Raven, NY.

Goldberg, G. (1985). Supplementary motor area structure and function: Review and hypotheses. *The Behavioral and Brain Sciences*, **8**, 567–616.

Goldman-Rakic, P. S. (1987). Development of cortical circuitry and cognitive function. *Child Development*, **58**, 601–22.

Goldman-Rakic, P. S. (1994). Specification of higher cortical functions. In *Atypical cognitive deficits in developmental disorders* (ed. S. H. Broman and J. Grafman), pp. 3–17. Lawrence Erlbaum Associates, Hillsdale, NJ.

Golomb, C. (1979). Pretense play: A cognitive perspective. In *Symbolic functioning in childhood* (ed. N. R. Smith and M. B. Franklin), pp. 101–16. Lawrence Erlbaum Associates, Hillsdale, NJ.

Hadwin, J., Baron-Cohen, S., Howlin, P., and Hill, K. (1996). Can we teach children with autism to understand emotions, belief, or pretence? *Development and Psychopathology*, **8**, 345–65.

Happé, F. G. E. (1995). The role of age and verbal ability in the theory of mind task performance of subjects with autism. *Child Development*, **66**, 843–55.

Harris, P. L. (1991). The work of the imagination. In *Natural theories of mind* (ed. A. Whiten), pp. 283–304. Blackwell, Oxford.

Harris, P. L. (1993). Pretending and planning. In *Understanding other minds: Perspectives from autism* (ed. S. Baron-Cohen, H. Tager-Flusberg, and D. Cohen), pp. 228–46. Oxford University Press.

Harris, P. L. (1994). Understanding pretence. In *Children's early understanding of mind* (ed. C. Lewis and P. Mitchell), pp. 235–59. Lawrence Erlbaum Associates, Hove.

Holroyd, S. and Baron-Cohen, S. (1993). How far can people with autism go in developing a theory of mind? *Journal of Autism and Developmental Disorders*, **23**, 379–85.

Hughes, C. (1996). Control of action and thought: Normal development and dysfunction in autism: A research note. *Journal of Child Psychology and Psychiatry*, **37**, 229–35.

Hughes, C. and Russell, J. (1993). Autistic children's difficulty with mental disengagement from an object: Its implications for theories of autism. *Developmental Psychology*, **29**, 498–510.

Hughes, C., Russell, J., and Robbins, T. R. (1994). Evidence for executive dysfunction in autism. *Neuropsychologia*, **32**, 477–92.

Huttenlocher, J. and Higgins, E. T. (1978). Issues in the study of symbolic development. In *Minnesota symposia on child psychology*, Vol. 11 (ed. W. A. Collins), pp. 98–140. Erlbaum, Hillsdale, NJ.

Jackowitz, E. R. and Watson, M. W. (1980). Development of object transformations in early pretend play. *Developmental Psychology*, 16, 543–9.

Jarrold C. (1993). An investigation into the pretend play shown by children with autism. Unpublished PhD thesis, University of Sheffield, UK.

Jarrold, C., Boucher, J., and Smith, P. K. (1993). Symbolic play in autism: A review. *Journal of Autism and Developmental Disorders*, 23, 281–307.

Jarrold, C., Boucher, J., and Smith, P. K. (1994a). Executive function deficits and the pretend play of children with autism: A research note. *Journal of Child Psychology and Psychiatry*, 35, 1473–82.

Jarrold, C., Carruthers, P., Smith, P. K., and Boucher, J. (1994b). Pretend play: Is it metarepresentational? *Mind and Language*, 9, 445–68.

Jarrold, C., Smith, P., Boucher, J., and Harris, P. (1994c). Comprehension of pretense in children with autism. *Journal of Autism and Developmental Disorders*, 24, 433–55.

Jarrold, C., Boucher, J. and Smith, P. K. (1996). Generativity deficits in pretend play in autism. *British Journal of Developmental Psychology*, 14, 275–300.

Jenkins, I. H., Brooks, D. J., Nixon, P. D., Frackowiak, R. S. J., and Passingham, R. E. (1994). Motor sequence learning: A study with positron emission tomography. *The Journal of Neuroscience*, 14, 3665–790.

Kavanaugh, R. D. and Harris, P. L. (1994). Imagining the outcome of pretend transformations: Assessing the competence of normal children and children with autism. *Developmental Psychology*, 30, 847–54.

Kimberg, D. Y. and Farah, M. J. (1993). A unified account of cognitive impairments following frontal lobe damage: The role of working memory in complex, organized behavior. *Journal of Experimental Psychology: General*, 122, 411–28.

Leslie, A. M. (1987). Pretence and representation: The origins of 'theory of mind'. *Psychological Review*, 94, 412–26.

Leslie, A. M. (1988). Some implications of pretence for mechanisms underlying the child's theory of mind. In *Developing theories of mind* (ed. J. W. Astington, P. L. Harris, and D. R. Olson), pp. 19–46. Cambridge University Press.

Leslie, A. M. and Frith, U. (1988). Autistic children's understanding of seeing, knowing and believing. *British Journal of Developmental Psychology*, 6, 315–24.

Leslie, A. M. and Frith, U. (1990). Prospects for a cognitive neuropsychology of autism: Hobson's choice. *Psychological Review*, 97, 122–31.

Leslie, A. M. and Roth, D. (1993). What autism teaches us about metarepresentation. In *Understanding other minds: Perspectives from autism* (ed. S. Baron-Cohen, H. Tager-Flusberg, and D. Cohen), 83–111. Oxford University Press.

Leslie, A. M. and Thaiss, L. (1992). Domain specificity in conceptual development: Neuropsychological evidence from autism. *Cognition*, 43, 225–51.

Levine, D. S., Leven, S. J., and Prueitt, P. S. (1992). Integration, disintegration, and the frontal lobes. In *Motivation, emotion, and goal direction in neural networks* (ed. D. S. Levine and S. J. Leven), 301–35. Lawrence Erlbaum Associates, Hillsdale, NJ.

Lewis, V. and Boucher, J. (1988). Spontaneous, instructed and elicited play in relatively able autistic children. *British Journal of Developmental Psychology*, 6, 325–39.

Lewis, V. and Boucher, J. (1991). Skill, content and generative strategies in autistic children's drawings. *British Journal of Developmental Psychology*, **9**, 393–416.

Lewis, V. and Boucher, J. (1995). Generativity in the play of young people with autism. *Journal of Autism and Developmental Disorders*, **25**, 105–21.

Libby, S., Powell, S., Messer, D., and Jordan, R. (1995). Spontaneous pretend play in children with autism: a reappraisal. *Paper presented at the British Psychological Society Developmental Section Annual Conference, Glasgow*, September 1995.

Lillard, A. S. (1993). Pretend play skills and the child's theory of mind. *Child Development*, **64**, 348–71.

Lowe, M. (1975). Trends in the development of representational play in infants from one to three years—an observational study. *Journal of Child Psychology and Psychiatry*, **16**, 33–47.

MacKay, D. M. (1978). The dynamics of perception. In *Cerebral correlates of conscious experience. INSERM Symposium No. 6.* (ed. P. A. Buser and A. Rougeul-Buser), pp. 53–68. Elsevier/North-Holland Biomedical Press.

Mundy, P., Sigman, M., Ungerer, J., and Sherman, T. (1986). Defining the social deficits of autism: The contribution of non-verbal communication measures. *Journal of Child Psychology and Psychiatry*, **27**, 657–69.

Norman, D. A. and Shallice, T. (1986). Attention to action: Willed and automatic control of behaviour. In *Consciousness and self-regulation* (ed. R. J. Davidson, G. E. Schwartz, and D. Shapiro), pp. 1–18. Plenum, NY.

Orgogozo, J. M. and Larsen, B. (1979). Activation of the supplementary motor area during voluntary movement in man suggests it works as a supramotor area. *Science*, **206**, 847–50.

Ozonoff, S., Pennington, B. F., and Rogers, S. J. (1991). Executive function deficits in high-functioning autistic individuals: Relationship to theory of mind. *Journal of Child Psychology and Psychiatry*, **32**, 1081–105.

Ozonoff, S., Strayer, D. L., McMahon, W. M., and Filloux, F. (1994). Executive function abilities in autism and Tourette syndrome: An information processing approach. *Journal of Child Psychology and Psychiatry*, **35**, 1015–32.

Passingham, R. E. (1993). *The frontal lobes and voluntary action.* Oxford University Press.

Passingham, R. E., Chen, Y. C., and Thaler, D. (1989). Supplementary motor cortex and self-initiated movement. In *Neural programming* (ed. M. Ito), pp. 13–24. Karger, Basel.

Pennington, B. F. (1994). The working memory function of the prefrontal cortices: Implications for developmental and individual differences in cognition. In *Future oriented processes in development* (ed. M. M. Haith, J. Benson, R. Roberts, and B. F. Pennington), pp. 243–89. University of Chicago Press.

Pennington, B. F. and Ozonoff, S. (1996). Executive functions and developmental psychopathology. *Journal of Child Psychology and Psychiatry*, **37**, 51–87.

Perner, J. (1991). *Understanding the representational mind.* MIT Press/Bradford Books, Cambridge, MA.

Perner, J., Frith, U., Leslie, A. M., and Leekam, S. R. (1989). Exploration of the autistic child's theory of mind: Knowledge, belief and communication. *Child Development*, **60**, 689–700.

Petersen, S. E., Fox, P. T., Posner, M. I., Mintun, M., and Raichle, M. E. (1988). Positron emission tomographic studies of the cortical anatomy of single-word processing. *Nature*, **331**, 585–9.

Piaget, J. (1962). *Play, dreams and imitation in childhood*. Routledge and Kegan Paul, London.

Prior, M. and Hoffman, W. (1990). Brief report: Neuropsychological testing of autistic children through an exploration with frontal lobe tests. *Journal of Autism and Developmental Disorders*, **20**, 581–90.

Pylyshyn, Z. W. (1978). When is attribution of beliefs justified? *Behavioural and Brain Sciences*, **1**, 592–3.

Riguet, C. B., Taylor, N. D., Benaroya, S., and Klein, L. S. (1981). Symbolic play in autistic, Down's and normal children of equivalent mental age. *Journal of Autism and Developmental Disorders*, **11**, 439–48.

Roland, P. E., Larsen, B., Lassen, N. A., and Skinhøj, E. (1980). Supplementary motor area and other cortical areas in organization of voluntary movements in man. *Journal of Neurophysiology*, **43**, 118–36.

Roland, P. E., Meyer, E., Shibasaki, T., Yamamoto, Y. L., and Thompson, C. J. (1982). Regional cerebral blood flow changes in cortex and basal ganglia during voluntary movements in normal human volunteers. *Journal of Neurophysiology*, **48**, 467–80.

Rumsey, J. M. (1985). Conceptual problem-solving in highly verbal nonretarded autistic men. *Journal of Autism and Developmental Disorders*, **15**, 23–36.

Rumsey, J. M. and Hamburger, S. D. (1988). Neuropsychological findings in high-functioning men with infantile autism, residual state. *Journal of Clinical and Experimental Neuropsychology*, **10**, 201–21.

Rumsey, J. M. and Hamburger, S. D. (1990). Neuropsychological divergence of high-level autism and severe dyslexia. *Journal of Autism and Developmental Disorders*, **20**, 155–68.

Russell, J. (1996). *Agency: its role in mental development*. Erlbaum (UK) Taylor and Francis, Hove.

Russell, J., Mauthner, N., Sharpe, S., and Tidswell, T. (1991). The 'windows task' as a measure of strategic deception in preschoolers and autistic subjects. *British Journal of Developmental Psychology*, **9**, 331–49.

Russell, J., Jarrold, C., and Henry, L. (1996). Working memory in autism. *Journal of Child Psychology and Psychiatry*, **37**, 673–86.

Scott, F. J. and Baron-Cohen, S. (1996). Imagining real and unreal things: evidence of a dissociation in autism. *Journal of Cognitive Neuroscience*, **8**, 371–82.

Shallice, T. (1988). *From Neuropsychology to Mental Structure*. Cambridge University Press.

Shallice, T. (1994). Multiple levels of control processes. *Attention and Performance*, **15**, 395–420.

Shallice, T. and Burgess, P. (1991). Higher-cognitive impairments and frontal lobe lesions in man. In *Frontal lobe function and dysfunction* (ed. H. S. Levin, H. M. Eisenberg, and A. L. Benton), pp. 125–38. Oxford University Press.

Sigman, M. and Ungerer, J. A. (1984). Cognitive and language skills in autistic, mentally retarded, and normal children. *Developmental Psychology*, **20**, 293–302.

Szatmari, P., Tuff, L., Finlayson, M. A. J., and Bartolucci, G. (1990). Asperger's syndrome and autism: Neurocognitive aspects. *Journal of the American Academy of Child and Adolescent Psychiatry*, **29**, 130–6.

Thaler, D., Chen, Y.-C., Nixon, P. D., Stern, C. E., and Passingham, R. E. (1995).

The functions of the medial premotor cortex: I. Simple learned movements. *Experimental Brain Research*, **102**, 445–60.

Turner, M. (1995a). Repetitive behaviour and generation of ideas in high functioning individuals with autism: Is there a link? *Paper presented at the Society for Research in Child Development, Biennial conference, Indianapolis*. March, 1995.

Turner, M. (1995b). *Stereotyped behaviour in autism*. Unpublished PhD thesis, University of Cambridge, UK.

Ungerer, J. A. and Sigman, M. (1981). Symbolic play and language comprehension in autistic children. *Journal of the American Academy of Child Psychiatry*, **20**, 318–37.

Ungerer, J. A., Zelazo, P. R., Kearsley, R. B., and O'Leary, K. (1981). Developmental changes in the representation of objects in symbolic play from 18 to 34 months of age. *Child Development*, **52**, 186–95.

Vygotsky, L. S. (1966). Play and its role in the mental development of the child. *Soviet Psychology*, **12**, 62–76.

Watson, M. W. and Fischer, K. W. (1977). A developmental sequence of agent use in late infancy. *Child Development*, **48**, 828–36.

Wing, L. (1978). Social, behavioural, and cognitive characteristics: An epidemiological approach. In *Autism, a reappraisal of concepts and treatment* (ed. M. Rutter and E. Schopler), pp. 27–45. Plenum, NY.

Wing, L., Gould, J., Yates, S. R., and Brierley, L. M. (1977). Symbolic play in severely mentally retarded and in autistic children. *Journal of Child Psychology and Psychiatry*, **18**, 167–78.

PART III

The nature and the uniqueness of the executive deficits in autism

5 Validity tests of the executive dysfunction hypothesis of autism

Bruce F. Pennington, Sally J. Rogers, Loisa Bennetto, Elizabeth McMahon Griffith, D.Taffy Reed, and Vivian Shyu

The goal of this chapter is to examine the validity of the hypothesis that executive dysfunction is the primary psychological cause of autism. We will: (1) review earlier work by our group that supports this hypothesis; (2) define executive functions and elaborate the executive dysfunction hypothesis; (3) present four recent validity tests of this hypothesis conducted by our group; and (4) consider metatheoretical issues that bear on the search for the primary psychological cause of this disorder.

Throughout this chapter we will also consider the validity of the main rival to the executive dysfunction hypothesis, namely the theory of mind or metarepresentational hypothesis, which has been elaborated by Baron Cohen (1988), Leslie (1987), and Morton and Frith (1995). We will see that neither hypothesis passes all the validity tests considered here, leading us to consider the metatheoretical issues mentioned above.

Earlier work supporting executive dysfunction

Over the past several years, there has been a substantial amount of empirical work focusing on executive functions in autism. Other chapters in this book and recent reviews (e.g. Pennington and Ozonoff 1996) document clearly that there are striking deficits on measures of executive functions in groups with autism. These deficits have been found in cross-sectional studies relative to both normal and developmentally disabled controls matched to the group with autism on IQ. Across studies, the average effect size (d)[1] of these group differences is about 1.00 (Pennington and Ozonoff 1996), which qualifies as a large effect (Cohen 1988). These deficits are also pervasive within the groups with autism that have been studied; they have been found in individuals both with and without mental retardation (MR); and they are found across a broad age range. All these results make it clear that executive dysfunction deficits need to be taken seriously in any comprehensive cognitive account of this disorder.

Our series of investigations into the executive function capacities of persons with autism began with an examination of the relationships between theory of mind and executive function performance in a group of high-functioning adolescents with autism and a clinical control group. In a set of studies by Sally Ozonoff, Bruce Pennington, and Sally Rogers, the relationship between theory of mind performance and executive function performance was established. Indeed, it was the (rather unexpected) power of these findings that motivated us to pursue the line of work described in this chapter.

In the first study (Ozonoff *et al.* 1991a), a group of 23 high-functioning people with autism, aged 8 to 20 years, was compared to a clinical control group of 20 subjects with various developmental disorders, particularly Attention Deficit Hyperactivity Disorder (ADHD) and dyslexia, matched on CA (chronological age), verbal IQ, SES, and sex. The subjects were compared on first- and second-order theory of mind tasks, emotion perception, executive function, and verbal memory tasks, as well as discriminant tasks involving spatial abilities and other control tasks. We hypothesized that the autistic group would be most impaired relative to controls on the theory of mind tasks, given the strong empirical support in the literature, and we expected to find that executive function deficits and emotion perception deficits would be secondary symptoms appearing in a subset of the subjects with autism. However, the findings did not support the primacy of theory of mind. Instead, we found that executive function deficits and second-order theory of mind deficits were significantly more widespread among the subjects with autism than were other deficits, and that only a subset of these subjects demonstrated a deficit in first-order theory of mind. Moreover, there were significant correlations (0.50 and 0.64) between first- and second-order theory of mind measures and an executive function composite score, which was the most potent discriminator of subjects with autism from controls.

The second study (Ozonoff *et al.* 1991b) split the autistic group into two: a group with Asperger's syndrome and a group with high-functioning autism (HFA). These two groups were then compared to the clinical control group, which had also been split in two and matched to the Asperger's and HFA groups. The HFA and the Asperger's groups differed in their deficit profiles when compared to their matched groups, with the Asperger's group demonstrating *no* theory of mind deficit. The only area in which both groups from the autism spectrum were deficient was in executive function. If we believe that the HFA and the Asperger's groups both lie on the autistic spectrum, then they should share the same primary deficit. The universality of the executive function deficits in both groups suggested that it might be a primary deficit in autism.

The third study (Ozonoff *et al.* 1993) examined the executive function and theory of mind performance of the subjects' siblings from the above two studies. No group differences on theory of mind tasks were found. However, three different analyses of the executive function measures provided convergent support for a potential subclinical marker in the executive function domain, and performance on the Tower of Hanoi task revealed significant differences between the groups correctly classifying 75% of both groups. However, the effect sizes on all measures were small, demonstrating a lack of power of these measures when used with non-impaired groups.

In summary, across our first three studies of executive function, we found (1) a close relationship between executive function and theory of mind, and (2) greater universality for the executive function deficit, leading us to consider the possibility that executive dysfunction is primary in autism and may account for theory of mind deficits.

There are two related, but distinguishable, ways in which the executive dysfunction hypothesis accounts for the intersubjectivity or theory of mind deficit in autism. One is that both executive functions and these aspects of early social cognition may rely on a frontally mediated, working memory system, which is important for integrating contextual cues over time and selectively and strategically shifting attentional set in response to context (Pennington 1994a). The other possibility is that many theory of mind tasks may really be executive function tasks. Russell *et al.* (1991) found a significantly higher rate of perseverative responding in an autistic group on the strategic deception task originally proposed by Premack and Woodruff (1978) to measure theory of mind in non-human primates. To evaluate whether an autistic individual's failure was caused by a theory of mind deficit or just by the inability to shift the cognitive set away from a present (and salient) stimulus, Russell and colleagues conducted several follow-up experiments (Hughes and Russell 1993; Russell *et al.* 1994). In one experiment, they manipulated the design to find whether the task required deception and whether the subjects' response was manual or verbal, maintaining the key feature that success on the task required a response to a salient, visible reward to be inhibited. They found that both autistic individuals and normal 3- (but not 4-) year-olds continued to fail the task in a perseverative manner. In another experiment, they found a similar problem with mental disengagement on an object retrieval task that did not involve theory of mind or deception (Hughes and Russell 1993, experiment 2).

Thus, failure on theory of mind tasks can be caused by an executive function deficit and not by a lack of understanding of others' minds. That is, most theory of mind tasks (like many Piagetian tasks) are conflict tasks. Failure on such tests may be caused either by a lack of the relevant concept or just by executive or strategic problems in conflict resolution.

Russell's work demonstrates that when the theory of mind component is removed but the element of conflict is maintained, both autistic subjects and young children still fail the task. A similar result has been obtained by Moore *et al.* (1995) in a study of a conflicting desire task in normally developing children. Taken together, the results from these two research groups support the hypothesis that performance on theory of mind tasks is related to a domain-general cognitive process, the executive function of inhibitory control, rather than to a domain-specific cognitive process, such as the expression-raiser postulated by Leslie (1987).

Although these findings question the primacy of the theory of mind deficit in autism, we still do not have convincing evidence that executive dysfunction is the proximal, cognitive *cause* of autism. While the results discussed above are consistent with that hypothesis, there are a number of possible threats to the validity of the executive dysfunction hypothesis. In this chapter, we will review these possible threats by presenting several of our recent studies that were designed to address these issues directly. Before presenting these studies, we will outline what we mean by the term 'executive functions' and how we understand executive dysfunction as a possible primary, cognitive cause of autism.

Elaborating the executive dysfunction hypothesis

Specifying the executive dysfunction hypothesis is important, because the scope of the term 'executive functions' can be quite broad, and different researchers have different notions of what the executive dysfunction hypothesis is. For instance, some proponents of a theory of mind theory of autism seem to believe that intact performance on the 'false-photo' task (Leekam and Perner 1991; Leslie and Thaiss 1992) rejects executive dysfunction as an explanation for impaired performance on standard theory of mind tasks. It does, but only if one narrowly defines the executive component of the false-photo and theory of mind tasks as inhibiting a response based on the most recent perceptual information (see also Russell, this volume). However, the two tasks also differ in their working memory requirements, in that the complexity of the mental representation that must be maintained in the face of new competing perceptual information differs across the two tasks. First of all, the test question across the two tasks differs in its syntactic complexity. There is an embedded clause in the false-belief task (What colour does Susan think Judy is?), but only a prepositional phrase in the false-photo task (In the picture, what colour is Judy?). Second, the camera and the photograph themselves are perceptually salient to the subjects in a way that the inferred beliefs of a doll or confederate are not. Finally, as discussed by Leekam and Perner (1991), the 'false' photo is not false at all. Unlike the doll with a false belief, it does not misrepresent current reality because it is not in the nature of cameras to make reference to current reality. So, opposite performance profiles between older children with autism and younger normal children could be explained by working memory and/or language deficits in the children with autism along with a greater understanding of a camera (due to their age).

Roberts *et al.* (1994) proposed that the probability of making an erroneous, but prepotent, response depends on the interaction of working memory demands and the strength of the prepotency; in fact, they demonstrated experimentally that manipulating working memory load dramatically alters the ease of inhibition, even in normal adults. So, unless the false-photo and theory of mind tasks were equated on *all* executive requirements, not just inhibition, an executive deficit would remain a competing explanation.

So what do we mean by the concept of executive functions? The empirical concept of executive functions derives mainly from research on patients and experimental animals with lesions to the prefrontal cortex, especially lesions to its dorsolateral portion. Such lesions generally disrupt the planning and execution of complex behaviours without disrupting more basic perceptual, motor, or mnemonic processes. The term 'executive functions' has been adopted as an umbrella term to refer to the cognitive processes involved in the planning and execution of complex behaviour, without necessarily specifying what those processes are more precisely. The term is also used even more broadly to refer to all behaviours disrupted by prefrontal lesions. Both uses lack theoretical precision.

Although the lists of symptoms and impaired tasks associated with prefrontal lesions can appear bewildering in their diversity, encouraging progress has been made in explaining this surface diversity with a few underlying cognitive processes. As just discussed, one such approach, called the interactive framework, posits that response selection in a given context depends on the interaction between the prepotency of various contending responses and the strength of working memory representations, which activate some responses and inhibit others (Roberts and Pennington 1996; Roberts *et al.* 1994). Hence, working memory representations provide constraints on action selection; these constraints may arise from immediate perception or from memory and may include goals and subgoals. This interactive approach is based on computational models of tasks impaired by prefrontal lesions (Cohen and Servan-Schreiber 1992; Kimberg and Farah 1993) and on the seminal work of Goldman-Rakic (1987a,b).

A related, although divergent, conception of executive function is presented in the work of Duncan and colleagues (Duncan 1995; Duncan *et al.* 1996), who describe the disruption of coherent, goal-directed behaviour after frontal lesions, especially in situations of novelty or weak environmental support. They introduced the term *goal neglect* to describe one aspect of behaviour after frontal lesions, namely disregard of a goal that has been understood and which is necessary for successful task performance. They also developed a simple experimental measure of goal neglect; patients with frontal lesions as well as normal individuals with lower fluid intelligence scores were impaired on this measure. The interactive framework would explain goal neglect as arising either from excessive demands on working memory, prepotency of salient but incorrect responses, or some combination of the two.

So, we are saying that executive dysfunction is basically a disruption in the planning and execution of complex behaviour due to limitations in working memory, or perhaps in some cases, to a specific inhibitory deficit.

Returning to autism, our executive dysfunction hypothesis is that in individuals with autism there is a severe, early disruption in the planning of complex behaviour, due to a severe deficit in working memory. Because this deficit occurs very early in development, it disrupts not only the planning of behaviour but also the acquisition and use of concepts that require the integration of information within a context and across time. Several concepts that are fundamental to social understanding require such integration. These concepts include a recognition of intentions in one's self and others, and their congruence or conflict. 'Interintentionality', as Stern (1985) proposes, is a cornerstone for theory of mind. The child's earliest experiences of inter-intentionality occur, for example, in imitative exchanges during the first months of life. A severe deficit in working memory would impair both the ability to imitate and the understanding of intentionality that arises from early imitative exchanges.

So, our executive dysfunction hypothesis could account for deficits in: (1) imitation; (2) joint attention; (3) theory of mind; and (4) symbolic play, which builds on both imitation and an understanding of goal-directed behaviour. It would also explain the motor stereotypies and behavioural rituals as practised, prepotent reactions that are not inhibited by a working memory representation of a more abstract goal for behaviour. Restricted and specialized interests would have a similar explanation. In addition, concreteness, inflexibility, and an impairment in discourse would all be readily explained by an executive dysfunction hypothesis. So, the executive dysfunction hypothesis has the potential to account for all the main symptoms of autism.

In what follows, we present four validity tests, being performed by our research group, of this executive dysfunction hypothesis of autism. Each of these tests has the potential to reject the executive dysfunction hypothesis, but none has the potential to confirm it. The four validity tests are listed below.

1. Are there executive deficits in a different cognitive domain?
2. Does executive dysfunction underlie other deficits in autism, such as those in joint attention and imitation?
3. Is executive dysfunction found very early in the development of children with autism?
4. Can the executive dysfunction theory be subsumed by another prominent cognitive theory, the central coherence theory?

The sections which follow address each validity test in turn. We will conclude with implications for future research.

Are there executive deficits in a different cognitive domain?

The studies reviewed in this and other chapters suggest that there may be a neuropsychological analogy, both in terms of test performance and symptoms, between individuals with autism and patients with frontal lobe lesions. How far can we extend this analogy? If we cannot extend it to a different domain, then the executive dysfunction hypothesis would be threatened. Instead of having primary underlying executive dysfunction that should affect performance in many domains, such an outcome would indicate that individuals with autism have executive problems that may be secondary or correlated with some other primary deficit.

Various cognitive domains could be chosen for this validity test, including discourse processes and motor planning or praxis, but we chose the domain of memory because there is a well-developed body of concepts, tasks, and results in that domain that allow one to test whether memory performance in autism is like that exhibited by patients with frontal lesions.

In this study (Bennetto *et al.* 1996), we conducted a comprehensive assessment of memory performance in autism, and examined whether individuals with autism demonstrate a pattern of memory performance similar to that observed in patients with frontal lesions. Similar patterns of memory performance would demonstrate an additional link between the cognitive deficits of individuals with autism and patients with frontal lesions, and would be consistent with the executive dysfunction hypothesis of autism.

Frontal lobe pathology is associated with a specific profile of memory dysfunction, which is distinct from the pattern of deficits associated with traditional limbic amnesia (Shimamura *et al.* 1991). This profile leads to specific predictions about how individuals with autism should behave if they have frontal deficits. In particular, patients with frontal lesions exhibit deficits on tasks that involve the organization, monitoring, or sequencing of information, including tasks that measure memory for temporal order, source memory, and free recall. Moscovitch (1994) has coined the term 'working with memory' to refer to these executive processes utilized by the memory system. In contrast, patients with frontal lesions are typically unimpaired on learning new information or recognition memory, which rely primarily on effective storage and consolidation of declarative information.

Memory and executive functions were tested in a sample of high-functioning adolescents with autism ($n = 18$). Their performance was compared to a sample of clinical comparison subjects, who were matched on age and verbal IQ. The groups were likewise similar in full-scale and performance IQ, gender ratio, and handedness.

The results of this study show that across a variety of memory tasks, subjects with autism demonstrated a pattern of memory functions similar to that observed in patients with frontal lesions. This pattern included impairment on temporal order memory, supraspan verbal learning, and the inability to maintain the appropriate context of the information they had learned (as demonstrated by source memory errors, among other things). In addition, subjects with autism showed a significant impairment on two standard executive function tasks, the Wisconsin Card Sorting Task and the Tower of Hanoi. In contrast, the subjects with autism were unimpaired on measures of short- and long-term recognition, cued recall, or new learning ability.

In particular, people with autism demonstrated a differential deficit in temporal order memory compared to recognition memory on an adaptation of the Corsi Memory Task (Milner *et al.* 1991). Memory for temporal order requires the organization of distinct memories and the retention of their temporal relationship to each other. This task provided a particularly strong test of differential deficit: a within-task manipulation, in which the contrasting conditions were equal in difficulty and variability in a normal population. In this task, words or pictures are presented singly on cards for the subject to remember. Periodically, there are probe trials in which two items are presented, one on top of the other on the same card separated by a question mark. The subject's task on each probe trial is the same, regardless of whether it is a recognition or a temporal order trial. Specifically, the subject must decide which of the two items appeared more recently. However, in recognition trials, only one of the two items has appeared before in the test, so the recency judgement is actually based on recognition memory. We found a significant group by condition-interaction effect on this task for words, such that the group with autism was significantly worse than controls on the temporal order condition but not on the recognition memory condition. This result provides strong evidence for a specific deficit in temporal order (or recency) memory in autism, at least for verbal stimuli. Since working memory functions are thought to be subserved by the prefrontal cortex (Goldman-Rakic 1987a,b), while other memory operations are not, this study provides further evidence of specific deficits in executive function in individuals with autism.

The subjects were also given the California Verbal Learning Test (CVLT; Delis *et al.* 1986), which measures learning and retention of verbal information, and provides information on learning processes, strategies, and patterns of errors. On this task, subjects with autism demonstrated a flatter learning curve across the initial learning trials than control children. While the two groups' performances were similar on early learning trials, subjects with autism were unable to increase their span on the last two trials. This may reflect the decreased ability of subjects with autism to use strategic organization or planning in recall. Furthermore, the pattern of errors made by children with autism on both recall and recognition trials of the CVLT is consistent with a deficit in source memory, in so far as the subjects with autism made more intrusion errors than the controls on recall trials. The nature of their intrusion errors reflected a failure to use the context of the current list to constrain responses. They recalled more words that had appeared on a previous but no longer correct list, and tended to recall words that were semantically similar to the target list. Similarly, subjects with autism endorsed significantly more false-positive items than controls on the recognition trial. They tended to endorse false-positive items that were semantically similar to the target list, but they did not endorse unrelated false-positive items. This pattern of errors suggests that previous exposure to target words primed the appropriate semantic categories, but the subjects with autism failed to use the context of the current task to deselect inappropriate responses. Finally, subjects with autism demonstrated intact performance on a digit span task, which measured auditory, verbal short-term memory.

Across a variety of cognitive tasks, subjects with autism have demonstrated a marked difficulty in maintaining and utilizing appropriate context. We hypothesized that this pattern of memory and executive function impairment is likely to reflect a more general deficit in working memory (WM). WM refers to the simultaneous processing and storage of information during complex cognitive tasks. WM permits one to solve problems that are transient, context-specific, and require the integration of information over space or time.

So, the results of this first validity test are positive. The executive dysfunction hypothesis can predict performance in a different cognitive domain. As mentioned previously, this kind of validity test could also be performed in other cognitive domains known to be affected in distinct ways by frontal lesions. Moreover, it is not clear how the theory of mind hypothesis would account for the 'frontal' memory deficits found in this study.

We next turn to the question of whether executive dysfunction can account for other deficits found in autism, specifically those in joint attention and imitation.

Does executive dysfunction underlie other deficits in autism?

After discovering a relationship between executive dysfunction and theory of mind deficits, which was discussed earlier, we then examined the relationship between executive dysfunction and earlier-developing aspects of social communication, including both joint attention and reciprocal social inter- action (McEvoy *et al.* 1993), and imitation and pantomime skills (Rogers *et al.* 1996). Since children with autism have deficits in these aspects of early social communication, and since there is evidence for the presence of some of these deficits by 12 months of age in the development of children with autism (Osterling and Dawson 1994), a successful theory of the primary psycholo- gical cause of autism must be able to show how that cause leads to these deficits in early social communication. Since the developmental onset of theory of mind (between the ages of 3 and 4 years) comes much later than these aspects of early social communication, the theory of mind theory must incorporate these early deficits as precursors or early indicators of the same underlying cognitive problem that causes deficits on theory of mind tasks. Likewise, the executive dysfunction theory must demonstrate that these deficits can be related to executive dysfunction, and that executive deficits appear early enough in the development of autism to cause these social communication deficits. In this section, we will examine whether these early social communication deficits can be related to executive dysfunction.

One of the most well-established deficits in young children with autism involves joint attention (Mundy *et al.* 1986), which refers to the coordination between a child's attention and his or her social partner's attention *vis-a-vis* an interesting event. Joint attention skills are demonstrated when a child follows another's point and searches for the interesting spectacle, or when a child holds up a toy and commands the mother's attention to the toy, or when a child, watching an interesting spectacle with a parent, looks back and forth from the spectacle to the parent's face. In normally developing children, the period of development of early executive function skills, such as performance on the A not B task and detour reaching, coincides with the period of development of joint attention skills, hence, it is possible that frontal lobe maturation might underlie the development of joint attention capacities (Butterworth and Grover 1988).

In order to test this possibility, we designed a study to examine the joint attention, social communication, and executive function skills of a group of young children with autism, aged 3 to 6. We compared them to two control groups: a group of children with developmental disabilities matched on non- verbal cognitive abilities, CA, and SES to the group with autism; and a group of normally developing children matched on verbal abilities and SES to the group with autism. A completely non-verbal executive function battery was designed by Robin McEvoy, based on existing work from both infant and primate studies. This battery covered a developmental range of 7 months to 6 years, and was piloted on a large group of normally developing children. Social-communicative behaviours were studied through the use of the Early Social Communication Skills or ESCS (Seibert *et al*. 1987)—this uses a semistructured play interview to elicit non-verbal communication for the purpose of regulating behaviour, establishing joint attention, and establishing and maintaining social interaction.

The group with autism demonstrated deficits in both joint attention and social interaction in comparison to both control groups, with joint attention being the most severely affected. The group with autism also showed significant deficits on spatial reversal, the one executive function task which had neither ceiling nor floor effects; they made significantly more perseverative responses than either control group on this task. When the relationship between the spatial reversal task and the social communicative behaviours was examined, significant correlations were found for both joint attention and social interaction for all three groups of children. While several interpretations of those relationships could be made, the interpretation which seemed to best fit both these data and other findings was that executive function skills, like working memory and inhibition, appear to underlie performance on social cognitive tasks in both normal development and in developmental psychopathology. These social cognitive tasks include joint attention and the maintenance of a reciprocal social interaction, including topic maintenance.

The second well-documented autism-specific deficit area that we have studied in relation to executive function involves imitation and pantomime skills. Unlike the relatively recent interest in theory of mind and joint attention, documentation of an imitation deficit in autism goes back to the early 1970s and has been replicated many times over the past 20 years. However, little theoretical importance was attached to these findings until recently. Both Dawson (Dawson 1991; Dawson and Lewy 1989) and Hobson (1993) discussed the possible significance of these imitation deficits in autism. Rogers and Pennington (1991) proposed a theoretical model of autism based on Stern's (1985) account of the normal development of intersubjectivity during the first year of life, which highlights imitation as the earliest example of reciprocal social exchanges in infancy. In the Rogers and Pennington (1991) model, autism is explained by a deficit in the formation and coordination of self–other representations which is postulated to undermine neonatal imitation, as well as other early social exchanges, thus leading to a failure in the development of intersubjectivity. A somewhat similar model for the development of autism was proposed by Meltzoff and Gopnik (1993). In the Rogers and Pennington paper, a possible relationship between imitation capacities and executive function abilities was also described.

We have recently completed a study of imitation and pantomime abilities (Rogers *et al.* 1996) in a group of 17 high-functioning adolescents with autism and a clinical control group of 15 subjects matched on SES, CA, and verbal IQ and made up mostly of subjects with ADHD and dyslexia. We tested two alternative hypotheses for the basis of the imitation and pantomime deficits found in previous studies of autism, namely a symbolic deficit hypothesis and an executive deficit hypothesis. Baron-Cohen (1988) hypothesized that imitation deficits are secondary to an underlying symbolic deficit related to the postulated primary metarepresentational deficit, whereas Rogers and Pennington (1991) proposed that they are secondary to an underlying executive deficit. The symbolic deficit hypothesis predicts differential impairment in subjects with autism on the imitation of meaningful gestures, whereas the executive deficit hypothesis predicts differential impairment on the imitation of sequential gestures, because imitating a sequence of movements requires more executive control. Therefore, we manipulated both memory and sequence in facial and manual imitation tasks; we also manipulated sequence in the pantomime tasks. Recognition memory and motor control tasks were matched to the experimental tasks.

The results provided no support for the symbolic deficit hypothesis in so far as meaning *aided* rather than hindered the performance of the group with autism. Deficits in non-meaningful imitation are difficult for the metarepresentational theory of autism to explain; while imitation does require some mental representation of the target movement, it does not require a metarepresentation.

There was partial support for the executive dysfunction hypothesis. The predicted Group × Sequence interaction effect was found: (1) across the meaningful conditions of the hand experiment, but not across the non-meaningful ones, resulting in a Group × Sequence × Meaning interaction; (2) in the pantomime experiment; but (3) not in the face experiment. Moreover, there were significant group differences on two non-sequential tasks: the non-meaningful, single-hand condition and the single pantomime condition. One could argue *post-hoc* that even the single movements on which there were group differences exceeded the working memory capacities of these subjects with autism; however, testing that hypothesis will require an experiment in which working memory requirements are manipulated within non-sequential imitation tasks.

Overall, the performance of subjects with autism reflected rather widespread deficits in imitation and pantomime. Imitation and pantomime tasks are considered classic tasks of praxis. (Praxis refers to the capacity for consciously formulating and then executing an intentional motor plan in a particular context, a capacity not necessary for conditioned, automatic, or reflexive movement patterns (Ayres 1985; Heilman 1979). Deficits involving both face and hand imitations and pantomime are commonly found in dyspraxic, neurologically impaired adults (DeRenzi *et al.* 1980; Kimura and Archibald 1974; Kolb and Milner 1981; Mateer and Kimura 1977). Indeed, the tasks used in this study are considered classic tests of praxis. Given the generalized deficits across the majority of these tasks shown by those individuals with autism, it is important to raise the question of a generalized dyspraxia in autism.

Several previous autism researchers (DeMyer *et al.* 1981; Jones and Prior 1985; Ohta 1987), presented with similar findings, have suggested that a dyspraxic deficit in autism is present and may interfere with even the simple motor activities involved in everyday life and normal non-verbal communication. A praxis hypothesis is not independent of an executive function hypothesis: executive function is involved in the execution of volitional movements, and persons with frontal lobe damage (which is generally associated with executive function deficits) demonstrate dyspraxia (Kolb and Milner 1981).

The question raised here is whether some other component of praxis, besides executive functions, are implicated in the dyspraxia found in autism. We have ruled out visual recognition memory, simple motor deficits, and motor initiation. We have not ruled out visual recall memory, but, had we ruled out a visual *recall* memory deficit, we would have, in effect, ruled out an executive deficit for the following reason. Visual recall memory in the context of imitation and pantomime tasks is not clearly distinguishable from the working memory and execution components of these tasks, which were discussed earlier. Recall memory requires the production of something in memory, in this case, a remembered action. In these tasks, production of a remembered action required holding the representation of the action in working memory while executing the action. Thus, it seems unparsimonious to postulate separate constructs of recall memory and working memory in the context of imitation and pantomime tasks.

We cannot totally exclude the possibility of a low-level motor impairment which makes complex motor tasks such as these differentially difficult. We cannot exclude a deficit in the cross-modal match between model and self that is required in imitation tasks (Meltzoff and Gopnik 1993), although the lack of group differences in several of our experimental conditions argues against a complete absence of the ability to form such cross-modal correspondences. Thus, more research is needed to specify the mechanisms underlying the imitation and pantomime deficit in autism.

Finally, our finding of a pantomime deficit, and the similarity between pantomime tasks and symbolic play, point to an important weakness in the explanation of the symbolic play deficits in autism provided by the metarepresentational theory. When a child represents an object in play that is not present, the child is pantomiming a movement with a substitute object or an imaginary object. In the pantomime condition in this study we are, in fact, asking subjects to *pretend* that they are ironing, drumming, etc. Since we also found deficits in the imitation of actions which do not involve representation of objects, but only require representation of body movements, it is possible that the symbolic play deficit in autism may have more to do with the representation and execution of body movements—with praxis—than with actions specifically focused on symbolized objects, contrary to the meta-representational hypothesis. In a similar vein, Jarrold *et al.* (1996) have provided evidence that a generativity deficit underlies the pretend play deficit in autism, rather than an inability to produce or understand pretence because of a metarepresentational deficit.

In summary, our research programme has systematically examined several major deficits in autism in relation to executive function performance. We have found significant relationships between executive function perfor-mance, on the one hand, and joint attention, reciprocal social interaction, and imitation, on the other, in addition to the significant relationships with the theory of mind discussed earlier.

These results, especially the imitation and pantomime results, also chal-lenge the metarepresentational theory of autism. However, some aspects of the imitation results go beyond the predictions of the executive dysfunction theory; hence, further work is needed to analyse the basis of the imitation and pantomime deficits in autism. Moreover, all the results thus far are cross-sectional; while executive dysfunction is correlated with various other key deficits in autism, we do not know if it precedes and predicts those deficits. That question is the focus of the next section.

Are there very early executive deficits?

The executive dysfunction hypothesis of autism is based on the premise that executive function deficits occur early in life and cause the disruption of development in other arenas, leading to the symptomatology commonly described in the diagnosis of autism. Previous studies (including ones discussed in this chapter) have investigated the relationship between execu-tive function deficits and deficits in other areas such as imitation, joint attention, and theory of mind. However, whether the executive function deficits are present in the earliest months of life prior to, or concurrent with, other defining features of autism has not yet been examined. While such a study would be extremely difficult to conduct, given the low incidence of autism in the population and the rarity of diagnosis prior to the early preschool years, few studies have even approached this issue by studying children with autism younger than school-age. Evidence of executive dys-function at early ages would greatly strengthen the case for an executive function deficit being the proximal, cognitive cause of autism, whereas evidence to the contrary would reject this hypothesis. The few studies that have examined executive function skills in very young children with autism have produced mixed results.

McEvoy *et al.* (1993) compared performance on four executive function tasks in a group of older preschoolers with autism to a developmental delay group matched on non-verbal and verbal abilities. Two tasks exhibited ceiling effects: A not B task with no delay, and Delayed Response; while a Delayed Alternation task showed floor effects. However, on the Spatial Reversal task, which had neither ceiling nor floor effects, children in the autism group made significantly more perseverative errors than controls.

This task, like the WCST, required the children to first establish and maintain a set pattern of response, and then to change the response set. A reward is hidden under one of two identical containers behind a screen, so that the child can not see the side of hiding. The child is allowed to choose a container, with no delay. The side of hiding changes only after the child makes four consecutive correct reaches. A total of 23 trials are given to each child. Scores from this task include: the number of correct responses; the number of sets of four correct reaches; the number of perseverative responses scored by WCST criteria (Heaton *et al.* 1993). This task is designed to build up a prepotent response (by keeping the side of hiding the same for four consecutive correct reaches), and then to make the person change their response pattern when the previous response is no longer successful in getting the reward, requiring inhibition of the prepotent response.

Consistent with the executive dysfunction deficit hypothesis, the children with autism in the McEvoy *et al.* (1993) study had difficulty shifting set and inhibiting the previously rewarded response, despite the fact that it was no longer productive, i.e. they perseverated on the previously correct response. The children with autism who completed this task had a mean age of 65 months, while the children in the control group were about a year younger with a mean chronological age of 51 months.

Surprisingly, a similar study of executive functions in even younger children, using three of the same tasks as in the study described above, found *no* evidence of executive function deficits in children with autism (Wehner and Rogers 1994). In this study, a group of 16 children with autism (mean age = 43 months) was compared to a developmentally delayed control group (*n* = 16; mean age = 45 months) matched on chronological age, and on verbal and non-verbal mental ages. On two tasks, A not B without a delay and Delayed Response, performance was again near ceiling. However, the two groups performed equally well, and not at ceiling or floor, on the Spatial Reversal task. This was the task which had differentiated between the two groups in the McEvoy *et al.* study.

To understand these discrepant results, we compared the performance of the two autistic groups from these studies. There is almost a 2-year chronological age difference between the two autistic groups. Surprisingly, the *older* group (in McEvoy *et al.* 1993) made more perseverative errors. This comparison raises the question of whether perseverative behaviour *increases* as children with autism grow older, a pattern opposite to normal development, for which there are data demonstrating improved performance on executive function measures as typically developing children mature (Diamond 1991; Levin *et al.* 1991: Llamas and Diamond 1991; Welsh *et al.* 1991). Although raising interesting questions about the development of executive functions in autism, this brief comparison of means must be interpreted cautiously because it is not only a cross-sectional, but also a cross-study, comparison.

Barth *et al.* (1995) have also recently completed a study in which they compared high- and low-functioning children with autism (mean ages = 63 and 65 months, respectively) to non-verbal IQ-matched controls on a Delayed Match to Sample task. They found no differences in performance on this task between the high-functioning autism group and the matched control group. Differences between the low-functioning autism group and their control group were found, but were eliminated when the data was re-analysed with non-verbal intelligence covaried out. While they interpret these results as evidence against an executive function hypothesis of autism, there is some debate in the literature regarding the correlation of this task with frontal lobe functions (Diamond *et al.*, in press); Goldman and Rosvold 1972).

The current study examined the development of performance on the Spatial Reversal task in a subset of the subjects from the Wehner and Rogers study, by re-testing them a year after the original data was collected. This study also examined the performance of young preschoolers (ages 36–60 months) on a broader range of tasks, suitable for children from infancy to early childhood, which have been linked to the functioning of the frontal cortices of the brain and meet the criteria specified in an earlier section of this chapter for tapping executive functions. These tasks require neither verbal responses nor verbal comprehension; they are designed to be self-explanatory and intrinsically motivating. They include A not B, Object Retrieval, 3-boxes stationary, 6-boxes stationary, 3-boxes scrambled, 6-boxes scrambled, A not B with invisible displacement, and Spatial Reversal (Diamond 1991; Diamond *et al.*, in press; Kaufman *et al.* 1989; Passingham 1985; Petrides and Milner 1982). Subjects are being recruited from the youngest children in the Wehner and Rogers study, so that there is some overlap in subject pool, but they are also being recruited from other sources.

For the results to support an executive dysfunction hypothesis of autism, the following pattern of findings will have to be observed:

1. The children with autism perform less well on the executive function tasks than the clinical control group, i.e. at a lower level than that expected for their mental ages. The differences in performance will increase as the executive demand of the tasks increases.
2. A significant proportion of subjects in the autism group will perform worse than the mean for the developmentally delayed group on executive function tasks.
3. On Spatial Reversal, the longitudinal trends will show an increase in performance by the developmentally delayed group, while the performance of the autism group will remain the same or decrease with age.

Preliminary results from this study are available for 18 children with autism and 17 children with developmental delays. These groups are matched on chronological age (51 months, verbal and non-verbal mental ages, and socioeconomic status. Surprisingly, analyses of the major dependent variables taken from each of the executive tasks do *not* indicate any significant differences in performance between the two groups, even on the perseveration variable from the Spatial Reversal task which differed between the groups in the McEvoy *et al.* (1993) study. However, both groups are performing below mental age expectations based on comparisons to cross-sectional, normal data from Diamond *et al.* (in press) suggesting that there are executive function deficits in children with mental retardation, irrespective of whether they have autism or not. Currently, there are not enough subjects for whom longitudinal data has been collected for us to determine the developmental trends on the Spatial Reversal task.

It is important to note, for purposes of discriminant validity, that the children with autism in this study are exhibiting joint attention deficits, another area of functioning often associated with autism. As discussed earlier, deficits in joint attention behaviours have been found across several studies of very young children with autism (Buitelaar *et al.* 1991; Mundy and Sigman 1989; Mundy *et al.* 1993). When this study is completed, information will be available on both groups' skills in the areas of executive function, joint attention, imitation, and play, allowing for comparisons as well as for an examination of the relationships among them.

Data are still being collected; however, the preliminary results appear to reject the executive dysfunction hypothesis of autism. This study addresses the question of whether executive function deficits are present early in the development of children with autism, and whether this is therefore a reasonable candidate for a primary symptom, a hypothesis called into question by the preliminary results. However, further study should be undertaken prior to the abandonment of this otherwise robust hypothesis.

One direction for future research includes examination of the types of tasks utilized in this study. Further exploration of many of these tasks is called for to confirm their ties with frontal or executive functions in the preschool years, since most of the work done in this area has focused on infants in the first year of life or adults. Another issue concerns possible domain-specificity of executive deficits in autism. The tasks used in this study were appropriate to very young children and children without language; thus the question arises of whether they were mediated by more spatially based representations of the task. Indeed, most of the tasks in this battery are considered to be classic, spatial working-memory tasks, whereas the tasks on which older subjects with autism are consistently impaired, such as the WCST and TOH, are not primarily spatial working-memory tasks, and may well depend more heavily on verbal working memory or some other executive function (Russell, this volume, for discussion). This alternative explanation predicts that older children with autism will be unimpaired on spatial working memory (which has not been tested) and that young children with autism will either be impaired on verbal working memory (which is difficult to disentangle from the general language delays found in such children) or on some other critical executive function.

Work is underway to specify further those skills involved in tasks currently grouped under the general executive function heading (Ozonoff et al. 1994; Roberts et al. 1994). Future research will need to explore this issue further to determine which, if any, of these skills are impaired early in the development of children with autism, and which adequately discriminate people with autism from other populations exhibiting executive function deficits. One hypothesis consistent with the current results is that executive function deficits (performance below MA expectation) is characteristic of mental retardation in general, but not of autism in particular.

We now turn to our final validity test, which concerns whether what we are calling executive dysfunction could be better understood as a deficit in central coherence. Central coherence is essentially global rather than local processing, processing the gist rather than the surface characteristics. So we are asking whether the construct of executive dysfunction can be replaced by the construct of weak central coherence in a theoretical account of autism. A given theoretical construct may be replaced by another if it is more parsimonious, coherent, or consistent with other theoretical constraints, even though each construct accounts for much of the same data equally well. Such theoretical replacement has occurred numerous times in the history of science.

Can the executive dysfunction theory be subsumed by the central coherence theory?

A theory of cognitive functioning in autism, referred to as the central coherence theory, has recently been proposed by U. Frith and colleagues

(Frith 1989; Frith and Happé 1994; Shah and Frith, 1983). While this theory is similar in some respects to a working memory theory of autism, it does make some fundamentally different predictions. The central coherence theory is part of a two-deficit theory, which proposes a modular theory of mind deficit along with a more global weakness in central coherence. The working memory theory, on the other hand, attempts to explain the full syndrome of autism with a single deficit; both general and seemingly specific deficits are accounted for by impaired working memory processes. One way to compare these two theories is by considering their predictions for the effects of a delay on performance. The working memory theory makes explicit predictions about the effects of having to hold information on-line over a delay. As currently stated, the theory of mind/central coherence theory does not, for it predicts that when a task necessitates the 'drawing together of diverse information to construct higher-level meaning in context' (Frith and Happé 1994, p. 121), individuals with autism will be impaired. The working memory theory predicts this impairment will be differentially greater in autism after a delay.

In an attempt to test the validity of the working memory theory of autism further and to clarify the relationship between it and the central coherence theory, we conducted a study that tested their competing predictions. We assessed the effects of delay on the performance of 15 subjects with autism and 15 verbal MA matched controls on modified versions of two tasks originally put forth as evidence for the central coherence theory: a Block Design task and a homograph ambiguity task. The working memory theory predicted that subjects with autism would show a significantly greater decrease in performance as the working memory demands increase (i.e. having to hold relevant information on-line to use it at a later time to achieve a goal). The central coherence theory did not predict this difficulty with delay, but it instead predicted that subjects with autism would perform worse on tasks demanding integration of information, regardless of delay.

An analysis of the cognitive components of the Block Design subtest provides some support for a lack of central coherence in autism. To complete this task, one must break each design down into segments; the child must find the smaller pieces that are embedded in the global design. This part of the task is difficult for young children, presumably because they have not yet learned to switch from global to local processing. However, the central coherence theory predicts that this step is unnecessary for the children with autism since they begin this task in a detached, local manner. Shah and Frith (1993) conducted an experiment in which each design was either unsegmented (usual form) or segmented. They found that the children with autism performed better than MA and CA matched controls in the unsegmented condition. However, the performance of children with autism did not change significantly in the segmented condition, while the performance of controls improved. Prior segmentation withdrew the need for the extra step the controls were originally having to complete. These authors concluded that a lack of central coherence in autism was supported.

Since specific conclusions about central coherence in autism are drawn from these Block Design results, a Modified Block Design task (MBD) was designed to simultaneously test the predictions made by this theory and the working memory theory. In this task, we implemented a manipulation of working memory, wherein subjects had to hold a visual representation of the target design on-line in order to correctly reproduce it. This independent variable had one present and two absent conditions. In the present condition, the design remained visible throughout each trial. In the first absent condition, the subjects had to reproduce the target design immediately following its withdrawal. With this manipulation, we assessed the impact of having to use the representation of a target design to guide performance, *without* a delay. In the second absent condition, the subjects had to hold the target design on-line over an 8-second delay, *and* use this visual representation to guide performance. All stimuli were presented in an unsegmented form, as this was the condition in which the subjects with autism were shown to have an advantage in the original study (Shah and Frith 1993).

For this task, the working memory theory predicted differential deficits in working memory for the subjects with autism. It predicted an interaction between the working memory variable (present, absent—no delay, absent—delay) and group, with the performance of subjects with autism being more significantly decreased by increases in working memory. When trying to test for differential group deficits, it is important to account for the alternative explanation that an interaction may be found only because the clinical group has a more generalized impairment that leads to increased difficulties with more complex tests (Chapman and Chapman 1978). In order to provide more support for a specific group deficit in working memory in autism, the difficulty of the designs in this MBD was varied across the three levels of the working memory variable to balance out the performance of normal controls. In other words, designs in the present condition were the most difficult (number of blocks in the design, complexity of design), while the designs in the two absent conditions were less difficult. Therefore, if the predicted interaction was obtained, it could more clearly be attributed to a differential group deficit in working memory.

A second factor was manipulated in our modified Block Design task, namely, the coherence of the designs themselves. The purpose of this manipulation was to test whether the subjects with autism were indeed processing the gestalt stimuli differently, as proposed by the central coherence theory. This second independent variable has two conditions: gestalt vs.

non-gestalt. Half the stimuli designs translate easily into a gestalt pattern (e.g. a square), and the other half are random patterns. The central coherence theory holds that individuals with autism process all designs, whether gestalt or non-gestalt, as disconnected local features; thus, this manipulation should not affect their performance over a delay. In contrast, the gestalt condition should benefit controls over a delay, because they should have less to hold on to over the delay in the gestalt condition (e.g. one red square as opposed to four red triangles) than the subjects with autism (e.g. always four red triangles). But, in the non-gestalt condition, the groups should be equivalent. In contrast, the working memory theory predicts that the performance of individuals with autism will decrease significantly as the delay interval increases, with no group-specific effects of gestalt vs. non-gestalt patterns. The central coherence theory predicted, then, that group would interact with the gestalt manipulation, while the WM manipulation would affect both groups equally. The working memory theory, on the other hand, predicted that group would interact with the WM manipulation, while the gestalt manipulation would affect both groups equally.

Another task that points to differences between children with autism and controls is a homograph ambiguity task. Here the subject is asked to read a sentence containing a homograph and some disambiguating context (DC), 'At the end of the play, he took a *bow*'. Happé (1991) found that subjects with autism made use of disambiguating phrases less than controls to determine the pronunciation of the homograph. The controls selected the correct, but less frequent, pronunciation when the DC occurred prior to the homograph, but not when it occured after it; whereas the subjects with autism generally did not do this. The explanation is that individuals with autism cannot extract the gist of the sentence, and, consequently, will most often say the dominant pronunciation of the homograph, despite the pronunciation suggested by the disambiguating context. Here, a lack of central coherence is said to have affected the performance of subjects with autism in that the *context* was not available to them.

A similar task called the Lexical Ambiguity task was used by Cohen *et al.* (unpublished) with schizophrenic subjects, as described in Cohen and Servan-Schrieber (1992). The subjects read sentences made up of two phrases, and then chose the meaning they thought the homograph carried in the sentence. The two phrases were presented one at a time, and were separated by a delay interval. One of the phrases contains an ambiguous homograph, and the other contains some disambiguating context (i.e. 'To keep chickens from running away,'—delay period—'you need to have a good PEN.'). The subject must be able to use the disambiguating context to choose the correct (subordinate vs. dominant) meaning of the homograph. The order in which the two phrases were presented served as the working memory manipulation. Following with Cohen *et al.*'s (1992) argument that working memory deficits account for the poor performance in the schizo-phrenic patient group, it was expected that such a task should be sensitive to the presence of the proposed working memory deficits in autism.

In the present study, a modified version of the Lexical Ambiguity task was used to address the differences between the two theories of autism. With this task, we assessed the ability of those people with autism to process contextual information to decide on the correct meaning of an ambiguous word, and thereby directly test the central coherence theory. Furthermore, the working memory manipulation used in the original Cohen *et al.* (unpublished) task was used to test predictions of the working memory theory. If working memory deficits do exist in autism, our subjects with autism should have had a harder time when they had to hold some information on line over a delay in order to inhibit the prepotent dominant meaning of a target homograph later. So the working memory theory predicted a group by delay interaction on this task, whereas the central coherence theory predicted only a main effect of group.

Results from the tests conducted on the MBD data supported neither the working memory theory's predictions nor the central coherence theory's predictions. There were no differences between groups at the present level of the WM variable (target design visible throughout the trial), across both the gestalt and non-gestalt conditions. Upon closer examination, it was found that the lack of differences at this level was attributable to some confounding ceiling effects. Since no specific predictions depended on this level of the working memory variable, a second analysis was conducted on the data from the two absent conditions, without the present condition data.

In a $2 \times 2 \times 2$ (group $\times$ gestalt $\times$ delay) ANOVA, we found significant main effects of group and gestalt, but a non-significant effect of delay, and no significant interactions. Contrary to the predictions of the WM theory, the group with autism did no worse with the increased delay in these two absent conditions. However, they did do worse overall. Some design issues make this result difficult to interpret. As discussed earlier, we varied the difficulty of the target designs across the working memory conditions to balance out the performance of control subjects. In order to achieve this, the designs in the absent, 8-second delay condition had to be made very simple to balance out the effects of the increased working memory demand. Unfortunately, it is believed that balancing the working memory levels actually made the 8-second delay designs so easy that our test was not sensitive enough to detect any incremental group differences here. In other words, we believe it is possible that these designs were so easy that any additional working memory demands there may have been from the absent—no delay condition to the absent—8-second delay condition may have been washed out. On the other hand, for the predicted group by working-memory, interaction effect to have been a convincing demonstration of a differential effect of working memory on the group with autism, balancing the contrasted conditions on difficulty was required. So a dilemma exists: the optimal design for sensitivity to a deficit is non-optimal for demonstrating specificity of a deficit. What we can say at this point is that, given these constraints, we did not find the specific group by working memory interaction that was predicted (the subjects with autism were expected to do increasingly worse as delay increased). This result, coupled with some of the results in the previous section, raises the question of whether delay is the most important WM manipulation in autism.

The MBD results did not support the central coherence theory's predictions, either. Recall that the central coherence theory would predict a group by gestalt interaction, because control subjects should process the gestalt figures as wholes whereas the subjects with autism should process them as separate pieces, the same as they do the non-gestalt designs. The significant main effect of gestalt showed that it was easier to hold a gestalt design on-line and reproduce it with blocks, than it was to hold a non-gestalt design on-line to be reproduced for *both* groups. Presumably, all subjects were storing the gestalt designs as integrated wholes, as opposed to the local, separate pieces presented by the non-gestalt designs. This pattern of results poses a challenge to the central coherence theory's claim that individuals with autism process gestalt objects as separate, disconnected pieces.

In summary, the MBD results failed to support the predictions of either the working memory theory or the central coherence theory. Subjects with autism do have a more difficult time reproducing designs when they are required to hold a representation of the target on-line, and use this to guide their performance, but this seems to be unaffected by delay. So, holding things in mind may be more difficult for them, even if delay is unimportant. In other words, any non-present target causes problems, but the delay *per se* does not. Additionally, the significant main effect of gestalt made it clear that reproducing gestalt targets was easier than non-gestalt targets for both groups. These results suggest that the subjects in the autistic group were able to process the gestalt figures as integrated 'wholes,' and show the same advantages of gestalt as did the controls.

The results from the 2 × 2 (group × context) ANOVA test conducted on the LAT data, on the other hand, did provide some support for the central coherence theory, but again the working memory theory's predictions were not upheld. There was a significant main effect of group, with those with autism making more errors than control subjects, but there was no effect of the placement of the disambiguating context (i.e. before or after the 8-second delay), and a non-significant interaction effect. This set results suggest two things. First, it looks like a working memory load in the form of delay does not affect the level at which an autistic individual is able to use context to disambiguate a homograph. This finding, again, challenges the delay aspect of the working memory theory. Second, there is evidence that the individuals with autism do have a more difficult time than matched controls when processing contextual information, regardless of changes in working memory demand. The significant group difference on the LAT provides some support for the predictions of the central coherence theory, while challenging the working memory theory's predictions concerning the effects of delay. However, it is important to note that coherence was not directly manipulated in this task. Therefore, while weaknesses in central coherence would be consistent with these results, these results do not provide evidence for such weaknesses being the cause of the poorer performance of the subjects with autism.

The sets of results from the MBD and the LAT taken together highlight some important issues. First, we found no evidence in either study of a differential impact of delay on the performance of the group with autism. The null spatial working memory results in the previous section bolster this conclusion, since several of those tasks involve a delay. As a final test of this conclusion about delay, we re-analysed the data from the adapted Corsi–Milner task above, which included three levels of a differential effect of delay before a test trial. Again, there was no clear evidence of differential effects of delay on the performance of the group with autism. So, integrating across studies, it appears fairly clear that the delay aspect of WM is unimportant in autism, leading us to abandon the hypothesis that the duration of the delay differentially affects performance in subjects with autism. Second, we found some evidence on the MBD tasks that runs counter to the predictions of the central coherence theory. Children with autism were *not* differentially affected by the coherence manipulation (gestalt vs. non-gestalt) regardless of the WM condition, showing that their processing is not entirely local. Third, across both tasks there is evidence that the autistic group is worse at keeping non-present information in mind, whether it be a sentence context or the elements of a design; and this could support a revised version of the working memory theory of autism.

In summary, the goal of this last validity test was to address the relationship between two currently separate cognitive theories of autism: namely, the central coherence theory and the working memory theory. Predictions of the two theories were pitted against one another in two separate tasks. This study has helped us refine these two theories, in that it seems likely that the impairments proposed by each do not exist at all levels of complexity. Taken together, these findings suggest that neither theory can currently be subsumed by the other, and that more work needs to be done to specify further both of the constructs and the specific effects they would be expected to have on the performance of individuals with autism.

Metatheoretical issues

The executive dysfunction hypothesis of autism has generated a considerable amount of research, including the four validity tests presented here. In the first two tests, the executive dysfunction hypothesis fares well. It predicts performance in a different domain, memory, and is related to the well-documented deficits in autism in domains such as theory of mind, joint attention, and imitation, although some aspects of the imitation/pantomime data are not readily explained by an executive dysfunction hypothesis. Of course, proving that executive deficits *cause* deficits in these other domains in autism is quite another matter, a task that faces the same difficulties as proving any given psychological deficit is primary in this disorder. The first two tests have also generated data which challenge the metarepresentational theory, (1) by means of a direct test through experimental manipulations (of meaning in the imitation tasks or of coherence in the modified Block Design task), (2) by suggesting an alternative explanation for the joint attention and theory of mind deficits in autism (which are possibly secondary to executive dysfunction), or (3) by documenting deficits, such as those in imitation and recency and source memory, which are not readily explained by the metarepresentational theory.

However, the results of the third validity test present a serious threat to the validity of the executive dysfunction hypothesis. In the youngest sample yet studied, executive deficits are not being found on a battery of mainly spatial working memory tasks, while joint attention deficits are. Either the executive deficits in autism do not include deficits in spatial working memory or executive deficits are not primary. If joint attention deficits are a precursor of the later theory of mind deficits, then the results of the third validity test favour the theory of mind theory over the executive dysfunction hypothesis.

The results of the fourth validity test, which compared the prediction of the central coherence and working memory theories, is inconclusive at present. The group by delay interaction predicted by the working memory theory was not found on either task, but a result contrary to the central coherence theory was found.

In summary, neither the executive dysfunction hypothesis nor its main rival, the metarepresentational hypothesis, comes out of these validity tests unscathed. Therefore, it may be time to develop some new hypotheses. Before attempting that task, we will consider some other threats to the validity of the executive dysfunction hypothesis.

One apparently serious threat to the executive dysfunction hypothesis, the discriminant validity problem, may be turning out to be less of a problem than it initially appeared. Both the severity and profile of executive deficits in autism are different from that found in ADHD or Fragile X in females

(Ozonoff this volume; Pennington, 1997; Pennington and Ozonoff 1996). Two other disorders, Tourette syndrome and conduct disorder (without ADHD), so far, do not exhibit consistent evidence of executive deficits, hence they are clearly distinct from autism. In other words, exactly the same executive deficit found in autism has not yet been found in another disorder. Two disorders which bear closer examination are mental retardation, especially given the results of the third validity test, and schizophrenia.

Another threat to validity concerns the effects of early focal frontal lesions. Although the existing database is fairly small and may suffer from ascertainment biases, we already know that early focal lesions to the prefrontal cortex (PFC) have not been reported as causing autism (see Eslinger, *et al.* 1997; Pennington and Ozonoff 1996). In contrast, conduct-disordered behaviour is a prominent sequela to such lesions, as are deficits on various executive function tasks. Studies of larger samples of children with early focal PFC lesions will be very fruitful for testing the role of the PFC in development. To account for the executive function deficits observed in populations with autism, one may have to predict either lesions in neural systems closely connected to the PFC, such as the basal ganglia, or even diffuse lesions.

It is important to remember that the neurological substrate in autism may not be a focal one. Instead, it may be a diffuse structural or metabolic difference in brain development. Adult patients with diffuse lesions also have executive dysfunction; we do not know whether this is because a diffuse lesion often includes the prefrontal cortex or because disrupting the connectivity of the *whole* brain mimics some of the effects of a focal frontal lesion, or both. In our efforts to understand normal and abnormal development, it is important to avoid becoming too fixated on localizationist hypotheses, since developmental variations in brain development are rarely localized. The rarity of localized changes in early brain development is both a problem and a promise, since the findings from developmental neuropsychology may help us re-think a modular, localizationist view of how the brain works (Pennington 1994b).

As stated repeatedly in this chapter, the most telling validity tests, such as in a prospective longitudinal study, are the most difficult to perform, and this applies equally to all the current contending candidates for the primary cognitive (or social or emotional) deficits in autism. Executive dysfunction could be secondary to some other primary deficit, either cognitive, social or emotional, or it could be a correlate of that deficit. For instance, the primary deficit in autism might be in some social skill that produces social avoidance. Social avoidance, in turn, would lead to fewer social interactions; and we would argue that social interactions provide unremitting practice in several executive functions. Reduced practice, in turn, would lead to worse executive function performance. Thus, all we really know is that executive function deficits are strongly correlated with autism, because the studies that have been done are only cross-sectional.

Proving a causal relationship will be difficult, since the methods for doing so in autism are generally unavailable. Two such methods are longitudinal studies and neurochemical manipulations. Longitudinal studies are always difficult to conduct and are particularly difficult in rare populations, such as in children with autism. A better understanding of neurobiological mechanisms can help remedy this problem, because it can allow one to test dose–response relationships and even sometimes manipulate the relevant neurobiological parameter. The classic example here is early treated phenylketonuria (PKU), in which a relationship between executive function deficits and dopamine depletion, caused by elevated phenylalanine levels, has been demonstrated (Diamond 1991b). Attention Deficit Hyperactivity Disorder (ADHD), because it responds to medications which affect dopamine transport, is also amenable to this strategy. Unfortunately, we cannot use this strategy in research into autism because we do not understand its neurobiological mechanisms sufficiently well.

So, the crucial longitudinal and truly experimental (involving manipulations of the presumed causal factor) validity tests are nearly impossible to perform in autism. Perhaps the best we can currently do is subject each of the candidate primary deficits to the kind of validity tests considered here, with the hope that some candidates will be eliminated. If they are not, then we will eventually reach a difficult theoretical impasse in which we are faced with too many candidates for the primary deficit, each with an impressive body of confirmatory findings, and insufficiently powerful means to distinguish them. Before then—all being well—advances in the genetics or neurology of autism will rescue us.

Before concluding, it is useful to examine a deeper validity issue, namely the validity of assumptions common to virtually all current efforts, to find the proximal psychological cause of autism. Some of these assumptions may be mistaken in a way that would lead to the impasse of having too many candidate primary deficits. As a way to highlight these assumptions, we will examine the general frameworks for analysis that have been used in autism and other neurodevelopmental disorders.

Errors in our explanatory frameworks?

One such framework has been developed by Pennington and colleagues (Pennington 1991; Pennington and Ozonoff 1991; Pennington and Welsh 1995) and another by Morton and Frith (1995). The first framework has four levels of analysis: aetiology, brain mechanisms, neuropsychological mechanisms, and symptoms, and it also specifies possible causal relationships between levels of analysis. It divides symptoms into primary, secondary, correlated, and artefactual; each type of symptom is defined by different causal relationships to underlying mechanisms at the three other levels of analysis. The Morton and Frith (1995) framework has three levels of analysis: biological, cognitive, and behavioural. Their last two levels of analysis are similar to the last two levels in the first framework, and their model likewise distinguishes between different kinds of symptoms and considers possible causal relationships between levels of analysis. An important function of their framework is to provide a theory-neutral, easily understood notation for diagramming theories and comparing them. Thus, although their framework is mainly applied to disorders whose cause appears to be biological, the framework can diagram theories in which the cause is completely non-biological, i.e. due to the social environment. In each of these frameworks, and in the empirical work derived from them, the focus has been on disorders in which there appears to be a unitary, specific, underlying cognitive deficit, largely because of a primary concern with cognitive development. A working assumption shared by all this work is that an underlying cognitive deficit (or deficits) is the proximal cause of the pattern of symptoms observed in a given developmental psychopathology. In other words, it is assumed that the effects of biology on observable behaviour (symptoms) is often mediated by underlying cognitive processes. Morton and Frith's account allows for a direct (i.e. not mediated by cognition) effect of brain mechanisms, and they give as examples two motor symptoms, tics in Tourette's syndrome and tremor in Parkinson's disease (of course, this implies that motor function is non-cognitive). It is also generally assumed that while there is likely to be heterogeneity in both aetiologies and even brain mechanisms in a given disorder, there will be homogeneity at the cognitive level in disorders such as dyslexia and autism.

Hence, the specific, underlying cognitive deficit in a given disorder will provide a powerful, parsimonious explanation of at least the core or primary signs and symptoms of the disorder, if not of the correlated and secondary ones as well. So the cognitive level of analysis is given priority in a unified explanation of a disorder. The primacy, homogeneity, and autonomy accorded to the cognitive level of analysis may, however, be mistaken. In these frameworks, biological causes are completely translated into a cognitive cause, which is optimistically regarded as unitary, thus allowing a powerful and comprehensive explanation of the disorder. So lurking in these frameworks is a kind of dualism; it is assumed that a neat line can be drawn between the biological and cognitive levels of analysis.

But what if this boundary is less neat, the cognitive cause is not unitary, or some of the biological effects on behaviour are not cognitive at all? Suppose, for example, that there is a general dopaminergic deficit in autism, as Damasio and Maurer (1978) originally proposed. More recent work on the relationship of dopamine to human behaviour (Luciana *et al.* 1992) suggests that such a deficit can affect three separate neural systems responsible, respectively, for working memory (prefrontal cortex), positive emotionality (limbic cortex), and motor programming including inhibition of motor stereotypes (basal ganglia). A dopaminergic deficit could result in a syndrome in which there were executive deficits, social isolation, and motor stereotypies, but there would be no unifying cognitive explanation for these various symptoms because the unifying deficit would be at the neurological level of analysis.

A second problem has to do with the modularity assumptions implicit in these frameworks, namely that there are independent components of mind to be discovered by examining the dissociations found within and across disorders like autism. But most developmental disorders, including autism, are a mix of specific and general cognitive deficits. Accounting for both kinds of deficits in a framework that assumes modularity presents problems.

Contrary then to what modularity theorists like Morton and Frith (1995) maintain, it may be appropriate to attempt to provide a single account of both the specific and general cognitive deficits in autism. Individuals with autism are impaired at many of the highest and most distinctively human aspects of cognition. These include imitation, joint attention, theory of mind, episodic memory, and an understanding of figurative language and the processing of gist rather than the surface levels of language. The pervasiveness of these impairments and the high correlation of autism with mental retardation (75% of individuals with autism are mentally retarded) argue against a domain-specific cognitive problem in autism. Instead, some very general and basic aspect of the human cognitive system seems to be affected.

Our initial efforts to characterize this cognitive deficit were guided by traditional neuropsychology, in so far as we were looking for a part of the brain, damage to which produces these kinds of cognitive problems. Hence, we were drawn to the frontal hypothesis of autism, first proposed by Damasio and Maurer (1978) and supported empirically by several independent studies. The frontal hypothesis is a localizationist hypothesis; in terms of modularity theory, it posits a deficit in central cognition, much like the central coherence deficit discussed by Frith. But the cognitive deficits it attempts to account for are not only produced by focal damage to the frontal lobes; focal damage in the basal ganglia (e.g. Huntington's dementia) as well as diffuse (e.g. mental retardation, closed head injury, and cognitive ageing) insults also produce these deficits. In fact, localizing such general and central cognitive processes seems like a dubious proposition altogether, since these processes are arguably an emergent property of the whole system (although they could be disrupted by a local change.) These cognitive processes allow a high degree of context specificity to action selection, but representing context requires simultaneously activating knowledge from multiple domains and across time. From a connectionist perspective, disruption of context specificity would reflect a failure of network dynamics to find the global best-fit among diverse constraints and the domination of performance by deeper and more local attractors. At a neural level, such a change in network dynamics could result from a general, diffuse change in the number of neurones, their connections, or their metabolic level. In this context, there are several recent findings about brain structure and function in autism that suggest a general diffuse change, including megalencephaly (Bailey *et al.* 1993; Piven *et al.* 1995) and an alteration in neuronal membrane metabolism (Minshew *et al.* 1993). However, we are still far away from an understanding of brain mechanisms in this disorder.

Of course, this connectionist theorizing about autism is quite preliminary, and daunting problems remain to be solved. By emphasizing what is general in the cognitive changes in autism, we may fail to account for what makes it a specific and distinct disorder. One can immediately ask why are all individuals with diffuse early brain insults not autistic, such as individuals with Down's syndrome, as well as how can there be individuals with autism with considerably above-average IQs?

In summary, the assumptions both of a unitary cognitive cause and of modularity are but two examples of how ideas embedded in our frameworks may be misleading us about the nature of both autism and cognitive development generally. For this reason, achieving a better theoretical account of autism will require not only dealing with theoretical problems within the cognitive level of analysis (e.g. those raised by assumptions of modularity), but it will also require us to consider theoretical issues concerning the relationships *between* levels of analysis. For instance, the maximally explanatory level of analysis in autism may turn out to be a level intermediate between brain and cognition, a *neurocomputational* level. Hence, work on a cognitive account of a disorder like autism must proceed in tandem with work on the appropriate framework for analysing both such disorders and normal development and with work on their neurobiology.

Note

1. The formula used for calculating effect size (d) was the difference in the means for the two groups divided by their average SD:

$$d = \frac{\overline{X}_1 - \overline{X}_2}{\sqrt{\frac{SD_1^2 + SD_2^2}{2}}}$$

No correction was made for the number in each group, since these were usually similar. This *d* estimate is conservative because the variance in the group with autism was frequently greater than that in controls; hence, using just the SD for the control group would have yielded a larger effect size.

Acknowledgements

This work was supported by NICHD grants P50 HD27802 and P30 HD04024, and NIMH grants 5 K02 MH00419 (RSA), 5 R37 MH38820 (MERIT), and R01 MH45916 to the first author. L. Bennetto and E. McMahon Griffith were supported by NIMH NRSA predoctoral fellowships (MH10470 and MH 11127). D. T. Reed was supported by an NIMH Institutional Postdoctoral Research Training Program (MH15442). Finally, some of the studies reported here were supported by the Developmental Psychobiology Research Group at the University of Colorado Health Sciences Center.

REFERENCES

Ayres, A. J. (1985). *Developmental dyspraxia and adult onset apraxia.* Sensory Integration International,Torrance, CA.

Bailey, A., Luthert, P., Bolton, P., LeCouteur, P., Rutter, M., and Harding, B. (1993). Letter: Autism and megalencephaly. *Lancet*, **341**, 1225–6.

Baron-Cohen, S. (1988). Social and pragmatic deficits in autism: Cognitive or affective? *Journal of Autism and Developmental Disorders*, **18**, 379–402.

Barth, C., Fein, D., and Waterhouse, L. (1995). Delayed match-to-sample performance in autistic children. *Developmental Neuropsychology*, **11**, 53–69.

Bennetto, L., Pennington, B. F., and Rogers, S. J. (1996). Intact and impaired memory functions in autism. *Child Development*, **67**, 1816–35.

Buitelaar, J., van Engeland, H., de Kogel, K., de Vries, H., and van Hooff, J. (1991). Differences in the structure of social behaviour of autistic children and non-autistic retarded controls. *Journal of Child Psychology and Psychiatry*, **32**, 995–1015.

Butterworth, G. and Grover, L. (1988). The origins of referential communication in human infancy. In *Thought without language* (ed. L. Weiskranz), pp. 5–24). Clarendon Press, Oxford.

Chapman, L. J. and Chapman, J. P. (1978). The measurement of differential deficit. *Journal of Psychiatric Research*, **14**, 303–11.

Cohen, J. (1988). *Statistical power analysis for the behavioural sciences*, 2nd edn. Erlbaum, Hillsdale, NJ.

Cohen, J. D. and Servan-Schreiber, D. (1992). Context, cortex, and dopamine: A connectionist approach to behavior and biology in schizophrenia. *Psychological Review*, **99**, 45–77.

Cohen, J. D., Targ, E., Kristoffersen, T., and Spiegel, D. The fabric of Thought Disorder: Disturbances in the processing of context. Unpublished manuscript.

Damasio, A. R. and Maurer, R. G. (1978). A neurological model for childhood autism. *Archives of Neurology*, **35**, 777–86.

Dawson, G. (1991). A psychobiological perspective on the early socio-emotional development of children with autism. In *Rochester symposium on developmental psychopathology: Volume 3: models and integrations* (ed. D. Cicchetti and S. L. Toth), pp. 207–34). University of Rochester, Rochester, NY.

Dawson, G. and Lewy, A. (1989). Arousal, attention, and the socioemotional impairments of individuals with autism. In *Autism: Nature, diagnosis, and treatment* (ed. G. Dawson), pp. 49–74). Guilford Press, NY.

Delis, D. C., Kramer, J. H., Kaplan, E., and Ober, B. A. (1986). The California verbal learning test—research edition. Psychological Corporation, NY.

DeMyer, M. K., Hingtgen, J. N., and Jackson, R. K. (1981). Infantile autism reviewed: A decade of research. *Schizophrenia Bulletin*, **7**, 388–451.

DeRenzi, E., Motti, F., and Nichelli, P. (1980). Imitating gestures: A quantitative approach to ideomotor apraxia. *Archives Neurological*, **37**, 6–10.

Diamond, A. (1991a). Neuropsychological insights into the meaning of object concept development. In The epigenesis of mind: Essays on biology and knowledge. (ed. Carey and Gelman), pp. 67–110. Erlbaum, Hillsdale, NJ.

Diamond, A. (1991b) Frontal lobe involvement in cognitive changes during the first year of life. In *Brain maturation and cognitive development* (ed. K. Gibson and A. Petersen), pp. 127–80. NY. Aldine/de Gruyter.

Diamond, A., Prevor, M., Callender, G., and Druin, D.P. (in press). Prefrontal cortex cognitive deficits in children treated early and continuously for PKU. *Monographs of the Society for Research in Child Development*.

Duncan, J. (1995). Attention, intelligence, and the frontal lobes. In *The cognitive neurosciences* (ed. M. S. Gazzaniga), pp. 721–33. MIT Press, Cambridge, MA.

Duncan, J., Emslie, H., and Williams, P. (1996). Intelligence and the frontal lobe: The organization of goal-directed behaviour. *Cognitive Psychology*. **30**, 257–303.

Eslinger, P., Biddle, K.R., and Grattan, L.M. (1997). Cognitive and social development in children with prefrontal cortex lesions. In *Development of the prefrontal cortex: Evolution, neurobiology, and Behaviour* (ed. N. Krasnegor, R. Lyon, and P. Goldman-Rakic). Brookes Publishing Company, Baltimore, MD. pp. 295–335.

Frith, U. (1989). *Autism: Explaining the enigma*. Basil Blackwell, Oxford.

Frith, U. and Happé, F. (1994). Autism: Beyond 'theory of mind'. *Cognition*, **50**, 115–32.

Goldman, P. S. and Rosvold, H. E. (1972). The effects of selective caudate lesions in infant and juvenile rhesus monkeys. *Brain Research*, **43**, 53–66.

Goldman-Rakic, P. S. (1987a). Circuitry of primate prefrontal cortex and regulation of behaviour by representational memory. In *Handbook of physiology: The nervous system* (ed. V. B. Mountcastle, F. Plum, and S. R. Geiger), pp. 373–417. American Physiological Society, Bethesda, MD.

Goldman-Rakic, P. (1987b). Development of cortical circuitry and cognitive function. *Child Development*, **58**, 601–22.

Happé, F. G. E. (1991). *Theory of mind and communication in autism*. Unpublished PhD, thesis, University of London.

Heaton, R. K., Chelune, G. J., Talley, J. L., Kay, G. G., and Curtiss, G. (1993). *Wisconsin card sorting test manual: Revised and expanded*. Psychological Assessment Resources, Odessa, FL.

Heilman, K. (1979). Apraxia. In *Clinical neuropsychology* (ed. K. M. Heilman and E. Valenstein), pp. 159–85). Guilford Press, NY.

Hobson, R. P. (1993). *Autism and the development of mind*. Erlbaum, Hillsdale, NJ.

Hughes, C. and Russell, J. (1993). Autistic children's difficulty with mental disengagement from an object: Its implications for theories of autism. *Developmental Psychology*, **29**, 498–510.

Jarrold, C., Boucher, J., and Smith, P. K. (1996). Generativity deficits in pretend play in autism. *British Journal of Developmental Psychology*, **14**, 275–300.

Jones, V. and Prior, M. (1985). Motor imitation abilities and neurological signs in autistic children. *Journal of Autism and Developmental Disorders*, **15**, 37–46.

Kaufman, P, Leckman, J., and Ort, S. (1989). Delayed Response performance in males with Fragile X. *Journal of Clinical and Experimental Neuropsychology*, **12**, 69.

Kimberg, D. Y. and Farah, M. J. (1993). A unified account of cognitive impairments following frontal lobe damage: The role of working memory in complex, organized behavior. *Journal of Experimental Psychology: General*, **122**, 411–28.

Kimura, D. and Archibald, Y. (1974). Motor functions of the left hemisphere. *Brain*, **97**, 337–50.

Kolb, B. and Milner, B. (1981). Performance of complex arm and facial movements after focal brain lesions. *Neuropsychologia*, **19**, 505–14.

Leekam, S.R. and Perner, J., (1991). Does the autistic child have a metarepresentational deficit? *Cognition*, **40**, 203–18.

Leslie, A. (1987). Pretence and representation: The origins of 'theory of mind'. *Psychological Review*, **94**, 412–26.

Leslie, A. M. and Thaiss, L. (1992). Domain specificity in conceptual development: Neuropsychological evidence from autism. *Cognition*, **43**, 225–51.

Levin, H., Culhane, K., Hartmann, J., Evankovich, K., Mattson, A., Harward, H., *et al.* (1991). Developmental changes in performance on tests of purported frontal lobe functioning. *Developmental Neuropsychology*, **7**, 377–95.

Llamas, C. and Diamond, A. (1991). *Development of frontal cortex abilities in children between 3–8 years of age*. Paper presented at the biennial meeting of Society for Research in Child Development, Seattle, WA.

Luciana, M., Depue, R. A., Arbisi, P., and Leon, A. (1992). Facilitation of working memory in humans by a D_2 dopamine receptor agonist. *Journal of Cognitive Neuroscience*, **4**, 58–68.

McEvoy, R. E., Rogers, S. J., and Pennington, B. F. (1993). Executive function and social communication deficits in young, autistic children. *Journal of Child Psychology and Psychiatry*, **34**, 563–78.

Mateer, C. and Kimura, D. (1977). Impairment of non-verbal oral movements in aphasia. *Brain and Language*, **4**, 262–76.

Meltzoff, A. N. and Gopnik, A. (1993). The role of imitation in understanding persons and developing a theory of mind. In *Understanding other minds: Perspectives from autism* (ed. S. Baron-Cohen, H. Tager-Flusberg, and D. J. Cohen), pp. 240–63. Oxford University Press, NY.

Milner, B., Corsi, P., and Leonard, G. (1991). Frontal-lobe contribution to recency judgments. *Neuropsychologia*, **29**, 601–18.

Minshew, N. J., Goldstein, G., Dombrowski, S.M., *et al.* (1993). A preliminary ^{31}P MRS study of autism: Evidence for undersynthesis and increased degradation of brain membranes. *Biological Psychiatry*, **33**, 762–73.

Moore, C., Jarrold, C., Russell, J., Lumb, A., Sapp, F., and MacCallum, F. (1995). Conflicting desire and the child's theory of mind. *Cognitive Development*, **10**, 467–82.

Morton, J. and Frith, U. (1995). Causal modelling: A structural approach to developmental psychopathology. In *Manual of developmental psychopathology*, Vol. I (ed. D. Cicchetti and D. J. Cohen), pp. 357–90. John Wiley & Sons, Inc., NY.

Moscovitch, M. (1994). Cognitive resources and dual-task interference effects at retrieval in normal people: The role of the frontal lobes and medial temporal cortex. *Neuropsychology*, **8**, 524–34.

Mundy, P. and Sigman, M. (1989). The theoretical implications of joint-attention deficits in autism. *Development and Psychopathology*, **1**, 173–83.

Mundy, P., Sigman, M., Ungerer, J., and Sherman, T. (1986). Defining the social deficits of autism: The contributions of non-verbal communication measures. *Journal of Child Psychology and Psychiatry*, **27**, 657—99.

Mundy, P., Sigman, M., and Kasari, C. (1993). Theory of mind and joint attention deficits in autism. In *Understanding other minds: Perspective from autism* (ed. S. Baron-Cohen, H. Tager-Flusberg, and D. Cohen), pp. 161–203. Oxford University Press.

Ohta, M. (1987). Cognitive disorders of infantile autism: A study employing the WISC, spatial relationships, conceptualization, and gesture imitations. *Journal of Autism and Developmental Disorders*, **17**, 45–62.

Osterling, J. and Dawson, G. (1994). Early recognition of children with autism: A study of first birthday home videotapes. *Journal of Autism and Developmental Disorders*, **24**, 247–57.

Ozonoff, S., Pennington, B. F., and Rogers, S. J. (1991a). Executive function deficits in high-functioning autistic individuals: Relationship to theory of mind. *Journal of Child Psychology and Psychiatry*, **32**, 1081–105.

Ozonoff, S., Rogers, S. J., and Pennington, B. F. (1991b). Asperger's syndrome: Evidence of an empirical distinction from high-functioning autism. *Journal of Child Psychology and Psychiatry*, **32**, 1107–22.

Ozonoff, S., Rogers, S. J., and Pennington, B. F. (1993). Can standard measures identify subclinical markers of autism? *Journal of Autism and Developmental Disorders*, **23**, 429–41.

Ozonoff, S., Strayer, D. L., McMahon, W. M., and Filloux, F. (1994). Executive function abilities in autism and Tourette syndrome: An information processing approach. *Journal of Child Psychology and Psychiatry*, **35**, 1015–32.

Passingham, R. (1985). Memory of monkeys (*Macaca mulatta*) with lesions in prefrontal cortex. *Behavioural Neuroscience*, **99**, 3–21.

Pennington, B. F. (1991). *Diagnosing learning disorders: A neuropsychological framework*. Guilford Press, NY.

Pennington, B.F. (1994a). The working memory function of the prefrontal cortices. Implications for developmental and individual differences in cognition. In *The development of future oriented processes* (ed. M. M. Haith, J. Benson, R. Roberts, and B. F. Pennington), pp. 243–89). University of Chicago Press.

Pennington, B. F. (1994b). Genetics of learning disabilities. *Journal of Child Neurology*, **10** (Supplement), 69–76.

Pennington, B. F. Dimensions of executive functions in normal and abnormal development (pp. 265–81). In *Development of the prefrontal cortex: Evolution, neurobiology, and behavior* (ed. N. Krasnegor, R. Lyon, and P. Goldman-Rakic) (1997). Brookes Publishing Company, Baltimore, MD.

Pennington, B. F. and Ozonoff, S. (1991). A neuroscientific perspective on continuity and discontinuity in developmental psychopathology. In *Rochester symposium on developmental psychopathology:* Vol. III (ed. D. Cicchetti), p.117–59). Cambridge University Press, NY.

Pennington, B. F. and Ozonoff, S. (1996). Annotation: Executive functions and developmental psychopathologies. *Journal of Child Psychology and Psychiatry*, **37**, 51–87.

Pennington, B. F. and Welsh, M. C. (1995). Neuropsychology and developmental psychopathology. In *Manual of developmental psychopathology*, Vol. I (ed. D. Cicchetti and D.J. Cohen), pp. 254–90. John Wiley, NY.

Petrides, M. and Milner, B. (1982). Deficits on subject-ordered tasks after frontal- and temporal-lobe lesions in man. *Neuropsychologia*, **20**, 249–62.

Piven, J., Arndt, S., Bailey, J., Havercamp, S., Andreasen, N.C., and Palmer, P. (1995). An MRI study of brain size in autism. *American Journal of Psychiatry*, **152**, 1145–9.

Premack, D. and Woodruff, G. (1978). Does the chimpanzee have a theory of mind? *Behavioural and Brain Sciences*, **1**, 515–26.

Roberts, R. J. and Pennington, B. F. (1996). An interactive framework for examining prefrontal cognitive processes. *Developmental Neuropsychology*, **12**, 105–26.

Roberts, R. J., Hager, L., and Heron, C. (1994). Prefrontal cognitive processes: working memory and inhibition in the Antisaccade task. *Journal of Experimental Psychology: General*, **123**, 374–93.

Rogers, S. J. and Pennington, B. F. (1991). A theoretical approach to the deficits in infantile autism. *Development and Psychopathology*, **3**, 137–63.

Rogers, S. J., Bennetto, L., McEvoy, R. E., and Pennington, B. F. (1996). Imitation and pantomime in high functioning adolescents with autism. *Child Development*, **67**, 2060–73.

Russell, J., Mauthner, N., Sharpe, S., and Tidswell, T. (1991). The 'windows task' as a measure of strategic deception in preschoolers and autistic subjects. *British Journal of Developmental Psychology*, **9**, 331–49.

Russell, J., Jarrold, C., and Potel, D. (1994). What makes strategic deception difficult for children—The deception or the strategy? *British Journal of Developmental Psychology*, **12**, 301–14.

Seibert, J. M., Hogan, A. E., and Mundy, P. C. (1987). Assessing social communication skills in infancy. *Topics in Early Childhood Special Education*, **7**, 32–48.

Shah, A. and Frith, U. (1983). An islet of ability in autistic children: A research note. *Journal of Child Psychology and Psychiatry*, **24**, 613–20.

Shah, A. and Frith, U. (1993). Why do autistic individuals show superior performance on the Block Design task? *Journal of Child Psychology and Psychiatry*, **34**, 1351–64.

Shimamura, A. P., Janowsky, J. S., and Squire, L. R. (1991). What is the role of frontal lobe damage in memory disorders? In *Frontal lobe function and injury* (ed. H. S. Levin, H. M. Eisenberg, and A. L. Benton), pp. 173–95. Oxford University Press, NY.

Stern, D. N. (1985). *The interpersonal world of the human infant*. Basic Books, NY.

Wehner, E. and Rogers, S. (1994) (March). *Attachment relationships of autistic and developmentally delayed children*. Paper presented at the bi-monthly meeting of the Developmental Psychobiology Research Group, Denver, CO.

Welsh, M., Pennington, B., and Groisser, D. (1991). A normative-developmental study of executive function: A window on prefrontal function in children. *Developmental Neuropsychology*, **7**, 131–49.

6 Components of executive function in autism and other disorders

Sally Ozonoff

While a converging body of evidence suggests that executive dysfunction is a central cognitive deficit of autism, a number of critical issues remain to be explored. First, the domain of executive function is globally defined and encompasses a broad array of cognitive operations that may be only loosely associated. The scope of the executive dysfunction in autism is not yet well understood. It is not clear, for example, if all executive operations are impaired or only a subset. Second, autism is not the only disorder in which executive functions are impaired; executive deficits have been reported in a variety of other developmental and neurological disorders and psychopatho logical conditions. This chapter explores these issues and suggests that some resolution may be brought to them through adoption of an information processing approach. Ways in which this framework can provide greater precision in both the definition of specific executive functions and the examination of their selective association with specific disorders will be explored. In addition to discussing autism, this chapter will consider the evidence for executive dysfunction in several other disorders, namely attention deficit hyperactivity disorder (ADHD), schizophrenia, Tourette syndrome (TS), and obsessive–compulsive disorder (OCD).

The discriminant validity problem

As summarized in other chapters in this volume, there have been several recent empirical reports of executive function (EF) deficits in autistic people. Rumsey (1985) was the first to explicitly examine this domain of functioning in individuals with autism, finding that normal-IQ, verbal adults with residual state autism were highly deficient on the Wisconsin Card Sorting Test (WCST), making significantly more perseverative responses than matched controls. This basic finding has been replicated in autistic individuals, having a range of ages and functioning levels, by several research teams using a variety of different EF measures (Hughes and Russell 1993;

Hughes *et al.* 1994; McEvoy *et al.* 1993; Ozonoff *et al.* 1991; Prior and Hoffman 1990; Rumsey and Hamburger 1988). Ozonoff *et al.* (1993) also found that executive function variables were best able to discriminate siblings of autistic subjects from siblings of learning disabled controls, indicating a possible subclinical marker for autism in the executive function domain. This growing body of research has led several investigators to hypothesize that executive function impairment, possibly mediated by prefrontal cortical dysfunction, underlies many symptoms of autism (Damasio and Maurer 1978; Harris 1993; Ozonoff 1995a; Pennington 1994).

The so-called 'executive function hypothesis of autism' is complicated, however, by findings of similar impairments in a variety of other conditions. Significant deficits on EF tasks are apparent in several psychiatric disorders, including conduct disorder (Hurt and Naglieri 1992; Lueger and Gill 1990), OCD (Head *et al.* 1989), and schizophrenia (Axelrod *et al.* 1994; Beatty *et al.* 1994). Executive deficits are also frequently found among individuals with developmental problems, including ADHD (Chelune *et al.* 1986), early-treated phenylketonuria (Diamond *et al.* 1992; Welsh *et al.* 1990), Tourette syndrome (Bornstein 1990; Gladstone *et al.* 1993), and Fragile X syndrome (Mazzocco *et al.* 1992, 1993), as well as among individuals with neurological conditions, such as Parkinson's disease (Owen *et al.* 1995). If executive function impairment is a general consequence of disorder, distinguishing 'normal' from 'abnormal', but not specifically associated with particular conditions, its significance for explaining the symptoms of autism is clearly diminished. It is, as yet, uncertain how disorders with different behavioural phenotypes can share the same cognitive underpinnings.

Several possibilities have been suggested by Pennington and colleagues in a series of papers that have explored this so-called 'discriminant validity question' (Pennington 1994; Pennington and Ozonoff 1996; Pennington *et al.* 1996). One possibility is that the severity of the underlying neural insult varies across conditions, accounting for variations in both executive function capabilities and behavioural symptomatology. The severity of the EF deficit underlying different conditions does appear to vary, with autism involving the greatest deviation from normality, and lesser severity associated with Fragile X, ADHD, Tourette syndrome, and conduct disorder (Pennington and Ozonoff 1996; Pennington *et al.* 1996). It is somewhat implausible, however, to attempt to explain all qualitative differences in the behavioural phenotypes of these disorders in a purely quantitative fashion.

A second possibility is that the timing of the onset of the executive dysfunction may account for disorder-specific symptom expression. For example, autism, schizophrenia, TS, and OCD clearly have very different patterns of symptomatic onset; these may, in turn, reflect different patterns of onset of cognitive dysfunction. Such speculations await future prospective studies to examine whether the timing of the expression of cognitive and behavioural symptoms coincides. Variations in onset patterns cannot explain phenotypic differences between autism and either PKU or Fragile X, however, as all of these conditions have onset at birth or shortly thereafter.

A third possibility is that definition and measurement problems have obscured relationships between specific types of executive impairment and specific disorders. This alternative explanation for the discriminant validity problem is the focus of this chapter. It will be proposed that when the broad domain of EF is parsed into more unitary components, we may find that specific disorders are associated with different profiles of executive function strength and weakness. In what follows, the general evidence implicating executive dysfunction in autism, ADHD, schizophrenia, TS, and OCD is reviewed first. Following this, the component process approach is described. Recent research using information processing paradigms with the five subject populations is then reviewed. Finally, the chapter concludes with a discussion of how this framework can reduce the measurement problems often associated with standard EF tasks and bring some clarity to the discriminant validity problem.

Table 6.1 summarizes previous EF research with samples diagnosed with autism, ADHD, schizophrenia, TS, and OCD. We chose six prototypical tasks for focus because they were the most widely used measures across the disorders.

Executive dysfunction in autism

As can be seen in Table 6.1, by far the most frequently used EF measure with autistic samples has been the WCST, a task generally considered to tap cognitive shifting ability. This task is administered by placing four cards, varying along the dimensions of colour, shape, and number, in front of the subject. A deck of cards varying along these same dimensions is presented and the subject is asked to match them with one of the four 'key' cards. The examiner provides feedback about the accuracy of responses, but the sorting strategy is not revealed to the subject. Once ten consecutive cards have been correctly placed, the underlying sorting principle changes, without notice or comment from the examiner, and responses according to the previous category now receive negative feedback. The primary dependent variable of interest is the number of perseverative responses, defined as the number of trials in which the subject continues sorting by a previously correct category despite negative feedback (Heaton 1981).

The great majority of studies find that individuals with autism perform poorly on the WCST relative to matched controls; deficits are usually evident as perseveration and difficulty shifting from one sorting strategy to another. Only two of ten investigations using the WCST with autistic individuals have

Table 6.1 Studies of EF in samples with autism, ADHD, schizophrenia, TS, and OCD: experimental control-group differences on selected measures

	Autism		ADHD	
	Group differences	No group differences	Group differences	No group differences
WCST	Bennetto et al. 1996 Ozonoff and McEvoy 1994 Ozonoff et al. 1991 Prior and Hoffmann 1990 Rumsey 1985 Rumsey and Hamburger 1988, 1990 Szatmari et al. 1990	Minshew et al. 1992 Schneider and Asarnow 1987	Boucugnani and Jones 1989 Chelune et al. 1986 Gorenstein et al. 1989 Shue and Douglas 1992	Barkley et al. 1992 Fischer et al. 1990 Grodzinsky and Diamond 1992 Loge et al. 1990 McGee et al. 1989 Pennington et al. 1993 Weyandt and Willis 1994
Trials B	Rumsey and Hamburger 1988	Minshew et al. 1992	Boucugnani and Jones 1989 Dykman and Ackerman 1991 Gorenstein et al. 1989 Shue and Douglas 1992	Barkley et al. 1992 Grodzinsky and Diamond 1992 McGee et al. 1989
Tower of Hanoi	Bennetto et al. 1996 Hughes et al. 1994 Ozonoff and McEvoy 1994 Ozonoff et al. 1991		Aman et al. (in press) Pennington et al. 1993 Weyandt and Willis 1994	
Maze tasks	Prior and Hoffman 1990		Carte et al. 1996 Grodzinsky and Diamond 1992 Kuehne et al. 1987 Robins 1992 Weyandt and Willis 1994	Barkley et al. 1992 McGee et al. 1989
MFFT	Waterhouse and Fein 1982		Cohen et al. 1972 Hopkins et al. 1979 Kuehne et al. 1987 Pennington et al. 1993 Robins 1992 Weyandt and Willis 1994	Fischer et al. 1990 Stoner and Glynn 1987

Table 6.1 continued

	Schizophrenia		TS	
	Group differences	No group differences	Group differences	No group differences
Stroop	Backley et al. 1992 Boucugnani and Jones 1989 Gcrenstein et al. 1989 Grodzinsky and Diamond 1992 Hcpkins et al. 1979 Lavoie and Charlebois 1994 Lufi et al. 1990 Reardon and Naglieri 1992	Brysor 1983 Eskes et al. 1990		Cohen et al. 1972
WCST	Axelrod et al. 1994 Beatty et al. 1994 Braff et al. 1991 Butler et al. 1992 Cleghorn et al. 1990 Fey 1951 Franke et al. 1992, 1993 Gambini et al. 1992 Hoff et al. 1992 Litman et al. 1991 Morice 1990 Morrison-Stewart et al. 1992 Raine et al. 1992 Saykin et al. 1994 Scarone et al. 1993 Seidman et al. 1991 Shoqeirat and Mayes 1988 Yurgelun-Todd and Kinney 1993		Gladstone et al. 1993	Bornstein 1990, 1991a Bornstein and Yang 1991 Randolph et al. 1993 Sutherland et al. 1982 Yeates and Bornstein 1994

Table 6.1 continued

	Schizophrenia		TS	
	Group differences	No group differences	Group differences	No group differences
Trails B	Braff et al. 1991 Franke et al. 1993 Galynker and Harvey 1992 Levander et al. 1985 Litman et al. 1991 Saykin et al. 1994 Yurgelun-Todd and Kinney 1993	Hoff et al. 1992	Channon et al. 1992	Bornstein 1991a Silverstein et al. 1995
Tower of Hanoi	Goldberg et al. 1990			
Maze tasks	Cleghorn et al. 1990 Murphy and DeWolfe 1989			
Stroop	Abramczyk et al. 1983 Carter et al. 1992 Everett et al. 1989 Hoff et al. 1992 Saykin et al. 1994 Wysocki and Sweet 1985	Carter et al. 1992 David 1993		Channon et al. 1992 Silverstein et al. 1995

Table 6.1 continued

	OCD	
	Group differences	No group differences
WCST	Christensen *et al.* 1992 Harvey 1987 Head *et al.* 1989	Boone *et al.* 1991 Gambini *et al.* 1993 Zielinski *et al.* 1991
Trails B	Martinot *et al.* 1990	Flor-Henry *et al.* 1979 Insel *et al.* 1983
Tower of Hanoi		
Maze tasks	Behar *et al.* 1984	Christensen *et al.* 1992
Stroop	Malloy 1987 Martinot *et al.* 1990	Boone *et al.* 1991 Hollander *et al.* 1993

failed to demonstrate this pattern; one of these studies contained a number of methodological limitations that may account for the null results. While Schneider and Asarnow (1987) failed to find autism-control group differences in perseveration on the WCST, their groups were not matched on intellectual ability, a variable that correlates highly with WCST performance (Ozonoff *et al.* 1991). In addition, all subjects perseverating throughout the test were eliminated. Approximately a quarter of the autistic subjects, but none of the controls, were excluded for this reason. These methodological issues likely contributed to the failure to find group differences in this study.

The Tower of Hanoi (Borys *et al.* 1982) is another EF measure that has been used frequently with autistic samples. This disc-transfer problem requires subjects to plan and carry out a sequence of moves that transforms a random arrangement of discs into a pyramidal goal configuration. Working memory appears essential to successful performance on this task, as intermediate disc configurations produced by different potential moves must be predicted, their implications for future disc configurations considered, and their utility toward eventual attainment of the goal state evaluated. All studies using this task (or other closely related measures, such as the Tower of London; Shallice 1982) with autistic individuals have found large performance decrements relative to control samples (see Table 6.1).

Relatively few studies have employed other traditional EF measures with autistic samples. The Matching Familiar Figures Test (MFFT) is a match-to-standard task developed to examine impulsivity (Kagan 1965). Subjects are shown a picture and four comparison figures, from among which they must choose the one that is identical. The comparison stimuli differ from each other and the standard in minor detail only. Response latency and accuracy are recorded. A pattern of short decision time, coupled with high error rate, is taken to indicate impulsivity. The one study using this task with autistic children found impulsive patterns of responding and poor performance relative to controls (Waterhouse and Fein 1982). Two studies have administered the Stroop Color-Word Test (Stroop 1935) to children with autism. This task measures the ability to selectively respond to one dimension of a multidimensional stimulus. In the critical colour-word interference condition of this task, subjects are given colour-words printed in mismatching ink (e.g. RED printed in green ink) and instructed to name the colour of the ink. This requires selective attention to a relatively less salient dimension of the stimulus, while inhibiting a more automatic response (Dempster 1991; MacLeod 1991). The interference created, evident as lower accuracy and longer reaction time, is known as the 'Stroop effect'. Both studies that administered this measure to autistic subjects found that the Stroop effect of the autistic group was similar in magnitude to that of controls (Bryson 1983; Eskes *et al.* 1990). While the designation of this task as a pure measure of inhibition is uncertain, one interpretation of these results is that inhibition is a relatively spared component of EF in individuals with autism. We will re-examine this interpretation later.

A variety of EF tasks other than those reported in Table 6.1 have been administered to individuals with autism. These studies (Hughes and Russell 1993; Hughes *et al.* 1994; McEvoy *et al.* 1993) are quite consistent with those summarized here in finding EF impairment. We turn next to the parallel literature on EF deficits in ADHD.

Executive dysfunction in ADHD

It has long been hypothesized that frontal lobe dysfunction, and subsequent executive impairments, are involved in the pathophysiology of ADHD (Mattes 1980; Zametkin and Rapoport 1987). In the last decade, exploration of executive-type deficits in children with ADHD has been a very active topic of research investigation, with roughly twice as many studies having been conducted with this population as with autism. In general, empirical studies have demonstrated executive impairments in ADHD, although somewhat less reliably than in autism. As illustrated in Table 6.1, performance is fairly consistently found to be deficient, relative to control samples, on the Tower of Hanoi, Stroop, MFFT, and maze tasks, with over 80% of studies documenting significant group differences. The WCST and the Trail Making Test-Part B, however, appear to be much less sensitive to the executive deficits of ADHD, with approximately half of the studies using each task failing to find performance decrements relative to controls.

One possible interpretation of these inconsistent findings is that the evidence for executive dysfunction in ADHD is less robust than that for autism. In a related vein, Barkley and colleagues (Barkley and Grodzinsky 1994; Barkley *et al.* 1992) recently reviewed the efficacy of executive function tasks in discriminating children with ADHD from those who are developing normally or who meet criteria for other disorders (e.g. learning disabilities, conduct disorder). The classification power of most EF measures was found to be surprisingly low (Barkley and Grodzinsky 1994), with the use of such tests for classification purposes resulting in a high rate of misdiagnosis. While these findings are a reflection of the all too real discriminant validity problem, they do not necessarily indicate that ADHD does not involve substantial executive impairment.

These inconsistent findings may make sense if one considers the domain of EF as consisting of several related, but dissociable, cognitive functions (e.g. inhibition, flexibility, planning, working memory, organization, etc.). The extent to which any one specific executive operation is required varies by task, so that one test may be a better or more pure measure of a particular executive function than is another test. If this is so, the pattern of results seen in Table 6.1 may indicate that the executive deficits of ADHD are not measured particularly well by the WCST and Trail Making Test, but are more prominently required by the Stroop, MFFT, Tower of Hanoi, and maze tasks (see also Pennington and Ozonoff 1996, for a discussion of this possibility). Indeed, it has been long been hypothesized that ADHD involves a primary deficit in the executive function of inhibition (Douglas 1983; Schachar *et al.* 1993), a cognitive operation that does not appear particularly important to WCST performance (Ozonoff and Strayer 1997). Conversely, children with ADHD may be generally capable on measures of flexibililty, such as the WCST and Trail Making Test. Thus, it appears that ADHD involves impairment in some aspects of EF, but not in all.

Executive dysfunction in schizophrenia

As illustrated in Table 6.1, there is strong evidence of robust group differences between schizophrenics and controls on measures presumed to tap the executive system, presenting perhaps the greatest challenge to the executive function hypothesis of autism. As with autism, the most widely used measure has been the WCST. Fey (1951) was the first to demonstrate that schizophrenics had difficulty on this test, perseverating significantly more than normal controls. Indeed, every study that has used this measure with this population since Fey's pioneering work has documented deficient performance, usually in the form of increased perseveration relative to controls, as can be seen from Table 6.1.

The Trail Making Test-Part B is thought to measure, at least in part, mental flexibility (Spreen and Strauss 1991). In this test, subjects must connect randomly arranged numbers and letters in alternating order (e.g. 1–A–2–B and so forth). In most studies with schizophrenics, performance on this test was found to be poor. Similarly, planning abilities, as measured by Tower of Hanoi-type problems and the Porteus Maze Test, have been found to be deficient in individuals with schizophrenia. And, in contrast to autism, the executive deficits of schizophrenia appear to extend to the domain of inhibition as well. Schizophrenic subjects demonstrate difficulty relative to controls on the Stroop test in six of eight studies reviewed.

In many of the investigations summarized in Table 6.1, however, deficits were not specific to the schizophrenic group, but were also seen in comparison samples of mood-disordered (Axelrod *et al.* 1994; Franke *et al.* 1993; Galynker and Harvey 1992; Morice 1990), brain-injured (Axelrod *et al.* 1994), and mixed psychiatric (Everett *et al.* 1989) patients. This provides a rather sobering picture of the discriminant validity problem, demonstrating not only clear overlap between the EF deficits of autism and schizophrenia, but also extension to affective and other disorders as well.

Executive dysfunction in TS

It has been hypothesized that the movements and utterances of TS may reflect failure of an inhibitory system mediated by executive dysfunction (Gedye 1991; Kane 1994; Leckman *et al.* 1991). As summarized in Table 6.1, however, studies of executive function ability in individuals with TS have been quite inconsistent in their findings. Most investigations failed to detect deficits on the WCST in individuals with TS (Bornstein 1990, 1991a; Bornstein and Yang 1991; Randolph *et al.* 1993; Sutherland *et al.* 1982; Yeates and Bornstein 1994), although one study has found impairment on this measure, relative to a comparison sample with OCD (Gladstone *et al.* 1993). Impairment on the Trail Making Test-Part B was found in one investigation (Channon *et al.* 1992), but not in two others (Bornstein 1991a; Silverstein *et al.* 1995). Both studies utilizing the Stroop test with TS individuals failed to find any performance differences relative to controls (Channon *et al.* 1992; Silverstein *et al.* 1995). Using measures other than those listed in Table 6.1, some investigations have found evidence of inhibitory deficits in TS (Baron-Cohen *et al.* 1994a), while others have not (Channon *et al.* 1992; Ozonoff *et al.* 1994).

One conclusion suggested by these inconsistent findings is that EF deficits are not as central a part of the cognitive phenotype of TS as they are for other disorders, such as autism. Furthermore, comorbidity issues and their implications for EF research have not been well dealt with in the TS literature. TS rarely occurs in isolation, but is often accompanied by comorbid ADHD, OCD, and autism (Leonard *et al.* 1992; Sverd 1991; Towbin and Riddle 1993), disorders that are themselves thought to involve executive impairment. Unfortunately, very few investigations of TS have carefully examined comorbidity issues. Those that have addressed this problem find that EF deficits are more prominent in individuals with TS plus a comorbid condition than in those with TS alone (Bornstein 1991b; Silverstein *et al.* 1995; Yeates and Bornstein 1994). This suggests that the EF deficits documented in the studies reviewed in Table 6.1 may be secondary to the comorbid conditions, rather than specific to TS, highlighting the critical importance of considering such confounding variables in all further EF studies of Tourette syndrome.

Executive dysfunction in OCD

Deficits presumed to reflect dysfunction of the executive system have been found in individuals with OCD, as with TS, somewhat inconsistently. As can be seen in Table 6.1, studies are almost equally split between those finding and failing to find deficient performance on the WCST, Trail Making Test, maze tasks, and the Stroop. A number of methodological issues likely contribute to this inconsistency, a matter to which we will turn in a moment. What is most important for the purposes of the present chapter, however, is that executive function studies of OCD also demonstrate overlap with the deficits of autism. To summarize, executive dysfunction is by no means restricted to autistic individuals.

Methodological issues

A number of design, methodological, and analytical issues have been proposed to account for both the discriminant validity problem and the inconsistent findings of EF deficits in certain disorders. One potentially confounding issue, alluded to above in the discussion of TS, is that most studies have not controlled for the presence of comorbid conditions which might impact executive dysfunction. ADHD, for example, can co-occur with Tourette syndrome and conduct disorder (Schachar 1991; Sverd, Curley, Jandorf and Volkersz 1988), both of which have been suggested to involve executive dysfunction. OCD can co-occur with Tourette syndrome and affective disorders (Leonard *et al.* 1992), both of which may be associated with executive impairments. Similarly, autism can co-occur with all of these conditions (McDougle *et al.* 1990; Sverd *et al.* 1993) and others which may involve EF impairment. Only a minority of studies have carefully screened samples for the presence of comorbid disorders, either excluding subjects with multiple diagnoses or statistically examining their effects on test performance (see Silverstein *et al.* 1995, for a discussion of this issue *vis-a-vis* Tourette syndrome). Thus, the extent to which deficits found on EF tasks in the studies reviewed above are specific to the primary disorders under investigation or are artefacts of coexisting conditions is not known.

Second, the adequacy of matching procedures varies widely across investigations. Some studies have matched their experimental and control samples on intellectual function, gender, age, and socioeconomic status, while others have not. These variables may exert influence on EF perfor- mance (Pennington and Ozonoff 1996) and thus it is critical to control for these in research investigations. Gambini *et al.* (1993), for example, found that group differences on the WCST between obsessive–compulsive subjects and normal controls were no longer statistically significant after correction for differences in educational level.

Furthermore, some of the studies reviewed above did not use a matched control sample (e.g. Bornstein 1990; Yeates and Bornstein 1994), instead comparing performance of the experimental group with published normative data. As noted by Boone *et al.* (1991), if subject samples differ significantly from normative samples on variables important to EF performance, such as intellectual and educational level, then use of normative data, rather than comparison to matched controls, may result in false-positive identification of EF deficits.

Finally, most investigations have treated EF as a unidimensional construct and have not differentiated and independently examined multiple components of the domain. Tasks used have been molar measures of EF that tap far more than one cognitive operation, usually without specific scoring systems that permit individual variance to be partialled out and examined independently. A good example of this problem is the WCST. While generally considered a test of cognitive flexibility, a variety of other operations are required for successful performance, including attribute identification, categorization, working memory, inhibition, selective attention, and utilization of verbal feedback provided in the context of a social interaction (Bond and Buchtel 1984; Dehaene and Changeux 1991; Ozonoff 1995b; Perrine 1993; van der Does and van den Bosch 1992).

This analysis can be extended to the other EF measures considered in this chapter. The Tower of Hanoi, for example, appears to require abstract reasoning, working memory capacity, recursive use of embedded if–then rules, means-end analysis, and planning. The MFFT appears to measure visual pattern analysis and attention to detail, in addition to inhibition of impulsive responses. The Trail Making Test requires mental flexibility, but also visual attention, sequencing ability, working memory, and motor function (Spreen and Strauss 1991). The Stroop has been described as measuring inhibition, interference-sensitivity, selective attention, and focused attention (Carte et al. 1996; Dempster 1991; Mirsky et al. 1991). Consequently, it is difficult to determine precisely why an individual performs poorly on any of these tests. Until this measurement imprecision is resolved, conclusions about the status of executive dysfunction in autism, schizophrenia, ADHD, TS, and OCD must be considered tentative. In the next section, we will explore whether employment of an information processing framework may help to resolve these measurement issues.

The information processing approach

The information processing approach is one of the dominant perspectives in the field of experimental cognitive psychology today. The main focus of this approach is an understanding of the component mental operations involved in the performance of cognitive tasks. The information processing perspective is not a specific model or theory, but rather a broad framework for understanding cognition. It provides relatively theory-independent methods and specific experimental paradigms for understanding complex behaviour (Anderson and Bower 1973; Ingram 1989). Thus, a variety of different cognitive models and constructs can be articulated and tested from within this framework.

One central methodological strategy of the information processing approach is *component process analysis* (Farah 1984; Friedrich and Rader 1996). The goal of component process analysis is decomposition of complex cognitive tasks into the elementary operations that appear to underlie them, the time course and relationship of these component processes to each other, and the internal representations, schemas, or codes they act upon (Friedrich and Rader 1996). The component process approach and the information processing paradigms it employs have been central to the fields of experimental psychology and cognitive neuropsychology for many years.

Several advantages of information processing tasks are apparent. They are typically administered by computer, permitting highly controlled stimulus presentation. All data collection is performed via computer as well, with precise reaction time and accuracy data automatically recorded. Thus, there is less opportunity for the administration and scoring errors that can occur during traditional neuropsychological testing. Additionally, these tasks typically measure very specific processes, such as target detection and response inhibition, reducing the measurement imprecision of standard neuropsychological measures. Researchers can use component process analyses to identify the underlying cognitive operations that appear requisite to the performance of a complex task, such as the WCST, and develop new experimental paradigms that isolate and selectively measure individual components. Thus, this approach may provide us with the method for parsing the large construct of executive function into more unitary and functionally independent cognitive operations, examining their association with specific disorders.

The information processing approach and autism

The first research team to employ computerized EF paradigms with autistic subjects was Hughes *et al.* (1994), who used the Intradimensional–Extradimensional (IDED) Shift task to assess set-shifting capacity. This task is, in many ways, similar to the WCST. It requires subjects to classify abstract patterns according to an initially unknown rule and then to shift to a new categorization principle after the previous sorting pattern receives negative feedback. It differs from and improves upon the WCST, however, in a number of critical ways. First, it does not require verbal ability or social interaction because both items and accuracy feedback are presented by computer. Second, the task is administered in multiple stages, with several internal controls built in to exclude alternative explanations of poor performance (e.g. discrimination learning, set-maintenance, rule reversal, transfer of learning, motor inhibition). This permits more precise identification of the underlying cognitive operations involved in task performance. Significant group differences were found on the IDED task, with the autistic sample reportedly engaging in highly perseverative and inflexible strategies (Hughes *et al.* 1994).

Courchesne *et al.* (1994) also employed information processing paradigms to study autistic people. They found that while non-retarded autistic adolescents performed as well as normal controls on a focused attention task, performance was highly deficient relative to controls on a shifting task that required rapid alternation of attentional focus between auditory and visual channels. Subjects were told to monitor one modality (either auditory or visual) until an oddball target was detected, respond to the target, and then immediately shift their attention to the other modality. False alarm errors occurred when subjects failed to disengage attention from the first modality and shift it to the second sensory channel, while misses occurred when subjects failed to quickly move and re-engage attention to the new channel, resulting in failure to detect new targets. Autistic subjects committed significantly more false alarm errors and misses than controls, suggesting deficits in both disengaging and moving attention.

Ozonoff and colleagues used a Go–NoGo paradigm to examine two component processes, flexibility and inhibition, that are often entangled in standard EF tests such as the WCST (Ozonoff *et al.* 1994). The Go–NoGo task consisted of three test conditions. The first required subjects to respond to a neutral cue, the 'go' stimulus (in this case, a circle), while simultaneously inhibiting responses to another neutral cue, the 'no-go' stimulus (a square). This condition is a standard Go–NoGo paradigm thought to require inhibition of motor responses (Drewe 1975), but no shifting of cognitive set. In the second condition, the 'go' and 'no-go' response designations reversed, so that now subjects were required to respond to the square, while inhibiting the previously reinforced, prepotent response to the circle. The final condition necessitated frequent shifting from one response pattern to another, placing high demands on cognitive flexibility.

The autistic group was unimpaired relative to controls on the standard Go–NoGo paradigm, suggesting that motor inhibition was intact. They were moderately impaired when inhibiting prepotent responses. The largest group differences were evident in the third condition, which required frequent shifting of cognitive set. In contrast, children with Tourette syndrome, matched on age and intellectual ability, experienced no difficulty in any of the three conditions (Ozonoff *et al.* 1994).

The results of this study suggested that both inhibition of prepotent responses and flexibility were impaired in autism (with the latter somewhat more deficient), while neither EF operation appeared to be a central disability of Tourette syndrome. Interpretation of these results was complicated, however, by a confounding of the inhibition and flexibility conditions. Specifically, it was necessary for subjects to shift set at the very beginning of the second phase and, thus, this condition did not selectively measure inhibition, as intended.

Ozonoff and Strayer (1997) conducted a second study to examine inhibitory functions in autism more closely and dissociate them from flexibility operations more completely. Two tasks, measuring different components of inhibition, were administered to a group of non-retarded children with autism and controls matched on age and IQ. In the Stopping task (Logan 1994; Logan et al. 1984), subjects were engaged in a simple primary task (e.g. categorizing words as animals or non-animals); on a subset of trials, an auditory signal was presented which indicated that responses should be inhibited on that trial (i.e. the word should not be categorized). This task is thought to measure the ability to control a voluntary motor response (Logan et al. 1984) and places little demand on flexibility operations.

The Negative Priming task (Tipper 1985) measured a more central, cognitive inhibitory mechanism (Neill et al. 1990). In this task, subjects saw a five-letter string (e.g. TVTVT) and were asked to judge whether the second and fourth letters were 'the same' or 'different'. On some trials, the target stimuli (letters 2 and 4) were the same as the distractor stimuli (letters 1, 3, and 5) from the immediately preceding trial. In general, when distractors from previous trials become targets on subsequent trials, performance of normal subjects is slower and less accurate than if the stimuli had not been seen previously (Tipper 1985). This disruption in performance is termed the *negative priming effect*.

Ozonoff and Strayer (1997) found that subjects with autism were unimpaired on both tests of inhibition relative to normally developing controls. On the Stopping task, no group differences were evident in the likelihood of responding on signal trials (i.e. when responses should have been withheld). On the Negative Priming task, when distractors on one trial became targets on the following trial, the act of previously ignoring these stimuli had similar effects on the reaction time and error rate of the two groups. The magnitude of the negative priming effect was equivalent in the autistic and control samples. Thus, across tasks measuring both motor and cognitive components of inhibition, the inhibitory ability of the autistic group was similar to that of matched normal controls. These results are convergent with the work of Burack and Iarocci (1995), who found no differences between autistic and matched mentally retarded individuals in their ability to inhibit the processing of distractor stimuli during an attentional task.

To conclude this discussion of the use of information processing paradigms with autistic individuals, it appears that they have helped to obtain some precision in the specification of the executive dysfunction involved in the disorder. It appears that flexibility operations are deficient in all paradigms that have been used (IDED, Attention Shift, Go–NoGo Flexibility condition). In contrast, inhibition deficits were not found in the work of Ozonoff and colleagues (Ozonoff and Strayer, 1997; Ozonoff *et al.* 1994), were ruled out as major contributors to poor performance in the IDED task of Hughes *et al.* (1994), were not found on the Stroop test (Bryson 1983; Eskes *et al.* 1990), and were not apparent during the attentional task of Burack and Iarocci (1995). This suggests that general inhibitory impairment is not central to the EF phenotype of autism.

The component process approach has also been used to explore the cognitive functioning of individuals with ADHD, schizophrenia, TS, and OCD. None of the information processing tasks on which autistic samples perform poorly have yet been used with these other groups. Fortuitously, however, three tasks on which autistic individuals perform well (e.g. the Stopping, Negative Priming, and Go–NoGo Inhibition tasks) have been used with the four other clinical groups considered in this chapter, allowing some critical contrasts to be made. We turn next to this literature.

The information processing approach and other disorders

Go–NoGo tasks

Go–NoGo paradigms have been used with all four groups, in each case administered in the standard manner thought to measure inhibition (e.g. in which subjects must respond to a 'go' stimulus while inhibiting responses to a 'no-go' stimulus). Trommer *et al.* (1988) found that children with attention deficit disorder (ADD) committed significantly more errors, failing to inhibit responses to the 'no-go' stimulus, than controls. The performance of ADD children without hyperactivity improved over the duration of the test, while that of hyperactive ADD children failed to improve with practice. Shue and Douglas (1992) also found that children with ADHD committed significantly more errors than controls in a Go–NoGo task.

Only one study has used this paradigm with schizophrenic subjects (Galbraith and Steffy 1980). The reaction time of process schizophrenic individuals was approximately 1000 milliseconds slower than that of normal controls in responding to the 'go' stimulus. Unfortunately, the statistical significance of this group difference was not reported, nor were error rates. It is quite likely, however, that the reported group differences were statistically significant, since the magnitude of the effect is very large. Previous studies have found reaction time differences of 50 milliseconds to significantly discriminate between groups on a similar Go–NoGo paradigm (Ozonoff *et al.* 1994).

Ozonoff *et al.* (1994) studied children with TS who did not meet criteria for any comorbid conditions (i.e. ADHD, OCD, learning disabilities, mood disorders, etc.). No deficits in the ability to inhibit responses on a Go–NoGo task were found, relative to normally developing controls matched on age and IQ.

The only study to employ a Go–NoGo task with OCD subjects did not report group differences in task performance, but was instead interested in frontal lobe activity, as measured by evoked potentials, during the task (Malloy *et al.* 1989). The primary variable of interest was the magnitude of the P300 component of the evoked potential during correct responses. The amplitude of the P300 component was significantly smaller in the orbital frontal region during performance of the task by OCD subjects, relative to controls matched on age, gender, handedness, and education.

To summarize, children with ADHD appear to be impaired on Go–NoGo tasks. The conclusions that can be reached for schizophrenia, TS, and OCD are limited by a dearth of studies and by the use of different dependent measures across investigations. There is some suggestion, however, that abnormalities exist in how individuals with schizophrenia and OCD process go and no-go stimuli. These results stand in contrast to the findings of Ozonoff *et al.* (1994) that performance of autistic children in the standard Go–NoGo task is unimpaired.

Stopping task

This paradigm, thought to measure voluntary inhibition of motor responses, has been used with children with ADHD by two different research teams. Schachar and Logan (1990) found that ADHD subjects were able to inhibit significantly fewer responses than matched normal controls. In addition, the estimated latency to respond to the stop-signal was significantly longer in the ADHD than the normal control group. These results were replicated by Aman *et al.* (1997). These findings contrast with the results of Ozonoff and Strayer (1997), who found that autistic individuals did not differ from matched controls on the Stopping task. This paradigm has not yet been employed with subjects with schizophrenia, TS, or OCD.

Negative Priming task

In the Negative Priming task, the primary variable of interest is reaction time to stimuli which served as distractors (e.g. were inhibited or ignored) on previous trials. Reduced negative priming indicates inferior cognitive inhibition (Neill *et al.* 1990). Reduced negative priming has been found in children with ADHD (McLaren 1989, reported in Houghton and Tipper 1994), and adults with schizophrenia (Beech *et al.* 1989), schizotypy (Beech and Claridge 1987; Beech *et al.* 1991; Peters *et al.* 1994), and OCD (Enright and Beech

1993). A recent study demonstrated that children with TS plus comorbid ADHD, OCD, or both, demonstrated greatly reduced negative priming relative to both children with TS alone and normally developing controls (Ozonoff, *et al.* under review). These results again stand in contrast to the unimpaired performance of autistic subjects reported by Ozonoff and Strayer (1997).

Table 6.2 summarizes the results of these information processing studies, illustrating the dissociation between the abilities and disabilities of autism, ADHD, schizophrenia, TS, and OCD on identical tasks.

Conclusions

Recent information processing studies suggest that component executive functions are dissociable and can be measured relatively independently. These studies provide the best empirical support for specific flexibility impairments in autism, with inhibition appearing to be a relatively less affected, or perhaps spared, ability. The robust group differences found on tasks such as the Tower of Hanoi and Tower of London may suggest that planning and working memory impairments are also central to autism. However, since only a few studies have yet been conducted and information processing-type tasks have not been widely utilized, this conclusion should be considered preliminary at the present time.

Information processing research also sheds light on the discriminant validity problem. There is emerging evidence that different neurodevelopmental and psychopathological disorders involve dysfunction of selective aspects of the executive system. The impairments in flexibility so typical of autism have not been found in subjects with Tourette syndrome (Ozonoff *et al.* 1994). In contrast, deficits in inhibition have been documented in subjects with ADHD, schizophrenia, and OCD using the same tasks on which autistic individuals perform well. There is some suggestion that the executive deficit of ADHD involves primarily inhibitory operations, while that in schizophrenia is more widespread, involving virtually all aspects of EF that have been investigated. Recent research on TS, using both traditional neuropsychological tests and more refined information processing measures, suggests that the pure form of the disorder may not involve executive dysfunction, with the deficits documented in some studies reflecting the presence of comorbid ADHD and OCD.

Thus, considering executive function as a multidimensional rather than a unitary construct has helped us obtain more precision in the nature of the dysfunction associated with autism, as well as providing a dissociation from other disorders. The possibility of double-dissociations and full differentiation among disorders, however, awaits future investigation. Particularly

Table 6.2 Performance of samples with autism, ADHD, schizophrenia, TS and OCD on selected information processing tasks.

	Standard Go-Nogo	Flexibility Go-Nogo	Stopping	Negative priming
Autism	– (Ozonoff et al. 1994)	+ (Ozonoff et al. 1994)	– (Ozonoff and Strayer 1997)	– (Ozonoff and Strayer 1997)
ADHD	+ (Shue and Douglas 1992) + (Trommer et al. 1988)		+ (Aman et al. in press) + (Schachar and Logan 1990)	+ (McLaren 1989)
Schizophrenia	+ (Galbraith and Steffy 1980)			+ (Beech et al. 1989)
TS	– (Ozonoff et al. 1994)	– (Ozonoff et al. 1994)		+ (Ozonoff et al. under review)
OCD	+ (Malloy et al. 1989)			+ (Enright and Beech 1993)

+ = deficit on task relative to control group; – = no significant group differences.

helpful will be studies that use the IDED paradigm of Hughes *et al.* (1994), the Attention Shifting task of Courchesne *et al.* (1994), or the Go–NoGo Flexibility condition of Ozonoff *et al.* (1994) with ADHD, schizophrenic, TS, and OCD individuals. The ultimate goal of this research is to obtain 'fingerprints' of the specific patterns of EF deficit associated with different disorders. The present review suggests that application of a component process framework to the study of executive function is not only fruitful, but necessary. Potentially interesting and informative group differences and selective patterns of deficit are all but obscured when traditional neuropsychological measures alone are employed.

Finally, the $64 000 question remains: How is executive impairment related to other cognitive and behavioural difficulties of autism? Are there causal links between executive deficits and other symptoms of the disorder? One clear difficulty of autistic individuals is that of mental state processing (also known as 'theory of mind'). Recently, it has been proposed that such social deficits may share similar underpinnings with executive function impairments. The work of Russell and colleagues first suggested that what appeared to be a theory of mind deficit, namely an inability to engage in deception, could be recast as an executive impairment, the inability to disengage from the immediate context and guide behaviour by internal rules instead (Hughes and Russell 1993; Russell *et al.* 1991). Similarly, Harris (1993) has suggested that the pretend-play impairment of autism may be an extension of a primary deficit in disengaging from environmental cues. A comparable analysis has been suggested by Frye *et al.* (1995) and Ozonoff (in press) who suggest that impairment in the capacity to employ 'if–then' strategic rules may lead to failure on both theory of mind and EF measures.

Other studies have found substantial correlations between social-cognitive and executive function abilities, suggesting again some interrelationship among the skills. McEvoy *et al.* (1993) found that executive function impairment and joint attention deficits were highly correlated; both abilities can be thought of as requiring some capacity to shift between competing alternatives (in the case of EF tasks, between two cognitive sets; in the case of joint attention, between two attentional perspectives). Ozonoff *et al.* (1991) found that EF scores were highly correlated with theory of mind ability in autistic people. EF capacity has also been found to be a strong predictor of social outcome and long-term prognosis in autistic individuals (Berger *et al.* 1993; Szatmari *et al.* 1989). Finally, very recent and exciting functional neuroimaging research suggests that theory of mind capacities may be subserved by the prefrontal cortex (Baron-Cohen *et al.* 1994b; Fletcher *et al.* 1995), potentially linking them to executive type impairments through proximity of the neural structures involved. These studies suggest that the social cognition and executive function deficits of autism may not be completely separable, independent islets of dysfunction.

A final goal of this chapter is to encourage the use of an information processing approach to explore further the contribution that EF deficits play in the larger behavioural and symptomatic picture of autism.

REFERENCES

Abramczyk, R. R., Jordan, D. E., and Hegel, M. (1983). 'Reverse' Stroop effect in the performance of schizophrenics. *Perceptual and Motor Skills*, **56**, 99–106.

Aman, C. J., Roberts, R. J., and Pennington, B. F. A neuropsychological examination of the underlying deficit in ADHD: The frontal lobe vs. right parietal lobe theories. *Developmental Psychology*. (In press.)

Anderson, J. R. and Bower, G. H. (1973). *Human associative memory*. Erlbaum, NY.

Axelrod, B. N., Goldman, R. S., Tompkins, L. M., and Jiron, C. C. (1994). Poor differential performance on the Wisconsin Card Sorting Test in schizophrenia, mood disorder, and traumatic brain injury. *Neuropsychiatry, Neuropsychology, and Behavioral Neurology*, **7**, 20–4.

Barkley, R. A. and Grodzinsky, G. M. (1994). Are tests of frontal lobe functions useful in the diagnosis of attention deficit disorders? *The Clinical Neuropsychologist*, **8**, 121–39.

Barkley, R. A., Grodzinsky, G., and DuPaul, G. J. (1992). Frontal lobe functions in attention deficit disorder with and without hyperactivity: A review and research report. *Journal of Abnormal Child Psychology*, **20**, 163–88.

Baron-Cohen, S., Cross, P., Crowson, M., and Robertson, M. (1994a). Can children with Gilles de la Tourette Syndrome edit their intentions? *Psychological Medicine*, **24**, 29–40.

Baron-Cohen, S., Ring, H., Moriarty, J., Schmitz, B., Costa, D., and Ell, P. (1994b) Recognition of mental state terms: Clinical findings in children with autism and a functional neuroimaging study of normal adults. *British Journal of Psychiatry*, **165**, 640–9.

Beatty, W. W., Jocic, Z., Monson, N., and Katzung, V. M. (1994). Problem solving by schizophrenic and schizoaffective patients on the Wisconsin and California Card Sorting Tests. *Neuropsychology*, **8**, 49–54.

Beech, A. and Claridge, G. (1987). Individual differences in negative priming: Relations with schizotypal personality traits. *British Journal of Psychology*, **78**, 349–56.

Beech, A., Powell, T., McWilliam, J., and Claridge, G. (1989). Evidence of reduced 'cognitive inhibition' in schizophrenia. *British Journal of Clinical Psychology*, **28**, 109–16.

Beech, A. R., McManus, D., Baylis, G., and Tipper, S. P. (1991). Individual differences in cognitive processes: Towards an explanation of schizophrenic symptomatology. *British Journal of Psychology*, **82**, 417–26.

Behar, D., Rapaport, J. L., Berg, C. J., Denckla, M. B., Mann, L., Cox, C., *et al.* (1984). Computerized tomography and neuropsychological test measures in adolescents with obsessive-compulsive disorder. *American Journal of Psychiatry*, **141**, 363–9.

Bennetto, L., Pennington, B. F., and Rogers, S. J. (1996). Intact and impaired memory functions in autism. *Child Development*, **67**, 1816–35.

Berger, H. J. C., van Spaendonck, K. P. M., Horstink, M. W. I. M., Buytenhuijs, E. L., Lammers, P. W. J. M., and Cools, A. R. (1993). Cognitive shifting as a predictor of progress in social understanding in high-functioning adolescents with autism: A prospective study. *Journal of Autism and Developmental Disorders*, **23**, 341–59.

Bond, J. A. and Buchtel, H. A. (1984). Comparison of the Wisconsin Card Sorting Test and the Halstead Category Test. *Journal of Clinical Psychology*, **40**, 1251–5.

Boone, K. B., Ananth, J., Philpott, L., Kaur, A., and Djenderedjian, A. (1991). Neuropsychological characteristics of nondepressed adults with obsessive-compulsive disorder. *Neuropsychiatry, Neuropsychology and Behavioral Neurology*, **4**, 96–109.

Bornstein, R. A. (1990). Neuropsychological performance in children with Tourette Syndrome. *Psychiatry Research*, **33**, 73–81.

Bornstein, R. A. (1991a). Neuropsychological performance in adults with Tourette syndrome. *Psychiatry Research*, **37**, 229–36.

Bornstein, R. A. (1991b). Neuropsychological correlates of obsessive characteristics in Tourette Syndrome. *Journal of Neuropsychiatry and Clinical Neurosciences*, **3**, 157–62.

Bornstein, R. A. and Yang, V. (1991). Neuropsychological performance in medicated and unmedicated patients with Tourette Disorder. *American Journal of Psychiatry*, **148**, 468–71.

Borys, S. V., Spitz, H. H., and Dorans, B. A. (1982). Tower of hanoi performance of retarded young adults and nonretarded children as a function of solution length and goal state. *Journal of Experimental Child Psychology*, **33**, 87–110.

Boucugnani, L. L. and Jones, R. W. (1989). Behaviors analogous to frontal lobe dysfunction in children with attention deficit hyperactivity disorder. *Archives of Clinical Neuropsychology*, **4**, 161–73.

Braff, D. L., Heaton, R. K., Kuck, J., Cullum, M., Moranville, J., Grant, I., *et al.* (1991). The generalized pattern of neuropsychological deficits in outpatients with chronic schizophrenia with heterogeneous Wisconsin Card Sorting Test results. *Archives of General Psychiatry*, **48**, 891–8.

Bryson, S. E. (1983). Interference effects in autistic children: Evidence for the comprehension of single stimuli. *Journal of Abnormal Psychology*, **92**, 250–4.

Burack, J. A. and Iarocci, G. (1995). *Visual filtering and covert orienting in developmentally disordered persons with and without autism*. Paper presented at the Society for Research in Child Development (March). Indianapolis, IN.

Butler, R. W., Jenkins, M. A., Sprock, J., and Braff, D. L. (1992). Wisconsin Card Sorting Test deficits in chronic paranoid schizophrenia: Evidence for a relatively discrete subgroup? *Schizophrenia Research*, **7**, 169–76.

Carte, E. T., Nigg, J. T., and Hinshaw, S. P. (1996). Neuropsychological functioning, motor speed, and language processing in boys with and without ADHD. *Journal of Abnormal Child Psychology*, **24**, 481–98.

Carter, C. S., Robertson, L. C., and Nordahl, T. E. (1992). Abnormal processing of irrelevant information in chronic schizophrenia: Selective enhancement of Stroop facilitation. *Psychiatry Research*, **41**, 137–46.

Channon, S., Flynn, D., and Robertson, M. M. (1992). Attentional deficits in Gilles de la Tourette syndrome. *Neuropsychiatry, Neuropsychology and Behavioral Neurology*, **5**, 170–7.

Chelune, G. J., Ferguson, W., Koon, R., and Dickey, T. O. (1986). Frontal lobe disinhibition in attention deficit disorder. *Child Psychiatry and Human Development*, **16**, 221–34.

Christensen, K. J., Kim, S. W., Dysken, M. W., and Hoover, K. M. (1992). Neuropsychological performance in obsessive-compulsive disorder. *Biological Psychiatry*, **31**, 4–18.

Cleghorn, J. M., Kaplan, R. D., Szechtman, B., Szechtmen, H., and Brown, G. M. (1990). Neuroleptic drug effects on cognitive function in schizophrenia. *Schizophrenia Research*, **3**, 211–19.

Cohen, N. J., Weiss, G., and Minde, K. (1972). Cognitive styles in adolescents previously diagnosed as hyperactive. *Journal of Child Psychology and Psychiatry*, **13**, 203–9.

Courchesne, E., Townsend, J., Akshoomoff, N.A., Saitoh, O., Yeung-Courchesne, R., Lincoln, A.J., et al. (1994). Impairment in shifting attention in autistic and cerebellar patients. *Behavioral Neuroscience*, **108**, 848–65.

Damasio, A. R. and Maurer, R. G. (1978). A neurological model for childhood autism. *Archives of Neurology*, **35**, 777–86.

David, A. S. (1993). Callosal transfer in schizophrenia: Too much or too little? *Journal of Abnormal Psychology*, **102**, 573–9.

Dehaene, S. and Changeux, J. P. (1991). The Wisconsin Card Sorting Test: Theoretical analysis and modeling in a neuronal network. *Cerebral Cortex*, **1**, 62–79.

Dempster, F. N. (1991). Inhibitory processes: A neglected dimension of intelligence. *Intelligence*, **15**, 157–73.

Diamond, A., Ciaramitaro, V., Donner, E., Hurwitz, W., Lee, E., Grover, W., et al. (1992). Prefrontal cortex cognitive deficits in early treated PKU: Results of a longitudinal study in children and of an animal model. *Society for Neuroscience Abstracts*, **18**, 1063.

Douglas, V. I. (1983). Attentional and cognitive problems. In *Developmental neuropsychiatry* (ed. M. Rutter), pp. 280–329. Guilford, NY.

Drewe, E. A. (1975). Go–NoGo learning after frontal lobe lesions in humans. *Cortex*, **11**, 8–16.

Dykman, R. A. and Ackerman, P. T. (1991). Attention deficit disorder and specific reading disability: Separate but often overlapping disorders. *Journal of Learning Disabilities*, **24**, 96–103.

Enright, S. J. and Beech, A. R. (1993). Reduced cognitive inhibition in obsessive-compulsive disorder. *British Journal of Clinical Psychology*, **32**, 67–74.

Eskes, G. A., Bryson, S. E., and McCormick, T. A. (1990). Comprehension of concrete and abstract words in autistic children. *Journal of Autism and Developmental Disorders*, **20**, 61–73.

Everett, J., Laplante, L., and Thomas, J. (1989). The selective attention deficit in schizophrenia: Limited resources or cognitive fatigue? *Journal of Nervous and Mental Disease*, **177**, 735–8.

Farah, M. J. (1984). The neurological basis of mental imagery: A componential analysis. *Cognition*, **18**, 245–72.

Fey, E. T. (1951). The performance of young schizophrenics and young normals on the Wisconsin Card Sorting Test. *Journal of Consulting Psychology*, **15**, 311–19.

Fischer, M., Barkley, R. A., Edelbrock, C. S., and Smallish, L. (1990). The adolescent outcome of hyperactive children diagnosed by research criteria: Academic, attentional, and neuropsychological status. *Journal of Consulting and Clinical Psychology*, **58**, 580–8.

Fletcher, P. C., Happé, F. G. E., Frith, U., Baker, S. C., Dolan, R. J., and Frackowiak, R. S. J. (1995). Other minds in the brain: A functional imaging study of theory of mind in story comprehension. *Cognition*, **57**, 2.

Flor-Henry, P., Yeudall, L. T., Koles, Z. J., and Howarth, B. G. (1979). Neuropsychological and power spectral EEG investigations of the obsessive-compulsive syndrome. *Biological Psychiatry*, **14**, 119–30.

Franke, P., Maier, W., Hain, C., and Klingler, T. (1992). Wisconsin Card Sorting Test: An indicator of vulnerability to schizophrenia? *Schizophrenia Research*, **6**, 243–9.

Franke, P., Maier, W., Hardt, J., Frieboes, R., Lichtermann, D., and Hain, C. (1993). Assessment of frontal lobe functioning in schizophrenia and unipolar major depression. *Psychopathology*, **26**, 76–84.

Friedrich, F. J. and Rader, S. (1996). Component process analysis in experimental and clinical neuropsychology. In *Theoretical foundations of clinical neuropsychology for clinical practitioners* (ed. M. Maruish and J. Moses), pp. 59–79. Lawrence Erlbaum, Hillsdale, NJ.

Frye, D., Zelazo, P. 0., and Palfai, T. (1995). Theory of mind and rule-based reasoning. *Cognitive Development*, **10**, 483–527.

Galbraith, K. J. and Steffy, R. A. (1980). Inhibition and redundancy-associated deficit in schizophrenic discrimination reaction time. *Canadian Journal of Behavioral Science*, **12**, 347–58.

Galynker, I. I. and Harvey, P. D. (1992). Neuropsychological screening in the psychiatric emergency room. *Comprehensive Psychiatry*, **33**, 291–5.

Gambini, O., Macciardi, F., Abbruzzese, M., and Scarone, S. (1992). Influence of education on WCST performances in schizophrenic patients. *International Journal of Neuroscience*, **67**, 105–9.

Gambini, O., Abbruzzese, M., and Scarone, S. (1993). Smooth pursuit and saccadic eye movements and Wisconsin Card Sorting Test performance in obsessive-compulsive disorder. *Psychiatry Research*, **48**, 191–200.

Gedye, A. (1991). Tourette Syndrome attributed to frontal lobe dysfunction: Numerous etiologies involved. *Journal of Clinical Psychology*, **47**, 233–52.

Gladstone, M., Carter, A. S., Schultz, R. T., Riddle, M., Scahill, L., and Pauls, D. L. (1993). *Neuropsychological functioning of children affected with Tourette Syndrome and obsessive compulsive disorder*. Paper presented at the meeting of the International Neuropsychological Society (February). Galveston, TX.

Goldberg, T. E., Saint-Cyr, J. A., and Weinberger, D. R. (1990). Assessment of procedural learning and problem-solving in schizophrenic patients by Tower of Hanoi type tasks. *Journal of Neuropsychiatry and Clinical Neuroscience*, **2**, 165–73.

Gorenstein, E. E., Mammato, C. A., and Sandy, J. M. (1989). Performance of inattentive-overactive children on selected measures of prefrontal-type function. *Journal of Clinical Psychology*, **45**, 619–32.

Grodzinsky, G. M. and Diamond, R. (1992). Frontal lobe functioning in boys with attention deficit hyperactivity disorder. *Developmental Neuropsychology*, **8**, 427–45.

Harris, P. (1993). Pretending and planning. In *Understanding other minds: Perspectives from autism* (ed. S. Baron-Cohen, H. Tager-Flusberg, and D.J. Cohen), pp. 228–46. Oxford University Press, NY.

Harvey, N. S. (1987). Neurological factors in obsessive-compulsive disorder. *British Journal of Psychiatry*, **150**, 567–8.

Head, D., Bolton, D., and Hymas, N. (1989). Deficit in cognitive shifting ability in patients with obsessive-compulsive disorder. *Biological Psychiatry*, **25**, 929–37.

Heaton, R. K. (1981). *Wisconsin Card Sorting Test Manual*. Psychological Assessment Resources, Odessa, FL.

Hoff, A. L., Riordan, H., O'Donnell, D. W., Morris, L., and DeLisi, L. E. (1992). Neuropsychological functioning of first-episode schizophreniform patients. *American Journal of Psychiatry*, **149**, 898–903.

Hollander, E., Cohen, L., Richards, M., and Mullen, L. (1993). A pilot study of the neuropsychology of obsessive-compulsive disorder and Parkinson's disease: Basal ganglia disorders. *Journal of Neuropsychiatry and Clinical Neurosciences*, **5**, 104–7.

Hopkins, J., Perlman, T., Hechtman, L., and Weiss, G. (1979). Cognitive style in adults originally diagnosed as hyperactives. *Journal of Child Psychology and Psychiatry*, **20**, 209–16.

Houghton, G. and Tipper, S. P. (1994). A model of inhibitory mechanisms in selective attention. In *Inhibitory processes in attention, memory, and language* (ed. D. Dagenbach and T.H. Carr), pp. 53–112. Academic Press, San Diego.

Hughes, C. and Russell, J. (1993). Autistic children's difficulty with mental disengagement from an object: Its implications for theories of autism. *Developmental Psychology*, **29**, 498–510.

Hughes, C., Russell, J., and Robbins, T. W. (1994). Evidence for executive dysfunction in autism. *Neuropsychologia*, **32**, 477–92.

Hurt, J. and Naglieri, J. A. (1992). Performance of delinquent and nondelinquent males on planning, attention, simultaneous and successive cognitive processing tasks. *Journal of Clinical Psychology*, **48**, 120–8.

Ingram, R. E. (1989). Information processing as a theoretical framework for child and adolescent psychiatry. In *Needs and prospects of child and adolescent psychiatry* (ed. M. H. Schmidt and H. Remschmidt), pp. 25–36. Hogrefe and Huber, Lewiston, NY.

Insel, T. R., Donnelly, E. F., Lalakea, M. L., Alterman, I. S., and Murphy, D. L. (1983). Neurological and neuropsychological studies of patients with obsessive-compulsive disorder. *Biological Psychiatry*, **18**, 741–51.

Kagan, J. (1965). Individual differences in the resolution of response uncertainty. *Journal of Personality and Social Psychology*, **2**, 154–60.

Kane, M. J. (1994). Premonitory urges as 'attentional tics' in Tourette syndrome. *Journal of the American Academy of Child and Adolescent Psychiatry*, **33**, 805–8.

Kuehne, C., Kehle, T. J., and McMahon, W. (1987). Differences between children with attention deficit disorder, children with specific learning disabilities, and normal children. *Journal of School Psychology*, **25**, 161–6.

Lavoie, M. E., and Charlebois, P. (1994). The discriminant validity of the Stroop color and word test: Toward a cost-effective strategy to distinguish subgroups of disruptive behavior preadolescents. *Psychology in the Schools*, **31**, 98–107.

Leckman, J. F., Knorr, A. M., Rasmusson, A. M., and Cohen, D.J. (1991). Basal ganglia research and Tourette's Syndrome. *Trends in Neuroscience*, **14**, 94.

Leonard, H. L., Swedo, S. E., Rapoport, J. L., Rickler, K. C., Topol, D., Lee, S., *et al.* (1992). Tourette Syndrome and obsessive-compulsive disorder. *Advances in Neurology*, **58**, 83–93.

Levander, S. E., Bartfai, A., and Schalling, D. (1985). Regional cortical dysfunction in schizophrenic patients studied by computerized neuropsychological methods. *Perceptual and Motor Skills*, **61**, 479–95.

Litman, R. E., Hommer, D. W., Clem, T., Ornsteen, M. L., Ollo, C., and Pickar, D. (1991). Correlation of Wisconsin Card Sorting Test performance with eye tracking in schizophrenia. *American Journal of Psychiatry*, **148**, 1580–2.

Logan, G. (1994). On the ability to inhibit thought and action: A user's guide to the stop-signal paradigm. In *Inhibitory processes in attention, memory and language* (ed. D. Dagenbach and T. H. Carr), pp. 189–239. Academic Press, San Diego.

Logan, G. D., Cowan, W. B., and Davis, K. A. (1984). On the ability to inhibit simple and choice reaction time responses: A model and a method. *Journal of Experimental Psychology: Human Perception and Performance*, **10**, 276–91.

Loge, D. V., Staton, R. D., and Beatty, W. M. (1990). Performance of children with ADHD on tests sensitive to frontal lobe dysfunction. *Journal of the American Academy of Child and Adolescent Psychiatry*, **29**, 540–5.

Lueger, R. J. and Gill, K. J. (1990). Frontal lobe cognitive dysfunction in conduct disorder adolescents. *Journal of Clinical Psychology*, **46**, 696–706.

Lufi, D., Cohen, A., and Parish-Plass, J. (1990). Identifying attention deficit hyperactivity disorder with the WISC-R and the Stroop color and word test. *Psychology in the Schools*, **27**, 28–34.

McDougle, C. J., Price, L. H., and Goodman, W. K. (1990). Fluvoxamine treatment of coincident autistic disorder and obsessive-compulsive disorder. *Journal of Autism and Developmental Disorders*, **20**, 537–43.

McEvoy, R. E., Rogers, S. J., and Pennington, B. F. (1993). Executive function and social communication deficits in young autistic children. *Journal of Child Psychology and Psychiatry*, **34**, 563–78.

McGee, R., Williams, S., Moffitt, T., and Erson, J. (1989). A comparison of 13-year-old boys with attention deficit and/or reading disorder on neuropsychological measures. *Journal of Abnormal Child Psychology*, **17**, 37–53.

McLaren, J. (1989). The development of selective and sustained attention in normal and attentionally disordered children. Unpublished doctoral dissertation, Dalousie University, Halifax, Nova Scotia.

MacLeod, C. (1991). Half a century of research on the Stroop effect: An integrative review. *Psychological Bulletin*, **109**, 163–203.

Malloy, P. (1987). Frontal lobe dysfunction in obsessive-compulsive disorder. In *The frontal lobes revisited* (ed. E. Perecman), pp. 207–23. IRBN Press, NY.

Malloy, P., Rasmussen, S., Braden, W., and Haier, R.J. (1989). Topographic evoked potential mapping in obsessive-compulsive disorder: Evidence of frontal lobe dysfunction. *Psychiatry Research*, **28**, 63–71.

Martinot, J. L., Allilaire, J. F., Mazoyer, B. M., Hantouche, E., Huret, J. D., Legaut-Demare, F., *et al.* (1990). Obsessive-compulsive disorder: A clinical, neuropsychological and positron emission tomography study. *Acta Psychiatrica Scandinavica*, **82**, 233–42.

Mattes, J. A. (1980). The role of frontal lobe dysfunction in childhood hyperkinesis. *Comprehensive Psychiatry*, **21**, 358–69.

Mazzocco, M. M. M., Hagerman, R. J., Cronister-Silverman, A., and Pennington, B. F. (1992). Specific frontal lobe deficits among women with the fragile X gene. *Journal of the American Academy of Child and Adolescent Psychiatry*, **31**, 1141–8.

Mazzocco, M. M. M., Pennington, B. F., and Hagerman, R. J. (1993). The neurocognitive phenotype of female carriers of fragile X: Additional evidence for specificity. *Developmental and Behavioral Pediatrics*, **14**, 328–35.

Minshew, N. J., Goldstein, G., Muenz, L. R., and Payton, L. R. (1992). Neuropsychological functioning in nonmentally retarded autistic individuals. *Journal of Clinical and Experimental Neuropsychology*, **14**, 749–61.

Mirsky, A. F., Anthony, B. J., Duncan, C. C., Ahearn, M. B., and Kellam, S. G. (1991). Analysis of the elements of attention: A neuropsychological approach. *Neuropsychology Review*, **2**, 109 45.

Morice, R. (1990). Cognitive inflexibility and prefrontal dysfunction in schizophrenia and mania. *British Journal of Psychiatry*, **157**, 50–4.

Morrison-Stewart, S. L., Williamson, P. C., Corning, W. C., and Kutcher, S. P. (1992). Frontal and nonfrontal lobe neuropsychological test performance and clinical symptomatology in schizophrenia. *Psychological Medicine*, **22**, 353–9.

Murphy, T. J. and DeWolfe, A. S. (1989). Planning abilities in alcoholics, process and reactive schizophrenics, and normals. *International Journal of the Addictions*, **24**, 435–44.

Neill, W. T., Lissner, L. S., and Beck, J. L. (1990). Negative priming in same-different matching: Further evidence for a central locus of inhibition. *Perception and Psychophysics*, **48**, 398 400.

Owen, A. M., Sahakian, B. J., Hodges, J. R., Summers, B. A., Polkey, C. E., and Robbins, T. W. (1995). Dopamine-dependent frontostriatal planning deficits in early Parkinson's disease. *Neuropsychology*, **9**, 126–40.

Ozonoff, S. (1995a). Executive functions in autism. In *Learning and cognition in autism* (ed. E. Schopler and G. B. Mesibov), pp. 199–219. Plenum, NY.

Ozonoff, S. (1995b). Reliability and validity of the Wisconsin Card Sorting Test in studies of autism. *Neuropsychology*, **9**, 491–500.

Ozonoff, S. Causal mechanisms of autism: Unifying perspectives from an information processing framework. In *Handbook of autism and pervasive developmental disorders* (2nd edn) (ed. D. J. Cohen and F. R. Volkmar). Wiley, NY. (In press.)

Ozonoff, S. and McEvoy, R. E. (1994). A longitudinal study of executive function and theory of mind development in autism. *Development and Psychopathology*, **6**, 415–31.

Ozonoff, S. and Strayer, D. L. (1997). Inhibitory function in nonretarded children with autism. *Journal of Autism and Developmental Disorders*, **27**, 59–77.

Ozonoff, S., Pennington, B. F., and Rogers, S. J. (1991). Executive function deficits in high-functioning autistic individuals: Relationship to theory of mind. *Journal of Child Psychology and Psychiatry*, **32**, 1081–105.

Ozonoff, S., Rogers, S. J., Farnham, J. M., and Pennington, B. F. (1993). Can standard measures identify subclinical markers of autism? *Journal of Autism and Developmental Disorders*, 23, 429–41.

Ozonoff, S., Strayer, D. L., McMahon, W. M., and Filloux, F. (1994). Executive function abilities in autism: An information processing approach. *Journal of Child Psychology and Psychiatry*, 35, 1015–31.

Ozonoff, S., Strayer, D. L., McMahon, W. M., and Filloux, F. Reduced negative priming in Tourette Syndrome: Contributions of severity and comorbidity. (In preparation.)

Pennington, B. F. (1994). The working memory function of the prefrontal cortices: Implications for developmental and individual differences in cognition. In *Future-oriented processes in development* (ed. M. M. Haith, J. Benson, R. Roberts, and B. F. Pennington), pp. 243–89. University of Chicago Press.

Pennington, B. F. Dimensions of executive functions in normal and abnormal development. In *Development of the prefrontal cortex: Evolution, neurobiology, and behavior* (ed. N. Krasnegor, R. Lyon, and P. Goldman-Rakic). Brookes Publishing Co., Baltimore. (In press.)

Pennington, B. F. and Ozonoff, S. (1996). Executive functions and developmental psychopathology. *Journal of Child Psychology and Psychiatry*, 37, 51–87.

Pennington, B. F., Groisser, D., and Welsh, M. C. (1993). Contrasting deficits in attention deficit hyperactivity disorder versus reading disability. *Developmental Psychology*, 29, 511–23.

Pennington, B. F., Bennetto, L., McAleer, O., and Roberts, R. J. (1996). Executive functions and working memory: Theoretical and measurement issues. In *Attention, memory, and executive function* (ed. G. R. Lyon and N. A. Krasnegor), pp. 327–48. Paul H. Brookes Publishing Co., Baltimore.

Perrine, K. (1993). Differential aspects of conceptual processing in the Category Test and Wisconsin Card Sorting Test. *Journal of Clinical and Experimental Neuropsychology*, 15, 461–73.

Peters, E. R., Pickering, A. D., and Hemsley, D. R. (1994). 'Cognitive inhibition' and positive symptomatology in schizotypy. *British Journal of Clinical Psychology*, 33, 33–48.

Prior, M. R. and Hoffmann, W. (1990). Neuropsychological testing of autistic children through an exploration with frontal lobe tests. *Journal of Autism and Developmental Disorders*, 20, 581–90.

Raine, A., Lencz, T., Reynolds, G. P., and Harrison, G. (1992). An evaluation of structural and functional prefrontal deficits in schizophrenia: MRI and neuropsychological measures. *Psychiatry Research and Neuroimaging*, 45, 123–37.

Randolph, C., Hyde, T. M., Gold, J. M., Goldberg, T. E., and Weinberger, D. R. (1993). Tourette syndrome in monozygotic twins: Relationship of tic severity to neuropsychological function. *Archives of Neurology*, 50, 725–8.

Reardon, S. M. and Naglieri, J. A. (1992). PASS cognitive processing characteristics of normal and ADHD males. *Journal of School Psychology*, 30, 151–63.

Robins, P. M. (1992). A comparison of behavioral and attentional function in children diagnosed as hyperactive or learning disabled. *Journal of Abnormal Child Psychology*, 20, 65–82.

Rumsey, J. M. (1985). Conceptual problem-solving in highly verbal, nonretarded autistic men. *Journal of Autism and Developmental Disorders*, 15, 23–36.

Rumsey, J. M. and Hamburger, S. D. (1988). Neuropsychological findings in high-functioning autistic men with infantile autism, residual state. *Journal of Clinical and Experimental Neuropsychology*, **10**, 201–21.

Rumsey, J. M. and Hamburger, S. D. (1990). Neuropsychological divergence of high-level autism and severe dyslexia. *Journal of Autism and Developmental Disorders*, **20**, 155–68.

Russell, J., Mauthner, N., Sharpe, S., and Tidswell, T. (1991). The 'windows task' as a measure of strategic deception in preschoolers and autistic subjects. *British Journal of Developmental Psychology*, **9**, 331–49.

Saykin, A. J., Shtasel, D. L., Gur, R. E., Kester, D. B., Mozley, L. H., Stafiniak, P., et al. (1994). Neuropsychological deficits in neuroleptic naive patients with first-episode schizophrenia. *Archives of General Psychiatry*, **51**, 124–31.

Scarone, S., Abbruzzese, M., and Gambini, O. (1993). The Wisconsin Card Sorting Test discriminates schizophrenic patients and their siblings. *Schizophrenia Research*, **10**, 103–7.

Schachar, R. (1991). Childhood hyperactivity. *Journal of Child Psychology and Psychiatry*, **32**, 155–91.

Schachar, R. and Logan, G. D. (1990). Impulsivity and inhibitory control in normal development and childhood psychopathology. *Developmental Psychology*, **26**, 710–20.

Schachar, R., Tannock, R., and Logan, G. (1993). Inhibitory control, impulsiveness, and attention deficit hyperactivity disorder. *Clinical Psychology Review*, **13**, 721–39.

Schneider, S. G. and Asarnow, R. F. (1987). A comparison of cognitive-neuropsychological impairments of nonretarded autistic and schizophrenic children. *Journal of Abnormal Child Psychology*, **15**, 29–46.

Seidman, L. J., Talbot, N. L., Kalinowski, A. G., and McCarley, R. W. (1991). Neuropsychological probes of fronto-limbic system dysfunction in schizophrenia: Olfactory identification and Wisconsin Card Sorting Test performance. *Schizophrenia Research*, **6**, 55–65.

Shallice, T. (1982). Specific impairments in planning. In *The neuropsychology of cognitive function* (ed. D. E. Broadbent and L. Weiskrantz), pp. 199–209). Royal Society, London.

Shoqeirat, M. A. and Mayes, A. R. (1988). Spatiotemporal memory and rate of forgetting in acute schizophrenics. *Psychological Medicine*, **18**, 843–53.

Shue, K. L. and Douglas, V. I. (1992). Attention deficit hyperactivity disorder and the frontal lobe syndrome. *Brain and Cognition*, **20**, 104–24.

Silverstein, S. M., Como, P. G., Palumbo, D. R., West, L. L., and Osborn, L. M. (1995). Multiple sources of attentional dysfunction in adults with Tourette Syndrome: Comparison with attention deficit hyperactivity disorder. *Neuropsychology*, **9**, 157–64.

Spreen, O. and Strauss, E. (1991). *A compendium of neuropsychological tests: Administration, norms, and commentary*. Oxford University Press, NY.

Stoner, S. B. and Glynn, M. A. (1987). Cognitive styles of school-age children showing attention deficit disorders with hyperactivity. *Psychological Reports*, **61**, 119–25.

Stroop, J. R. (1935). Studies of interference in serial verbal reactions. *Journal of Experimental Psychology*, **18**, 643–62.

Sutherland, R. J., Kolb, B., Schoel, W. M., Whishaw, I. Q., and Davies, D. (1982). Neuropsychological assessment of children and adults with Tourette syndrome: A comparison with learning disabilities and schizophrenia. In *Gilles de la Tourette syndrome* (ed. A. J. Friedhoff and T. N. Chase), pp. 311–22. Raven Press, NY.

Sverd, J. (1991). Tourette syndrome and autistic disorder: A significant relationship. *American Journal of Medical Genetics*, **39**, 173–9.

Sverd, J., Curley, A. D., Jandorf, L., and Volkersz, L. (1988). Behavior disorder and attention deficits in boys with Tourette syndrome. *Journal of the American Academy of Child and Adolescent Psychiatry*, **27**, 413–17.

Sverd, J., Montero, G., and Gurevich, N. (1993). Cases for an association between Tourette Syndrome, autistic disorder, and schizophrenia-like disorder. *Journal of Autism and Developmental Disorders*, **23**, 407–13.

Szatmari, P., Bartolucci, G., Bremner, R., Bond, S., and Rich, S. (1989). A follow-up study of high-functioning autistic children. *Journal of Autism and Developmental Disorders*, **19**, 213–25.

Szatmari, P., Tuff, L., Finlayson, M. A. J., and Bartolucci, G. (1990). Asperger's syndrome and autism: Neurocognitive aspects. *Journal of the American Academy of Child and Adolescent Psychiatry*, **29**, 130–6.

Tipper, S. P. (1985). The negative priming effect: Inhibitory priming by ignored objects. *Quarterly Journal of Experimental Psychology*, **37**, 571–90.

Towbin, K. E. and Riddle, M. A. (1993). Attention deficit hyperactivity disorder. In *Handbook of Tourette syndrome and related tic and behavioral disorders* (ed. R. Kurlan), pp. 89–109. Marcel-Dekker, NY.

Trommer, B. L., Hoeppner, J. B., Lorber, R., and Armstrong, K. J. (1988). The go–no-go paradigm in attention deficit disorder. *Annals of Neurology*, **24**, 610–14.

van der Does, A. W. and van den Bosch, R. J. (1992). What determines Wisconsin Card Sorting Test performance in schizophrenia? *Clinical Psychology Review*, **12**, 567–83.

Waterhouse, L., and Fein, D. (1982). Language skills in developmentally disabled children. *Brain and Language*, **15**, 307–33.

Welsh, M. C., Pennington, B. F., and Groisser, D. B. (1991). A normative-developmental study of executive function: A window on prefrontal function in children. *Developmental Neuropsychology*, **7**, 131–49.

Weyandt, L. L. and Willis, W. G. (1994). Executive functions in school-aged children: Potential efficacy of tasks in discriminating clinical groups. *Developmental Neuropsychology*, **10**, 27–38.

Wysocki, J. J. and Sweet, J. J. (1985). Identification of brain-damaged, schizophrenic, and normal medical patients using a brief neuropsychological screening battery. *International Journal of Clinical Neuropsychology*, **7**, 40–9.

Yeates, K. O. and Bornstein, R. A. (1994). Attention deficit disorder and neuropsychological functioning in children with Tourette's syndrome. *Neuropsychology*, **8**, 65–74.

Yurgelun-Todd, D. A. and Kinney, D. K. (1993). Patterns of neuropsychological deficits that discriminate schizophrenic individuals from siblings and control subjects. *Journal of Neuropsychiatry and Clinical Neurosciences*, **5**, 294–300.

Zametkin, A. J. and Rapoport, J. L. (1987). Neurobiology of attention deficit disorder with hyperactivity. *Journal of American Academy of Child and Adolescent Psychiatry*, **26**, 616–86.

Zielinski, C. M., Taylor, M. A., and Juzwin, K. R. (1991). Neuropsychological deficits in obsessive-compulsive disorder. *Neuropsychiatry, Neuropsychology and Behavioral Neurology*, **4**, 110–26.

PART IV

Agency, self-awareness, and autism

7 Motor-images, self-consciousness, and autism[1]

Elisabeth Pacherie

How does agency relate to self-awareness? What does agency contribute to our understanding of mental states? Recently, there has been a renewal of interest on the part of both philosophers and psychologists in the role played by agency in the development of self-world dualism; that is to say in the emergence both of a conception of an objective world existing independently of our perception of it and of a conception of ourselves as agents in that world who entertain representations (accurate or inaccurate) about it. It seems that our theorizing about these questions could benefit from considering recent studies of the neurophysiology of action and of the nature of motor intention and imagery. Moreover, such neurophysiological work could also shed light on the neuropsychological origins of psychopathologies in which executive and mentalizing deficits are associated. One such pathology is schizophrenia (C. D. Frith 1992)—another is autism.

In this chapter I argue that a capacity for action plays a major role in the structuring of a unitary experience of the world and in the development of self-world dualism. I further argue that conscious access to the content of their motor representations gives subjects a primitive form of awareness of the relationship between their representations and their actions and of their status as agents and as owners of representations. It provides, furthermore, the basis for a progressive elaboration of these notions. Finally, I will suggest that a number of the difficulties encountered by individuals with autism may have their common origin in an impairment of action representations.

In the first section, I give a brief review of a number of studies indicating that individuals with autism experience both mentalizing and executive difficulties, as well as a review of the current debate concerning the relationships between the two kinds of dysfunctions. In the second section, a number of proposals stemming from work in the neurophysiology of action will be presented and discussed. The third section considers the bearing of these proposals on problems confronted by psychologists and philosophers of action. Here I will endeavour to show how we can make use of those ideas to defend a particular philosophical theory of action and show how they can shed light on the relationship between action and the development of self-awareness and theory of mind. In the final section, I return to autism in order to offer a tentative taxonomy of a number of executive dysfunctions from the perspective of the theory of action advocated in the previous section. I then suggest that the executive difficulties encountered in subjects with autism may have their source in a specific impairment of their motor representations and examine what consequences would ensue from such an impairment.

Mentalizing and executive difficulties in autism

We find in autism a combination of executive and mentalizing difficulties. An important question, now hotly debated, is whether the two kinds of difficulties are causally linked or whether they can be assigned a common neuropsychological cause. Two main contenders for the role of primary impairment are deficits in the innately specified theory of mind 'module' and deficits in the kind of executive functioning on which the development of self-awareness depends.[2] The theory of mind approach holds that in children with autism the ability to attribute mental states to themselves and to others as a way of explaining and predicting behaviour fails to develop in a normal way. It contends that theory of mind difficulties lead to impoverished pretend play (Leslie 1987) and poor performance on executive tasks (Carruthers 1996). Empirical support for mentalizing deficits in autism has been provided by a number of empirical studies designed to tap children's understanding of mental states. Those studies led to the following findings. Children with autism have great difficulties correctly predicting the beliefs of others (Baron-Cohen *et al.* 1985; Leekam and Perner 1991; Leslie and Thaiss 1992). They have a specific difficulty in understanding psychological but not physical causality (Baron-Cohen *et al.* 1986). Although they can understand simple desires (Baron-Cohen 1991), they have difficulties predicting the desires of others when they conflict with their own (Harris and Muncer 1988). They show little or no spontaneous pretend play (Baron-Cohen 1987; Lewis and Boucher 1988; Sigman and Ungerer 1984). They are less able than controls to distinguish between mental and physical states and to understand the mental functions of the brain (Baron-Cohen 1989).

On the other hand, the executive function approach holds that the primary impairment in autism may be an impairment in executive function, defined as: 'the ability to maintain an appropriate problem-solving set for attainment of a future goal, [that] includes behaviours such as planning, impulse control, inhibition of prepotent but irrelevant responses, set maintenance, organized search, and flexibility of thought and action' (Ozonoff *et al.* 1991, p. 1083). It suggests, in turn, that the problems encountered by subjects with autism on theory of mind and on pretence may be traced back to executive function deficits. The most direct evidence supporting executive function deficits in autism comes from studies on problem-solving and set-shifting. Subjects with autism have been found to perform poorly on the Wisconsin Card Sorting Task (Ozonoff *et al.* 1991; Prior and Hoffman 1990; Rumsey 1985) and on the Tower of Hanoi problem (Ozonoff *et al.* 1991; Hughes *et al.* 1994). Supportive findings have also been obtained by Russell and colleagues (Hughes and Russell 1993; Russell *et al.* 1991) in their experiments with the 'windows' task. In this, the children were shown two boxes; each box had a window so that the contents were visible. One box was empty, the other contained a sweet. To win the sweet the children had to indicate the empty box. It turned out that many children with autism perseveratively made an incorrect response throughout 20 trials. According to Russell and his colleagues, the poor performance of subjects with autism on this task is a clear indication of their difficulties with inhibiting incorrect but prepotent strategies. Individuals with autism also show memory deficits similar to those seen in patients with frontal lobe impairments, performing poorly on memory tasks that require active, strategic processing, such as temporal ordering, source memory and free recall (Bennetto *et al.* 1996).

Other experimental data that may be viewed as evidence of an executive deficit are the poor performance of children with autism in imitation tasks (see Pennington *et al.*, Chapter 5) and their difficulties in a task where they had to remember whether they or another person had performed certain actions. Several studies reviewed by Meltzoff and Gopnik (1993) have found that children with autism perform less well than controls on motor imitation of both pure body movements and actions on objects, and are particularly impaired on the imitation of simple body movements (Curcio 1978; Dawson and Adams 1984; DeMyer *et al.* 1972; Jones and Prior 1985; Sigman and Ungerer 1984).

Some forms of memory impairment in autism can also be explained in executive terms. Russell and Jarrold (in press) found that children with autism were dramatically impaired on the so-called Alternating Placement task designed to test memory for actions. In that task, the experimenter and the child each had a doll to manipulate, making up four agents—two real agents and two proxy. Each agent had six picture cards to place on a grid. In the test phase, the subjects had to remember whether a card had been placed by themselves or by the experimenter and also to remember whether the card had been placed on their own (or the experimenter's) behalf or on behalf of a doll-partner. The performance of the children with autism was very poor, and, in contrast with the controls, they were worse at remembering the cards they themselves had placed than the cards placed by the experimenter and also less successful at recalling which cards they had laid themselves in contrast to which cards had been laid on behalf of their doll-partner. These authors also ran a second experiment with three new conditions: (1) a 'child-moves' condition in which the child had to move cards from four locations on to the board; (2) an 'experimenter-moves' condition in which the child had to watch the experimenter moving the cards; and (3) an 'automated' condition in which the child had to watch the cards moving on to a central board from four locations on a computer screen. In these three conditions where they did not have to distinguish between their own and others' placements, the children with autism were not significantly impaired. According to Russell and Jarrold, these data are evidence for a self-monitoring deficit in autism (see Russell, this volume).

Although the evidence for executive dysfunctions in autism is compelling, and although the results of Russell and Jarrold hint at the existence of a developmental causal link between an early executive deficit (impairment in self-monitoring) and a later mentalizing deficit (impairment in self-aware-ness), the exact nature of the relationship between the executive difficulties experienced by children with autism and their impairment in self-awareness largely remains to be discovered. As noted by Russell and Jarrold, this is partly because 'executive function' is not a precise notion but an umbrella term covering all the processes involved in the regulation of physical and mental action. This is also partly because the notion of an impairment of self-awareness is not very precise either. It can refer just as well to an impairment in the conscious, reflexive grasp of one's long-term identity as it can to much more primitive impairments that are prior to and independent of any reflexive understanding of one's agency and mental states; and, of course, there are many intermediate possibilities between these two extreme cases. Thus, it remains to be determined how the tasks used to probe for executive dysfunctions relate to one another psychologically, and how the different forms of self-awareness impairment relate to one another and to the executive dysfunctions that may be supposed to underlie them.

One way to proceed in this enterprise of clarification, is to take advantage of recent convergent insights into the relationship between intentions and actions coming from neurophysiology and from the philosophy of action.

The nature of motor intentions and imagery

Jeannerod (1994a) offers a very stimulating synthesis of an important body of neurophysiological work on the nature of motor intention and imagery. In particular, he presents evidence in favour of the four following theses:

1. Actions are driven by an internally represented goal rather than directly by the external world.

2. There exists a close functional equivalence between motor preparation and motor imagery and both rely on the same motor representation system.
3. Motor representations have a specific content, involving two main components: a representation of the body in action as a generator of forces and a representation of a goal of action encoded in a *pragmatic* mode, distinct from *semantic* modes of representation (these terms will be explained below.)
4. The motor representations activated during motor preparation for (and motor imagery of) a specific action are also activated when the subject observes someone else performing the same action.

Let us take a closer look at these four theses. The first emphasizes a central version of the motor theory, in so far as motor intentions are thought to be largely endogenous rather than generated by peripheral mechanisms propagating to central levels. This is not to deny that motor representations can rely, at least in part, on knowledge resulting from our experience of the outside world, but it is to claim that there is no direct transformation of perceptual input into outgoing activity. A representational step intervenes that must involve the two components stated in the third thesis.

The second thesis suggests a close equivalence between motor preparation and motor imagery, conceived as a type of internal imagery, a first-person process pertaining to the representation of the self in action, with the subject feeling him or herself executing a given action. Jeannerod's conception of motor imagery is based on an analogy with visual imagery. A great deal of data on visual imagery suggest that mental images retain a number of the visual and spatial characteristics of visual perception (for a review, see Finke 1989). These data have been taken as supporting the idea that visual imagery and visual perception rely on the same neural substrate, at least at the higher levels of information processing. Jeannerod considers that this interpretation of visual imagery could be generalized to mental representations in other modalities and, specifically, to motor imagery. As he puts it:

> According to this view, motor imagery would be related to motor physiology in the same way visual imagery is related to visual physiology. Motor imagery would accordingly be part of a broader phenomenon (the motor representation) related to intending and preparing movements. (Jeannerod 1994a, p. 189.)

Jeannerod insists that a clear distinction should be drawn between motor imagery and other kinds of imagery including dynamic visual imagery, such as mental rotation (Shepard and Metzler 1971) or mental scanning (Kosslyn *et al.* 1978). In order to delimit his use of the term motor imagery, he appeals to the internal and external imagery distinction used by sports psychologists. According to sports psychologists (Mahoney and Avener 1987), internal imagery is a first-person process involving mostly a kinaesthetic representation of the action, whereas external imagery is a third-person process involving a visual representation of that action or of the space in which it takes place. Jeannerod conceives of motor imagery as belonging to the former type, i.e. as pertaining to the self in action, with the subject feeling himself executing a given action. Examples of motor imagery tasks would be imagining oneself walking to a target placed at a given distance (Decety *et al.* 1989), imagining catching a ball, or imagining writing one's name. Jeannerod acknowledges, however, that since motor imagery often relates to actions taking place within represented visual space (as in the task in Decety's experiment, where blindfolded subjects were asked to imagine walking to a previously inspected target), it cannot be entirely segregated from visual imagery. Nevertheless, motor imagery remains distinct from visual imagery in so far as it always involves a kinaesthetic representation of the self in action as an essential element.

Three different sources of empirical evidence support Jeannerod's claim of a functional equivalence between motor preparation and motor imagery. First, motor imagery has been found to have positive effects on motor learning and training (for a review, see Feltz and Landers 1983). Second, motor preparation and imagery have been shown to share the same neural mechanisms. In particular, the supplementary motor area is activated during both imagined and executed movements (Fox *et al.* 1987). Third, the same physiological correlates (increased heart rate and pulmonary ventilation) have been found in both motor imagery and preparation (for a review, see Requin *et al.* 1991).

According to Jeannerod what distinguishes motor imagery from motor preparation, besides the obvious fact that the latter (but not the former) is followed by actual execution, is that they have different subjective contents. Motor preparation is an entirely non-conscious process of which only the final result is open to the subject's judgement, whereas, by contrast, the content of motor images can be accessed consciously. Jeannerod thinks, however, that this difference might be one of degree rather than of kind, and suggests that the transition from non-conscious to conscious is a matter of timing in the following sense:

> . . . if motor preparation (normally very brief) could be prolonged, the intention to act would become progressively a motor image of the same action. If it were the case, the nonconscious to conscious transition would be determined solely by the time allowed for the preparation processes to access awareness. Actions that fail or are cancelled at the last moment could involve a nonconscious program that is transformed into a conscious image

> . . . if the action were actually executed, the content of the motor representation would not reach consciousness because it would be cancelled as soon as the corresponding movements were executed (perhaps by the incoming signals generated by the execution itself). By contrast, if only motor imagery occurred with execution blocked or delayed, the representation would be protected from cancellation and would become accessible to conscious processing. (Jeannerod 1994a, p. 190.)

Before examining the content of motor representations in more detail, we should first clarify the status of motor representations and motor images with respect to the whole of motor preparation. Jeannerod warns us against the artificial separation between movement representations, assumed to pertain to a physiological approach, and action representations, assumed to pertain to a psychological approach. His claim is that there is no such dichotomy:

> The system that plans the action and its expected effects is continuous with the executive mechanisms. The representation of the action is therefore distributed at several levels of the action system. (Jeannerod 1994a, p. 231.)

More precisely, there is a hierarchy of motor representations such that the goals and parameters of the actions coded for at the higher levels act as constraints on the lower levels of motor representation. One way to think of this motor organization is to draw an analogy with visual processing, where the relationships between levels of motor preparation are the mirror images of the relationships between levels of perceptual processing. That is, whereas in visual processing the flow of constraints travels mainly in an ascending fashion, with the output of lower levels serving as input for higher levels, in motor preparation the flow of constraints travels mainly in the opposite direction, with the parameters encoded at the higher levels constraining the way processes operate at lower levels.

Another aspect of the analogy with visual processing concerns the accessibility to consciousness of the content of representations computed at different levels of processing. In the case of vision, only representations computed at higher levels of visual processing seem to be accessible to consciousness. Thus, according to Jackendoff (1987), the content of the conscious visual experience corresponds to the 2.5D sketch in Marr's theory of vision (Marr 1982); by contrast, neither the content of the primal sketch nor the content of the 2D sketch are consciously accessible. Since we know much less about motor processing and its organization, it would be premature to claim that only representations at one or another level of motor processing are consciously accessible. It is, however, reasonable to assume that aspects of movements that are encoded at higher levels of motor representations will be more easily accessed than those encoded at lower levels. Hence, the content of motor images will presumably correspond to the content of the higher levels of motor representation. We now turn to the problem of specifying what this content is.

The third thesis picks out two aspects of the content of motor representations. The first concerns the representation of the body in action. Jeannerod points out that the motor representation is a representation of the acting self that involves a representation of the body as a generator of acting forces, not just a representation of the effects of those forces on the external world. Let me call this aspect of the motor representation the self-referential component or pole. Experimental studies reviewed by Jeannerod (Decety *et al.* 1993; Gandevia 1982, 1987; Gandevia and McCloskey 1977; McCloskey *et al.* 1983) suggest that the amount of force needed to produce the desired motor effect is encoded in this component of the representation. Moreover, experiments with completely, or partially, paralysed patients (Gandevia 1982; Jeannerod 1994b; Scheerer 1987) suggest that the programming of force has a subjective correlate—the sensation of effort. Empirical evidence also suggests that the central representation of action encodes certain parameters of movement execution dictated by kinematic rules (Decety and Michel 1989; Georgopoulos and Massey 1987; Georgopoulos *et al.* 1989; Viviani and McCollum 1983) and biomechanical constraints (Rosenbaum and Jorgensen 1992; Rosenbaum *et al.* 1990; Shiffrar and Freyd 1990).

The second essential aspect of a motor representation is a representation of the goal of action. In accordance with the 'schema' theory of action,[3] Jeannerod develops the idea that this goal-related component of the motor representation includes a representation of both the external object towards which it is directed, and the final state of the organism when that object has been reached. In simple, object-oriented actions (i. e. when objects are goals for actions), the visual attributes of those objects are represented in a specific, pragmatic mode used for the selection of appropriate movements and distinct from other modes of representation used for other aspects of object-oriented behaviour (categorization, recognition, etc.). Jeannerod's distinction between pragmatic and semantic modes of visual processing has its roots in Ungerleider and Mishkin's (1982) distinction between 'what' and 'where' systems of visual information processing, involved in the processing of object perception and in the processing of spatial analysis, respectively. This distinction is based on neurobiological studies of the visual system indicating that, in addition to a subcortical route which is of primary importance in lower mammals, there are two main visual processing routes in the primate cortex that appear to be specialized for different classes of information. According to the classical formulation of the distinction, the 'where' system (corresponding to the corticodorsal pathway) is specialized in the processing of information concerning stimulus location and codes this information in viewer-centred coordinates, whereas the 'what' system (corresponding to the ventrocortical pathway) is specialized in the processing of information concerning object identification—thus enabling recognition and individuation—and codes this information in object-centred coordinates. Recent work (Atkinson 1993; Braddick 1993, McCarthy 1993), however, suggests that the distinction is too coarse and that there are, in fact, multiple 'what' and 'where' systems. McCarthy (1993), for instance, considers specific types of tasks and different subtypes of neurological impairments as a means of analysing the very different ways in which the constructs of 'what' and 'where' have been used; her conclusion is that most of the neurological evidence does not fit the neat packaging of separate 'what' and 'where' processing.

Jeannerod accepts the idea of a 'what' system, responsible for what he calls the semantic mode of object representation and corresponding to the ventrocortical pathway where objects are described in object-centred coordinates. His notion of pragmatic processing, however, does not correspond to the 'where' system, as traditionally construed. First, Jeannerod contends that the motor representation includes much more than the spatial aspects of the movements. He draws a distinction between spatially oriented actions (like reaching), which are coded in viewer-centred coordinates, and object-oriented actions (like grasping and manipulating), which are, in his view, coded in object-centred coordinates. Second, he contends that recent neurological data point to a division of labour between the ventral and dorsal pathways that differs from what was initially suggested by Ungerleider and Mishkin (1982). Thus, Goodale et al. (1991) reported the case of a patient whose occipito-temporal lesion was likely to have interrupted the ventral pathway. Although the patient was unable to recognize objects, she was quite accurate when instructed to take these target objects. She was able not only to reach the object location, but she also preshaped her hand accurately according to the object's size and shape. Similarly, patients who exhibit blindsight may be able to reach accurately and to preshape their hand according to the object shape and size, provided they adopt an automatic mode of response (McCarthy 1993; Perenin and Jeannerod 1978). By contrast, lesions in the dorsal pathway do not alter object recognition, but they do alter arm movement during reaching as well as finger movements during preshaping and grasping (Jakobson et al. 1991; Jeannerod 1986; Perenin and Vighetto 1988). According to Jeannerod, the existence of such double dissociations confirms the hypothesis of selective semantic and pragmatic representation mechanisms and suggests that the dorsal pathway is involved not only in spatial processing but also in pragmatic processing. Thus, whereas Jeannerod's notion of semantic processing corresponds to the 'what' system, his system for pragmatic processing is not equivalent to the 'where' system. Rather it constitutes a third kind of information processing, which could be called a 'how' system. Pragmatic representations differ from 'where' representations narrowly conceived in so far as (1) they encode not only information about object location, but also information about object attributes, and (2) they encode this information in object-centred coordinates. They differ from 'what' or semantic representations in that (1) they are processed in the dorsal pathway rather than in the ventral pathway, and (2) they provide information for visually guided action rather than for visual identification.

In order to clarify what exactly is meant by pragmatic representations, one can appeal to Campbell's notion of causal indexicality (Campbell 1993, 1994). Campbell points out that many notions are causally significant in so far as judgements made using them have some significance for the ways in which the world will behave, and for how it would behave in various possible circumstances. A subclass of these notions has the further characteristic that a grasp of their causal significance consists in one's practical grasp of their immediate implications for one's own actions. Notions in this subclass are what Campbell calls causally indexical notions. Predicates such as 'is a weight I can easily lift', 'is too hot for me to handle', or 'is within my reach' are offered by Campbell as examples of causally indexical predicates. He notes, however, that although these examples make use of the first person and use notions of weight and temperature, use of indexical terms need not depend upon self-consciousness or grasp of non-indexical notions. Thus, unstructured uses of 'is heavy', 'is hot', or 'is within reach' may be taken as more primitive examples of causally indexical terms in so far as they have immediate implications for the subject's actions. Campbell's notion of causal indexicality fits nicely with Jeannerod's idea of a pragmatic mode of representation of objects; and I think it would not be betraying Jeannerod's position to say that pragmatic representations of objects are causally indexical representations, where objects' attributes are treated in terms of their immediate implications for action, that is to the extent to which they afford specific motor patterns. Thus, Jeannerod's claim that a large number of object attributes (shape, size, compliance, texture, and so on) are relevant to both pragmatic and semantic representations, could be rephrased using Campbell's terminology by saying that those attributes can be represented in either a causally indexical or in a non-indexical way. For instance, the same shape could be represented as 'an elongated rectangle' (semantic mode) or as 'graspable with thumb and forefinger' (pragmatic mode).[4]

To sum up, Jeannerod suggests that a motor representation of a goal object includes both a visuospatial component pertaining to its spatial location and an object-centred component determining how to deal with it. He also suggests that the function of those representations 'falls between' a sensory function (extracting from the environment attributes of objects or situations relevant to a given action) and a motor one (encoding certain aspects of that action). In other words, in a pragmatic representation, object attributes are treated in a causally indexical way, or, to use a different terminology, as 'affordances' (Gibson 1979), activating predetermined motor patterns.

Jeannerod suggests that the same general framework used for simple object-oriented actions remains applicable to higher-order representations encoding long-term action plans. The lower-level, object-oriented motor representations should be considered as constituents of more complex action representations, that will also need to involve higher-order schemas for controlling the selection, the activation, the inhibition, and the sequencing of elementary motor schemas.

Finally, the fourth thesis (the same motor representations are activated both during motor preparation for—and motor imagery of—a specific action and when the subject observes someone else performing the same action) is based on findings by Rizzolatti and his group (Di Pellegrino et al. 1992; Rizzolatti et al. 1988) with monkeys. These workers have described a class of neurones in the rostral part of the inferior premotor cortex (area F5) that fire prior to and during specific actions performed by the animal and that also fire while the monkey observes the experimenter performing the same action. This suggests that watching others' movements is not just to observe some visual pattern, but is to generate a motor image of oneself doing the same thing as the observed actor.

Action representations, self-consciousness, and understanding of mind

The four theses presented in the previous section suggest ways of approaching several problems confronted by philosophers and psychologists. To appreciate their import, it may be useful to consider their bearing on the current debates in the philosophy of action.

According to the currently popular Causal Theory of Actions,[5] what distinguishes actions from mere happenings is the nature of their causal antecedents. Genuine actions are events with a distinctive mental cause. More precisely, according to Brand's formulation of the Causal Theory, '[a subject] S's Aing is an action if there is a [nonactional mental event] M of S such that (i) M caused S's Aing and (ii) M is appropriate to S's Aing' (Brand 1984, p. 7). The requirement in Brand's clause (i) that M be a non-actional mental event is meant to distinguish the Causal Theory from the Mental Action Theory, the latter theory claiming that the action is to be identified with the initial mental event in a causal sequence consisting of mental events and behaviours. In the Causal Theory, the relevant causal antecedent is typically conceived as a complex of some of the subject's beliefs and desires. According to Davidson (1963), for instance, the causal antecedent of an action is a combination of a pro-attitude toward actions of a certain kind and a belief that that kind of action can be performed. Brand's clause (ii), in the specification of the Causal Theory, says that the content of the non-actional mental event relates to the performance of an action. Assuming that A is the action and that the relevant mental event is a combination of a belief and a desire, this means that the desire should be a desire that one As and the belief a belief that one can do so.

However, this simple version of the Causal Theory is faced with several difficulties. First, as a number of philosophers (Brand 1984; Davis 1979; Searle 1983) have remarked, many actions, in particular automatic ones, do not seem to be preceded by any intention to perform them, at least if the intention (i.e. on the Causal Theory the belief–desire pair) is meant to be conscious or introspectively available. To borrow an example from Searle (1983), suppose I am sitting in a chair reflecting on a philosophical problem, and I suddenly get up and start pacing about the room; although my getting up and pacing about are actions of mine, in order to do them I do not need to form an intention to do them prior to doing them. In the same vein, although my typing the present sentence may have been preceded by an intention to do so, I did not have a distinct intention for each key I pressed. Indeed, it may be presumed that my having such distinct intentions would have interfered with my performance (see Russell, this volume, for further discussion).

Second, the Causal Theory faces the problem of causal deviance or waywardness.[6] To borrow an example from Davidson (1973), a climber might want to rid himself of the weight and danger of holding another man on a rope, and he might know that by loosening his hold on the rope he could rid himself of the weight and danger. This belief and want might so unnerve him as to cause him to loosen his hold. Yet it might be the case that he never chose to loosen his hold, nor did he do it intentionally. The problem here is that not every causal relation between seemingly appropriate mental antecedents and resultant events qualifies the latter as actions. The challenge then is to specify the causal connection that must hold between the antecedent mental event and the resultant behaviour for the latter to qualify as an action.

A third objection to the Causal Theory is that it fails to account for the specific features of our knowledge of our own actions. According to Frankfurt (1978), since the theory claims that the main difference between actions and simple events lies in their causal antecedents, it implies that actions and simple events are not intrinsically different. As a consequence, the theory must assume that a person knows that he or she is performing an action not in virtue of his or her immediate awareness that he or she is moving, but because he or she knows what the antecedent conditions causing his or her behaviour are. Thus, the Causal Theory cannot envisage, as a criterion of action, that the person may stand in a specific relationship to his or her bodily movements during the time when he or she is presumed to be acting.

Finally, a fourth objection to the Causal Theory is that it merely postulates that appropriate mental events cause actions, but does not explain how it is possible for such mental events to cause actions, what the properties of the non-actional events are that cause the correlated behaviour (Brand 1984). The Causal Theory claims that the content of the antecedent mental event must be appropriate to the action. Yet, having a representation of a future action, however detailed, is compatible with not acting, even if the world is completely friendly toward that action. As Livet (1996) contends, simply listing a series of initial states, intermediary states, and final states, and stipulating functions that define transformations from one state to another does not amount to a causal explanation of an action. Indeed, what is given is no more than a formal description of an action. For a causal explanation to be provided, what is required in addition is that the actual processes operating to realize those functions be specified.

In order to answer these problems, a number of philosophers have proposed that we distinguish between two types of intentions, variously called intentions-in-action vs. prior intentions (Searle 1983), present-directed intentions vs. future directed intentions (Bratman 1987), immediate intentions vs. prospective intentions (Brand 1984), or intentions-in-actions vs. intention-representations (Livet, submitted). In what follows, I shall retain Searle's terminology. Although the revised versions of the Causal Theory that are based on a distinction between two types of intentions differ on some points, they all agree that the relevant causal antecedent of an action is the intention-in-action that proximately causes the physiological chain leading to overt behaviour. The label 'intention-in-action' is indeed quite appropriate in that it highlights an important aspect of this conception of the causation of action, namely that the intention does not terminate with the onset of action but continues until the action is completed. On this view, the intention does not simply trigger the action, it is involved in its guiding and monitoring.[7]

Let us examine how this proposal can help solve the difficulties mentioned earlier. To begin with, it provides a straightforward answer to the first problem I pointed out (that many actions do not seem to be preceded by any intention to perform them). According to the revised Causal Theory, all actions have intentions-in-action, but they do not all have prior intentions. Moreover, although intentions-in-action can be conscious, that is accompanied by what Searle (1983) calls an 'experience of acting', this does not need to be the case. Thus, on the modified causal account, for a bit of behaviour to qualify as an action, it is both necessary and sufficient that it be caused by an intention-in-action, and it does not matter whether the latter is accompanied by an experience of acting or not. The modified Causal Theory also provides at least a partial answer to the problem of causal deviance or waywardness. On this view, what is criterial for an event to qualify as an action is not that it be caused by a prior intention, but that it be caused by an intention-in-action. Thus, in Davidson's example, the climber's loosening his hold does not count as an action despite its being caused by a prior intention to do so, because the intervening events in the causal chain that links the prior intention to the resultant bodily behaviour do not include an intention-in-action that one performs that bodily movement. However, for a complete answer to the problem of causal deviance to be provided, more needs to be said. In cases where the agent is acting on his prior intention, there must be a close connection between the prior intention and the intention-in-action and we need to spell out what this connection is. This problem will be discussed at length below.

The revised Causal Theory also seems to answer the third objection concerning our knowledge of our own actions. In so far as the intention-in-action is involved in the guidance and monitoring of the action, it does not terminate with the onset of action, but continues as long as the guidance and monitoring continues. As a consequence, it seems possible to reconcile the view that the main difference between actions and simple events lies in their causal antecedents with the idea that we are immediately aware that we are acting and that this awareness has a non-perceptual source. According to the present account, this awareness takes the form of an experience of acting, that is a conscious presentation of the intentional content of the intention-in-action. As Searle insists, this awareness of acting should not be confused with the perceptual awareness (proprioceptive or otherwise) of our bodily movements. There can be an experience of acting without there being actual bodily movements, as in the famous case described by William James (1950) where a patient with an anaesthetized arm was asked to close his eyes and then to raise his arm. Unknown to him his arm was held to prevent it from moving and when he opened his eyes, he was surprised to discover that there was no arm movement. Conversely, a patient can be caused to move his hand by applying an electrode to the motor cortex of one hemisphere (Penfield 1975), in which case the patients feels his arm moving but reports no experience of acting.

For the fourth objection to the Causal Theory to be answered, we still need to specify what the properties of the intention-in-action are that cause the correlated behaviour. If we take an intention-in-action to be a representation specifying a sequence of states corresponding to the successive steps in the realization of an action, we will have a formal description of the action but no causal explanation of it. Unfortunately, the advocates of the revised Causal Theory remain rather vague as to what the internal structure of the intention-in-action consists of, except for saying (Searle 1983) that it has an intentional content and that it must be causally self-referential. For the revised version of the Causal Theory to provide a satisfactory explanation of the causation of action, we still need an adequate account of the nature and structure of intentions-in-action.

According to Livet (1996), Jeannerod's neurophysiological model of motor representations provides such an account. As we have seen in the previous section, motor representations as described by Jeannerod encode information in a pragmatic rather a semantic format. Object attributes are treated as 'affordances' that activate certain predetermined motor schemas. Pragmatic representations encode goals in terms of differences between the location of the target and the position of the body that can be cancelled by movements satisfying certain cinematic and biomechanical constraints. These representations are thus essentially relational and interactive, what they represent is not just the goal of the action, conceived as a final state, or even the sequence of states that correspond to the successive steps in the realization of an action, but also the processes through which those steps are achieved. As Livet puts it, 'the goal is given under a mode of presentation, namely the form of the process' (Livet 1996, p. 6). As a consequence, the motor intention in Jeannerod's model is better seen as corresponding to Searle's intention-in-action than as corresponding to a prior intention.

Now, if we agree that the motor intention in Jeannerod's neurophysiological model corresponds to the intention-in-action in Searle's philosophical account, it seems natural to extend the correspondence by considering the conscious motor image in Jeannerod's model to be the counterpart of Searle's experience of acting. Indeed, Jeannerod's conception of the relationship between motor intentions and motor images is quite similar to Searle's view of the relationship between intentions-in-action and experience of acting. Both consider that the intention-in-action (motor intention) can exist without any experience of acting (motor image) and both consider that the difference between an intention-in-action (motor intention) and an experience of acting (motor image) is not one of intentional content, but one of subjective content (i.e. the former is normally unconscious while the latter is, by essence, a conscious experience). There are, however, three differences between their accounts. One is that although Searle remarks that actions are sometimes performed without any conscious experience of acting, he offers no explanation for this fact, whereas, as we have seen in the previous section, Jeannerod attempts to explain it in terms of the time needed for a motor intention to become a motor image. The second is that, according to

Jeannerod, motor preparation involves a hierarchy of motor representations, with the content of the motor image corresponding to the content of the higher-level motor representations. The third is that, as we shall see below, Searle characterizes the content of an intention-in-action mainly in terms of its conditions of satisfaction and remains silent on the topic of the mode of representation used for the encoding of this content, whereas, by contrast, this topic is central in Jeannerod's model, where the emphasis is put on the pragmatic nature of motor representations.

What remains to be accounted for, however, is the nature of the connection between prior intentions and intentions-in-action. Searle characterizes intentions-in-action and prior intentions in the following way:

> . . . the contents of the prior intention and the intention in action look quite different, because, though both are causally self-referential, the prior intention represents the whole action as the rest of its conditions of satisfaction, but the intention in action presents, but does not *re*present, the physical movement and not the whole action as the rest of its conditions of satisfaction. In the former case the whole action is the 'Intentional object'; in the latter case the movement is the 'Intentional object'. . . . Another difference is that in any real-life situation the intention in action will be much more determinate than the prior intention. (Searle 1983, p. 93.)

Let us take a closer look at Searle's characterization.Searle characterizes both intentions-in-action and prior intentions in terms of their intentional content, as given by their conditions of satisfaction. He first notes that both prior intentions and intentions-in-action are causally self-referential; that is, their conditions of satisfaction require that the intentional states themselves play a causal role in bringing about the rest of their conditions of satisfaction. However, he points out three differences between intentions-in-actions and prior intentions. The first difference concerns the rest of their conditions of satisfaction. Searle claims that whereas the content of intentions-in-action represents physical movements, the content of prior intentions represents whole actions, that is, not just a physical movement, but the causal sequence consisting of the intention-in-action causing the physical movement. Thus, to borrow one of his examples, the conditions of satisfaction of my prior intention to raise my arm can be expressed as follows:

> An intention-in-action which is a presentation of my arm going up causes my arm to go up as a result of this prior intention.

By contrast, the condition of satisfaction of the intention-in-action is simply that:

> My arm goes up as a result of this intention-in-action.

The second difference between prior intentions and intentions-in-actions is that the former represent their conditions of satisfaction whereas the latter present them. Searle's characterization of the distinction between presentations and representations is not very precise however. He first introduces the distinction in the context of a discussion of the differences between perceptual experiences and beliefs, in order to mark a contrast between the ways in which perceptual experiences and beliefs are related to their object. The perceptual experience is said to provide a direct access to its object. As Searle puts it: 'The experience has a kind of directness, immediacy and involuntariness which is not shared by a belief I might have about the object in its absence. It seems therefore unnatural to describe visual experiences as representations' (Searle 1983, p. 46). Searle does not want to deny that presentations are representations. Indeed, he insists that they satisfy all the defining conditions of representations (they have intentional content, conditions of satisfaction, direction of fit, etc.). Rather, presentations are a subclass of representations, characterized by their specific relationship to their intentional object. Searle later draws an analogy between perception and action, claiming that the formal relationships between the visual memory of a flower, the visual experience of the flower, and the flower are the mirror image of the relationships between the prior intention to raise my arm, the intention-in-action of raising my arm, and my arm rising. That is, the direction of fit (mind-to-world in visual perception vs. world-to-mind in action) as well as the direction of causation (world-to-mind in visual perception vs. mind-to-world in action) are inverted, but the prior intention (representation) is to the intention-in action (presentation) as the perceptual memory (representation) is to the perceptual experience (presentation).

Finally, Searle points out that the content of an intention-of-action is much more determinate than the content of the prior intention, meaning that my intention-in-action to raise my arm, for instance, will include not only that my arm goes up, but that it goes up in a certain way, at a certain speed, etc. Although he does not expand on this point, I think it is essential. Indeed, what is at stake is not merely a difference in the degree of determinacy in so far as such a difference could be cancelled by spelling out the prior intention in more detail; rather, it is a difference in the representational mode used to specify the content. The content of a prior intention contains a description of a type of action. It is a kind of conceptual content. By contrast, the content of the intention-in-action is a kind of non-conceptual content. I could raise my arm slowly or rapidly, I could raise my arm by first raising my hand, then my forearm and then my arm, or I could run this sequence in the reverse order. Different intentions-in-actions would have to cause these movements, but they would also satisfy the description 'my raising my arm'. In order to make this point clearer, we can draw the analogy between perception and action in a way slightly different from Searle's, saying that the prior intention is to the intention-in-action as the perceptual belief (rather than the perceptual memory) is to the perceptual experience. To adapt an example from Peacocke (1992), if you are looking at a range of mountains, you may form the perceptual belief that some are rounded, some are jagged. But the content of your visual experience in respect to the shape of the mountains is far more specific than that description suggests. The perceptual belief involving the concepts *round* and *jagged* would cover many different fine-grained contents that your experience could have. Similarly, my prior intention to raise my arm, where the action concept *raising one's arm* is a component of the content of the prior intention covers many fine-grained contents that the corresponding intention-in-action could have. And although we could use very fine-grained concepts to capture the fine-grained content of the intention-in-action, this does not entail that these concepts themselves are somehow components of the content of the intention-in-action nor that the concepts must be possessed by the agent for him to perform the intention-in-action.

Assuming that the present characterization of intentions-in-action and prior intentions, based on Searle's analysis, is on the right track, the fact that an organism be capable of acting and thus that it have intentions-in-actions is no warranty that it be capable of forming conscious prior intentions. The content of the prior intention represents the whole action, that is, it involves both a representation of the intention-in-action and a description of the physical movements that this intention-in-action is to cause—i.e. a representation of the content of the intention-in-action. Moreover, whereas the representational content of the intention-in-action is a non-conceptual kind of content, its description at the level of the prior intention makes use of action concepts. Thus for an organism to be able to form prior intentions, it is, moreover, necessary for it to have some conscious grasp of what an intention-in-action is and for it to possess action concepts. As a consequence, our Searle-based account of the formal relationships between prior intentions and intentions-in-action needs to be supplemented by an explanation of what it takes to have a conscious grasp of intentions-in-action and to possess action concepts.

That we have such an explanation is indeed crucial if we want to be able to say something about the relationship between agency and self-awareness. Agency appears necessary for an experience of an objective world, and thus for a self-world duality to emerge. As noted by Russell (1995), the experience of reversibility plays a key role in such an emergence.[8] That it should sometimes be possible to reverse the flow of our perceptions or to cancel a modification of our perceptual input by making active compensatory movements[9] and thus to maintain or construct certain invariants is a

necessary condition of a self-world distinction. The experience of reversibility
or irreversibility requires the operation of action-monitoring mechanisms
and of cognitive processes able to extract correlations between motor
activities and the properties of the perceptual input. Such mechanisms
may be more or less primitive or sophisticated according to whether they
allow for the construction or preservation of more or less complex types of
invariants or forms of compensation.[10]

However, those mechanisms can presumably be conceived to operate at
subpersonal levels. Thus, with consistency one can claim that an organism
could be endowed with such mechanisms and yet enjoy no conscious
awareness of an objective world independent of its perception nor of itself
as an agent acting in that world. In other words, those mechanisms may be
necessary and/or sufficient for an organism to behave in a flexible and
appropriate manner in the world and yet *not* be sufficient for the organism to
be ascribed a conscious grasp of itself as an agent and of the world as
objective. What remains to be explained is what further conditions are
needed for an organism to enjoy the conscious representations of itself as
an agent and of the world as distinct from itself that human beings are able to
entertain.

What we need to do is to bridge the gap between prior intentions and
intentions-in-action. Given the analysis of the relationships between prior
intentions and intentions-in-action set forth above, this means that we must
explain both how it is possible for an organism to have a conscious grasp of
its intentions-in-action and of their role in bringing about actions and how its
mastery of action concepts is related to the non-conceptual content of its
intentions-in-action. Returning once again to the analogy between action
and perception, we can see that the second problem is analogous to the
problem of explaining how observational concepts are related to perceptual
content. My strategy for dealing with action concepts will share features with
the strategy Peacocke (1992) deploys for answering the problem of the
anchoring of perceptual concepts. Before examining this second problem
in more detail, I shall try to answer the first one, for I think that the key
element in its solution is also a key element in the solution of the second
problem.

I take this key element to be Jeannerod's notion of a conscious motor
image. Jeannerod defends the thesis of a functional equivalence between
motor preparation and motor imagery. According to the thesis, recall, the
motor image is the conscious counterpart of the internal motor representation. More precisely, the content of the motor representation (that is
normally unconscious) becomes conscious when execution is blocked or
delayed or when the action fails. Motor intentions, as described in the second
section of this chapter, are relational models that include both information

about the external world—the objects in the world towards which the action is directed and the final state of the environment once the goal is attained—and information about the agent him- or herself as a generator of acting forces. Thus, when the unconscious motor intention is converted into a conscious motor image, the subject becomes aware not just of what is being intended (the goal) but of his or her body as a generator of acting forces. Of course this does not mean that the motor image, by itself, provides the agent with a *concept* of him- or herself as an agent, and with concepts of action, but it provides him or her with some form of conscious, though non-conceptual, grasp of his or her agency.

Indeed, the fact—if it is a fact—that the motor representation becomes conscious when execution is delayed or blocked presents an important advantage. In the normal case (when the action succeeds), the motor intention (the cause) is concomitant with the movement (its effect). When execution is blocked or delayed, the intention-in-action is temporally separated from its effect. Thus, motor images would give us conscious access to the intention-in-action in its purest form, uncontaminated by feedback linked to execution. It may then be suggested that the temporal gap between the intention-in-action, that gets converted into a conscious motor image, and the execution is what allows one to build a notion of oneself as the agent responsible for the continuity between intention and action. To sum up, my tentative solution to the problem of explaining how it is possible for an organism to have a conscious grasp of its intentions-in-action and of their role in bringing about actions is based on the idea that motor representations get converted into motor intentions when execution is blocked or delayed. The motor image provides the organism with an awareness of what is intended and with a conscious grasp of his body as a generator of acting forces. Moreover, the existence of a temporal gap between intention and action makes it possible to separate out cause and effect, and allows for a notion of the agent as responsible for the continuity between intention and action to be constructed.

Let us now turn to our second problem; that is, explaining how the mastery of action concept is related to the non-conceptual content of intentions-in-action. Recall that I claimed that prior intentions have conceptual content whereas intentions-in-action have non-conceptual content. In order to account for the connection between prior intentions and intentions-in-action, it is necessary to explain how a subject can possess action concepts and how, when a prior intention causes an intention-in-action, the conceptual content of the prior intention can be converted into the non-conceptual content of an intention-in-action.[11] One strategy to account for the possession of a set of concepts is to claim that possession of this set depends asymmetrically on the possession of a set of more basic concepts.

However, as remarked by Peacocke (1992), since our repertoire of primitive, unstructured concepts is finite, this strategy has its limits. There will be at least one set of concepts that does not stand in the asymmetrical relationship of dependence to any other set. Peacocke claims that relatively observational concepts that have peculiarly close links with perception are very plausible candidate elements for one such set. Similarly, I contend that, given the close connection between prior intentions and intentions-in-action, there must be a conceptually basic set of action concepts.[12]

Peacocke (1992) distinguishes between two layers of non-conceptual representational content that a perceptual experience has: scenario-content and protopropositional content. His notion of protopropositional content is of special interest given our purposes. It serves as a basis for the anchoring of relatively observational, perceptual-shape concepts such as *square, cuboid, diamond-shaped*, or *cylindrical*, that can be possessed without the subject's awareness of any geometrical definition. As described by Peacocke, a protopropositional content contains an individual or individuals together with a property or relation (rather than concepts thereof) and represents the property or relation as holding of the individual or individuals. To put it in a different way, protopropositional content constitutes a layer of perceptual content where certain properties or relations of a visual scene are made salient. To borrow one of Peacocke's examples, for something to be perceived as square, the symmetry about the bisectors of its sides must be perceived, whereas for the same thing to be perceived as diamond-shaped, the symmetry about a line that bisects the object's corners must be perceived. The difference between perceiving something as a square and perceiving it as a regular diamond is a difference between the protopropositional contents of the two perceptions. Thus a condition for a thinker to possess the concept 'square' is that he or she be able to have perceptual experiences with a certain type of protopropositional content (concerning the straightness of certain lines, the symmetry of the figure about the bisectors of those lines, the identity of certain lengths, etc.), and that he or she be disposed to form the belief that the demonstratively presented object is square when he or she has an experience with this kind of protopropositional content. .

It would certainly be overextending the analogy between perception and action to try to give an account of basic action concepts that would run exactly parallel to Peacocke's account of perceptual concepts. However, the important point in Peacocke's account, that is certainly also relevant for an account of basic action concepts, is that we could not be said to have mastery of certain concepts unless we were able to have experiences—the non-conceptual representational content of which make certain properties or relations of what is experienced salient. What this means is that in order to ground basic action concepts, we need to identify a level of non-conceptual content where properties and relations, that are essential for the individuation of those concepts, are made salient. Once again, I think that motor images are good candidates for such a level of content. Recall that, according to Jeannerod, motor preparation involves a hierarchy of motor representations, with the parameters of the action that are coded for at the higher levels acting as constraints on the lower levels of motor representation, and that the content of motor images corresponds to the content of the higher-level motor representations. To put it another way, the higher levels of motor representations encode, and thus make salient, the goal of the action as well as some relatively global movement parameters, whereas lower-level motor representations work out the details, so to speak. Thus, if the conscious motor image gives us access to the content of higher-level motor representations, it indeed provides us with a representation of an action where its essential features are highlighted.

In so far as our knowledge of the nature and particulars of motor representations and motor imagery is much less advanced than our knowledge of their perceptual counterparts, this account remains rather speculative. But, if true, it has important consequences for the individuation of basic action concepts, namely that mastery of such concepts require that they be anchored in the content of motor images, and that a subject should not be granted possession of such concepts unless he has motor images. This does not mean that having motor images is sufficient for having motor concepts, just as it is not sufficient that a creature enjoys perceptual experiences with protopropositional content for it to possess perceptual concepts. It is quite possible to conceive of creatures that enjoy experiences with structured non-conceptual content of the type described by Peacocke and yet lack the cognitive resources needed to construct concepts from that basis. The idea is, rather, that even a creature endowed with the cognitive resources needed to construct concepts would fail to construct certain concepts if, for some reason or other, it did not have experiences with a certain type of structured non-conceptual content.

As illustrated in Fig. 7.1, my claim so far has been that motor images function as a bridge between intentions-in-action and prior intentions, in the sense both of providing an agent with some form of conscious, though non-conceptual, grasp of his or her agency (in the form of a grasp of his of her intentions-in-action and of their role in bringing about actions), and of providing him or her with a level of structured non-conceptual content for the anchoring of basic action concepts. The importance of motor imagery as a bridge between intentions-in-action and prior intentions can be further emphasized by considering two other aspects of its role.

So far, I have been considering motor imagery only in the context of motor images that arise as a result of execution being accidentally blocked or

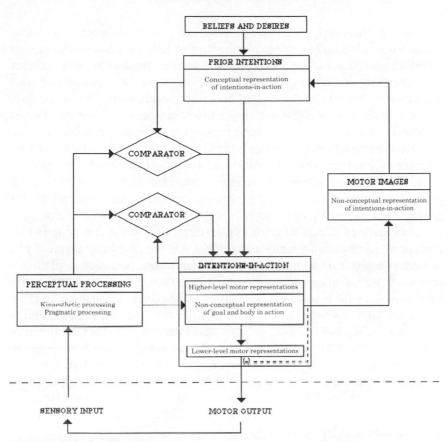

Fig. 7.1 Relationships between prior intentions, intentions-in-action, and motor images. The broken line represents the link between inhibition of execution and production of motor images.

delayed. However, mental images can also arise as a result not of an accident but of execution being purposively blocked. To distinguish the latter from the former, we can speak of motor simulation. What distinguishes motor images from motor simulation is not their content, but the fact that the latter are under the voluntary control of the subjects, in the same sense in which the visual images evoked by subjects in visual imagery tasks—for instance, the mental rotation tasks of Shepard and Metzler (1971)—are under their voluntary control. If, as I suggested, motor images function as a bridge between intentions-in-action and prior intentions, mental simulation could help widen and consolidate this bridge. On the one hand, if the content of motor images provides a basis for the conscious grasp by a subject of his or her agency and for the anchoring of action concepts, motor simulation would allow for an extension of this basis. On the other hand, the practice of motor simulation would constitute a tool for consolidating the link between prior intentions and intentions-in-action and for making possible the construction of more complex prior intentions, in particular, action plans. For instance, a novice piano player must think of the position of each of his or her fingers when playing a chord. However, after a while, playing a major triad becomes automatic; the pianist does not have to form a prior intention to position the fingers in such and such a way, but simply to form the intention of playing a major triad. At a later stage, he or she may not even have to think in terms of individual chords, but only, for instance, in terms of a plagal cadence in F minor. This can be the result of actual practice, but it can also be, at least in part, the result of mental rehearsal. Motor simulation can also help us to mentally test our action plans. The coherence of the combinations of actions envisaged in our action plans can be tested by attempting corresponding motor simulations, and our plans may eventually be revised as a result of such simulations.[13] Seen in this way, action plans are complex prior intentions and not motor simulations of actions, but they are built, in part, on the basis of such simulations. Motor simulation also allows us, on this account, to develop a more systematic grasp of the forms of reversibility and irreversibility that we can experience. It makes it possible for us to organize our perceptual experience more coherently. Motor simulation and planning can be conceived as mental experiments designed to extract and to test new correlations between our motor activities and the dynamic properties of perceptual input in different modalities. In other words, they provide for a continuation at the personal level of the work done at the subpersonal levels by the mechanisms alluded to earlier.

The second point I want to consider concerns the role played by motor imagery in the development of an understanding of other minds. How do we come to deal with objects and people in different ways? How do we come to consider others as having desires, intentions, and beliefs and to see their behaviours as contingent on their mental states? My hypothesis exploits the fourth Jeannerod-derived claim presented in the second section of this chapter—that identical representations underlie the preparation and simulation of our own actions and the observation of actions by others. If indeed conscious access to the content of our motor representations provides the basis for an apprehension of ourselves as agents and owners of representations, and if the observation of an action performed by someone else activates a mental representation identical to the one activated during motor preparation for the same action, then similar processes would underlie apprehension of oneself and of others as agents and owners of representations.

Obviously the claim that observing someone else acting activates in us a motor representation identical to the one activated in us during preparation for the same action cannot give us the whole story. What else is needed? What is still in need of an explanation is how, on that basis, we come to see the other as an agent and owner of representations. In order to understand how it is possible for a subject observing another acting to take that further step, we need to appreciate the similarities and differences between the present case and the case discussed earlier in this section of a subject coming to a form of understanding of his or her own agency. I claimed that a subject could come to such an understanding as a result of motor representations being converted into motor intentions when execution is blocked or delayed. More precisely, I claimed both that the motor image provides the subject with an awareness of what is intended and with a conscious grasp of his or her body as a generator of acting forces, and that the existence of a temporal gap between intention and action makes it possible to separate out cause and effect and allows for a notion of the agent as responsible for the continuity between intention and action to be constructed.

According to the present hypothesis, when a subject sees someone else acting, he or she generates a motor representation identical to the one he or she *would* generate *if* he or she were preparing for that action. Since the motor representation is not followed by actual execution on his or her part, it is likely to be converted into a conscious motor image, hence the observer is aware of an intention-in-action. The difference between this and the former case, however, is that although there is also a gap between the intention-in-action as experienced by the observer, it is of a different kind. Although the observer does not personally perform the action, the action is actually performed. In such a case, the subject cannot consider him- or herself as responsible for the continuity between the experienced intention-in-action and the action. In order to solve the dissonance experienced, the observer must consider the person or animal observed as responsible for the continuity between the intention and the action, and in order to do so the observer must ascribe to the person or animal the intention-in-action that he or she experiences.

Let me conclude this section by returning briefly to the problem of action concepts. In the tentative account of the possession of action concepts that I sketched earlier, I wilfully neglected an important constraint that all concepts must fulfil, namely what Evans (1982) called the Generality Constraint. The Generality Constraint states that for a thinker to be said to possess a concept F, it must be possible for that person to entertain the thoughts Fa, Fb, Fc, etc. where a, b, c belong to a range of individuals of which the concept can significantly be said to be true or false. It follows from this principle that a subject could not be said to possess the concept of an action A, if he or she were not capable of entertaining the thought Aa, with a denoting an individual other than him- or herself. As a consequence, if, as I suggested earlier, motor images are to provide the level of non-conceptual content needed for anchoring the basic action concepts, it is indeed essential that we have motor images not only of our own actions, but also of the actions of other individuals. One last word of caution, just as I was careful to insist that conscious access to the content of our motor representations is a necessary but not a sufficient condition for the possession of a concept of oneself as an agent and for the possession of action concepts, I should insist here that the fact that a motor representation is activated and that a motor image may be formed during the observation of others acting is not a sufficient condition for the possession of concepts of others as agents or for the possession of action concepts. In both cases, further cognitive resources are required and, maybe, as Russell (1996) suggests, the development of linguistic competence is needed for concepts of self, others, and mental kinds to crystallize. What I claim is that motor images of our own actions, and of actions performed by others, provide a basis for the development and application of such concepts.

Action representation impairments in autism

I will now try to provide a tentative taxonomy of a number of executive dysfunctions from the perspective of the distinction between prior intentions and intentions-in-action. I would like to suggest that different forms of executive dysfunctions may be related to either impairments of intentions-in-action, or prior intentions, or their connection.

A first possible type of executive dysfunction could concern the intention-in-action itself. An individual may have difficulties performing an action because his system of motor representation is deviant or impaired. For instance, the mechanisms in charge of computing lower-level motor representations on the basis of the constraints provided by higher-level motor representations may be impaired. Alternatively, the mechanisms in charge of adjusting and correcting the movements in response to feedback in the course of execution may be impaired. However, this does not seem to be the main locus of the executive difficulties encountered by individuals with autism, in so far as children with autism do not appear to be specifically impaired on general sensorimotor intelligence. They do not seem to be delayed in tool-use or object-manipulation, and their sensorimotor coordination seems to be intact (Curcio 1978; Sigman and Ungerer 1981, 1984).

The fact that the patterns of performance of children with autism in executive tasks (such as the Tower of Hanoi, the Wisconsin Card Sorting Tasks, or the memory tasks that require an active, strategic process) are similar to that of patients with frontal lobe impairment may tempt us into thinking that the primary executive impairment in autism is one of planning. But such a diagnosis remains insufficient. The symptomatology of individuals with autism is not the same as the symptomatology of frontal subjects, including those with early 'frontal' lobe damage. In support of this claim, a study by Price *et al.* (1990) indicates that, although subjects who have suffered bilateral prefrontal damage early in life subsequently exhibit severely aberrant behaviour, they do not appear autistic (see Pennington *et al.*, Chapter 5). Their actions are impulsive, triggered by the immediate stimulus, characterized by lack of judgement and shallow foresight. Indeed, they have major deficits in the maturation of judgement, insight, abstract reasoning, perspective taking, empathy and moral development. However, memory, language and visuospatial skills appear normal. Besides, although this area of knowledge was not specifically tested, the descriptions offered of the cases suggest that those 'frontal' subjects present with no specific impairment in self-attributing actions. This suggests that the planning difficulties observed in both 'frontal' patients and subjects with autism may have different characters.

Let me consider this difference. Performing a preplanned action involves first constructing a plan (forming a complex prior intention) and then carrying it out (forming the intentions-in-action that correspond to the successive steps of the plan and executing them). A planning deficit may concern either the construction of complex prior intentions, the construction of the corresponding intentions-in-action, the control of the unfolding action by the previously constructed prior intention in the course of execution, or the construction of a link ensuring continuity between prior intentions and corresponding intentions-in-action. Let me give some illustrations. Construction of a plan may involve a recursive loop between prior intentions and motor imagery. A prior intention is formed (it is tested by carrying out a motor simulation of a corresponding intention-in-action), it may be adjusted or corrected as a result of this process of simulation and so forth until its formulation appears satisfactory. This is probably what happens when a normal subject is first confronted with the Tower of Hanoi problem. Such a process of construction would be disrupted, however, by a dysfunction of the mechanisms in charge of the control of inhibition. One possible consequence of such a dysfunction would be to make it impossible to generate mental imagery without it immediately leading to motor execution. The construction of plans by a reciprocal interchange between prior intentions and motor simulation would then be made almost impossible. As another possibility, a subject may be able to form a complex prior intention and to launch a corresponding intention-in-action, and yet the prior intention may become ineffective once the action has been launched. It would then be unable to control its course or to ensure the relay between the intentions-in-action corresponding to the successive steps of the plan. What would be in question in such a case would not be the loop between prior intentions and motor simulations during the construction of the plan, but rather the control loop between prior intentions and intentions-in-action during execution. Fig. 7.2 illustrates these possibilities.

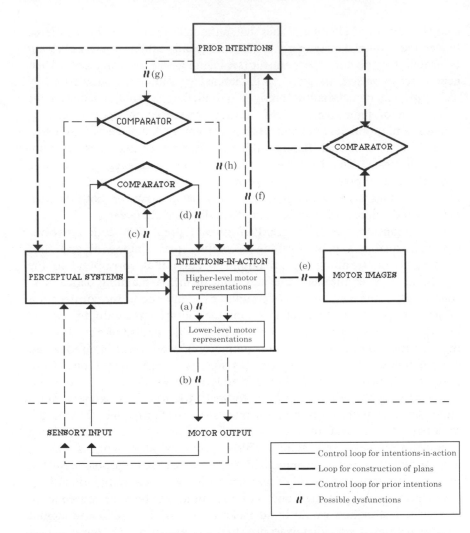

Fig. 7.2 Different types of executive dysfunctions. Several possible impairments in the production and control of action are represented. A first possible type of dysfunction concerns the intention-in-action loop: (a) and (b) represent possible impairments at different levels of motor preparation; (c) and (d) represent possible impairments in the guiding and monitoring of action during execution. Impairments could also concern the production of action plans. In particular, (e) is especially relevant to autism: if people with autism find it difficult to generate motor images in the first place, they should be impaired in the construction of plans, and difficulties in converting prior intentions into intentions-in-action (represented by (f)) may be a consequence of a primary impairment at (e). Finally, impairments could also concern the execution and control of actions based on prior intentions. Dysfunctions at (g) or (h) may be responsible for the planning difficulties observed in frontal patients.

It has been suggested (Shallice 1988) that the planning difficulties confronted by 'frontal' patients may be explained by an impairment of the
inhibitory control normally governing elementary motor schemas. In this
case, as soon as it is formed, a prior intention would trigger action, without it
being possible for the intention to control its course or to prevent a drift. To
put it slightly differently, prior intentions normally have two functions: to
trigger actions and to control their unfolding once triggered. In 'frontal'
patients, prior intentions fulfil their first function, and in this sense we can
say that the continuity between prior intentions and intentions-in-action is
present, but they do not fulfil their second function, that of controlling
actions once launched. By contrast, I would like to suggest that the executive
impairment in subjects with autism is of a more basic kind, in that it concerns
the construction of a bridge ensuring continuity between prior intentions and
intentions-in-action. I claimed in the third section of this chapter, that our
conscious motor images are the main bridge between prior intentions and
intentions-in-action. Those motor images give us conscious access to the
content of our intentions-in-action, provide a basis for the anchoring of
action concepts, and serve as a grounding for the development of a notion of
the agent as responsible for the continuity between prior intentions and
intentions-in-action. My tentative proposal is that a number of difficulties
encountered by children with autism may have their source in the lability of
motor representations. Such a lability would prevent the normal emergence
of conscious motor images and thus prevent the construction of a robust
notion by individuals with autism of themselves as the agents responsible for
the continuity between their intentions and their actions. This does not mean
that subjects with autism have no notion of what a prior intention is. Such a
notion can be inculcated, in part, through language and social learning, but
in their case it would not be properly grounded in their own experience of
action.

The present hypothesis could also throw some light on the nature of the
link between the executive difficulties that subjects with autism share with
'frontal' patients—such as planning difficulties—and other executive difficulties encountered in autism—such as their impairment in imitation tasks or
in the Alternating Placement task described earlier. As I mentioned in the
first section, several studies reviewed by Meltzoff and Gopnik (1993) have
found that children with autism perform more poorly than controls on motor
imitation tasks, but are more impaired on imitation of body movement (for
instance, touching their nose with a finger, hopping, walking on tiptoe) than
on imitation of actions on objects (stacking cubes, stirring with a spoon in a
cup, lacing shoes, etc.).[14] How do we account for the fact that their
impairment is more serious on imitation of pure bodily movement than
on imitation of actions on objects? As we have just seen, children with autism

do not appear specifically impaired on general sensorimotor intelligence; they do not seemed to be delayed in tool-use or object permanence. This suggests that the pragmatic treatment of information is not impaired in autism. Object affordances are recognized and they trigger the corresponding elementary motor schemas. Preservation of pragmatic processing of visual information may explain why the performance of children with autism is less impaired on imitation of actions on objects than on body movement imitation. In the former case, but not in the latter, a target-object is present and provides some of the information needed to construct a motor representation of an action and later control its execution. That is, when a target-object is present, a visuopragmatic representation of this object can be constructed, this representation can trigger corresponding motor schemas, and the execution of the action can be controlled by comparison of the visuopragmatic representation with visual feedback. In contrast, in the imitation of pure bodily movement, there is no visible object-goal and thus no opportunity to exploit the object's affordances to construct a motor representation. In order to imitate the body movement demonstrated by the experimenter, the subject would have to construct and retain a motor image of the observed action and to act on its basis. Such a task should not pose a special problem for a subject capable of forming conscious motor images, since this image would give him or her access to the intention-in-action needed to perform the action. In contrast, a subject with an impaired capacity for motor imagery should encounter difficulties in such a task. One prediction that can be made on the basis of the present hypothesis is that children with autism should be more impaired on imitation of strange or inappropriate actions on objects (like drinking from a book or writing with a plate) than on imitation of usual actions, for in the former cases the affordances of the objects would give them no clue as to what action they should perform and they would have to rely on motor images of the action demonstrated by the experimenter. Let us note that lack or poverty of pretend-play may be explained along the same lines. Pretend-play, and especially symbolic pretend-play (where one object may be substituted for another, where imaginary entities are created), can be regarded as a form of overt simulation, the result of an externalization of motor simulation. Hence, if motor simulation is difficult for children with autism, pretend-play should also be.

Russell and Jarrold's Alternating Placement task described earlier indicates that children with autism have severe difficulties in self-attributing past actions. Russell and Jarrold's interpretation of this result is in terms of an impairment in self-monitoring: in individuals with such an impairment, experiencing one's own actions would not be as psychologically distinctive (with respect to experiencing the actions of others) as it is in individuals who are not impaired in this regard. This claim marries well with my own claim that individuals with autism are impaired in motor imagery. For a subject to apprehend himself as responsible for an action, he must view the action as caused by an intention-in-action of his self, and motor images are what give us conscious access to our own intentions-in-action. To answer the question whether he was responsible for the placement of a card, the subject would have to evoke motor images of his past intentions-in-action and to see whether one of these corresponds to the action of placing that card. If a subject has difficulty constructing motor images in the first place, he should be impaired in a task that requires remembering those.

Finally, the hypothesis that an impairment in motor imagery would disrupt the connection between prior intentions and intentions-in-actions may also help to account for some aspects of high-level perseverative behaviour in autism as revealed by Russell's 'windows' task. In a study using the 'windows' task with children of normal intelligence, but with a diagnosis of Asperger syndrome, Wareham (1994) found one subject who could articulate the rule perfectly and yet perseveratively pointed to the baited box on every trial. In other words, there seemed to be a dissociation between the content of the prior intention as conveyed by the instruction in the form of a rule and the intention-in-action controlled by the salient features of the immediate situation. Perseveration could be explained in this case by saying, not that the subject is unable to inhibit a more salient, but incorrect response in favour of a less salient but more relevant one (implying a competition between two intentions-in-action) but rather by saying that the subject is unable to transform the prior intention given by the rule into an intention-in-action. He or she would then perseverate in their inappropriate response (pointing to the baited box), not because it is more salient than its competitors, but because the corresponding intention-in-action is the only one available.

In the third section, I made a number of claims concerning the role played by intentions-in-action, motor imagery and prior intentions in the emergence of self-awareness, in the development of an understanding of mental functions and in achieving a more coherent organization of perceptual experience. I suggested that motor images as described in the second section provide subjects with a conscious, although non-conceptual grasp of their own agency and provide the ground for a further elaboration of a conscious representation of the self. I also suggested that motor images work as a bridge between intentions-in-action and prior intentions and provide the level of non-conceptual content appropriate for the anchoring of action concepts. If, as the present hypothesis suggests, motor imagery is impaired in subjects with autism, they would not have access to all the information available to normal subjects and should, in particular, have difficulties getting a conscious grasp of their agency and working out the link between prior intentions, intentions-in-action, and actions. In other words, their conscious experience would not provide them with all the material necessary for an understanding of their mental functioning and for an apprehension of themselves as agents ensuring the continuity between prior intentions and intentions-in-action. Such an impairment would also make it very difficult for them to simulate actions and build action plans. Moreover, the present hypothesis could also help to explain, if we accept the proposal put forth at the end of the third section, why subjects with autism have problems understanding the mental states of others. According to that proposal, in order to attribute agency and intentions to others, a subject has to be able to construct motor images when observing an action being performed by someone else and to ascribe to the observed actor the intention-in-action revealed by his or her motor image. If the capacity to form motor images is impaired in individuals with autism, they will lack the basis for such an ascription.

To sum up, the general thesis developed in this chapter is that impaired agency can result in impaired self-awareness and poor understanding of mental functions. I have tried to defend a view of the nature of the causal links between executive and mentalizing difficulties in autism, based on a conception of motor representations and motor imagery borrowed from work in the neurophysiology of action. I proposed that those deficits could have their common source in an impairment of the mechanisms of motor imagery. An important reason why motor images may appear as an essential link between executive deficits and mentalizing deficits is that they constitute a contact point between prior intentions and intentions-in-action, and contain the informational material needed for the elaboration by the subject of a notion of him- or herself as an agent and an owner of representations. If, in autism, motor representations are too labile to become converted into conscious motor images, children with autism would not be provided with the experiential base on which those notions are built. On the present hypothesis the meta-representational and/or theory of mind deficits in autism are not primary; they are the consequence of impairments at the more elementary level of motor representations.

Notes

1. Earlier versions of this chapter were presented at a conference on *Philosophy of action and neuroscience*, at the University of Strasbourg and the Collège de France, in February 1996, and at a workshop on *Philosophy and Psychiatry* in Hôtel-Dieu, Paris, in April 1996. I am indebted to participants for their comments. Many thanks to John

Campbell, Steven Davis, Pierre Livet, and Joëlle Proust for their helpful comments and discussions. I am very grateful to James Russell for extensive comments and suggestions.

2. For a thorough examination of the theory of mind hypothesis of autism, see Baron-Cohen *et al.* (1993). For a review of executive difficulties in autism, see Ozonoff *et al.* (1991) and Harris (1993).

3. As noted by Jeannerod (1994a), the 'schema' theory has a long history. It was first developed by Head (1920) to account for the maintenance and regulation of posture. It was later adopted by others to account for further aspects of motor control and learning. See Schmidt (1982) for a recent formulation of this view.

4. It should be noted that Campbell's discussion of causal indexicality is mainly concerned with causally indexical concepts. I think, however, that the notion of causal indexicality has a wider scope and that there can be causally indexical representations that are not conceptual. Indexical properties can be represented without the representation containing concepts of those properties. In particular, although motor representations in Jeannerod's sense can be described as causally indexical representations, they are not conceptual representations.

5. The most prominent proponents of the Causal Theory of Action are Davidson (1963, 1973, 1978) and Goldman (1970). The origin of the current interest in the Causal Theory can be traced back to Davidson's 1963 paper 'Actions, reasons and causes'. Versions of the Causal Theory have also been advocated by Sellars (1966, 1973), Castañeda (1975, 1980), Searle (1979, 1983), and Brand (1984).

6. For a detailed analysis of the problem of causal deviance, see Brand 1984, p. 17 *et sq.*

7. It should be noted, however, that although the conception of action defended by Frankfurt (1978) is quite similar to the approach just sketched, he does not consider himself a proponent of a Causal Theory of Action. The reason why he rejects this label is that he thinks that the Causal Theory is committed to the idea that the mental cause of an action should precede the movement and not be concomitant with it. It should also be noted that, at variance with the standard versions of the Causal Theory, Searle (1983) identifies the action not just with the bodily movement but with the entire causal sequence consisting of the intention-in-action causing the bodily movement.

8. In recent papers, Baldwin (1995) and Russell (1995) both argue that the experience of agency is necessary for the experience of objectivity. Their accounts differ in that Baldwin emphasizes the link between motor action and objectivity and takes the experience of limitations to our bodily power (felt resistance) as a condition for a conception of causality

to emerge, whereas Russell takes it that non-physical interactions between our body and the world (e.g. eye-movements) are sufficient for us to regard objects as refractory. I was independently drawn to similar conclusions (Pacherie 1997) by consideration of a modern variant of Molyneux's question inspired by the tactile vision substitution system devised by Bach-y-Rita and his co-workers (Collins and Bach-y-Rita 1973; White *et al.* 1970). Tests with this device demonstrated the great importance of self-generated movements by the observer; those movements appeared necessary for the experienced phenomena to be attributed to a stable outside world.

9. The notion of compensation is borrowed from Poincaré (1905, 1907, 1930), a leading exponent of the theory that movements, and especially compensatory movements, play an essential role in the emergence of a conscious experience of space and objectivity.

10. The famous study by von Holst and Mittelstaedt (1950, translated in Gallistel 1980) of the optokinetic reaction in the fruit fly provides an example of a primitive action-monitoring mechanism that these authors called efference copying. The animal attempts to maintain a stable visual field by turning in the direction of world movements. von Holst and Mittelstaedt set out to explain why, however, the optokinetic reaction does not return the animal to its former position whenever a movement is initiated. They postulated the operation of an efference copy mechanism. A copy of the motor command is sent to the optokinetic unit. The optokinetic unit treats the signal as though it were a command originating within the optokinetic unit itself. However, the reafferent visual signal and the efference copy signal cancel each other and the turn goes ahead unperturbed. von Holst and Mittelstaedt provided evidence in favour of the hypothetical mechanism, by twisting the heads of the flies. This reverses the sign of the reafferent signal. The efference copy and the reafference no longer cancel, they reinforce. The unfortunate flies continuously turn in small circles. Efference copying thus appears as a very primitive mechanism for distinguishing real from apparent changes in sensory input. The mechanisms of action monitoring become more complex in more complex organisms, as demonstrated, for instance, by investigations using extensive perturbations such as inversions or reversals in the visual field of mammals. Human beings and other mammals, as opposed to insects and lower vertebrates, are capable of behavioural compensation, that is to say, they are capable of behaving almost normally after more or less extensive practice under inverted or reversed vision (Ewert 1930; Held 1968; Kohler 1955; Rock 1966 Smith and Smith 1962; Stratton 1896, 1897; Taub 1968;). By contrast, smaller perturbations, such as those produced by prisms that shift the optical

array about 10 to 20 degrees, trigger perceptual recalibration even in non-mammals. Rossi (1968), for instance, demonstrated that newly hatched chicks were able to adjust their pecking to small prismatic displacements.

11. Livet's (submitted) distinction between intentions-in-action and intention-representations is explicitly meant to mark the contrast between two types of content. Intention-representations are descriptions of actions involving action concepts, whereas intentions-in-action are internal models (motor representations) of movements. Whereas Livet's intentions-in-action correspond to Searle's intentions-in-actions, his intention-representations should not be equated with prior intentions. Intention-representations do not always precede and cause intentions-in-actions, an intention-representation can also be a retrospective description of an earlier intention-in-action. For instance, intention-representations can be inferred on the basis of the motor images we form of our motor intentions when execution is blocked, or on the basis of the motor images we form when we observe someone else acting. In such cases, intention-representations are interpretations rather than causes of intentions-in-action. We may have to distinguish between intention-representations as prior intentions and intention-representations as interpretations in terms of their different cognitive roles, but one characteristic they share is that their content is conceptual.

12. Although action concepts are likely to be concepts of actions involving simple bodily movement, such as the concept of raising one's arm, they should not be confused with movement concepts. Take, for instance, the two events of my raising my arm and of my arm going up as a result of being pulled by a string, the same movement concept (the rising of an arm) can be used in a (partial) description of each of the two events, but the action concept (raising one's arm) can only appropriately be used to describe the first event.

It is also important to note that for a subject to possess an action concept it is not required that he or she be able to think of the type of action picked out by the concept in a non-indexical way. It is enough that the subject be able to think of an action as being that action, where the demonstrative picks out properties made salient in a motor image.

13. See Berthoz (1996) for a stimulating view of the role of mental simulation for decision in perception and in the control of movement, and for a description of the different levels of neural organization at which mechanisms involved in decision-making can be found.

14. These examples are taken from DeMyer et al. (1972).

REFERENCES

Atkinson, J. (1993). A neurobiological approach to the development of 'where' and 'what' systems for spatial representation in human infants. In *Spatial representation* (ed. N. Eilan, R. McCarthy, and B. Brewer), pp. 325–39. Blackwell, Oxford.

Baldwin, T. (1995). Objectivity, causality, and agency. In *The body and the self* (ed. J. L. Bermúdez, A. Marcel, and N. Eilan), pp. 107–25. MIT Press, Cambridge, MA.

Baron-Cohen, S. (1987). Autism and symbolic play. *British Journal of Developmental Psychology*, **5**, 139–48.

Baron-Cohen, S. (1989). Are autistic children behaviorists? An examination of their mental-physical and appearance-reality distinctions. *Journal of Autism and Developmental Disorders*, **19**, 579–600.

Baron-Cohen, S. (1991). Do people with autism understand what causes emotion? *Child Development*, **62**, 385–95.

Baron-Cohen, S., Leslie, A. M., and Frith, U. (1985). Does the autistic child have a 'theory of mind'? *Cognition*, **21**, 37–46.

Baron-Cohen, S., Leslie, A. M., and Frith, U. (1986). Mechanical, behavioural and intentional understanding of picture stories in autistic children. *British Journal of Developmental Psychology*, **4**, 113–25.

Baron-Cohen, S., Tager-Flusberg, H., and Cohen, D. J. (1993). *Understanding other minds*. Oxford University Press, Oxford.

Bennetto, L., Pennington, B. F., and Rogers, S. J. (1996). Intact and impaired memory functions in autism. *Child Development*, **67**, 1816–35.

Berthoz, A. (1996). Neural basis of decision in perception and in the control of movement. In *Neurobiology of decision-making* (ed. A. R. Damasio *et al.*), pp. 83–100. Springer-Verlag, Berlin, Heidelberg.

Braddick, O. (1993). Computing 'where' and 'what' in the visual system. In *Spatial representation* (ed. N. Eilan, R. McCarthy, and B. Brewer), pp. 340–55. Blackwell, Oxford.

Brand, M. (1984). *Intending and acting*. MIT Press, Cambridge, MA.

Bratman, M. (1987). *Intention, plans, and practical reasoning*. Harvard University Press, Cambridge, MA.

Campbell, J. (1993). The role of physical objects in spatial thinking. In *Spatial representation* (ed. N. Eilan, R. McCarthy, and B. Brewer), pp. 65–95. Blackwell, Oxford.

Campbell, J. (1994). *Past, space and self*. MIT Press, Cambridge, MA.

Carruthers, P. (1996). Autism as mind-blindness: and elaboration and partial defense. In *Theories of theories of mind* (ed. P. Carruthers and P.K. Smith), pp. 257–73. Cambridge University Press, Cambridge.

Castañeda, H.-N. (1975). *Thinking and doing*. D. Reidel, Dordrecht, Holland.

Castañeda, H.-N. (1980). The doing of thinking: intending and willing. In *Action and responsibility* (ed. M. Bradie and M. Brand), pp. 80–92. Bowling Green State University Press, Bowling Green, OH.

Collins, C. C. and Bach-y-Rita, P. (1973). Transmission of pictorial information through the skin. *Advances in Biological and Medical Physics*, **14**, 285–315.

Curcio, F. (1978). Sensorimotor functioning and communication in mute autistic children. *Journal of Autism and Childhood Schizophrenia*, **8**, 281–92.

Davidson, D. (1963). Actions, reasons, and causes. *Journal of Philosophy*, **60**, 685–700. (Reprinted in Davidson 1980, pp. 3–19.)

Davidson, D. (1973). Freedom to act. In *Essays on freedom of action* (ed. T. Honderich), pp. 137–56. Routledge and Kegan Paul, London. (Reprinted in Davidson 1980, pp. 63–81)

Davidson, D. (1978). Intending. In *Philosophy of history and action* (ed. Y. Yovel), pp. 41–60. D. Reidel, Dordrecht, Holland. (Reprinted in Davidson 1980, pp. 83–102.)

Davidson, D. (1980). *Essays on actions and events*. Oxford University Press, Oxford.

Davis, L. H. (1979). *Theory of action*. Prentice-Hall, Englewood Cliffs, NJ.

Dawson, G. and Adams, A. (1984). Imitation and social responsiveness in autistic children. *Journal of Abnormal Child Psychology*, **12**, 209 26.

Decety, J. and Michel, F. (1989). Comparative analysis of actual and mental movement times in two graphic tasks. *Brain and Cognition*, **11**, 87–97.

Decety, J., Jeannerod, M., and Prablanc, C. (1989). The timing of of mentally represented actions. *Behavioural Brain Research*, **34**, 35–42.

Decety, J., Jeannerod, M., Durozard, D., and Baverel, G. (1993). Central activation of autonomic effectors during mental simulation of motor actions. *Journal of Physiology*, **461**, 549–63.

DeMyer, M. K., Alpern, G. D., Barton, S., DeMyer, W. E., Churchill, D. W., Hingtgen, J. N., *et al.* (1972). Imitation in autistic, early schizophrenic, and non-psychotic subnormal children. *Journal of Autism and Childhood Schizophrenia*, **2**, 264–87.

Di Pellegrino, G., Fadiga, L., Fogassi, L., Gallese, V., and Rizzolatti, G. (1992). Understanding motor events: a neurophysiological study. *Experimental Brain Research*, **91**, 176–80.

Evans, G. (1982). *The varieties of reference*. Clarendon Press, Oxford.

Ewert, P. H. (1930). A study of the effect of inverted retinal stimulation upon spatially coordinated behavior. *Genetic Psychology monographs*, **7**, 177–363.

Feltz, D. L. and Landers, D. M. (1983). The effects of mental practice on motor skill learning and performance. A meta-analysis. *Journal of Sport Psychology*, **5**, 25–57.

Finke, R. A. (1989). *Principles of visual imagery*. MIT Press, Cambridge, MA.

Fox, P. T., Pardo, J. V., Petersen, S. E, and Raichle, M. E. (1987). Supplementary motor and premotor responses to actual and imagined hand movements with positron emission tomography. *Society for Neuroscience Abstracts*, **13**, 1433.

Frankfurt, H. G. (1978). The problem of action. *American Philosophical Quarterly*, **15**, 157–62.

Frith, C. D. (1992). *The cognitive neuropsychology of schizophrenia*. Lawrence Erlbaum, Hove.

Frith, U. (1989). *Autism: explaining the enigma*. Blackwell, Oxford.

Gandevia, S. C. (1982). The perception of motor commands of effort during muscular paralysis. *Brain*, **105**, 151–9.

Gandevia, S. C. (1987). Roles for perceived voluntary commands in motor control. *Trends in Neuroscience*, **10**, 81–5.

Gandevia, S. C. and McCloskey, D. I. (1977). Changes in motor commands, as shown by changes in perceived heaviness, during partial curarization and peripheral anaesthesia in man. *Journal of Physiology*, **272**, 673–89.

Georgopoulos, A. P. and Massey, J. T. (1987). Cognitive spatial-motor processes. *Experimental Brain Research*, **65**, 361–70.

Georgopoulos, A. P., Crutcher, M. D., and Schwartz, A. B. (1989). Cognitive spatial motor processes: 3. Motor cortical prediction of movement direction during an instructed delay period. *Experimental Brain Research*, **75**, 183–94.

Gibson, J. J. (1979). *The ecological approach to visual perception*. Houghton-Mifflin, Boston.

Goldman, A. (1970). *A theory of human action*. Prentice-Hall, Englewood Cliffs, NJ.

Goodale, M. A., Milner, A. D., Jakobson, L. S., and Carey, D. P. (1991). A neurological dissociation between perceiving objects and grasping them. *Nature*, **349**, 154–6.

Harris, P. L. and Muncer, A. (1988). Autistic children's understanding of belief and desires. Paper presented at the British Psychological Society Section Conference, September. Coleg Harlech.

Harris, P. L. (1993). Pretending and planning. In *Understanding other minds* (ed. S. Baron-Cohen, H. Tager-Flusberg, and D. J. Cohen), pp. 228–46. Oxford University Press, Oxford.

Head, H. (1920). *Studies in neurology*. Oxford University Press, London.

Held, R. (1968). Plasticity in sensorimotor coordination. In *The neuropsychology of spatially oriented behavior* (ed. S. J. Freedman), pp. 57–62. The Dorsey Press, Homewood, IL.

Hughes, C. and Russell, J. (1993). Autistic children's difficulty with mental disengagement from an object: its implications for theories of autism. *Developmental Psychology*, **29**, 498–510.

Hughes, C., Russell, J., and Robbins, T. W. (1994). Evidence for executive dysfunction in autism. *Neuropsychologia*, **32**, 477–92.

Jackendoff, R. (1987). *Conciousness and the computational mind*. MIT Press, Cambridge, MA.

Jakobson, L. S., Archibald, Y. M., Carey, D. P., and Goodale, M. A. (1991). A kinematic analysis of reaching and grasping movements in a patient recovering from optic ataxia. *Neuropsychologia*, **29**, 803–9.

James, W. (1950). *The principles of psychology*. Dover, NY.

Jeannerod, M. (1986). The formation of finger grip during prehension. A cortically mediated visuomotor pattern. *Behavioural Brain Research*, **19**, 99–116.

Jeannerod, M. (1994a). The representing brain: neural correlates of motor intention and imagery. *Behavioral and Brain Sciences*, **17**, 187–246.

Jeannerod, M. (1994b). A theory of representation-driven actions. In *The perceived self: Ecological and interpersonal sources of self-knowledge* (ed. U. Neisser). Cambridge University Press, Cambridge.

Jones, V. and Prior, M. (1985). Motor imitation abilities and neurological signs in autistic children. *Journal of Autism and Developmental Disorders*, **13**, 37–46.

Kohler, I. (1955). Experiments with prolonged optical distorsions. *Acta Psychologica*, **11**, 176–8.

Kosslyn, S. M., Ball, T. M, and Reiser, B. J. (1978). Visual images preserve metric spatial information. Evidence from studies of image scanning. *Journal of Experimental Psychology: Human Perception and Performance*, **4**, 47–60.

Leekam, S. and Perner, J. (1991). Does the autistic children have a theory of representation? *Cognition*, **40**, 203–18.

Leslie, A. M. (1987). Pretence and representation: the origins of 'theory of mind'. *Psychological Review*, **94**, 412–26.

Leslie, A. M. and Thaiss, L. (1992). Domain specificity in conceptual development: neuropsychological evidence from autism. *Cognition*, **43**, 225–51.

Lewis, V. and Boucher, J. (1988). Spontaneous, instructed and elicited play in relatively able autistic children. *British Journal of Developmental Psychology*, **6**, 315–24.

Livet, P. (1996). Modèles de la motricité et théorie de l'action. *Rapports et Documents du CREA*, n 9610.

Livet, P. Les deux intentions de l'action. (Submitted)

McCarthy, R. (1993). Assembling routines and addressing representations: An alternative conceptualization of 'what' and 'where' in the human brain. In *Spatial representation* (ed. N. Eilan, R. McCarthy, and B. Brewer), pp. 373–99. Blackwell, Oxford.

McCloskey, D. I., Colebatch, J. G., Potter, E. K., and Burke, D. (1983). Judgements about onset of rapid voluntary movements in man. *Journal of Neurophysiology*, **49**, 851–63.

Mahoney, M. J. and Avener, M. (1987). Psychology of the elite athlete. An explorative study, **1**, 135–41.

Marr, D. (1982). *Vision*. W. H. Freeman and Company, NY.

Meltzoff, A. and Gopnik, A. (1993). The role of imitation in understanding persons and developing a theory of mind. In *Understanding other minds* (ed. S. Baron-Cohen, H. Tager-Flusberg, and D. J. Cohen), pp. 335–66. Oxford University Press, Oxford.

Ozonoff, S., Pennington, B. F., and Rogers, S. J. (1991). Executive function deficits in high-functioning autistic individuals: relationships to theory of mind. *Journal of Child Psychology and Psychiatry*, **32**, 1081–105.

Pacherie, E. (1997). Du problème de Molyneux au problème de Bach-y-Rita. In *Perception et Intermodalité, Approches actuelles du Problème de Molyneux* (ed. J. Proust), pp. 255–93. PUF, Paris.

Peacocke, C. (1992). *A study of concepts*. MIT Press, Cambridge, MA.

Penfield, W. (1975). *The mystery of the mind*. Princeton University Press, Princeton, NJ.

Perenin, M. T. and Jeannerod, M. (1978). Visual function within the hemianopicfield following early cerebral hemidecortication in man. 1. Spatial localization. *Neuropsychologia*, **16**, 1–13.

Perenin, M. T. and Vighetto, A. (1988). Optic ataxia: A specific disruption in visuomotor mechanisms. I. Differents aspects of the deficit in reaching for objects. *Brain*, **111**, 643–74.

Poincaré, H. (1905). *La valeur de la science*. Flammarion, Paris.

Poincaré, H.(1907). *La science et l'hypothèse*. Flammarion, Paris.

Poincaré, H.(1930). *Dernières pensées*. Flammarion, Paris.

Price, B. H, Daffner, K. R, Stowe, R. M., and Mesulam, M. M. (1990). The comportmental learning disabilities of early frontal lobe damage. *Brain*, **113**, 1383–93.

Prior, M. and Hoffman, W. (1990). Brief report: neuropsychological testing of autistic children through an exploration with frontal lobe tests. *Journal of Autism and Developmental Disorders*, **20**, 581–90.

Requin, J., Brener, J., and Ring, C. (1991). Preparation for action. In *Psychophysiology of human information processing* (ed. J. R. Jennings and M. G. H. Coles), pp. 357–448. Wiley, NY.

Rizzolatti, G., Carmada, R., Gentilucci, M. Luppino, G., and Matelli, M. (1988). Functional organization of area 6 in the macaque monkey. II Area F5 and the control of distal movements. *Experimental Brain Research*, **71**, 491–507.

Rock, I. (1966). *The nature of perceptual adaptation*. Basic Books, NY.

Rosenbaum, D. A. and Jorgensen, M. J. (1992). Planning macroscopic aspects of manual control. *Human Movement Science*, **11**, 61–9.

Rosenbaum, D. A., Marchak, F., Barnes, H. J., Vaughan, J., Slotta, J. D., and Jorgensen, M. J. (1990). Constraints for action selection. Overhand versus underhand grips. In *Attention and Performance XIII: Motor representation and control* (ed. M. Jeannerod), pp. 321–42. Lawrence Erlbaum, Hillsdale, NJ.

Rossi, P. J. (1968). Adaptation and negative after effect to lateral optical displacement in newly hatched chicks. *Science*, **160**, 430–2.

Rumsey, J. M. (1985). Conceptual problem-solving in highly verbal, nonretarded autistic men. *Journal of Autism and Developmental Disorders*, **15**, 23–36.

Russell, J. (1995). At two with nature: agency and the development of self-world dualism. In *The body and the self* (ed. J. L. Bermúdez, A. Marcel, and N. Eilan), pp. 127–51. MIT Press, Cambridge, MA.

Russell, J. (1996). *Agency: its role in mental development*. Lawrence Erlbaum, Hove.

Russell, J. and Jarrold, C. (in press) Memory for actions in children with autism: Self versus other *British Journal of Developmental Psychology*.

Russell, J., Mauthner, N., Sharpe, S., and Tiddswell, T. (1991). The 'windows task' as a measure of strategic deception in preschoolers and autistic subjects. *British Journal of Developmental Psychology*, **9**, 331–49.

Scheerer, E. (1987). Muscle sense and innervation feelings. A chapter in the history of perception and action. In *Perspectives on perception and action* (ed. H. Heuer and A. F. Sanders), pp. 171–94. Lawrence Erlbaum, Hillsdale, NJ.

Schmidt, R. A. (1982). *Motor control and learning*. Human Kinetics Publishers, Champaign, IL.

Searle, J. (1979). The intentionality of intention and action. *Inquiry*, **22**, 253–80.

Searle, J. (1981). Intentionality and method. *Journal of Philosophy*, **78**, 720–33.

Searle, J. (1983). *Intentionality*. Cambridge University Press, Cambridge.

Sellars, W. (1966). Thought and action. In *Freedom and determinism* (ed. K. Lehrer), pp. 105–39. Random House, NY.

Sellars, W. (1973). Action and events. *Nous*, **7**, 179–202.

Shallice, T. (1988). From neuropsychology to mental structure. Cambridge University Press, Cambridge.

Shepard, R. N. and Metzler, J. (1971). Mental rotation of three-dimensional objects. *Science*, **171**, 701–3.

Shiffrar, M. and Freyd, J. J. (1990). Apparent motion of the human body. *Psychological Science*, **1**, 257–64.

Sigman, M. and Ungerer, J. A. (1981). Sensorimotor skills and language comprehension in autistic children. *Journal of Abnormal Child Psychology*, **9**, 149–65.

Sigman, M. and Ungerer, J. A. (1984). Cognitive and language skills in autistic, mentally retarded and normal children. *Developmental Psychology*, **20**, 293–302.

Smith, K. U. and Smith, W. M. (1962). *Perception and motion*. W. B. Saunders, London.

Stratton, G. M. (1896). Some preliminary experiments on vision without inversion of the retinal image. *Psychological Review*, **3**, 611–17.

Stratton, G. M. (1897). Upright vision and the retinal image. *Psychological Review*, **4**, 182–7.

Taub, E. (1968). Prism compensation as a learning phenomenon: a phylogenetic perspective. In *The neuropsychology of spatially oriented behavior* (ed. S. J. Freedman), pp. 77–106. The Dorsey Press, Homewood, IL.

Ungerleider, L. G. and Mishkin, M. (1982). Two cortical visual systems. In *Analysis of visual behavior* (ed. D. J. Ingle, M. A. Goodale, and R. J. W. Mansfield). MIT Press, Cambridge, MA.

Viviani, P. and McCollum, G. (1983). The relation between linear extent and velocity in drawing movements. *Neuroscience*, **10**, 211–18.

von Holst, E. and Mittelstaedt, H. (1950). Das reafferenzprinzip. Wechselwirkung zwischen Zentralnervensystem und Peripherie. *Naturwissenschaften*, **37**, 464–76. (transl. R. D. Martin, reprinted in C. R. Gallistel (1980). *The organization of action*, pp. 176–209. Lawrence Erlbaum, Hillsdale, NJ.)

Wareham, A. (1994). Executive function and mental concepts in children with Asperger's syndrome. Unpublished M. Phil. thesis. University of Cambridge.

White, B.W., Saunders, F.A., Scadden, L., Bach-Y-Rita, P., and Collins, C. C. (1970). Seeing with the skin. *Perception and Psychophysics*, **7**, 23–7.

8 How executive disorders can bring about an inadequate 'theory of mind'

James Russell

Autism not only manifests itself as a severe executive disorder, with deficits arguably more severe than those found in other clinical populations, but it is characterized by a profile of executive dysfunctions that appears to be unique (see Chapters 5 and 6). Persons with autism also, of course, have severe, and arguably unique, impairments in mentalizing (Baron-Cohen *et al.* 1993). My starting assumption will accordingly be that both executive and mentalizing impairments are fundamental components of autism and that a major task for cognitive theories of the disorder is to give an account of how the two are related. While acknowledging that impairments in mentalizing might affect executive functioning, I will describe how executive deficits might impact upon mentalizing—arguing first in a fairly *a priori* style and then from the evidence.

The qualification 'cognitive' in 'cognitive theories of autism' is important for the following reason. Those who take executive dysfunctions to be primary share with those who argue that the core deficit is in 'theory of mind' a commitment to provide an explanation at the cognitive level (see Morton and Frith 1995). (Although, for my purposes, 'psychological' is a better term than 'cognitive', because I want this explanatory level to encompass not only information-processing and epistemic states but also phenomenology.)

A rejection of arguments at the 'cognitive' level would, in this context, mean saying that if two kinds of impairment exist within a disorder then we must seek an explanation for this fact at the level of brain anatomy and physiology *alone*—perhaps in terms of shared circuitry between an 'executive' centre and a 'mentalizing' centre. On this approach, we ignore how one kind of impairment might impact upon another psychologically, with only interactions at the neural level being countenanced. But this is unwise, given that the brain is an open system whose development not only determines experience but is determined by it. Accordingly, a developmental dysfunction in neural domain X might cause the individual to experience self and world in an inadequate way, and this inadequate experience (the psychological level) might affect behaviour and mental life within cognitive domain Y—and perhaps lead to behavioural dysfunctions associated with this domain. At the same time, of course, things are happening at the neural level; but this does not mean that the relationship between the two impairments can only be explained *at* that level. In other words, one does not go straight from surface symptoms to the neurophysiology.

Needless to say, in making this point I am not dismissing research on the neural substrates of autism! The point is entirely about how we explain the relationship between types of impairment, and indeed it parallels the thinking of some neurobiologists. Thus Robbins (Chapter 2) argues that neurobiological theories of autism must accept the necessity for 'horizontal integration' between neural theories of autism as well as for 'vertical integration' between neural and cognitive theories. In this chapter I am attempting some horizontal integration between two cognitive theories of autism and making the case that early executive impairments can impact upon the acquisition of a theory of mind. Theories that favour a causal linkage in the opposite direction will be touched upon at the end.

This chapter falls into two parts. In the first part I describe a conceptual linkage between agency and self-awareness and give reasons for thinking that disorders of agency will give rise to disorders of self-awareness. In the second part I review the evidence for this view that has emerged from experimental studies of autism, concentrating on the process of action-monitoring. Before proceeding, however, I need to insert a caveat. What follows is by no means supposed to be a 'theory of autism'. Rather, autism is being used as a test case for a general account of the relationship between agency and self-awareness in development. This means, of course, that the predictions which fall from this account extend beyond autism: in *any* population of children in which there is the kind of disordered agency described here one should find a disordered conception of mentality.

Agency and self-awareness

Four facts about agency

In this section I will describe four features of agency and then discuss how they impact upon self-awareness, though allowing this term to be ambiguous for the time being. To a degree this section will be a streamlined and somewhat modified version of something I have said in greater detail elsewhere (Russell 1996, Part 2). It is more than this, however, because the implications for what I will call a 'pretheoretical self-awareness'—and hence for autism—are spelt out here.

The concept of 'agency' is not identical to that of 'executive functioning'. 'Executive functioning' refers to the set of mental processes necessary for the control of action (and of thought, in so far as thought is mental action), while 'agency', as I will use the term, refers to the fact that adequate executive functioning determines the subject's experiences. *'Agency' refers to subjects' ability to change their perceptual inputs at will.* This is what the exercise of agency gives us. For example, subjects with adequate executive functioning can freely choose what to look at. They can, for example, glance around a room as opposed to having their attention captured by the objects within it. With this in mind, we will consider four features of agency. The first two features describe what the nervous system must enable and the second two describe modes of experience that the exercise of agency gives the subject.

Action-monitoring—locating the cause of altered inputs within one's body (feature A)

Staying within the visual modality, there are only two ways in which our inputs can be caused to change. Either there is an environmental event (e.g. an object moves towards us, something explodes) or we move our body, thereby giving us a different perspective on the environment. These bodily movements can, of course, range widely—anything from a slight leftward glance to flying to the moon.

The organism must necessarily code which of these visual changes were brought about by its actions and which were caused by the world, for unless this were done no fundamental distinction could be drawn between objectively caused experiences and subjectively determined ones.[1] You may think this is simple enough. All the nervous system needs to do is to record that all those visual changes preceded by motor commands are self-caused and all those that are not are world-caused. For example, an object begins to loom; but just before this there were motor commands to walk forward, so this change in input is coded as self-caused not world-caused. Conversely, an object begins to loom towards the organism when there have been no motor commands, so the nervous system 'concludes' that there the visual change is world-caused. But it cannot be a simple as this.

The main problem is that the nervous system has to record correspondences between motor commands *of a certain kind* and visual inputs *of a certain kind*. It is not enough merely to record that a change of some kind in the visual input was preceded by a motor command of some kind: the two have to map precisely. And to the extent that this mapping is not exact, self-generated visual experiences will be unpredictable. According to Helmholz we have evolved the following solution to this problem. When the nervous system produces a motor command to, say, move the head in a certain way it makes a copy of this command and this copy is calibrated against the resulting visual input. For example, after looking straight at an object we look to the left, thus causing the image of the object to move to the right of our visual field. We do not, however, take the object itself to have moved. The reason is that we produce an *efference copy* of the motor command to move the eyes which is then matched against the resulting visual input—and the mapping is precise. If the motor command is (a fanciful example) 'move 6 units to the left', and if the visual input is 'image moves 6 units to the right' then these two cancel and the nervous system concludes that nothing has changed in the world. Note that the following must be true of the efference copy: it must be in a code that can be matched against the visual input. In the present case this code must be either a-modal or visual. In support of the latter possibility Held (1961) claimed that motor commands are copied into a visual form—a 'visual schema'—for comparing against the visual input. I shall return to this idea when the evidence for efference-copying impairments in autism is discussed.

I am going to use the more general term 'action-monitoring' to describe the process through which changes in experience are taken to have been caused by the self and not the world, rather than the term 'efference-copying'—for the following reason. Efference copying is a very primitive process— indeed, it is achieved by fruit flies (von Holst and Mittelstaedt 1977). And, of course, this primitive character is exactly what one would expect if it is the process that enables organisms to discriminate between self-determined and world-determined changes in input; without this distinction they would quickly succumb.

It is primitive, however, in the sense that it can be applied to *re*-actions to stimuli just as well as to goal-directed movements; in fact it was evoked by von Holst and Mittelstaedt to explain why flies do not become paralysed when they produce 'optokinetic' reactions to stimuli (tracking stimuli which move across the visual field). We need a richer conception and a different term which does full justice to the fact that actions are applied to the world rather than evoked by it. Imagine, for example, a toddler exploring a playroom. Her attention will be captured by attractive toys or by other children; but to a large extent she will intentionally move from place to place and from object to object. Maybe we do not want to say that the behaviour is goal-directed. Perhaps one might place the behaviour somewhere between planning 'in the head' and then acting and simply being tugged here and there by salient features of the environment. For a number of reasons (to be discussed later) it is misleading to say that an intention to do something 'precedes' the doing of it and that the notion of 'intention in action' (Searle 1983; and see Pacherie's chapter in this volume) is sometimes to be preferred above, to coin a phrase, that of 'intention *then* action'.

The claim is, therefore, that all kinds of bodily movement are monitored, both those evoked by stimuli and those that are intentional: the basic logic of efference copying can be applied in all cases. This is a large and seemingly extravagant claim to make, however, and I shall be saying more about it under feature C below.

'Instigation': the self-determination of perceptual sequences (feature B)

The best way to understand this feature is in terms of the distinction just drawn between monitored movements of the body called out by the world (the case of the fly) and monitored actions generated by the subject (the case of the toddler). In the first case, the organism takes its bodily movements to be the cause of the altered perceptual inputs, but these movements are not what we would want to call 'intentional'. It generates motor commands; but there can surely be motor commands without anything that we would want to call 'intentions'. Thus, a puppet-like organism which never moved except in response to exogenous signals to its motor system might possess a nervous system that monitored its actions sufficiently well to distinguish between changes in input that were determined by movements of its body (in response to distal stimulation) and those that were not due to bodily movements.

In contrast to this situation, we can consider an organism that is in control of its movements. There is, of course, no uncontentious definition of being 'in control'; and I am not even going to offer a contentious one because we can proceed without it. What feature B describes is not the fact of being in control but rather the experiential *result* of being a creature that is in control of its movements, as opposed to reacting to inputs or ballistically running-through packages of movements. A creature that is in control of what it does *is able to determine for itself the sequences of perceptual inputs it enjoys from moment to moment*. Moreover, being able to determine these sequences means being able to repeat them at will—it can glance from A to B and then back to A and continue to do so for as long as it likes. This feature of intentional movement was what James Mark Baldwin, and later Jean Piaget, referred to as 'circular', that is, circular in the sense of affording the possibility of returning to the starting point.

Being able to determine its own movements, then, enables the subject to enjoy two kinds of perceptual sequences, as the author of one and the subject of another: those that are *reversible* and those that are *irreversible*. This distinction is owing to Kant. Irreversible perceptual sequences are typically caused by events in the world. For example, when a cat walks across my room from left to right I am not in a position to repeat the perceptual sequence (I must wait upon the cat); although I can, of course, look from the left to the right of the room and back again as often as I like. I am not saying, by the way, that the *only* difference between reversible and irreversible sequences is that the former have their source in the body and the latter have their source in the world, because we can undergo sequences of bodily sensation (such as a dull ache followed by a shooting pain) that are within the body and yet irreversible. The point is, rather, that, for a given state of the environment, agents can repeat what they have just done and thus experience what they have just experienced. The clearest example here is that of changing visual fixations by eye and head movements; for many kinds of bodily movement are not reversible for entirely physical reasons (e.g. we can dive into a pool but cannot dive out again). In fact, the notion of reversibility has much the clearest application to the kinds of action that are difficult to distinguish from attentional acts, given that a mark of self-determined attention—as opposed to the capture by stimuli—is its reversibility.

Much more work would need to be done to spell out properly the relationship between self-determined perceptual sequences and reversibility, and between world-determined sequences and irreversibility (for this see Russell 1996, Part 2.2), but enough has been done to set up some empirical claims. What feature B boils down to is the fact that agents experience a tension between two kind of perceptual sequences—those they control and those the world imposes on them. Unless a subject is able to instigate actions this tension will never be experienced; and this—my empirical claim—will impact upon the development of subjectivity.

The presence of action-monitoring and instigation enables the agent to be related to his or her actions in two ways. These will now be described.

Non-observational knowledge of actions (feature C)

If a subject is in control of herself she does not have to observe her actions to know what they are. Her actions are not phenomena to be observed, as it were, from a third-person perspective as if through a kind of inner eye. This fact emerges from the monitored and instigated nature of actions.

With regard to action-monitoring, the endogenous causes of action are not, as we have seen, like triggers whose job is done once the movement begins—as if intentions launched actions and then evaporated. The agent does not simply intend something and then, as it were, sit back and hope that the attempt comes off. Imagine that it were otherwise: first intending to move in a certain way, then a bodily movement, then finally checking the memory of what was intended against the bodily movement. What is missing here is the fact of continuous control of the body.

When describing action-monitoring, I assumed a parallel between the monitoring of motor commands through efference copying and the monitoring of intentions. This is completely inadequate as it stands, for a motor command *can* be regarded as a trigger; and the last thing we want to do—the point of the previous paragraph—is to regard an intention in this way. So how do we hold on simultaneously to the views (1) that intentions, like motor commands, are monitored and (2) intentions cannot be regarded as the 'triggers' of action.

We must steer clear of the notion that intention-monitoring is a kind of self-observation—just like efference copying, as it were, 'but conscious'—and realize that what makes a bodily movement intentional is precisely that we do *not* have to watch ourselves to know its nature. But why do we need the notion of 'monitoring' at all? Why would nature have evolved such a belt-and-braces system? Perhaps the mark of an intentional bodily movement, in fact, is that it does not *need* to be monitored. I shall now say why this view is fundamentally mistaken.

Consider the distinction between basic actions and goal-directed actions. Basic actions are actions like moving one's arm upwards: they are movements of the body that are ends in themselves (cf. Piaget's 'primary circular reactions'). Goal-directed actions, on the other hand, are actions performed so as to bring about a change in the environment (e.g. raising one's arm to reach a cup or to hail a taxi). Now while basic actions are not the expressions of goals—we do not *try* to raise our arm and then happily succeed—they are nevertheless expressions of intentions. The intention to raise the arm in just *this* way 'runs ahead', as it were, of the bodily movement, and if it did not our movements could always surprise us. The claim I will make is that what makes this 'running ahead' possible is a subpersonal mechanism: the nervous system 'making predictions'[2] about the bodily outcome of its motor commands. These predictions are copies of the motor commands in a form that can be matched against the feedback from the movement, and so long as they are fulfilled we are in control of our body (and can perhaps reflect on this fact), while at the instant they fail we have lost control of ourselves (and perhaps feel we have done so). In other words, being in control is the result of monitoring at the subpersonal level: it is the result of the matching between motor outputs and proprioceptive and exteroceptive inputs—the meshing of predictions with outcomes.

Imagine what the result would be if there were no monitoring of actions. The nervous system would be faced with two incommensurable sources of information—efference and afference, the motor commands to move the arm in just this way and the kinaesthetic result of doing so (and perhaps accompanying exteroceptive inputs of how the arm now looks). What action-monitoring achieves is the making of these two sources of information commensurable, through the production of a copy of the motor command in a form matchable against the sensory feedback from the movement. (If such a system did not exist then subjects really *would* have to watch themselves to find out what action their nervous system had brought about, as it were 'on their behalf'). There is no room, therefore, in the picture of agency I am sketching for the notion of self-observation. No room for questions such as 'How did you know that you intended to move your arm in just that way?' or 'Why didn't you think that you intended to move it in a different way?'.

I now consider how instigation (feature B) contributes to the non-observational knowledge of our actions. To the extent that the agent does X rather than Y intentionally, her knowledge of what she intended to do is 'immediate'—meaning not being mediated by concepts. The toddler in our earlier example intentionally picks up one toy rather than another, but in doing so does not have to represent to herself concepts such as 'intention', 'choice', 'preference'; indeed the notion of 'representation' is quite out of place here. The agent does X, and in so far as it is done intentionally, what is intended is transparent.

One can say then that action-monitoring and instigation together make it possible for agents to be in control of their bodies *and thus in control of their perceptual inputs in so far as these result from bodily movements*. An individual will fail to be in control if there is, as it were, a gap between her intention and her bodily movement such that she has to observe herself to find out what she is doing or whether an intention has come to fruition. Agency evaporates as soon the subject becomes a self-observer. We do not need to be self-observers because: (1) the meshing of efference and afference via monitoring mechanisms ensures that we experience self-control rather than mental acts of intending followed by observation of their results; and (2) the nature of our intentions is known immediately, not via a representational medium.

It is worth hammering home the point that action-monitoring and self-observation are opposites, despite the fact that the terms sound similar. Action-monitoring is a subpersonal process that enables subjects to discriminate between self-determined and world-determined changes in input. It can give rise to a mode of experience (the experience of being the cause of altered inputs and the experience of being in control), but it is not itself a mode of experience any more than the functioning of the, say, oculomotor system is a mode of experience. Self-observation, on the other hand, *is* a mode of experience—in fact one should say a *pathological* mode of experience—in which we watch ourselves, as it were, dispassionately to see what we are doing or whether we have succeeded in doing what we wanted to do. By contrast, we do, of course, find out what is happening in the environment by observing it. The fact that we know our actions without observation is, then, one process through which we appreciate the difference between what is true of the world and what is true of us—and ultimately what is true of the world versus what is true of our minds.

Finally, it is necessary to locate the present point in relation to Norman and Shallice's (1980) influential model of the executive system; predictably this model has received a great deal of attention in this book. Their model is not, as it were, 'contention scheduling with an homunculus sitting on top', because it describes the process of self-monitoring *not self-observation*.

Privileged knowledge of goals (feature D)

Let us return to the distinction between basic actions, such as lifting an arm or pursing the lips, and goal-directed behaviour, such as changing a light bulb or demisting a windscreen. As discussed, in goal-directed behaviour the movements of the body are the means towards an end; whereas in basic actions the movements and the ends are one. We can, of course, observe goal-directed behaviour in others, and indeed our nervous systems are almost certainly configured innately to perceive some kinds of action as goal directed and some kinds of action as not (Gergely *et al.* 1995, for data suggesting that the input to such a system may be very abstract). We can, however, be mistaken about the nature of the goals we perceive in others: the person fiddling with the light-socket may be planting a bugging device and the person apparently cleaning the windscreen may be a vandal. We cannot, however, be wrong about our own on-line goals. (I say 'on-line' goals here in order to avoid the problem of self-deception.) We can lose sight of them and they can be supplanted without our being aware of the fact, but in the moment of acting in a goal-directed fashion we know incorrigibly what the goal is; and while another may know about this goal, there is scope for error. That is to say, if it seems to me that I am trying to achieve X then that is just what I am trying to achieve. What I take my immediate goal to be, in other words, *exhausts it nature.*

This incorrigibility about goals affords another distinction: that between first-person and third-person knowledge of agency, one incorrigible the other corrigible. By the way, and recalling what was said earlier about knowledge without observation, I am not denying that the agent's awareness of her goals is a matter of having mental representations. A goal is, after all, a representation of a future state of affairs. The point was rather that the notion of representation is out of place when describing the process of choosing to do A rather B and in being in control of oneself when doing it. The point was that intention and being in control cannot be explicated in terms of having the right kinds of representation and having one's behaviour guided by them.

There are, then, two important senses in which the first-person experience of agency differs from the third-person perception of another's agency. To experience oneself as being in control of what happens next, and then determining it, is immediate (unmediated by concepts), and to have a goal is to have a kind of knowledge that is infallible. The latter has something of a Cartesian flavour—it comes from O'Shaughnessy (1980) who calls it 'conditional Cartesianism'—and I admit that the term 'knowledge' is somewhat out of place.

Successful agency and pretheoretical self-awareness

In this section I will describe a form of self-awareness that can be ascribed to a subject whose nervous system enables action-monitoring and instigation, and which therefore knows its actions without observation and has incorrigible knowledge of its goals. What must be avoided here is the smuggling in of folk-psychological concepts; because the aim is to describe the kind of first-person experience that *grounds* folk psychology. Of course, to those who think that a child's knowledge of folk psychology exists in an innate module (the 'theory of mind mechanism' of Leslie 1987) the idea that a mode of experience might 'ground' its maturation would sound absurd: this module is a *sui generis* entity that matures autonomously (although it may require triggering from the environment or from other modules). But it should not sound absurd. For even if we knew for sure that such a module existed, it really would be absurd to assume that this is *all* the child needs for a theory of mind. What use would an innate conception of agency be to a creature which was not itself an agent? (For a detailed defence of this view see Russell 1996, Section 3.3 (iii).)

Another potential worry hovers over the phrase 'pretheoretical self-awareness' itself. Isn't this a contradiction? To be 'self-aware' would seem to require possession of a concept of self—a concept of something of which the agent is reflexively aware; and yet this is supposed to be *pre*theoretical. A full answer to this point should emerge in the rest of this section, but something needs to be said right now. I am assuming that a subject can be self-aware without thereby being in a position to exercise the network of concepts involved in having a 'theory of mind'. Such a subject will be able, at least, to distinguish self from other, self from object, experience responsibility for determining its perceptual inputs, and all without any conception of itself as a believer, knower, intender, desirer, and so forth—let alone any conception of how these attitudes are interrelated. Indeed we may want to withdraw still further from ascribing a conception of self to a subject of this kind and say that having a concept of X requires knowing something about the criteria through which Xs are identified—which enables us to judge, in a more or less rational way, whether something is an X. This is a form of self-awareness falling far short of this.

What lies at the heart of the present sense of 'self-awareness' is *ownership*—the ability to regard experiences as one's own. You may think this is a rather empty kind of ability. Who *else* could they belong to! What I have in mind here is the fact that agents are directly responsible for the character of some of their experiences, namely those that are self-determined rather than world-determined (see feature B above). I will describe the present sense of self-awareness under three headings: bodily awareness; the 'immediate' experience of willing; and the integration of knowing and willing.

Bodily awareness

It emerged from the discussion of action-monitoring and knowledge without observation that intentions and movements of the body are not related as causes to effects. There exists no disembodied intention causally (and mysteriously) related to a mechanical outcome. In lapsing into this mistaken way of thinking we lose all purchase on the notion of subjects being in control of themselves. When we, for example, glance around a room or twiddle our fingers or wave our arms we are not producing a series of atomistic micro-intentions that happily map to a series of movements. Rather, we exercise control over our body and may do so in a manner that need not be goal-directed. That is to say, the body is the *expression* of the will, rather than its puppet, and when we act we have the experience of intentions coming to fruition (O'Shaughnessy's phrase) rather than the experience of things working out bodily as we intend them to.

This is by no means an original point. Schopenhauer wrote: 'I cannot imagine this will without this body'; while later Nietzsche said: 'Behind your thoughts and feelings . . . there stands a mighty ruler, an unknown sage— whose name is self. In your body he dwells; he is your body.' In a somewhat different vein, Wittgenstein (1953) insisted that a willed bodily movement is not the outcome of a kind of *wishing*, and that: 'It cannot stop anywhere short of the action.' (615). He went on to describe the absurdity of the 'agent wills body responds' picture in the following terms:

> Let us not forget this: when 'I raise my arm', my arm goes up. And the problem arises: what is left over if I subtract the fact that my arm goes up from the fact that I raise my arm? (Are the kinaesthetic sensations my willing?)' (621).

> When I raise my arm I do not usually *try* to raise it. (622)

> 'How do you know that you have raised your arm?'—'I feel it.' 'So what you recognise is the feeling? And are you certain that you recognise it right?— You are certain that you have raised your arm; isn't this a criterion, the measure of the recognition?' (625)

Two related points are made in the Wittgenstein passage. First, there is no ethereal mental act of willing that can be hived off from the bodily movement to which it is responsive. Second, 'knowing' what we have done is not like the kind of knowledge (recall I said earlier it is not really 'knowledge' at all) that we glean by observation—which, unlike this, always admits the possibility of uncertainty and error. It is reasonable to say, then, that successful agents experience the body as the expression, as the physical manifestation, of their intentions, not as something separate from them: there is for them a fundamental unity between volition and bodily awareness.

This inspires the claim that children too young to apply mental predicates to themselves can nevertheless experience the body not merely as an organic object responsive to their desires, but as a kind of mental object. Therefore, my proposal is that the bodily awareness that is the product of successful agency provides a grounding for self-awareness: early self-awareness is indissociable from bodily awareness. For very young children to regard their experiences *as* their own, therefore, they must regard their body as their own, and take it to be not an owned object to which they are intimately connected but the physical manifestation of their will. For this reason, changes in the child's experience caused by movements of the body are taken to be caused not by an object (the body) which happens to be very responsive to volitional events but caused, as it were, 'directly' by a willing centre.

The 'immediate' experience of willing

As we have already seen—most recently in the latter part of the Wittgenstein quotation—knowing what we are doing (e.g. raising an arm) is not like perceiving something as X or recognizing something as an instance of X. It does not involve the application of concepts, and it does not accordingly have a representational character.

What needs to be emphasized here is the fact that the experience of agency, and thus the agent's experience of freely determining perceptual inputs through bodily movements, does not require the exercise of psychological concepts such as 'agent', 'intention', and 'desire'. This is not to say that this experience can be enjoyed by a subject *with no concepts at all*. Indeed, as I have argued elsewhere, following Piaget, the development of the concept of an object depends upon subjects experiencing the limits within which they can determine the nature of their perceptual inputs, and it depends upon experiencing something as refractory (Russell 1995; also see T. Baldwin 1995). Agency can only be experienced within a world of objects—the body must be experienced as a special kind of object—and so must involve the exercise of concepts of space, time, and cause-and effect; but it does not depend upon the exercise of psychological concepts.

It could be objected that the sense of self-awareness under discussion is so 'thin' that saying that it occurs pretheoretically is saying rather little. Perhaps this bodily-based, immediate self-awareness is indeed a necessary condition for 'true', theory-involving self-awareness, but necessary conditions are two-a-penny. (One necessary condition for being a rational human is the possession of a head.)

The answer to this objection is implicit in what has already been said.

Everybody agrees that the *concept* of agency is necessary for the development of a theory of mind. What is under discussion here is the extension of that concept, not some low-level, common-denominator-style necessary condition for developing such a concept. What the above discussion entails is that the extension of the concept of an agent is surely not a set of perceptual invariants *in the bodily movements of others.*

Complete integration of willing and apprehending

The 'self' of which the subject is aware cannot be a purely willing self but must also be something that has knowledge of the world through observation. The self, though, is not a *composite* of the volitional and the cognitive: it involves the complete integration of the two. In other words, that which determines its own perceptual inputs through action and strives to alter the world through action is also that which knows things about the world. For the point of acting is to change the world as *I* perceive it or believe it to be, while the capacity to apprehend states of the world will determine the form these actions take.[3] Accordingly, if the child is to have first-person thoughts then the 'I' must have the same reference in 'I do . . .' or 'I try . . .' as the 'I' in 'I see . . .' or 'I know . . .'. Incoming information converges on and volition emanates from the same psychological 'point'.

This might be seen as an unexceptional claim about the relationship between volition and apprehension. There is, however, a moral to be drawn from it, one somewhat similar to the moral on the previous page. It is that the volitional face of the first person cannot be treated as a kind of knowledge: it is not knowledge about psychological categories—about what it takes to be a believer, say, and how this relates to being a desirer. One does not need to possess the concept of intending in order to intend X or that of that desiring in order to desire Y; and it is the experience of intending, *not reflexive awareness of oneself as an intender*, that is supposed to be completely integrated with apprehension.

Here is an objection. Apprehenders are concept-users, so how can something that involves the exercise of concepts (apprehension) be completely integrated with something that, on the present view, does not (volition)? What is required—the objection runs—is knowledge of folk-psychological categories to bridge these two. It is the possession of a (perhaps innate) folk-psychology theory that makes this integration between the willing and the apprehending self possible.

But no such 'bridge' is required. How we apprehend the world gives us reasons for acting; but taking action is something guided by these reasons directly, not something requiring a further set of psychological, self-reflective reasons. (The mountain is climbed 'because it is there' not because we can reflect on the fact that we 'believe' that taking these steps will fulfil our 'desire' for a good view.) There is no requirement to apprehend folk-psychological categories such as belief and desire, in addition to, say, spatial, temporal, causal, and physical categories. For example, a toddler who is able to search for an object following its invisible displacement does so on the basis of his knowledge that it is still there under the same blue, but displaced, cup; and if he were a little older he could tell us what he is doing. He has reasons for acting in other words. But in no sense do these reasons exploit a conceptual grasp of agency. (Recall what was said earlier about knowledge of our actions being non-observational). The toddler lifts the blue cup because he thinks the trinket is under it, not because he knows how his desire for the object's return and his current beliefs interact to cause him to do so. (Contrast his spatial knowledge of the relationship between the trinket and the cup.) In short, what is integrated with physical, spatial, and temporal concepts in self-awareness is not something conceptual.

What is impaired in autism? Action-monitoring and beyond

I have been arguing that there is a conceptual link between, on the one hand, the successful monitoring of actions and their instigation and, on the other, agents' non-observational knowledge of their actions and incorrigible knowledge of their goals. I have also suggested that being related to one's actions in this way grounds a mode of a self-awareness requiring no grasp of psychological concepts. It is, therefore, a non-theoretical, or, in the case of young children a pretheoretical self-awareness given that, if they develop normally, children will acquire a form of self-awareness that *is* concept-exercising. But what if they do not develop normally? As I said at the beginning, the aim here is not to put forward 'a theory of autism', but rather to give reasons for believing that children with executive dysfunctions will have delayed or deviant understanding of mentality. This is because the development of a 'theory' of mind is dependent upon the adequate development of something that is not theoretical—the 'something' that I described in the first section.

The main empirical claim arising from this discussion is a very simple one: there should be an association between deficits in mentalizing and deficits in the monitoring and instigation of actions. What are action-monitoring deficits supposed to encompass? The definition is broad enough to cover everything from deficits in the efference copying of endogenously caused movements to those in the higher level processes that C. D. Frith calls 'intention-monitoring' and 'central-monitoring' and processes that workers on memory such as Marcia Johnson call 'self-monitoring'. (Their work is discussed below.) I will be assuming that there are no *qualitative* differences between these levels. They are all subpersonal processes. And they all involve, in different ways, the nervous system's feeding forward predictions about the outcomes of physical and mental actions. Speaking subpersonally, the motor cortex launches movements and the prefrontal lobes launch intentions, and both kinds of process are monitored via copying and feedforward mechanisms. Put like this the claim is unsatisfactory, but it is good enough get my empirical claims off the ground.[4]

Two further terminological points. First, I will take 'deficits in mentalizing' to mean a weak or absent grasp of mental categories of the kind found in autism (as opposed to understanding mental categories but failing adequately to attribute thought and volition to the self and others, as found in schizophrenia). Second, with due acknowledgement of the fact that different workers can mean different things by the phrase 'executive functions' I will be using the term 'executive' as equivalent to monitoring and instigation. Does this not ignore the contribution of other facets of executive functioning? Both from *a priori* considerations about what is required for an adequate executive system and from the results of factor-analytical studies (e.g. Pennington, in press) these can be said to be: *inhibition, mental flexibility* (or 'set-shifting'), and *working memory*. (See Jarrold's Chapter 4 for a discussion of inhibition, Ozonoff's Chapter 6 for mental flexibility, and Pennington *et al.*'s Chapter 5 for working memory.)

Turning first to inhibition, we can define this as: 'the ability to suppress a prepotent but incorrect response called out by a salient stimulus or by information made salient through learning'. This is subsumed under the notion of instigation, and explaining why this is so will get us closer to the heart of instigation. Instigation is not simply taking action: it is taking action that is not evoked by stimuli and is not the expression of a habit. It does not have to be goal-directed, but it must express a choice. For example, in choosing one of two equally attractive alternatives we do something intentional and rational (if we like them both equally it doesn't matter which we pick), but that particular (A over B) choice was not made in pursuit of a goal of having A rather than B. Also, because instigation need not be goal-directed it does not fall naturally within the ambit of a folk-psychological explanation in terms of practical inferences involving beliefs and desires. (This is not, however, to say that it is a more *primitive* form of behaviour than goal-directed behaviour. For example, being capable of random behaviour requires considerable cognitive sophistication; but we surely do not wish to explain each act—each, say, stroke of the pen or tap of the keyboard—in terms of the coming together of certain beliefs and certain desires.)

If, then, instigation is being defined as the capacity to take actions that are not evoked externally or driven by habits then it is clear that a capacity to instigate depends upon a capacity to inhibit. The relationship between the two concepts is not symmetrical, however. For while it makes no sense to say that a creature is a successful instigator and an unsuccessful inhibitor (as the former requires the latter) it is certainly possible for individuals to be successful inhibitors and unsuccessful instigators: they do nothing.

I turn next to mental flexibility. As gauged in tasks such as the WCST and the IDED shift task, this requires the abandonment of one schema and the engagement of a new one. This will obviously not work if the agent has not adequately monitored the outcome of the erroneous response and if he or she is unable to instigate a strategy.

Third, I will define working memory as: 'the ability to hold in mind past states of the environment and past actions while currently performing an action'. On the present view, working memory does not lie at the heart of the executive system but is, rather, what makes complex actions possible. That is, monitoring can only be said to be a form of memory at a metaphorical level; while holding information on-line is not a form of instigation (feeding data through a rehearsal loop clearly cannot count as instigation). But without adequate working memory the subject would always be acting, as it were, in the continuous present. There would be monitoring and instigation, but actions would be lacking a context. This implies that monitoring and instigation of action can be impaired while working memory is intact.

In the first part of this second section I will review the evidence for the presence of monitoring impairments in autism. What of instigation? Perhaps the purest test of instigation is one in which the subject is required to take random actions—actions that are self-determined rather than determined by task-relative goals or by the immediate environment. Turner (Chapter 3) reviews the evidence for there being such an impairment in autism. And, of course, the topic of instigation has received a good deal of attention in recent autism research under the heading 'generativity' (see Chapter 4). Action-monitoring, however, has been neglected; and so it will be my focus.

When the evidence for a monitoring impairment has been reviewed I will look at formal tests of executive functioning and of theory of mind to ask, in the first place, how monitoring and instigation difficulties manifest them-selves and, in the second place, whether failure on the false-belief task can be said to have an executive component.

Are children with autism impaired in action-monitoring?

It is clearly inadequate, in the present context, to say that children with autism must have monitoring dysfunctions by virtue of the fact that they perform poorly on tests of executive functioning, all of which tap monitoring abilities. For these tasks tap a number of cognitive operations in addition to monitoring. Rather, we need direct evidence for a monitoring impairment. The evidence for such an impairment is not overwhelming at the present time—but it exists.

Motor skill

Hermelin and O'Connor (1975) performed a study whose main aim was to compare the skills of congenitally blind and sighted children (with average mental ages of around 10 years) in reproducing the terminus and the distance of certain bodily movements. However, because some of their subjects were children with autism and because the performance of these children was similar to that of the blind children on one of the tasks, they produced evidence for a monitoring impairment in autism—for reasons which will emerge. Three groups of children (congenitally blind, normally developing, and relatively high-functioning children with autism) performed two location-estimation tasks and one distance-estimation task. In all three they had to move a pointer vertically on a rod, and in all three the children with autism and the normally developing children wore blindfolds. In one of the location tasks the children had to move the pointer from the bottom of the rod to a location which had previously been marked by a stopper, and in the other they had to do the same thing but beginning from a new starting point halfway between the bottom and the previous position of the stopper. In the second task, then, they had to move the pointer about half as far as in the first. Note that these tasks require the children to end a movement at an *absolute* point in space. There were no group differences on this task.

In the distance-estimation task the children, as before, began by moving the pointer from the bottom of the rod to a number of locations marked by a stopper, and then, as in the second task, the pointer was repositioned halfway between the bottom of the rod and the stopper's earlier position. This time, however, the task was to move the pointer the same *distance* as before; they had to stop, in contrast to the location tasks, at different absolute positions. There were group differences on this task. The children with autism and the blind children were less successful than the normally developing children. Both groups tended to underestimate the longer distances, and the children with autism also tended to overshoot at shorter distances.

Why does this count as evidence for an efference-copying deficit? The efference copy is produced at the same time as the motor command and must be matched, in a comparator, against afferent signals resulting from the movement. If these afferent signals are visual (signals specifying, in this case, what an arm movement looks like) then, if the comparator is to do its work, the code in which the efference copy is produced must be commensurable with the visual modality. As I mentioned before (feature A) there are two alternatives: either afferent signal and efferent copy are compared amodally, or an efference copy is made in a visual code. As we have seen the latter alternative is the one favoured by Held (1961). On Held's theory, motor signals are accompanied by copies in a visual code (a 'visual schema') because the copies have to be matched against visual input. Obviously, the congenitally blind will be unable to construct visual schemata; and if children with autism are similarly unable to construct efference copies in the form of visual schemata they will, when they are blindfolded, perform similarly to the blind. The normally developing, sighted children, by contrast, *will* be able to reproduce distances by using representations of how a movement of that distance *looks*—even when they are blindfolded.

Why were there no group differences on the two location tasks? Because they could be performed without recruiting visual schemata of movements. What the children had to do in this case was to remember the absolute point at which they had received exteroceptive feedback, needing only to remember 'at this point in space the movement must stop'. In reproducing a distance, in contrast, memories of exteroceptive feedback are not available; what is necessary is a memory of the course of the movement itself.

Some earlier data, however, complicate this picture. A study by U. Frith and Hermelin (1969) produced data that, on the surface, appear to say the *opposite* thing about the motor skills of children with autism. In this experiment children with autism (mental ages between 4 and 6 years) were in fact *less* dependent on visual feedback than were the other two groups. Frith and Hermelin had given children with autism, mentally handicapped children, and normally developing children (all matched for verbal mental age) a tracking task with or without visual feedback. This task required tracking a metal stylus as quickly as possible inside grooves cut in perspex. Broadly speaking, the children with autism made less efficient use of visual information and more efficient use of purely motor (kinaesthetic) feedback than did the controls. But, if what was argued in the previous paragraph is correct, should we not expect children with autism to be more, not less, dependent upon visual feedback than controls? No, because the tasks used in the two experiments were of quite different types. In the tracking task the children received immediate exteroceptive feedback from each micro-movement of the stylus, and so there was no need to prepare and monitor movements of a given distance, velocity, or kind.

This does not immediately explain why the children with autism were less dependent upon visual feedback in the Frith and Hermelin task. Consider, however, the developmental consequences of being unable to generate codes for relating movements to their visible outcomes. Children will be faced with two incommensurable sources of information—visual and motor—and the consequence is likely to be that they will become overreliant upon non-visual (especially kinaesthetic and exteroceptive) information about their movements. Therefore, the data from these two studies, far from contradicting, complement each other.

What these two studies tell us about action-monitoring is, however, somewhat indirect, in the sense that neither had been designed as studies of action-monitoring; and so the theoretical spin of the previous paragraph is not that of their authors. In the next study I report, the situation is different. Chris Jarrold and I (Russell and Jarrold, in press, a) borrowed a paradigm from the literature of schizophrenia which twice had been used to investigate action-monitoring impairments in that disorder (Frith and Done 1989; Malenka *et al.* 1981) and which we used to look at action-monitoring in autism.

This is the rationale behind the paradigm. We know that normal adults are capable of correcting errors so quickly that they cannot be doing so by relying on exteroceptive feedback (Rabbitt 1966); they must be utilizing a central copy (C. Frith's phrase) of the launched action before receiving exteroceptive feedback. In the experiments performed by Malenka *et al.* and by Frith and Done the subjects had to learn a response-outcome contingency which was sufficiently difficult to provoke errors but easy enough for these errors to be correctable before their outcome was experienced. The Frith and Done task—on which my study with Jarrold was based—was a computer game in which a man was seen to fire shots at a bird whose position could change from the left to the right side of the screen. The missile travelled slowly, and if the subject saw that it was travelling in the wrong direction he or she could change its direction by pressing the key which should have been pressed originally. I will refer to corrections in this case (in which the trajectory was visible) as the 'external' corrections. In contrast to this, there was a condition in which the subjects were unable to see the direction in which the missile was headed until it hit or missed the target. Again this invisible missile travelled slowly, so corrections were possible. But now, of course, successful correction depends upon the subject knowing which of the two keys had been pressed and the result of pressing them. I will call these 'internal' corrections.

Both of these studies showed that subjects with schizophrenia were specifically impaired in their ability to make internal corrections, that is to say, corrections that utilized a central copy of the action. Malenka *et al.* reported similar problems in (hallucinating) subjects with alcoholism, and Frith and Done showed that their subjects with schizophrenia were significantly more likely to fail to correct internal errors if they reported delusions of alien control and auditory hallucinations. According to C. D. Frith (1992) impairments in action-monitoring are directly responsible for these symptoms. This is because a delusion of alien control will result when there is little, if any, experienced responsibility for one's own actions, while an auditory hallucination will result when the patient does not feel responsible for the verbalized thoughts that she 'hears' herself thinking.

In our task, children with autism, together with two control groups of normally developing children and children with moderate learning difficulties, played a computer game in which they saw, in the centre of the screen, two cartoon birds holding tennis racquets. One bird was on a blue horizontal strip and the other on a yellow horizontal strip, with one strip (and therefore one bird) being above the other. Shortly after this a bag appeared, dangling from either the left- or the right-hand side of either the blue or the yellow strip. The players knew that one key on the computer controlled the bird on the blue strip and the other controlled the bird on the yellow strip. Accordingly, if the bag appeared on the yellow strip, the appropriate key had to be pressed in order to make the bird serve the tennis ball towards the bag. There was, however, the possibility of response competition in the task, sufficient to provoke errors. This occurred whenever the bag appeared on the opposite side of the screen to the correct key.

The children were encouraged to press the key as quickly as they could as soon as the bag appeared on the screen, and they received a warning signal (the computer said 'Too slow!') if the reaction time was too long. In one condition, the children could see the ball's trajectory and in the other condition a screen obliterated the bird and the ball's trajectory, leaving only the bag visible. In both cases, errors could be corrected between the service of the ball and its leaving the screen, but in the latter case, of course, these corrections had to be internal: they depended upon the children maintaining a record of which key had been pressed.

The performance of the children with autism was clearly different to that of the mentally handicapped and of the normally developing children; but their pattern of responding did not parallel that of schizophrenic subjects. Where Malenka et al. and Frith and Done found that schizophrenics corrected a similar proportion of external errors to the controls but failed to correct more internal errors, we found that children with autism corrected fewer errors of both kinds. They made a very similar number of errors to the control groups but failed to correct around three times as many errors of both kinds.

I will explain these data in the same terms in which I explained the data from Hermelin and O'Connor's and Frith and Hermelin's studies: the children with autism were failing to construct visual schemata for their actions. In the first place, failures to correct internal errors were the result of the fact that an absent or weak visual schema of the action (e.g. pressing the right-hand key) would result in a weak memory trace of that action. The child would therefore have to be reliant on a proprioceptive representation of what had been done. The failure to correct external errors, on the other hand, can be explained in terms of the fact that children with autism are less likely than other children to utilize visual feedback from their actions in order to correct themselves. In other words, the existence of a difficulty with internal correction is consistent with the Hermelin and O'Connor data, while the difficulty with external correction is consistent with the Frith and Hermelin data. It must be borne in mind, however, that these facts should be regarded as two sides of the same coin. As I argued earlier, those who fail to construct adequate visual codes for relating launched actions to their visible outcomes may come to rely on motor feedback rather than on visual feedback in order to avoid confusion between two sources of incommensurable information.

Finally, the kind of parallel that this work suggests between autism and congenital blindness allows us to explain why congenitally blind children can present with autism-like symptoms (e.g. Chess 1971; Fraiberg 1977; Rogers and Newhart-Larson 1989). Hobson (1993) explains this association by arguing that congenital blindness deprives the child of the intersubjective experiences necessary for the adequate development of self. In contrast, the present position is that congenitally blind children lack adequate experience of how their agency affects their perceptual experiences, and that self-hood cannot develop adequately without this experience.

Higher-level action-monitoring and 'self-monitoring' in memory

I now turn to evidence for monitoring impairments at a higher cognitive level—at the level of judging what one had intended and done. Phillips *et al.* (in press) modified a task which had originally been designed by Shultz and Wells (1985) to study normally developing children's understanding of what it means to intend an outcome. Children with autism and mentally handicapped children with mental ages of around 6 years played a game in which they fired a gun at some coloured tin cans lined up on a wall. Some of the cans contained a prize and some of them did not, and the children were ignorant of which ones contained prizes. Before each trial they had to choose the colour of the can at which they would aim. The game was rigged in such a way that sometimes the children would succeed in hitting the one being aimed at and sometime they would not; while the can which fell either contained or did not contain a prize. Accordingly, both hitting the aimed-for can and hitting the wrong can could result in prizes. After a can had fallen and its contents revealed the children were asked: 'Which colour did you mean to shoot? The [say] red one or the [say] yellow one?'. Obviously, they had to resist saying that they had aimed to shoot the can which actually fell if that was not the one they had aimed at. There was little difference between the performance of children with autism and controls in the case where the intended can was hit: both performed well. However, in the case where a can other than the intended one was hit (and a prize was either won or not won) the children with autism were much less successful. Indeed, when a prize was fortuitously won, they were no better than chance at saying whether or not they had intended to hit that can.

Phillips *et al.* favour an explanation of this result in terms of a theory-of-mind impairment, suggesting that children with autism answer as they do because they lack a proper understanding of the nature of intention.

However, the data can be explained, at least as well, in terms of a monitoring impairment. On this view they failed adequately to monitor their intention and thereby failed to encode it for later recall. I would further speculate that children with autism with mental ages of above 6 years—the age of the subjects—generally do understand what it means to intend to shoot at a target.

The evidence Jarrold and I collected for higher-level monitoring problems in autism is of two kinds—memory for one's own actions, and memory for cognitive effort. These are aspects of what is more likely to be called *self-monitoring* in the current literature, meaning the ability to make 'internal records of cognitive operations' (Johnson and Raye 1981). In the first study (Russell and Jarrold, in press, b), children with autism, mentally handicapped children, and normally developing children received 'the alternating placement task'. In this task, the child and an experimenter take it in turns to distribute picture cards from four corners of a board. Each picture card is placed on top of its equivalent on the board and each player has a doll on whose behalf he or she plays the cards—making up the four locations. The child has then to return the cards to their original 'owners'. Children with autism are very clearly impaired on this task relative to both of the control groups. Impairment is what one would expect if they are failing to code a placement *as* their own; for if subjects fail to do this adequately then they will be more likely to conflate a placement made by themselves with ones made by another person.

We tested this conjecture in a second study that had the following rationale. If children with autism are conflating placements that they had made themselves with those made by others because they fail to monitor their actions as their own, then they should *not* be impaired when self–other discriminations do not have to be made. Accordingly, we gave the children three placement-memory tasks of the following kind: (1) placing all the cards themselves;[5] (2) watching the experimenter place all the cards himself; (3) watching the cards moving on to a central board on a computer screen. In support of the monitoring-impairment view, the children were not significantly worse on these tasks than were the control subjects. The data do, however, have to be qualified. Although the children with autism were clearly unimpaired in case (1)—where they moved the cards themselves—they were not far short of being significantly worse than the mentally handicapped children in the two cases where they watched the cards being moved (by an agent or on a screen); the children with autism were worse than the mentally handicapped controls at $p < 0.1$.. The absolute group differences in these two cases were small. This raises the possibility that a task involving placement and replacement may be making cognitive demands on children with autism that confound whatever difficulties they might have with self-monitoring. There are a number of possibilities, and perhaps the most plausible is that children with autism have difficulty attending to external events of this kind.

Consequently, we would need to run more conventional 'source-monitoring' tasks (e.g. Conway and Dewhurst 1995) in which such confounding factors loom less large. In these tasks, either the experimenter or the child performs an action on an object, after which the following kinds of memory question can be given: (1) Which action was performed on object X? (2) Which object received action Y? (3) *Who* performed action X on object Y? Our prediction would be that only in the third case would children with autism be impaired.

I now turn to the second kind of self-monitoring task which we performed—memory for cognitive effort. One would expect that recall by those subjects who are able to lay down adequate records of their cognitive operations should be affected by the amount of cognitive work that went into laying down the trace (see footnote 4). For example, when the subject has to generate the name of an item after being told, for example, that it is the name of an animal that moos and provides us with milk, then 'cow' is more memorable than if the experimenter had simply presented the word or a picture. This is what is found. It is called the 'generation effect' (Slamenka and Graf 1978). Moreover, the generation of low-frequency words results in better recall than the generation of high-frequency words, because more cognitive effort is involved in the former case (Johnson *et al.* 1981).

Normal adults are better at source (self-versus-other) attribution tasks in which they have to say whether it was they or the experimenter who generated a word, where the words to be generated are low-frequency rather than high-frequency (Johnson *et al.* 1981). Hallucinating subjects with schizophrenia, by contrast, while being no less accurate on overall self–other source attributions, are more likely than normal controls to ascribe their self-generated, low-frequency words to the experimenter (Bentall *et al.* 1991).

The question which Jarrold and I asked (Russell and Jarrold 1997) was the simpler one of whether children with autism show the generation effect. In the task Jarrold devised, children discovered the contents of a series of boxes presented on a computer screen. In the two most relevant conditions, they were either shown the contents or they had to generate the names themselves. For example, the experimenter would, in the first case, click open the box to show a cat, and in the second he would say: 'In the blue box is an animal that goes miaow', after which the child generated a name and the experimenter opened the box. At test, children with autism, together with the usual control groups, were shown all the items in the boxes at the bottom of the screen and then had to say from which boxes they had emerged. There were no group differences here; and this is what we would expect from our data on placement, in which placement by self and other did not alternate. What is relevant to the present question is that while the normally developing children and the mentally handicapped children were better at recalling the boxes whose contents they had generated the children with autism were not. It would be misleading, however, to conclude flatly that the two control groups showed the generation effect and the children with autism did not, because while there was a statistically significant group difference the absolute differences were small. Moreover, there were no differential effects of generation (i.e. all three groups were better in that condition) when the task was one of freely recalling the contents rather than of matching contents to boxes. (Perhaps this is because free recall is inherently effortful, unlike the somewhat paired-associate task of matching contents to boxes, and so this fact can swap our generation effects.)

These two memory experiments provide suggestive, though not compelling, evidence for the following claim. Children with autism find it especially difficult to make memorial discriminations between their own and others' actions, and their recall is less likely to benefit from expending extra cognitive effort at the time of encoding. These facts are consistent with the presence of self-monitoring difficulties.

Imitation

Let us consider the role of action-monitoring in imitation. If we are to imitate the actions of another person it is necessary to monitor our own actions. If the subject is to copy a modelled movement then she must not only attend and retain the modelled action but must regulate her own productions in relation to an internal model of what is observed, matching product with model (Bandura 1977). It is necessary not merely to have a visual schema of the model's action but also to be able to match, on-line, the movements of one's own body against this schema. In order to do this, the agent must be in a position to match a representation of what is being intended (I am moving my arm just like *this* . . .) against what is being, or has been, observed. It is difficult to see how this could be achieved unless the agent has a visual schema of his or her intended movements. It is not *impossible* to imagine how it could be done without such schemata because the agent might achieve the match by keeping an eye on his or her own arm movements and matching these against the model's. But this 'imitation through self observation' is doomed to be a hit-and-miss affair in so far as the agent will have only weak knowledge—lacking visual schemata—of what the visible results of intentionally moving in a certain way will be before performing the action. In short, imitation requires the agent to know *without observation* what he or she is doing (see feature C above), and this would seem to require knowledge of what a limb movement will look like *before it is performed*.

Compare this with the situation where our task is not to imitate another's movement but rather to determine whether our spontaneous actions are being imitated, or to determine which of two experimenters is imitating us. In this case, the production of visual schemata of our actions is *not* necessary for success. Why not? All we need to do here is to make a movement, record the fact that it has been made through self-observation (note: self-*observation*, not self-monitoring), and then note the parallel between what we have observed ourselves doing and what we see another body doing. The point is that it is not necessary to match a visual schema of an intention with what is observed; indeed our movements could just as well be unintentional—a nervous tick or a sneeze.

I am not denying that a kind of bodily awareness comes into play when a subject recognizes that he or she is being imitated. I am, though, denying that the kind of bodily awareness described on p. 266 has to be involved. For example, the ability of the 16-month-old children studied by Meltzoff (1990) to discriminate an imitating from a non-imitating experimenter would seem to mark a significant advance in bodily awareness. After all, the successful toddlers can be said to have been taking a 'third-person' view of themselves sufficient to draw a parallel between what they did and what another had just done. My point is, rather, that matching immediate knowledge of one's actions is not necessary for success in the way in which it is when the child is imitating a model. The matching can be done *post hoc*: my body has done X, one experimenter is doing X and another is doing Y.[6] By contrast, when the child is the imitator rather than the imitated we have the following: the model has done X, I must intentionally do X. The intentional doing of X is unlikely to be achieved by self-observation for reasons given above.

I now turn to the evidence. There is an imitation deficit in autism which takes the form of failure to imitate a model's actions (Smith and Bryson 1994, for a review; and see Chapter 5) rather than of insensitivity to being imitated (Dawson and Adams 1984; Tiegerman and Primavera 1984). This is as predicted. Also, recall that it is not impossible for an individual with inadequate action-monitoring to imitate a model, because the imitation can be achieved visually—by matching how one's limbs look in relation to the limbs of others. At least one study suggests that this is indeed how certain children with autism imitate. Ohta (1987) reports that a large proportion of her sample of autistic children achieved so-called 'partial imitation' of manual gestures, meaning that when subjects were facing the model they produced gestures which *reversed* the orientation of their own hands so as to make them look the same as the hands of the models. Thus, if the model's palms moved towards the subject the subject moved her own open palms towards herself—a case of visual matching.

The present account makes a very clear prediction: subjects with autism should have profound difficulties imitating gestures when they cannot see their limbs. This claim can be sharpened a little by considering some data that appear to repudiate it. Charman and Baron-Cohen (1994) report that children with autism (mean verbal mental age around 4 years) were unimpaired relative to matched mentally handicapped children when they had to imitate the two following 'unfamiliar invisible gestures'—pulling down on both earlobes, and clapping both hands on to the back of the head. What is notable about these actions, however, is that they are very simple movements directed straight towards parts of the body, and so, for this reason, the modelling of them is tantamount to the instruction 'do this to that'. All a subject has to do to succeed is to follow that non-verbal instruction. There is all the difference in the world between imitating movements of this kind and imitating the kinds of actions that may be said to require the exercise of a body schema, in the sense of 'a superordinate representation of the interface between sensory and motor processes that both internally and externally specify a posture' (Bairstow 1986; see Campbell 1995, for discussion). If what I have said about efference copying and about bodily awareness—p. 266—is correct and if the proposals about autism are correct we should expect the body schema of persons with autism to be poorly specified. Of course one cannot say *a priori* which kinds of imitation require an adequate body schema and which do not—a simple dance, or an unusual pose, or waving then chopping movements of the arms perhaps—but one can stipulate that the movements must be novel and not directed towards objects or towards body parts. Supportive data are reported in Chapter 5: children with autism were found to be specifically impaired when imitating meaningless rather than meaningful actions.

It is clear, then, that this account aligns itself with those (e.g. Dawson and Lewy 1989) who regard the imitation difficulties in autism as rooted in dysfunctional information-processing rather than rooted in a mentalizing or social deficit. At the same time it diverges from the view, expressed by Barresi and Moore (1996) and by Meltzoff and Gopnik (1993), that deficiencies in imitation contribute to the failure to develop an adequate 'theory of mind'. The present position is that the imitation deficit and the mentalizing deficit are both rooted in inadequate action-monitoring.

Bridge

My assumption throughout has been that mentalizing difficulties are rooted in impoverished self-awareness. In the first section I argued that because action-monitoring and instigation are the elements of executive functioning the impairment of which is most likely to impact upon the development of self-awareness, it is these elements that are likely to be impaired in autism. Up to this point I have been reviewing the evidence for action-monitoring impairments in autism.

In order to place this evidence in context, I shall now consider why children with autism fail formal tests of executive functioning and of 'theory of mind'. In the first place, it is not sufficient to say 'it's because they are poor at monitoring and instigation' for, given the complexity of the tasks, there are many ways that such difficulties might be manifested. In the second place, it is not sufficient to say 'it's because their understanding of mental life is weak' for, given the structure of many mentalizing tasks, it looks likely that these tests measure executive functioning as well as the understanding of mental states.

The dual requirements to inhibit and to hold in mind

Pennington *et al.* (Chapter 5) and others argue that an executive task should contain both prepotency and the need to maintain a rule in working memory. (At the start of the second section I suggested that action-monitoring and instigation might underlie such demands.) There are, however, a number of reasons why subjects should be especially challenged by this pair of demands. In the first subsection I suggest that it is the combination *per se* that is important *in the case of autism*; and in the second I describe how this combination affects mentalizing ability with reference to the false-belief task.

Prepotency plus working memoryand verbal coding

Do children with autism have distinct problems with the inhibition of prepotent responses and with working memory, or do they only experience difficulties when the two are combined? Turning first to inhibition, the answer which Ozonoff (Chapter 6) gives is that they do have not problems with inhibition *per se*. It is subjects with ADHD and with OCD who tend to be impaired on tasks such as Go–NoGo, Stopping, and Negative Priming— tasks that all require inhibition and encourage impulsive responses. Children with autism are generally found to be unimpaired on these tasks. There are, however, impaired on the third phase of the Go–NoGo task which requires mental flexibility, as Ozonoff describes.

Second, do children with autism have specific difficulties with working memory? The data are contradictory. Working memory was defined earlier as: 'the ability to hold in mind past states of the environment and past actions while currently performing an action'. A good example of a working memory task is the so-called Case-counting task (Case *et al.* 1982), in which subjects have to count the dots on a series of cards and then recall the totals. That is to say, they have to perform the mental operation of counting while maintaining a memory of previous totals. Bennetto *et al.* (1996) have recently reported that adolescents and young adults with autism are impaired on this task while being unimpaired on a number of other kinds of memory task. Our data were, however, quite different (Russell *et al.* 1996). In addition to the Case-counting task we gave our subjects two further working memory tasks. One was a task where they had to point to the odd man out from three vertically arranged stimuli whilst holding in mind the different locations from trial to trial (based on a task previously used by Hitch and McAuley 1991). The second was an adding-up version of Daneman and Carpenter's (1980) sentence-completion task in which the children had to do very simple sums such as '2 + 1 = ?' while holding in mind the previous totals. The performance of our children with autism was certainly not inferior to that of mentally handicapped controls.

The reason our data conflict with those of Bennetto et al. may lie in the nature of the two subject populations. Bennetto et al.'s autistic subjects were adolescents and adults with intelligence quotients within the normal range, whereas ours were children (plus some adolescents) with autism who were also mentally handicapped. Accordingly, where we were comparing the performance of mentally handicapped children with autism against that of mentally handicapped children without autism, Bennetto et al. were comparing the performance of their autistic subjects against that of subjects who were not mentally handicapped. What is the significance of this fact? In our study, the normally developing children had performed better than the two clinical groups, so it is possible that working memory difficulties are a marker for many kinds of mental disorder—even when the IQ is around normal. This would explain the Bennetto et al. result.

Whether or not this point is correct, it can be said that while the Bennetto et al. study was more sensitive than ours, in the sense that their subjects were relatively 'pure' cases of autism, our study was more conservative.[7] It was conservative in the sense that if a form of cognitive impairment is funda- mental to autism one would expect it to appear in the presence of mental handicap. It should be manifest in children with both autism and mental handicap relative to children with mental handicap alone. Recall that in research on theory of mind impairments the subjects with autism are generally mentally handicapped (e.g. Baron-Cohen et al. 1985). Moreover, the large majority of persons with autism are mentally handicapped. One may reasonably conclude, therefore, that working memory impairments, relative to controls, only distinguish subjects with autism who are of normal intelligence. Some recent data collected by Michelle Turner (unpublished) reinforces this point. Using the spatial working memory test from the computerized CANTAB battery (see Chapter 2) she found that low-func- tioning subjects were not impaired relative to controls but that high- functioning subjects were impaired.

I conclude, therefore, that working memory impairments are unlikely to be fundamental to autism. When coupled with the fact that subjects with autism do not seem to find inhibition difficult when there are no accompanying working memory requirements, it can be concluded that it is the combination of working memory and the inhibition of prepotent responses that challenges them. This is not a contentious point, but it is certainly an important one. I now address the question of what might underlie this difficulty; and here I will be saying something contentious.

A subject might understand and be capable of articulating a rule, but this rule's representation in working memory may be too weak to guide behaviour under conditions in which the task is pulling the subject away from following it. This 'pulling away' may be caused by salient objects, learned responses, or salient knowledge—any of which can bias the subject towards error. Furthermore, it may be the case that what, in the normal case, enables the rule to override prepotency is the fact that the subject encodes it in natural language. For example, in the Hughes and Russell (1993, experiment 2) 'box' task, subjects had to hold in mind the fact that they must throw a switch on the side of the box before reaching in to retrieve a marble. If they do not do this but instead reach directly the marble disappears. (This is because the direct reach breaks a light-beam which causes the marble to drop down out of sight; the switch turns off the beam and makes retrieving the marble possible.) An obvious way to 'strengthen' the representation of rule is by saying to oneself during the trials something like 'switch then reach'. Perhaps the reason why this task does not challenge older preschool children but does challenge younger ones is that the older children are becoming able to use inner speech for self instruction. Needless to say, this idea is nothing if not unoriginal (Luria and Yudovich 1971).

This leaves, of course, the awkward question of how one should regard executive tasks on which preverbal children and animals *succeed*. The best-known of these is Piaget's A-not-B task, failed by infants up to the age of about 12 months. In this, subjects retrieve an object a few times from behind occluder A, after which they see it transferred from behind A to behind B and are then (perhaps after a short delay) allowed to search again. Younger infants continue to search at A. Diamond (1991) argues that this is an executive task in the sense that it both encourages a prepotent response (search at A) and requires that a representation be maintained in working memory before the action is taken (the movement of the object from A to B). (The likelihood of error increases with the delay between hiding at B and allowing search.)

Piaget's invisible displacement tasks also count as executive tasks that can be performed by infants whose verbal skills are far too modest to afford inner speech. (It has been suggested that apes too can perform them: Natale and Antinucci 1989; Parker 1991, Table 2 therein.) Invisible displacement tasks take a number of forms. For example, if containers A and B are transposed without the object being revealed infants below about 18 months will search behind B, which now occupies the same location that A had previously occupied. In fact, difficulties with invisible displacement continue *well into the third year of life*, as Hood (1995) has shown using the 'tubes task'. In the simplest condition of this task a ball is dropped into an opaque tube that curves diagonally down into a catch-tray. Directly beneath the mouth of this tube is another catch-tray that is not, of course, connected to the tube. Normally developing children below about 3 years will, when the ball is dropped into the mouth of the tube, search in the catch-tray that is not connected to the tube but which is directly beneath the tube's mouth. (This is not simply an impulsive error because the children do not tend to correct themselves and visit the appropriate catch-tray immediately after their initial search.) On this task there is clearly a prepotent response: searching, on the principle that things fall vertically, immediately beneath the place where the ball disappeared. And this is in competition with task demands that must be held in mind—following the actual course of the tube into which the ball was put.

These tasks are certainly executive in so far as they tap the control of action rather than the possession of knowledge, but there is a very clear difference between what the Hughes and Russell box task requires of subjects and what tasks like A-not-B and 'tubes' require of them. It boils down to this. In tasks like the box task the rule that is in competition with a prepotent response is an *arbitrary* rule — all true rules are. That is to say, there is no natural, causal link between the response (switching) and the successful action (retrieving): there is no reason *why* the switch should be thrown. (It would be quite different, of course, if the subject knew the inner workings of the box.) Indeed, if we recall the structure of the most frequently used executive tasks such as WCST and the TOH and the TOL we also see that the rules which have to be held in mind are arbitrary. For example: 'sort by the new dimension and ignore the old' (WCST); 'when moving a ball to a stick first move any balls already there to another stick if it should be placed below them' (TOL). These are rules without rationales.

Of course, in tasks like A-not-B and tubes the situation is quite different. There is every reason why a subject should search where something was last hidden (A-not-B) and search at the outlet of a tube into which a ball was put rather than vertically beneath its mouth. *The rules are exhausted by their rationales: they are not really rules at all.* For this reason it cannot be said that these Piaget-inspired tasks demand the maintenance of rules in working memory. In the tubes task, moreover, the term 'working memory' has rather little foothold if we take the definition I used earlier: 'the ability to hold in mind past states of the environment and past actions while currently performing an action'.

Let us now cast the net a little wider and look at two other tasks which attract the label 'executive' but which do not include arbitrary rules—

detour-reaching and delayed-response tasks. In the first place, Lockman (1984) and Diamond (1991) have shown that infants below about 15 months of age have difficulty reaching round a barrier to obtain an object when the barrier is transparent but not when it is opaque. Viewed executively, they are failing to inhibit the habitual strategy of reaching along the line of sight. In the second task (delayed response) the subject, who is likely to be a monkey or a human infant, sees a desired object hidden behind a cover either on its left or right on each trial, after which a screen is dropped. He or she must then hold in mind the location of the object before making a response. The first requires the inhibition of a prepotent response without working memory and the latter requires working memory without the inhibition of prepotent response. In the latter of the two, moreover, one cannot even assume that they are mediated by the prefrontal cortex because the hippocampus is implicated in the performance of delayed-response tasks with longer delays (Squire 1992).

The structural difference is, then, very clear between the kind of executive tasks which are frequently given to patients with frontal lesions, people with mental disorders, and verbal children (e.g. WCST, TOL) and the kind of executive test given to preverbal children and animals. The former tasks involve the holding in mind of arbitrary rules and the latter do not; in the latter it is debatable whether working memory capacities are being tapped at all (tubes), or it is clear that they are not (detour-reaching), or that working memory is being tapped but not inhibition of a prepotent response (delayed response). The fundamental divergence between them, however, is that over the matter of arbitrary rules.

Before returning to the possible role of inner speech in executive tasks that include arbitrary rules I will make the following generalization: The only kind of executive tasks on which persons with autism are impaired is the kind with arbitrary rules. First, young children with autism (mean age 43 months) have been found to be unimpaired on the A-not-B task, on the delayed response task, and on the Spatial Reversal task (Wehner and Rogers 1994; see also Chapter 5). Moreover, Chris Jarrold and I (unpublished data) found that children with autism who had been mental-age-matched to Hood's sample of normally developing preschoolers were not impaired on the tubes task. Indeed, the children with autism tended to outperform normal children on the more difficult (multi-tube) problems.

This implies that there are likely to be clinical populations of children that are impaired on executive tasks *without* arbitrary rules. This is indeed the case, and Diamond's (1996) research on children with phenylketonuria (PKU) provides the clearest example. The development of severe mental retardation is avoided in these children by altering their diet, but doing so does not prevent cognitive impairments brought about by a lack of dopaminergic innervation to the prefrontal cortex. What is relevant to our immediate purpose is that PKU children were found to be impaired on the A-not-B with visible displacement and on A-not-B with invisible displacement. (They were impaired on other tasks too, and I will mention one of them later.) The difficulty that PKU children have with invisible displacement is reinforced by Hood's (personal communication) recent finding that they are impaired on the tubes task. On all three of these tasks, recall that children with autism are not impaired.

What, then, does all this imply about the role of verbal thought in executive tasks? Natural language would appear to be the ideal medium in which to represent arbitrary rules. If we want to remember, say, to sort by shape and ignore colour or remember to throw a switch before reaching then one is at a great advantage if this rule can be encoded in working memory in a verbal form. Could such a rule not be encoded by a non-symbolic medium such a visual imagery? Perhaps, but one can be sceptical about how a medium without symbolic content can, as it were, tell us what to do. (See Carruthers (1996a) on why inner language may be necessary to 'thinking in pictures'.)

My claim is, then, that the reason people with autism are challenged by formal tests of executive functioning is that they are unable to use inner speech to regulate their behaviour. I am assuming that, similar to normally developing children performing WCST-like tests (Zalazo et al. 1996), they can *represent* the rule verbally but that their knowledge of that rule does not guide their behaviour. They cannot use language in the service of self-monitoring. Perhaps it is no accident that Luria (Luria and Homskaya 1964) was not only among the first to propose the prefrontal cortex as a centre of executive control but was also a subscriber to the view that the development of self-regulation is, after a certain age, a verbal process.

The present hypothesis is consistent with the results of a study by Hurlburt et al. (1994). In this study, three high-functioning persons with autism (two of them passing second-order false belief) and control subjects were asked to wear a small device during the day which emitted a beep at random intervals. The subjects had to 'freeze the contents of their awareness' and take notes as soon as the beep sounded. As one would expect, the normal subjects reported a good deal of inner speech. By contrast, two of the persons with autism reported visual images but no inner verbalizations, while the third reported no subjective experiences at all.

Before ending this section, I need to confront two difficulties with the present thesis about inner speech. The first is about its internal coherence and the second about recalcitrant data. Taking the conceptual difficulty first, it is obviously necessary to relate my claims about inner speech to this chapter's main motif—pretheoretical self-awareness and its failure to develop in autism. A proper defence would require another essay (one exists: Russell, in press), but here is the synecdoche. To self-instruct one must possess a capacity for first-person thought, and the referent of this thought cannot itself be a verbal construction. 'I' is in the paradoxical position of being both the speaker and the listener in self-talk; and the addressor–addressee cannot itself be something linguistic. Inadequate development of the cognitive substrate for first-person thought ensures that the capacity for self-talk will not develop adequately. In slogan form: the development of verbal self-regulation depends upon the preverbal development of action-monitoring and instigation.

The objection could still be raised, however, that if children with autism have action-monitoring and instigation difficulties then they should be impaired on any task that requires goal-directed action. They *should*, on this view, be impaired on Piagetian object retrieval tasks. This is a major challenge to my thesis, and in answering it some retrenchment is necessary. The ability to retrieve objects that have gone out of sight is, as Piaget claimed, an index of self-world dualism—the ability to cognize objects as independent of one's experience of them. But I earlier assumed that self-world dualism is dependent upon adequate action-monitoring and instigation. (This was not made explicit, but it is very explicit in Russell (1996).) My thesis must therefore be that in the first 12 or even 18 months of life the development of agency often proceeds normally in children who will later be diagnosed as having autism. In fact,this fits quite well with the evidence, because the earliest that autism is normally detected is shortly after the first birthday, when stereotypies appear and the child starts to attend away from people and towards objects; while 18 months is quite a common age of onset (Eriksson and de Chateau 1992; Osterling and Dawson 1994). In terms of the present thesis, this implies that fundamental conceptions of the physical world are normally secure in autism and that the deviant development of self-aware-ness takes place *against a background of this.*

The point bears upon action-monitoring in the following way. The development of object permanence depends upon the development of adequate action-monitoring in the first year or so of life; for the developing infant must locate the causes of its actions in its own body. This does not mean, however, that older children who 'have' object permanence need to produce visual schemata of their actions whenever they have to retrieve an object. As I argued when discussing the Hermelin and O'Connor (1975) study, some motor tasks tap this ability and some do not. The thesis is therefore constrained to say that the action-monitoring problems experienced by children with autism must develop in the second year of life and that these difficulties must accordingly be *at a relatively high level.* For example, they affect imitation of models but not the ability to keep track of invisible displacements.

I now come to the recalcitrant data. The present thesis would be undermined if it were found that in some situations children with autism can indeed act in accordance with arbitrary rules while inhibiting a prepotent response. As before, some relevant studies have been performed both by the Denver group and by the Cambridge group. As Pennington *et al.* report in their chapter, Wehner and Rogers (1994) found that a group of children with autism (mean age of 43 months) were unimpaired on the Spatial Reversal task in which the side of hiding a reward is changed from one of two locations to the other after every four trials. This rule would seem to be 'arbitrary' on the above definition.

In the second place, subjects with autism are *un*impaired on the Stroop task (Bryson 1983; Eskes *et al.* 1990) where they have to say the colour of the ink in which a word is printed instead of reading the word (e.g. the word 'red' is printed in green ink—say 'green'). In order to check that these negative results were not due to the fact that the Stroop test probes processes specific to reading rather than broadly executive processes, Jarrold and I (unpublished data) gave the following task to children with autism and to mentally handicapped controls. It was an adaptation of a task devised by Gerstadt *et al.* (1994) called the 'day–night' task. In this, subjects have to say the word 'day' when presented with a card showing a night-sky and the word 'night' when shown a picture of a sunny sky, while in the control condition they have to attach these words to arbitrary designs. We compared the performance of children with autism within the verbal mental age range of 5 and 8 years against that of normally developing and mentally handicapped children. The children with autism were neither less accurate than the control groups nor slower than them.[8]

I doubt, however, that this is this a case of 'Ugly Facts Destroy Beautiful Hypothesis'. In the first place, the Spatial Reversal task does not so much involve prepotency plus a working memory rule as simple response alternation—learning to reverse a response after four hits. Moreover, as Pennington *et al.* report (Chapter 5), an earlier study by McEvoy *et al.* (1993) showed that *older* autistic children were indeed impaired on this task relative to controls. This can be explained by the fact that the controls improved on this task with age by utilizing inner speech, whereas the children with autism were not in a position to do so. (I admit that this does not explain why the older group produced more perseverations than the younger group; but, as Pennington *et al.* point out, this comparison is not only cross-sectional but also cross-study.)

Note also, that the present hypothesis (autistic children only impaired on executive tasks with arbitrary rules) explains the lack of group differences in Pennington *et al.*'s preliminary report of their study involving eight executive tasks which were 'self-explanatory and intrinsically motivating' . This phrase means that the tasks did not contain arbitrary rules. In addition, note that the autistic children in the study had joint attention impairments; these are a common feature of the disorder. On the present view, failing to follow the direction of another's gaze might be explained in terms of an inadequate bodily schema which is, in part, a consequence of inadequate action-monitoring. Joint attention deficits will probably not yield to the same account as that offered above for imitation deficits. But the fact remains that children with difficulties in regulating their own action and attention are clearly going to be impaired in regulating these in relation to others.

Second, why are children unimpaired on the day–night task and on the Stroop task? To my knowledge, these are the only executive tasks in which the output is verbal: they involve the control of verbalization not of action. For this reason, it is unlikely that when unimpaired subjects succeed on them they do so by holding a rule in verbal working memory, given that interference is likely to occur between representations within the same modality—output and rehearsal. On the Baddeley and Hitch model of working memory the subject would be speaking at the same time as keeping the rule refreshed in the articulatory loop. (This is the line of reasoning used by Baddeley (1986, p. 203) to explain why 'fluent internal rehearsal' is not possible when children have to name stimuli.) A verbal rule is, in short, little help; and so non-autistic subjects' performance becomes similar to that of subjects with autism.

Needless to say, this account will look like special pleading in the absence of more data. One piece of supporting data which can be cited, however, is that emerging from Diamond's (1996) study of executive functioning in children with PKU, mentioned above: these children were found to be impaired on the day–night task. (Children with PKU, recall, are also impaired on the A-not-B and the 'tubes' tasks—executive tasks without arbitrary rules.) This is consistent with the executive impairment in PKU being unconnected with verbal self-regulation—in contrast to the case with autism. A similar contrast exists between autism and Williams' syndrome. Janette Atkinson (unpublished data, Psychology Dept, University College London) has shown that children with Williams' syndrome—these are children who are highly sociable but who show some everyday 'frontal features' such as perseveration—are impaired on the day–night task. One might suggest that, whatever executive problems these superverbal children have, they are not caused or compounded by impairments of verbal self-regulation. Most important, neither PKU children nor Williams' children have mentalizing problems.

Prepotency plus working memory . . . and the false-belief task

In this section I examine the possibility that the problems which children with autism experience with mentalizing tasks such as those of false belief (Baron-Cohen et al. 1985) may be due, at least in part, to executive factors. I am not saying that their difficulties can thus be explained away. Rather, I am saying that many of the tasks on which their grasp of mental concepts is assessed confound mentalizing demands with executive demands. Individuals with autism clearly have mentalizing difficulties—the aim of this chapter is to explain how these come about—but some of the tasks on which their mentalizing abilities are assessed look awfully like executive tasks. I will present some data and then turn to the question of why children with autism do *not*, broadly speaking, fail Zaitchik's (1990) false-photograph task; for this too would *appear* to be an executive task.

In the false-belief task of Wimmer and Perner (1983) the subject sees a protagonist place an object at place A and then depart. The object is then moved from place A to place B, after which the protagonist returns. Once we have ensured that the subject remembers the original location, that the object has moved, and that the protagonist is ignorant of this fact,[9] we can ask where the protagonist will look for the object or where he thinks it is now located. Children with autism are clearly impaired on this task (see Baron-Cohen *et al.* 1993, for the continuing story). However, because failing this task means saying that the protagonist will search where the object is currently located ('at B') it is easy to regard this as a case of answering in terms of one's own knowledge when one should answer in terms of the protagonist's belief ('at A'). On the assumption that what one currently knows is more cognitively salient than another's false belief, this can, in turn, be regarded as yielding to the prepotent response.

When, however, we push the analogy with executive tasks further and look for working memory requirements and 'arbitrary' rules this situation is less encouraging. Subjects must clearly hold in mind the protagonist's and the object's recent histories at the time of framing an answer to the question, but this narrative has nothing arbitrary about it; and so the analogy with the kind of executive tasks on which children with autism are normally impaired breaks down. Moreover, the response which the children have to make is verbal (see pp. 289–90), and even if they point to a location their answer is to a single question and so the analogy with standard executive tasks is further weakened.

This seems to leave three possible accounts of why children with autism are impaired on the false-belief task:

1. They have a specific difficulty with answering questions about belief.
2. They have a global difficulty with questions about mentality, even if these do not require a grasp of the representational character of mind.
3. Their difficulties are executive, in the loose sense of requiring an answer in terms of the weaker (though correct) of two representations. (I say 'loose sense' because there is no mention here of arbitrary rules in working memory.)

As a way of spelling out and assessing these three views I will report data from the so-called 'conflicting desire' task. The rationale behind this task is the following. In the false-belief task a subject who possesses the concept of belief has two competing representations before the mind when asked the test question—a representation of what he or she believes and a representation of what the protagonist believes. In order to answer correctly the cognitive salience of the former must be suppressed. In other words, a prepotent response must be inhibited. Now if the subject's difficulty is indeed with suppressing the salience of his or her own mental state, rather than with the concept of belief, then he or she should experience the same kind of difficulty with a task in which two conflicting desires (one's own and another's) have to be taken into account. If the level of difficulty is similar in the two cases then we will have reason to believe that the difficulty is not with belief *per se*.

The distinction between a belief and a desire task is important for another reason. As Perner (1991) points out, understanding belief requires some grasp of the metarepresentational character of thought—in thinking 'X', the thinker takes reality to be a certain way, and this affords the possibility of error. Thus, in thinking that the object has moved from A to B the protagonist takes reality to be in a certain way, a mental representation that is only in the running for truth. Desire, however, is quite different. If I desire, say, a cheeseburger, I am not taking reality to be a certain way and neither is my desire only the running for truth: it makes no claim about reality. And while desires can be expressed as propositional attitudes ('I desire that a cheeseburger be in my hand'), unlike beliefs they need not be: we cannot say 'I believe a cheeseburger'. In short, understanding what it means to desire an object requires no metarepresentational grasp (in Perner's sense).

Given this, we can address position (1): that children with autism have specific difficulties understanding the concept of belief. For reasons I have just given, the modularist position is, in fact, that the difficulty experienced by children with autism is with grasping the metarepresentational character of mind—rather than belief *per se*. (In fact, all propositional attitudes fan out from belief.[10]) I will now describe a prediction that is entailed by the modularist view. In the false-belief task there is a conflict between the child's own true belief and the protagonist's false belief about the state of reality. The reason why 3-year-olds and older children with autism fail this task, on the modularist view, is that they cannot understand how belief is operating in this situation. They do not, on this view, fail for the (broadly executive) reason that they cannot organize their answer in relation to their strong representation of their own knowledge and their weak representation of another's belief. The modularist's prediction must be the following. Children with autism should *not* be impaired when they are faced with a conflict between their own and another's desires rather than between their own and other's beliefs. If their difficulty is with grasping the metarepresentational character of some mental states then this task should not challenge them: desires are not metarepresentational. Let us turn first to data from normally developing children.

In collaboration with Chris Moore (Moore *et al.* 1995), we showed that, contrary to the modularists' prediction, a conflicting desires task is just as difficult for normally developing pre-schoolers as the standard false-belief ('conflicting belief') tasks. In one experiment the children played a game against a puppet in which, at test, each player needs a differently coloured card from the pack. When asked which card the puppet opponent needed they were just as likely to give the colour of the card that they themselves needed as they were to ascribe a true belief to the protagonist on the false-belief task. More recently, Rebecca Saltmarsh and I (1997) gave a task of this kind to a group of children with autism and to a control group of mentally handicapped children and compared their performance on it with their performance on the false-belief task. The principal finding was that the performance of the children with autism was similar on both tasks, although they needed a much higher verbal mental age to pass them than the mentally handicapped children, as one would expect.

This result leaves hypotheses (2) and (3) intact. One might indeed combine them and say that, while children with autism are not strongly prey to prepotency *per se* (i.e. when they do not have to hold rules in working memory) and while they may have no difficulty understanding simple desires (Phillips *et al.* 1995) their grasp of mental life is sufficiently weak and their executive difficulties sufficiently pervasive that any task with both mental and executive elements challenges them. If this is so, the consequences for everyday life are easy to imagine. Social perspective-taking necessitates the setting aside of one's own beliefs and desires while keeping track of those of other people. This is what persons with autism clearly fail to do. I have been arguing that this failure does not, in itself, imply that an innate theory of mind module has failed to develop adequately. Indeed, to say that it does so is to go far beyond the data.

The final issue to be dealt in this section concerns the relative ease with which children with autism complete Zaitchik's (1990) false-photograph task. Recall that this task has a similar narrative structure to the false-belief task while requiring the subject to understand photographic, rather than mental, representation. A Polaroid photograph takes a picture of situation A; while the picture is developing the situation is changed to B; and the child is asked what the developed photograph will show. Normal 3-year-olds say that situation B will be represented in the photograph, analogous with their saying that a protagonist will search at place B in the false-belief task. Children with autism are found to be *un*impaired on this task and on similar tasks with two-dimensional representations (Leekham and Perner 1991; Leslie and Thaiss 1992). Now if the case can be made that the false-photograph task is indeed an executive task this would be strong evidence for the modularist position as against the present one.

As Baron-Cohen and Swettenham (in press) argue, the false-photograph task can be regarded as an executive task on the grounds that current reality (situation B) would be expected to be more cognitively salient than an unseen representation of a prior situation (A): reference to B is set up as the prepotent response. (This is, of course, 'executive' only on the more relaxed interpretation of this term that does not demand an arbitrary rule to be held in mind.) This claim is reasonable, but far from compelling. When the test question is asked the subject is faced with two representations: a three-dimensional representation (e.g. of a girl in a yellow dress—a doll) and a two-dimensional representation (e.g. a picture of the doll in a red dress). Is a three-dimensional representation more cognitively salient than a two-dimensional one? Possibly. But is the difference in salience as great as that between my true belief and another's false belief, or between what I want and what another person wants?

I am, of course, trading here on intuitions about relative salience. However, it is surely more than a mere intuition that something being present is more salient than nothing being present. Accordingly, if the false-photograph task were run in the following way it would be difficult to deny that it encouraged a prepotent response. Initially, the camera takes a picture of a *blank* wall, after which a doll is placed on the spot where the camera was pointing. The subject is then asked what is in the photograph that has just been developed.[11] (Indeed one could go the whole hog and include a working memory requirement such as the rule that pictures with dolls in them go in one box and pictures with nothing in them go in a different box.) The prediction would have to be, of course, that these manipulations would have a far greater effect on children with autism than on control subjects, and indeed that once steps are taken to ensure that the false-photograph task presents a clear executive challenge to the children with autism their performance will begin to look similar to that on the false-belief task. I cannot pretend that the issues are clear-cut here. But tasks like the false-belief task are not themselves clear-cut: they contain a mixture of mentalizing and executive demands.

Two points emerge from this discussion. First, it is naïve to think that the dramatic difficulty with the false-belief task (and its cognates) experienced by many people with autism is proof that they '*lack* a theory of mind'. The magnitude of the failure could be due to the fact that this task challenges both their executive and their mentalizing abilities. Second, it is precipitate to argue (e.g. Baron-Cohen and Swettenham, in press) that the general success of children with autism on the false-photograph task is a major blow to the kind of account being presented here.

The conclusion

In the first part of this chapter I argued that the monitoring of actions and the ability to act at will are necessary ingredients to the development of a 'pretheoretical' form of self-awareness. Next, I argued that this form of self-awareness must be in place if the individual is to gain an adequate grasp of mental concepts. I said nothing about how these concepts normally develop, and took no sides on the issue of whether there is something which might be called a 'theory of mind module'. This was because the principal aim of the chapter was to demonstrate that the failure of mental understanding to develop normally is not in itself evidence that there is an innate theory of mind module in human beings. Autism is not an existence proof of such a module. Moreover, an advantage which the present position has over the modularist position is that it explains the co-existence of executive and mentalizing impairments in autism quite naturally.

In the second part of the paper I reviewed the evidence for the existence of action-monitoring impairments in autism. (See Chapters 3 and 4 for discussions of the impairments of action-instigation.) I concluded that the evidence is sparse but promising. In the remainder, I developed the idea that the kinds of executive task on which persons with autism are typically impaired are those that not only encourage a prepotent but wrong response but also require the subject to hold in mind an arbitrary rule. I also suggested that the ability to regulate one's behaviour by inner speech depends upon the adequate development of pretheoretical self-awareness. Finally, I argued that, because tasks like false belief confound executive with mentalizing requirements, it is unwise to regard failure on this task as evidence for lacking a theory of mind; and the same goes for normally developing children of course.

It would be misleading, however, to leave things there without acknowledging the fact—mentioned at the start—that a plausible thesis can be set up that moves in the opposite direction. This is the thesis that the executive dysfunctions in autism can be traced to inadequate theory of mind. Indeed, as I said at the start, attempts at 'horizontal integration' between cognitive theories are to be preferred to imperialistic attempts to explain all cognitive manifestations of autism in the same terms. The present thesis certainly does not preclude the possibility that children with autism may have innate impairments in their abilities to parse intentional events in the social world. But while it is necessary to acknowledge that impaired mentalizing ability might impact upon executive functioning, one must defend the integrity of the present position nevertheless.

The case for mentalizing-to-executive causation is made by Carruthers (1996b) in relation to autism, by C. D. Frith (1992) with regard to schizophrenia, and it is implicit in Perner's (1991, Chapter 9) discussion of the dependency of the development of self-control on the development of the metarepresentational insight.[12] The core assumption here is that executive control requires individuals to 'stand back' mentally from what they are engaged in, viewing their actions within a broader project, and that doing this requires a theoretical grasp of what it means to be a mind engaged in such reflection. To put it another way, action-monitoring requires self-monitoring, self-monitoring requires a concept of self, and a *concept* of self requires a theory of mental life. On this view, the link I tried to make above between self-awareness and verbal self-regulation would be described in terms of the possession of an innate theory: talking to the self to regulate its behaviour requires an innate theory of a self's mental states.

It is too late in the day to embark upon a full discussion of this view. I will say this though:[13] the notion of a 'theory of mind' seems to be fatally overstretched here. Let us take again an executive task on which children with autism are dramatically impaired—the 'box' task (Hughes and Russell 1993) that requires a switch-then-reach sequence. To succeed, the subject must embed the goal (retrieve the marble) within an arbitrary or non-natural subgoal (throwing a switch on the box). Put like this the demands are executive: they gauge the ability to act from the appropriate representation rather than gauging the possession of concepts. On the other hand, however, this is a superficial description of what is going on, because if we dig deeper we see that this embedding requires knowledge of belief–desire psychology and so what is at stake here is indeed the possession of concepts. Well, is it? Does folk psychology go this deep? The assumption being made by those who think that executive tasks really do tap mentalizing abilities is that once behaviour can be said to have a second-order character—once a subject is required to represent to itself what it is doing and what needs to be done— theory-of-mind talk must immediately be ushered in. Is this assumption justified? We can certainly describe what the subject is doing in terms of folk-psychological categories and generalizations ('I *want* to get the marble but I *think* that a direct reach will make it disappear so I must . . .'). But one can explain any kind of behaviour in these terms; and this fact captures both the everyday utility and the scientific vacuity of folk psychology.

Even if acting on the basis of an arbitrary rule, whilst suppressing the prepotent response, requires a grasp of belief–desire psychology, it is still possible that the difficulty that children with autism have with executive tasks is executive in nature. They may have a theory on which they cannot act. Perhaps any linguistic performance, whether social or self-directed, depends upon a minimal grasp of belief–desire psychology; but one can have an adequate grasp of what one must do and what needs to be done and fail to do it for executive reasons. We know that this is the case for normal 3-year-olds performing on an extradimensional shift task (Zelazo *et al.* 1996). Moreover, if it is indeed the case that children with autism have problems with action-monitoring at the level of motor control (evidence reviewed above) how are these to be explained in folk-psychological terms? We are, of course, waiting on more and stronger evidence here, but if it is forthcoming and if the conceptual links between action-monitoring and self-awareness are as I described then we have the tools to explain mentalizing impairments in subpersonal terms. And surely we must ultimately deliver a subpersonal account of the disorder. (Speculating about the brain-locus of 'the theory of mind module' will not be good enough.)

There is a final reason for preferring an approach to autism that is subpersonal and executive over one which explains the disorder in terms of a lack of a personal-level theory. It is a paradoxical sort of reason because it manages to be at once provocative and self-evident. For a very large proportion of children with autism the question of whether or not they have a theory of mind simply cannot arise. They have no language, they engage in self-injuring behaviour, and they exhibit a discontent so profound that only emotive descriptions can capture its character. The world must indeed be a frightening place to those who cannot control their experiences of it.

Notes

1. This claim needs a detailed defence. It receives one in Russell (1996).
2. For a neural-network model of this process see Jordan and Rumelhart (1992).
3. Here I am staying very close to Janaway (1983).
4. What is the nature of the mental actions that are supposed to be monitored? Will any kind of thought do? Is every mental occurrence monitored by copying and feedforward mechanisms? Take the case of verbalized thoughts in inner speech. C. D. Frith's (1992) account of auditory hallucinations in schizophrenia depends upon the claim that verbal thoughts, like actions, are monitored; when they fail to be monitored, hallucinations result. But as Campbell (in press) has argued, what normally gives rise to a verbalized thought are other thoughts, in so far as a thought is an element in a rational sequence. To the extent that a tokened mental sentence is physically caused so it will typically be caused by other tokened sentences, and these causal relation-ships are a product of the deductive relationships between them, not a

product of motor instructions. There is no analogue to a resting body springing into action. (Campbell favours a higher-level account of auditory hallucinations in terms of deficits of metarepresentation, *qua* failure to represent oneself as having certain long-standing dispositional beliefs. Given this, the patient fails to recognize certain occurrent thoughts as products of these dispositional beliefs.) Because of the difficulties noted by Campbell, it is wise to limit the notion of mental action to those mental processes where one can speak of, in Frith's phrase, 'mental effort'. For example, we are asked to list all the capital cities beginning with the letter 'K', or we are asked to generate a novel use for an ice-cream cone, or we try to remember how we got home last night. These mental efforts can be said to be monitored—on the present account.

5. It might be argued that the monitoring-deficit account does, in fact, have to predict errors on this condition, on the grounds that an action that is inadequately coded, in terms of the intention that launched it, is likely to be less distinctive than one which received such a coding, and is therefore easier to confuse with a similar action also produced by the self. But this is implausible. Successfully coding all four actions as self-generated does not make each one any more distinctive from the others; and what the subject must do here is to encode the distinctive character of each action (e.g. that the cat picture came from the yellow location).

6. I certainly do not want to dismiss the significance of this study to the development of bodily awareness in the normal case (see Campbell 1995). What I am saying is that it is possible for subjects—in particular children with autism—to detect that they are being imitated without recruiting the kind of action-monitoring capacities being described here. Almost certainly, normal children *do* recruit them. The fact that they show, what Meltzoff calls, 'testing behaviour' (taking an action and watching to see if the experimenter copies it) suggests they do.

7. In fact the claim that autism-plus-normal-IQ represents the 'pure' case of autism can itself be questioned. The assumption here is that mentally handicapped subjects have autism and mental handicap in addition. But one can equally well say that, whenever autism is severe, mental handicap will be inevitable. This follows, in fact, from the present position, and it implies that it is persons with autism with low intelligence who represent the 'pure' case. It is also worth bearing in mind that 'mental handicap' does not label a *sui generis* disorder; and so it can be inappropriate to treat it as an additive factor.

8. It would be misleading, however, to say that there were no group differences. On the experimental (Stroop-like) conditions the variances of the scores from the autistic group were far higher than for the control groups; but not for the control (non-Stroop) condition.

9. Lumb and Russell (1996) have shown, in a series of experiments, that success on this ignorance question virtually guarantees success on the belief question. This raises the possibility that, as Wimmer and Weichbold (1994) have argued, the essential difficulty is knowing how perception leads to knowledge. Once the subject grasps this fact he or she is not challenged by questions about false belief.

10. We cannot hope that, expect that, pretend that, wish that, and so forth, without also having certain beliefs. We can, conversely, have a belief while hoping, etc. nothing.

11. Rebecca Saltmarsh and I have recently given this task to children with autism. At the time of writing, we have yet to test control subjects. The version with prepotency (photograph taken of a blank screen, after which the doll stands before the camera) was found to be more difficult. What is more interesting, however, is the great difficulty that the children experienced with the control question: 'Where was [the doll] when I took the photograph?'. The correct answer is that it was behind the scenes rather than before the camera. Many of the children with autism insisted that the doll was in front of the camera. They could not, therefore, inhibit an answer in terms of their current state of knowledge.

12. Baron-Cohen's (1989) argument that lacking a theory of mind leads to social anxiety and thus to stereotypies is discussed in Turner's chapter (Chapter 3). The difficulties with this view are reviewed there so I shall not touch upon them.

13. In Russell (in press) I discuss this view fully, and also describe some common ground between executive and mentalizing theories.

Acknowledgements

The research described here was supported by a grant from the Wellcome Trust. I am grateful to a number of people for their comments on an earlier version of this paper, especially to Chas Fernyhough, Al Lumb, and Rebecca Saltmarsh.

REFERENCES

Baddeley, A. (1986). *Working memory*. Cambridge University Press, Cambridge.

Bairstow, P. (1986). Postural control. In *Motor skill development in children* (ed. H. T. A. Whiting and M. G. Wade), pp. 24–42. Nijhoff, Dordrecht.

Baldwin, T. (1995). Objectivity, causality, and agency. In *The body and the self* (ed. J. Bermúdez, A. J. Marcel, and N. Eilan), pp. 108–25. MIT Press, Cambridge, MA.

Bandura, A. (1991). Self-efficacy: Towards a unifying theory of behaviour change. *Psychological Review*, **84**, 191–215.

Baron-Cohen, S. (1989). Do autistic children have obsessions and compulsions? *British Journal of Clinical Psychology*, **9**, 193–200.

Baron-Cohen, S. and Swettenham, J. Theory of mind in autism: Its relationship to executive function and central coherence. In *Handbook of autism and pervasive developmental disorders* (2nd edn) (ed. D. Cohen and F. Volkmar.). John Wiley, NY. (In press.)

Baron-Cohen, S., Leslie, A. M., and Frith, U. (1985). Does the autistic child have a 'theory of mind'? *Cognition*, **21**, 37–46.

Baron-Cohen, S., Tager-Flusberg, H., and Cohen, D. J. (1993). *Understanding other minds: Perspectives from autism*. Oxford University Press, Oxford.

Barresi, J. and Moore, C. (1996). Intentional relations and social understanding. *Behavioural and Brain Sciences*, **19**, 107–22.

Bennetto, L., Pennington, B. F., and Roger, S. J. (1996). Intact and impaired memory functions in autism. *Child Development*, **67**, 1816–35.

Bentall, R. P., Baker, G. A., and Havers, S. (1991). Reality monitoring and psychotic hallucinations. *British Journal of Clinical Psychology*, **30**, 213–22.

Bryson, S. E. (1983). Interference effects in autistic children: Evidence for the comprehension of single stimuli. *Journal of Abnormal Psychology*, **92**, 250–4.

Campbell, J. (1995). The body image and self-consciousness. In *The body and the self* (ed. J. Bermúdez, A. J. Marcel, and N. Eilan). MIT Press, Cambridge, MA.

Campbell, J. Frith's model of schizophrenia. In *Agency and psychopathology* (ed. J. Proust and M. Grivois). Presses Universitaire de France, Paris. (In press.)

Carruthers, P. (1996a). *Language, thought, and consciousness*. Cambridge University Press, Cambridge.

Carruthers, P. (1996b). Autism as mind-blindness: An elaboration and a partial defence. In *Theories of theories of mind* (ed. P. Carruthers), pp. 257–73. Cambridge University Press, Cambridge.

Case, R., Kurtland, D. M., and Goldberg, J. (1982). Operational efficiency and the growth of short-term memory span. *Journal of Experimental Child Psychology*, **33**, 386–404.

Charman, T. and Baron-Cohen, S. (1992). Understanding drawings and beliefs: A further test of the metarepresentational theory of autism. *Journal of Child Psychology and Psychiatry*, **33**, 11–5–1112.

Charman, T. and Baron-Cohen, S. (1994). Another look at imitation in autism. *Development and Psychopathology*, **6**, 403–13.

Chess, S. (1971). Autism in children with congenital rubella. *Journal of Autism and Childhood Schizophrenia*, **1**, 33–47.

Conway, M. and Dewhurst, S. A. (1995). Remembering, familiarity, and source monitoring. *Quarterly Journal of Experimental Psychology*, **48A**, 125–40.

Daneman, M. and Carpenter, P. A. (1980). Individual differences in working memory and reading. *Journal of Verbal Learning and Verbal Behaviour*, **19**, 450–66.

Dawson, G. and Adams, A. (1984). Imitation and social responsiveness in autistic children. *Journal of Abnormal Child Psychology*, **12**, 209–26.

Dawson, G. and Lewy, A. (1989). Reciprocal subcortical–cortical influences in autism. In *Autism: Nature, diagnosis, and treatment* (ed. G. Dawson), pp. 49–74. Guildford Press, NY.

Diamond, A. (1991). Neuropsychological insights into the meaning of object concept development. In *The epigenesis of mind* (ed. S. Carey and R. Gelman.), pp. 67–110. Lawrence Erlbaum Associates, Hillsdale, NJ.

Diamond, A. (1996). Evidence for the importance of dopamine for prefrontal functions early in life. *Philosophical Transactions of the Royal Society: Biological Sciences*, **352**, 1483–94.

Eriksson, A-S. and de Chateau, P. (1992). Brief report: A girl aged two years and seven months with autistic disorder videotaped at birth. *Journal of Autism and Developmental Disorders*, **22**, 127–9.

Eskes, G. A., Bryson, S. E., and McCormick, T. A. (1990). Comprehension of concrete and abstract words in autistic children. *Journal of Autism and Developmental Disorders*, **20**, 61–73.

Fraiberg, S. (1977). Congenital sensory and motor deficits and ego formation. *Annual of Psychoanalysis*, **5**, 169–94.

Frith, C. D. (1992). *The cognitive neuropsychology of schizophrenia*. Erlbaum UK, Hove.

Frith, C. D. and Done, D. J. (1989). Experiences of alien control in schizophrenia reflect a disorder of central monitoring of action. *Psychological Medicine*, **19**, 353–63.

Frith, U. and Hermelin, B. (1969). The role of visual and motor cues for normal, subnormal and autistic children. *Journal of Child Psychology and Psychiatry*, **10**, 153–63.

Gergely, G., Nádasdy, Z., Csibra, G., and Bíro, S. (1995). *Cognition*, **56**, 165–93.

Gerstadt, C. L., Hong, Y. J., and Diamond, A. (1994). The relationship between cognition and action: Performance of children 3-and-a-half to 7 years on a Stroop-like day–night task. *Cognition*, **53**, 129–53.

Held, R. (1961). Exposure history as a factor in maintaining stability of perception and distance information. *Journal of Nervous and Mental Diseases*, **132**, 26–32.

Hermelin, B. and O'Connor, N. (1975). Location and distance estimates by blind and sighted children. *Quarterly Journal of Experimental Psychology*, **27**, 295–301.

Hitch, G. J. and McAuley, E. (1991). Working memory in children with specific arithmetical learning difficulties. *British Journal of Psychology*, **82**, 375–86.

Hobson, P. (1993). *Autism and the development of mind*. Erlbaum UK, Hove.

Hood, B. (1995). Gravity rules for 2–4 year olds? *Cognitive Development*, **10**, 577–98.

Hughes, C. and Russell, J. (1993). Autistic children's difficulty with mental disengagement from an object: Implications for theories of autism. *Developmental Psychology*, **29**, 498–510.

Hulbert, R., Happé, F., and Frith, U. (1994). Sampling the form of inner experience of three adults with Asperger Syndrome. *Psychological Medicine*, **24**, 385–95.

Janaway, C. (1983). The subject and the objective order. *Proceedings of the Aristotelian Society*, **84**, 147–65.

Johnson, M. K. and Raye, C. L. (1981). Reality monitoring. *Psychological Review*, **88**, 67–85.

Johnson, M. K., Raye, C. L., Foley, H. J., and Foley, M. A. (1981). Cognitive operations and decision bias in reality monitoring. *American Journal of Psychology*, **94**, 37–64.

Jordan, M. I. and Rumelhart, D. E. (1992). Forward models: Supervised learning with a distal teacher. *Cognitive Science*, **16**, 307–54.

Leekam, S. and Perner, J. (1991). Does the autistic child have a theory of representation? *Cognition*, **94**, 203–18.

Leslie, A. M. (1987). Pretence and representation: The origins of 'theory of mind'. *Psychological Review*, **94**, 412–26.

Leslie, A. M. and Thaiss, L. (1992). Domain specificity in conceptual development: Neuropsychological evidence from autism. *Cognition*, **43**, 225–51.

Lockman, J. J. (1984). The development of detour ability during infancy. *Child Development*, **55**, 482–91

Lumb, A. and Russell, J. (1996). Does the false belief task really measure children understanding of knowledge acquisition? Poster presented at the annual meeting of the BPS Developmental Section, Oxford, September , 1996.

Luria, A. R. and Homskaya, E.D. (1964). Disturbance in the regulative role of speech with frontal lesions. In *The frontal granular cortex and behaviour* (ed. J. M. Warren and K. Akert), pp. 353–71. McGraw-Hill, NY.

Luria, A. R. and Yudovich, F. (1971). *Speech and the development of mental processes in the child*. Penguin Books, Harmondsworth.

McEvoy, R. E., Rogers, S. J., and Pennington, B. F. (1993). Executive function and social communication deficits in young, autistic children. *Journal of Child Psychology and Psychiatry*, **34**, 563–78.

Malenka, R. C., Angel, R. W., Hamptom, B., and Berger, P. A. (1981). Impaired central error-correcting behaviour in schizophrenia. *Archives of General Psychiatry*, **39**, 101–7.

Meltzoff, A. N. (1990). Foundations for a developing concept of self: The role of imitation in relating self to other and the value of social mirroring, social modelling, and self practice in infancy. In *The self in transition: Infancy to childhood* (ed. D. Ciccetti and M. Beeghly), pp. 139–64. University of Chicago Press, Chicago.

Meltzoff, A. N. and Gopnik, A. (1993). The role of imitation in understanding persons and developing a theory of mind. In *Understanding other minds* (ed. S. Baron-Cohen, H. Tager-Flusberg, and D. J. Cohen.). Oxford University Press, NY.

Moore, C., Jarrold, C., Russell, J., Lumb, A., Sapp, F., and MacCallum, F. (1995). Conflicting desires and the child's theory of mind. *Cognitive Development*, **10**, 467–82.

Morton, J. and Frith, U. (1995). Causal modelling: A structural approach to developmental psychopathology. In *Manual of developmental psychopathology*, Vol. 1 (ed. D. Cicchetti and D. J. Cohen.), pp. 357–90. John Wiley, NY.

Natale, F. and Antinucci, F. (1989). Stage 6 object-concept and representation. In *Cognitive structure and development in nonhuman primates* (ed. F. Antinucci.), pp. 36–49. Lawrence Erlbaum Associates, Hillsdale, NJ.

Norman, D. and Shallice, T. (1980). *Attention to action: Willed and automatic control of behaviour*. Centre for Human Information Processing, Technical Report No. 99, University of California, San Diego.

Ohta, M. (1987). Cognitive disorders in infantile autism: A study employing the WISC, spatial relationships conceptualization, and gesture imitation. *Journal of Autism and Developmental Disorders*, **17**, 45–62.

O'Shaughnessy, B. (1980). *The will*, Vol. 2. Cambridge University Press, Cambridge.

Osterling, J. and Dawson, G. (1994). Early recognition of children with autism: A study of first birthday home videos. *Journal of Autism and Developmental Disorders*, **24**, 247–59.

Parker, S. (1991). A developmental approach to the origins of self-recognition in great apes. *Human Evolution*, **6**, 435–49.

Pennington, B. F. Dimensions of executive functions in normal and abnormal development. In *Development of the prefrontal cortex: Evolution, neurobiology, and behaviour*. Brooks Publishing Company, Baltimore, MD. (In press.)

Perner, J. (1991). *Understanding the representational mind*. MIT Press, Cambridge, MA.

Phillips, W., Baron-Cohen, S., and Rutter, M. (1995). To what extent can children with autism understand desire? *Development and Psychopathology*, **7**, 151–69.

Phillips, W., Baron-Cohen, S., and Rutter, M. Understanding intention in normal development and in autism. *British Journal of Developmental Psychology*. (In press.)

Rabbitt, P. M. A. (1966). Error-correction time without external signals. *Nature*, **212**, 438–40.

Rogers, S. J. und Newhart-Larson, S. (1989). Characteristics of infantile autism in five children with Leber's congenital amaurosis. *Developmental Medicine and Child Neurology*, **31**, 598–608.

Russell, J. (1995). At two with nature: Agency and the development of self-world dualism. In *The body and the self* (ed. J. Bermúdez, A. J. Marcel, and N. Eilan), pp. 127–51. MIT Press, Cambridge, MA.

Russell, J. (1996). *Agency: Its role in mental development*. The Psychology Press, Hove.

Russell, J. 'Poor ToMM': Modules, metarepresentation and executive dysfunctions in autism. In *Agency and psychopathology* (ed. J. Proust and M. Grivois). Presses Universitaire de France, Paris. (In press.)

Russell, J. and Jarrold, C. (in press, a). Error-correction problems in autism: Evidence for a central monitoring impairment? *Journal of Autism and Developmental Disorders*.

Russell, J. and Jarrold, C. (in press, b). Memory for actions in children with autism: Self versus other. *British Journal of Developmental Psychology*.

Russell, J. and Jarrold, C. (1997). Do children with autism show the generation effect? (In preparation.)

Russell, J., Jarrold, C., and Henry, L. (1996). Working memory in children with autism and with moderate learning difficulties. *Journal of Child Psychology and Psychiatry*, **37**, 673–96.

Russell, J. and Saltmarsh, R. (1997). Do children with autism understand conflicting desires? Poster presented at the annual conference of the Society for Research in Child Development, Washington DC. April.

Searle, J. (1983). *Intentionality*. Cambridge University Press, Cambridge.

Shultz, T. R. and Wells. D. (1985). Judging the intentionality of action-outcomes. *Developmental Psychology*, **21**, 83–9.

Slamenka, N. J. and Graf, P. (1978). The generation effect: Delineation of a phenomenon. *Journal of Experimental Psychology: Human Learning and Memory*, **4**, 592–604.

Smith, I. M. and Bryson, S. E. (1994). Imitation and action in autism: A critical review. *Psychological Bulletin*, **116**, 259–73.

Squire, L. R. (1992). Memory in the hippocampus: A synthesis of findings with rats, monkeys, and humans. *Psychological Review*, **99**, 195–231.

Tiegerman, E. and Primavera, L. (1984). Imitating in the autistic child: Facilitating communicative gaze behaviour. *Journal of Autism and Developmental Disorders*, **11**, 427–38.

von Holst, E. and Mittlestaedt, H. (1977). Das Reafferenzprinzipzwischen Zentralnervensystem und Peripherie. In *The behavioural physiology of animals and man: Selected papers of E. von Holst* (trans. R. D. Martin). University of Miami Press, Coral Cables.

Wehner, E. and Rogers, S. (1994, March). Attachment relationships of autistic and developmentally delayed children. Paper presented at the bi-monthly meeting of the Developmental Psychobiology Research Group, Denvers, CO.

Wimmer, H. and Perner, J. (1983). Beliefs about beliefs: Representation and constraining functions of wrong beliefs in young children's understanding of deception. *Cognition*, **13**, 103–28.

Wimmer, H. and Weichbold, V. (1994). Children's theory of mind: Fodor's heuristics examined. *Cognition*, **53**, 45–57.

Wittgenstein, L. (1953). *Philosophical investigations*. Basil Blackwell, Oxford.

Zaitchik, D. (1990). When representations conflict with reality: The preschooler's problem with false belief and 'false' photographs. *Cognition*, **35**, 41–68.

Zelazo, P. D., Frye, D., and Rapus, T. (1996). An age-related dissociation between knowing rules and using them. *Cognitive Development*, **11**, 37–63.

Author index

Subject index